"This is a book to read for anyone who wants to understand the reason of regional differences, their historical reasons, and recent social-political consequences of the conflicts within Europe and including the crisis of the European Union."

– **László Valki**, *Professor of International Law, Eotvos Lorand University, Budapest*

"This comparative study is the successful and stimulating culmination of Professor Berend's prolonged work on and contribution to our understanding of the forces that explain Europe's recent past and economic experience. It will feed into and stimulate the vital debate about the idea and experience of 'Europe.'"

– **Barry Supple**, *Emeritus Professor of Economic History, University of Cambridge, UK*

Economic History of a Divided Europe

This book presents the sharp regional differences within the integrating European continent. Four regions – Northwestern Europe, Southern Europe, Central Europe, and Eastern-Southeastern Europe – represent high, medium, and relatively less-developed levels of economic advancement. These disparities have emerged as a result of historical differences that produced and reinforced cultural and behavioral differences.

The author examines the distinctions between the regions, looks at how these differences transpired and became so retrenched, and answers the question of why some countries were able to elevate to higher levels of economic development while others could not. This book is unique in that it provides a timely historical analysis of the main causes of the most pressing conflicts in Europe today. Readers will come away from this book with a deeper understanding of the sharp divergence in economic standing between the four different regions of Europe, as well as knowledge about how institutional corruption and other cultural features exacerbated these variations. The book also offers a better understanding of major European Union conflicts between member countries and between member and nonmember countries, as well as the rise of autocratic regimes in certain countries. The book begins with a short history of European integration throughout European civilization and then goes on to discuss the modern reality of integration and attempts to homogenize the Continent that divided into four different macro-regions.

It will primarily appeal to scholars, researchers and students studying Europe from various fields, including economics, business, history, political science, and sociology, as well as a general readership interested in Europe's past, present, and future.

Ivan T. Berend is a distinguished research professor at the University of California, Los Angeles (UCLA), USA. He is a member of the American Academy of Arts and Sciences; the British Academy; the Academy of Europe; and the Austrian, Hungarian, Bulgarian, and Czech Academies of Sciences. He was president of the International Historical Association between 1995 and 2000 and is author of 35 books.

Routledge Studies in the European Economy

Greek Employment Relations in Crisis
Problems, Challenges and Prospects
Edited by Horen Voskeritsian, Panos Kapotas and Christina Niforou

Centrally Planned Economies
Theory and Practice in Socialist Czechoslovakia
Edited by Libor Žídek

SME Finance and the Economic Crisis
The Case of Greece
Alina Hyz

Russian Trade Policy
Achievements, Challenges and Prospects
Edited by Sergei Sutyrin, Olga Y. Trofimenko and Alexandra Koval

Digital Transformation and Public Services
Societal Impacts in Sweden and Beyond
Edited by Anthony Larsson and Robin Teigland

Economic Policy, Crisis and Innovation
Beyond Austerity in Europe
Edited by Maria Cristina Marcuzzo, Antonella Palumbo and Paola Villa

The Economics of Monetary Unions
Past Experiences and the Eurozone
Edited by Juan E. Castañeda, Alessandro Roselli and Geoffrey E. Wood

Economic History of a Divided Europe
Four Diverse Regions in an Integrating Continent
Ivan T. Berend

For more information about this series, please visit: www.routledge.com/series/SE0431

Economic History of a Divided Europe

Four Diverse Regions in an Integrating Continent

Ivan T. Berend

Routledge
Taylor & Francis Group
LONDON AND NEW YORK

First published 2020
by Routledge
2 Park Square, Milton Park, Abingdon, Oxon OX14 4RN

and by Routledge
52 Vanderbilt Avenue, New York, NY 10017

Routledge is an imprint of the Taylor & Francis Group, an informa business

British Library Cataloguing-in-Publication Data
A catalogue record for this book is available from the British Library

Library of Congress Cataloging-in-Publication Data
Names: Berend, T. Iván (Tibor Iván), 1930– author.
Title: Economic history of a divided Europe: four diverse regions in an integrating continent/Ivan T. Berend.
Description: Abingdon, Oxon; New York, NY: Routledge, 2020. |
Series: Routledge studies in the European economy |
Includes bibliographical references and index.
Identifiers: LCCN 2019050362 (print) | LCCN 2019050363 (ebook) |
Subjects: LCSH: Europe–Economic conditions. |
Regional disparities–Europe.
Classification: LCC HC240 .B394675 2020 (print) |
LCC HC240 (ebook) | DDC 330.94–dc23
LC record available at https://lccn.loc.gov/2019050362
LC ebook record available at https://lccn.loc.gov/2019050363

ISBN: 978-0-367-89650-8 (hbk)
ISBN: 978-1-003-02031-8 (ebk)

Typeset in Bembo
by Newgen Publishing UK

Contents

Illustrations

Figure

Tables

Introduction

Europe, its civilizations and historical regions

Europe and its civilization

Today, Europe's 44 states (as the United Nations calculates, including six city- or mini-states such as San Marino or the Vatican City) represent as many as nearly one-quarter of the world's roughly 200 states (the United Nations has 193 member states). While its landed area of 10.18 million square kilometers (3,931 million square miles) is just seven percent of the world's territory, it is home to 852 million people, roughly 11 percent of the world's population.
Despite its relatively small area, Europe represents a special civilization. Together with its name, it was born from the ancient time Greek and then Roman civilizations. The Roman empire with its highest level of ancient civilization gradually enlarged and covered most of Western and parts of Central Europe, up to the dividing eastern border, the "limes" of River Danube, which separated the eastern half of the continent from the empire. This development culminated in a Christian-European civilization, represented by the Carolingian empire of the eighth and early ninth centuries, ruled by the legendary Charlemagne, who converted pagans and beheaded those who resisted. In the tenth century, the Carolingian empire was replaced by the emergent Holy Roman Empire, a much less centralized formation, which also incorporated vast parts of Western and Central Europe into its almost thousand-year reign.

From the early 19th to the mid-20th century, there were further attempts to conquer and unify Europe, but these efforts were largely overshadowed by the primacy of small sovereign nation-states. The concept of independent, sovereign states was established by the Treaty of Westphalia (1648), ending the Eight Years' and the Thirty Years' wars, one of the most devastating wars in the 400 years almost permanent warfare in Europe. This treaty became the sacrosanct legitimation of independent states by establishing a new political order in Europe, based upon the concept of coexisting sovereign states. "Westphalian sovereignty" became the central concept of international law and a basic principle of the emerging modern world. The divisions between states became even more distinct after the American and French revolutions of the late 18th century, which birthed the *nation* and precipitated the 19th- and 20th-century linguistic and cultural homogenization of the populations of *nation-states* by schools, media and national armies.

Nevertheless, parallel with the separation of individual nation-states, recognition of the marked similarity of the countries and peoples in the Western half of Europe was clearly and continuously expressed from the late 18th century. The French Montesquieu, who traveled outside Europe, compared the similarity of Western European countries and societies to a "single republic." A century after the Treaty of Westphalia, Voltaire, in his *Le Siècle de Louise XIV*, also described Europe as "a kind of great republic divided into several states." In his view, "[Europeans] all have the same religious foundation, even if divided into several confessions. They all have the same principle of public law and politics, unknown in other parts of the world." Two decades later, Jean-Jacques Rousseau expressed a similar view: "There are no longer Frenchmen, Germans, and Spaniard, or even English, but only European."

In spite of the increasing separation and conflict between European nations in the first half of the 20th century, many prominent scholars rejected a nation-centric view of the world in favor of a focus on the history of *civilizations*. According to his two-volume *Der untergang des Abendlandes* (1918–1922), German historian-philosopher Oswald Spengler describes eight "high cultures" that developed into civilizations in human history: Babylonian, Egyptians, Chinese, Indian, Mesoamerican, and Arabian, and two separate European civilizations: the classic Greco-Roman and, after the 18th century, the "Faustian" *Western Civilization*.

Writing a few decades after Spengler, British historian Arnold J. Toynbee published his monumental 12-volume *A Study of History* (1930–1960) about the rise and decline of 23 distinct civilizations. He also identified civilizations according to cultural characteristics and not along the lines of modern nation-states, and he treated Western Europe as a single unit, the *Western Civilization*. He considered this unit, including all of the nations that have existed in Western Europe since the collapse of the Roman empire, to be one single civilization. Importantly, his grouping excluded the "Orthodox" Eastern civilization of Russia and the Balkans. This distinction was not new. It was already made by the Russian Nikolai Y. Danilevski, a leading ideologue of the Pan-Slav movement in the second half of the 19th century, who published his *Russia and Europe* in 1869, in which he described the Slavic-Orthodox civilization as separate and superior to the "Romano-German" Western one.

The idea and reality of European integration

The concept of a homogenous Western civilization led to the recognition of the need to integrate and unite Europe. This idea gradually emerged and led to the organization of several movements in the late 19th and early 20th centuries. The famous French writer Victor Hugo enthusiastically supported the idea of a united Europe. In particular, in speeches delivered at a series of conferences Hugo advocated for the federalization of Europe and addressed the audience as "citizens of the United States of Europe." Following the First World War and in spite of the recent hostility and conflict between nations, Count Richard von Coudenhove-Kalergi founded a Pan-European Movement and published a *Paneuropa Manifesto* in 1923. In 1929, French Prime Minister Aristide Briand filed a League of Nations initiative suggesting the unification of Europe. These calls for integration all failed and, instead, the most murderous and devastating long second world war (1939–1945) decimated Europe.[1]

Nevertheless, World War II also led to radical positive change. As early as 1941, a strong idea suggested the federative reorganization of Europe after the war, predicated on the rejection of confrontational nation-states. This historical requirement of eliminate the nation-states and federalize Europe was seen as the only possible future of the continent after the war. This idea of a united, federal Europe was declared, characteristically, by two political prisoners of Ventotene, Mussolini's Italian fascist prison-island.[2] Several antifascist resistance movements throughout Europe advocated for the same federalist idea during the last years of the war and immediately after.[3] Following the war, the idea of opening a new, peaceful, unifying chapter of European history gained mass support, and leading British, Italian, French, Belgian, Dutch and German politicians turned to the idea of integration and dreamed about a future federal Europe.

The Cold War between the United States (together with its allies) and the Soviet Union (with its satellites) emerged at the end of World War II and frightened Europeans with the imminent eruption of World War III. In response, Winston Churchill, the leading politician of Western Europe at the time, urged the continent to form a "United States of Europe" in a famous speech in Zurich in 1946.[4] Under Presidents Truman and Eisenhower, the United States as the dominant superpower put this agenda into the middle of its postwar diplomacy and pushed this initiative toward realization.[5] In 1948, the American Marshall Plan, a major aid program for rebuilding Europe, set the precedent for cooperation among the aid recipients. The process of integration began in the 1950s.

Two-thirds of a century has now passed since the beginning of the historic project of unification, first with the Schuman Declaration and then the Treaty of Paris (1951), which laid the foundation for the European Coal and Steel Community (ECSC). Six northwestern European countries – France, Germany, Belgium, the Netherlands, Luxembourg, and Italy signed integration agreements. (Italy was not a northwestern country, but northern Italy traditionally belonged to that group.) These founding countries were quite similar in their economic level and, in spite of the immediate fascist and Nazi episodes behind Italy and Germany, also shared a similar Western value system and democratic political experience. Within a few years of the establishment of the ECSC, the same six countries signed the Treaty of Rome (1957) to establish the European Economic Community and targeted an "ever closer union."

From the 1970s, the European Economic Community, which became the European Union (EU) in 1993, started enlarging. By 2013, the EU had already incorporated 28 member countries, while another 5 – Turkey and the countries of the Western Balkans – stood before the door of the EU as officially recognized candidate countries for future membership. Other countries including Norway, Iceland, Switzerland, and Lichtenstein, although are not members of the Union are closely connected to the Union and its Single Market through several agreements. These countries even pay a membership fee and adopt the rules of the EU.

If we consider that among the nonmember and unassociated countries are four mini-states (Vatican City, Andorra, Monaco and San Marino) and that some others are transcontinental states (Russia and Turkey) that are only partly European and partly – or even mostly – Asian, then it seems to be a reasonable estimation that about 80 percent of Europe is connected with the European Union. Thus, the integration process became a huge success.

In spite of integration, major macro-regional differences

A few years before the first steps of integration were taken on March 5, 1946 Winston Churchill delivered his "iron curtain" speech in Fulton, United States. He famously stated:

> From Stettin in the Baltic to Trieste in the Adriatic, an iron curtain has descended across the Continent. Behind that line … the populations … lie in what I must call the Soviet sphere, and all are subject … not only to Soviet influence but to a very high and, in many cases, increasing measure of control from Moscow.[6]

Churchill, first after the war, declared the division of Europe to two different parts, separated by an "iron curtain." He was politically right. This divide actually became a major factor promoting urgent integration to strengthen the Western alliance against the assumed Soviet danger.

However, between 1989 and 1991, the Soviet Bloc and then the Soviet Union itself collapsed. This opened new possibilities but also new difficulties for the European Union. Europe was deeply divided. Churchill, as much as he was right, was actually wrong in speaking about how the iron curtain had "descended" at that time. That curtain had existed there during the entire modern period and is still there today. The Hungarian journal *Gazdaság* (Economy) published an article on September 21, 2018 entitled "Why are East-Europeans dying earlier than Westerners?" The first sentences of the article state:

> A sharp dividing line cuts Europe into two between Szczecin in Poland and Trieste in Italy, approximately. Although Europeans have long lives, the differences within Europe are huge. At the one end, the average life expectancy of Spaniards in Madrid is 85 years, while the average life span in Severozapaten, Bulgaria is only 73 years. In Hungary, the life expectancy is 75.7 years.[7]

Health organizations, the article explains, point to bad habits in the eastern half of the continent, among them extreme smoking and drinking, as well as the inferior health services of the entire region.

Indeed, a kind of "iron curtain" separated Europe during the entirety of European history and especially during the modern age. In the later 19th century, people on the Western side of Europe lived in democratizing political systems that were also industrial societies; these people were literate, much better educated, and lived longer. In contrast, on the Eastern side the societies were still agricultural. The population experienced autocratic regimes and lived shorter lives; a great part of the population was still illiterate. Even as late as 1913, the economic level and the living standards were much higher in the West. The East did not surpass half of this developmental difference: in huge parts of the region development reached less than a third of the Western level.

Nevertheless, in reality, the situation in Europe was much more difficult and diverse. Quite marked differences existed not only along east–west divides but also south–west ones. In other words, Europe was never a consistent and homogenous historical unit. The long and rather different historical trajectories of European countries and regions always separated Western Europe from the peripheries of the continent. Integration actually began in the area with the highest levels and most homogenous economic development, often called the region of "Western civilization." Today, remarkably, the largest part of the peripheral ring around the Western core – the entire Irish, Mediterranean, Central European and Baltic area and parts of the Balkans – belongs to the European Union. Despite this progress, even three generations into the process of integration, Europe is far from homogenous. It remains easy to distinguish between regions with markedly different economic and social-cultural-political characteristics.

Both within and outside of the European Union, neglecting the numberless micro-regions within the macro-regions – less developed enclaves, rust-belts, sparsely populated Nordic areas and isolated rural backyards in advanced countries as well as small advanced areas and Western type of capital cities in backward countries[8] – I will discuss *four macro-regions* that can be distinguished on the continent. I have distinguished the macro-regions into areas with relatively consistent development levels, which differ significantly from one another. The economic and educational levels of each of these regions are relatively similar, as are their standards of living and lifestyle, measured by per capita income or gross domestic product (GDP) and Human Development Index (HDI). They also have somewhat comparable social-cultural-behavioral patterns, and their institutions, laws and political systems resemble one another.

One of these macro-regions consists of the North-Western European countries. This closely linked area spans from Northern Italy to Britain, the Benelux countries (Belgium, the Netherlands, and Luxembourg) to Scandinavia (Sweden, Norway, and Denmark), Switzerland, to France and Germany. The countries of this region have similarly strong and modern economies, and all of them belong to the highest income level and richest group of countries in the world. In this way, they are rather distinct from the peripheral regions.

Countries in Southern and Eastern Europe exhibit different characteristics. Their economies have several major weaknesses and vulnerabilities. These countries are economically relatively less developed, their income levels are classified as low or medium, and they are often poor. Their social-cultural characteristics differ from those of the North-Western region. The latter, for example, maintained relatively strong discipline when it comes to taxation, while most of the people in Southern and Eastern regions consider tax evasion to be a virtue. The Western region boasts a better educational system and a more educated population. While Finland, Belgium and Britain spend 6–7 percent of their higher GDP on public education, Spain, Italy, Slovakia and Romania spend only 3–4 percent on public education. While the pupil's unit cost for secondary education is $7,000 in France, it is only $400 in Poland.

Children spent much more years in education in Western Europe where in Luxembourg, Norway, Sweden, and Britain 48–51 percent of the age group participates in tertiary education, while in Italy, the Czech Republic, Poland, Croatia, Slovakia, and Hungary only 22–30 percent do so. Moreover, in France and the Netherlands, 100 percent of the preschool age group participated in early education, while in Croatia and Greece this share is only 71–75 percent.[9]

Western Europe has relatively smaller illegal, nonregistered "black economy" and lower levels of corruption. The peripheries have still weaker institutions and the rule of law even less dominant. Their population is less educated, and a non-European corruption practice the worst in the world. The western macro-region has a strong free-market economy, regulated by laws and stable institutions, and stable democracies. To varying degrees, people on the peripheries respect less neither institutions nor the rule of law, and often consider their own state an enemy. Instead of relying on state institutions, they prefer to cultivate traditional kinship relations among individuals and family groups. In the peripheries, the state is interventionist and owns or operates the economy in an often authoritarian way. In contrast to the West, freedom is restricted and sometimes brutally suppressed.

In this book, I describe the *four macro-regions* as they emerged historically, separated from one other both in in the early 20th and early 21st centuries: (1) the advanced core of northwest Europe; (2) the Mediterranean-Irish region, from East to South surrounding the northwest, a formerly peripheral area that has made significant progress to catch-up with the core and in the mid-2010s elevated to high-income level, although reaching only 63 percent of the GDP level of the northwestern core; (3) the Central European and Baltic periphery has an income level only less than 32 percent of the cores; (4) and the combined Russian (together with other independent, former Soviet republics), Turkish and Balkan periphery, the least developed area in Europe that represents only somewhat more than 11 percent of the northwestern and 35 percent of the Central European GDP.

While the physical distance between the two capital cities of Luxembourg and Moldova *(Chişinău),* or Luxembourg and Ukraine (Kiev) is hardly more than 1,700 and 2,000 kilometers, respectively, the per capita income levels of Luxembourg ($102,000) and Moldova ($2,100) or Ukraine (less than $2,300) are at light-year distance from each other.

The latter two, relatively more backward macro-regions largely belonged to the Soviet Bloc and thus had neither market economies nor multiparty political democracies for most or at least part of the 20th century. In recent decades, they have attempted the difficult transition from nonmarket, authoritarian regimes toward market democracies.

Is the Central and Eastern European backwardness the legacy of communism?

Some scholarly interpretations around the turn of the millennium connected the peripheral backwardness of the Central-Eastern European and Baltic periphery and even more so the Russian-Balkan region, with its legacy of communism. When analyzing the beginning of postcommunist transformation a quarter century ago, Berkeley scholar Ken Jowitt stated: "Whatever the results of the current turmoil in Eastern Europe, one thing is clear: the new institutional patterns will be shaped by the 'inheritance' and legacy of forty years of Leninist rule."[10] Twenty years later, the *New York Times* reported about Romania's serious political troubles and spoke similarly about the legacy of the corrupt authoritarian regime of Nicolae Ceaușescu and attributed the country's problems to the persistence the legacy of communism. This view was quite widespread. In 2011 two authors reviewed about 400 studies on the recent decades of Eastern Europe's transformation and summarized the idea that "there is hardly any outcome of interest in Eastern Europe and Eurasia that has not been linked in some way to the legacies … inherited from communism." However, they concluded: "A closer look at any of the studies that have probed communist-era legacies in depth shows that … some of the communist-era variations may be explained in part by differences in pre-communist structures, norms and institutions."[11]

Attempts to explain the early-21st-century phenomena and characteristics of various European regions by means of the immediate historical background of the 20th century and explaining some peripheral characteristics in Eastern Europe by the immediate Soviet-type economic-political legacy is nothing but superficial.

The "longue durée" approach

History, warned the giant historical minds of Marc Bloch and Lucien Fabvre, as well as their successor Fernand Braudel, is an endless process where the present is only the last point at the transitory end of a long development process. In order to understand history, one has to turn to the "*longue durée*" as they suggested. Quoting Braudel's words: "History is the sum of all possible histories … those of yesterday, today, and tomorrow. The only mistake would be to *choose one of these histories* to the exclusion of all the others." He also explained that "old attitudes of thought and action, resistant frameworks die hard, at times against all logic."[12]

Moving beyond the inadequate explanation that early-21st-century phenomena are merely the legacies of the immediate past decades, this book addresses the much deeper roots of historical difference between European regions. It is a legitimate question to ask: did communism create Russia, or did Russia define communism? Governor Miklós Horthy's capitalism in interwar Hungary was a corrupt, exclusive and authoritarian regime in alliance with Hitler and Mussolini. Postwar Hungarian communism exhibited several similar characteristics, although they were then and are still presented as antagonistic and oppositional regimes. Boleslaw Bierut's Stalinism in the 1950s or Wojciech Jaruzelski's Martial Law Poland in the 1980s exhibited similarities with the post-1931 one-party system in Pilsudski's Poland and the military junta of the colonels in the second half of the 1930s. The crony capitalism of Eastern Europe was distorted and socialism was born as deformed Stalinism, both of which were relatively backward, corrupt, authoritarian, and discriminatory. Electoral systems were crippled by open ballots, one-party regimes and other corruptions. As "God made man in his own image," to paraphrase the bible, Russia made any social-political system in its own image. We have to turn to the *longue durée,* the long historic trends, to understand regional differences in Europe. These trends will be discussed in Chapter 1.

Evaluating and measuring peripheral backwardness

I use the commonly used term "periphery" to describe relatively backward European regions. This is, however, only a *metaphor* in this book, since I do not employ its traditional usage, which originates in "core-periphery" or "world system" theories. The term "periphery," in various forms, appeared in early-20th-century scholarship and political pamphlets, and its usage increased in frequency after World War II following the 1950s collapse of the colonial system and the establishment of several independent new states in the so-called Third World or "developing countries." The less developed regions of Europe including Mediterranean and Eastern Europe were also incorporated into the "peripheries." (The "world system" theory called these regions "semi-peripheries" in the 20th century.)

The use of the term "periphery" in connection with certain European regions almost disappeared from the economic-political vocabulary in recent decades following European integration, the collapse of communism and the transformation of the former Soviet Bloc countries along the Western model. In the wake of the 2008 financial-economic crisis, however, the term reentered common parlance. The Mediterranean and Central-Eastern European regions were once again described as "peripheries," indicating their dramatic collapse and persistent weaknesses, which contrast sharply with the northwestern "core."

In Chapters 1 and 2, I briefly summarize the traditional core-periphery theories and their interpretation of the relationship between less developed peripheral regions and the advanced core. While these theories begin to explain the connections between these areas and their different economic standards,

I level two important critiques against them: they fail to explain the real reasons behind advanced development in some countries, and they neglect the factors that led to relative backwardness in others. I offer explanations for these developments based on a *longue durée* view of the history of the various regions. I also disagree with the one-sided approach of the core-periphery theories stressing only the exploitative character of the connection that permanently reproduces dependency. I focus instead on the ambivalent character of the relationship, exploitative which is virtually reproducing itself on the one hand, but positive and stimulating on the other that may help the elevation from backwardness (discussed in Chapters 1 and 2).

The use of the terms core and peripheries in this book thus serves no other purpose than to metaphorically distinguish between advanced and less developed regions. Instead of core, periphery or semi-periphery, I use the terminology introduced by the World Bank: *high-income, medium-income and low-income* countries and regions,[13] although I do not use the exact *income clusters* introduced by the World Bank for the entire world and all of the continents.[14] Because this is a book about Europe, it requires attention to a uniquely European cluster. The exact dollar value of these clusters and categories, expressed by per capita GDP levels, naturally varies over time. At the beginning of the 20th century, according to the income clusters I am using in this book, the most developed high-income countries had a per capita income level of around $4,000 (in 1990 dollar value), while the figure for the middle-income countries was about $2,000–2,500. In contrast, the per capita income of the low-income European countries was only around $1,000.

A century later, at the beginning of the 21st century, these figures were much higher. To get a realistic picture, we must to exclude the two extremes, namely the super high-income countries of Qatar and Luxembourg with their $120,000–100,000 per capita income levels, as well as the extremely low-income, non-European countries such as Sumatra, Congo, and Niger with their $400–1,000 income level. Using in the text the new estimations, made in the summer of 2017, I calculated the average income level of the world's 190 countries to be $10,562 per capita.[15] Of the world's countries, the *upper 20 percent* – nearly 40 countries – had per capita income levels above $20,000. This is the group I determine to be the high-income zone in Europe, while according to the World Bank's categorization countries above income level of $12,736 are considered to be high-income countries in 2014. At the *lower half* of the income scale (below the world's average income level of $10,526) is 95 countries with an average per capita income of $5,500. I categorize those countries that have an income level between these two extremes – that is, between $20,000 and $10,526 – as *middle-income* countries, differently from the World Bank's range of $1,045 and $12,736. In my evaluation, the threshold for low-income level in Europe is actually $10,526 per capita, different from the World Bank's demarcation of $1,045. Again, these differences reflect the fact that the World Bank's figures take a global sample and thus the numbers are lower than they should be for Europe.

The exact US dollar amounts in 1913 and 2016 need some explanation. In part, they reflect inflation, the difference between the disparate values of the dollar from one century to the next, which are quite significant. The US dollar had an average inflation rate of 3.14 percent per year in the century between 1913 and 2016. Consequently, $100 in 1913 is worth $2,424.31 in 2016. The other element that influences the dollar's value is, of course, the increase in GDP that occurred across all income categories during the 20th century. Regardless of the exact dollar values, the distance among the regions, expressed in per capita income level in US dollars, are hardly changed or mostly even increased. At the beginning of the 20th century, as described earlier, the middle-income countries had only roughly half, and the low-income countries one-quarter of the per capita income of the high-income regions, differences that persisted until the early 21st century, illustrating the relative backwardness of the peripheral regions. In some cases the gap even increased. In 1913, the least developed region of Europe reached 33 percent of the northwestern GDP level, today only hardly more than 11 percent of it.

It goes without saying that such a drastic difference in income levels resulted in radically different lifestyles and life possibilities. I have to add: the European peripheral countries, if we compare Europe to the entire world in the early 21st century, are mostly high- and medium-income level, while the Russian-Turkish-Balkans region lies at the top of the low-income zone. A few of the countries of that region (former Soviet republics) earned only about $2,000 on average per capita, an extremely low-income level.

In quantifying the income levels of the four regions of early-21st-century Europe, the topic of this book, we register the following differences:

At the top, *Northwest Europe* (11 countries) have an unweighted average per capita income of $49,317. This region is at the border of the group of super-rich countries (above $50,000 income level) and four of them (Switzerland, Norway, and Denmark, and, very near to them, Sweden) belong to the super-rich category.

The *Mediterranean-Irish* region (5 countries) earns on average $31,198 per capita. Consequently, this region belongs to the high-income group above $20,000 (although Ireland belongs to the super-rich category), but their average income is only somewhat more than 63 percent of the northwest countries, and they exhibit various weaknesses and vulnerabilities.

The *Central European and Baltic* region (9 countries) has an average income of $15,635, and thus lies in the middle-income zone, with roughly 32 percent of the income of the northwest. Only one country of this group, Slovenia, advanced to the bottom of the high-income zone.

The *Russian-Turkish-Balkan* region, together with the Western successor states of the Soviet Union – Belarus, Ukraine, and Moldova, but without the eastern and non-European former Soviet republics in the Caucasus and Asia – altogether 11 countries, belongs to the top of the low-income zone with an average per capita income of $6,241, more than half of the world average but only 13 percent of northwest Europe's and 40 percent of the income level of the Central European-Baltic region. Three countries (Russia, Turkey, and Romania) from this region are or are very near the border of the middle-income zone.[16]

The terms of backwardness, its measurement and generalization

At this point, I have to briefly clarify three methodological and terminological questions. One of them is the problem of the measurement of backwardness by per capita income level. In this book, advancement and backwardness is measured by per capita GDP, everything produced in agriculture, industry and services in a country. This measurement is, of course, somewhat one-sided, neglecting hundreds of other factors that influence progress and characterize backwardness. Measuring development level by GDP alone has generated criticisms for decades. However, the only correction that was made about two decades ago, which resulted in a somewhat more complex measurement, is the so-called HDI. In addition to income level, HDI also takes health and educational levels into consideration by calculating average life span and years spent in school. Based on the Gallup World Poll, the United Nations also presented a life satisfaction or "happiness ranking" developed from data point comes from questions that asks people in 156 countries to rate their lives on a scale of zero to ten – with zero being the worst possible life and ten being the best possible life. The latest rankings show that among the first 30 most satisfied countries of the world, led by Finland and Denmark, 17 northwestern European countries are listed. Hungary, Estonia, and Portugal are in the middle zone, at around 60th place, while Albania lies at 107th and Ukraine is in 133rd place.[17]

All of these new indexes prove that a GDP per capita index is not as one-sided as it may seem. Several examinations prove that various other factors of human development, including nourishment, housing, health, education, even water consumption, length of leisure time and traveling abroad, or satisfaction with life are closely connected to GDP levels. Higher GDP means, with few exceptions, higher consumption, longer vacations, higher educational levels, etc. In other words, the per capita GDP index reflects general development levels quite well.

Why some connections between higher income (GDP) level and other spheres of life such as higher consumption, better housing and more traveling are evident, GDP level, indirectly, is also connected with the political system of a country. At first glance, this is less apparent, but the connection is strong. Seymour Lipset's well-known study called the attention to this connection as early as1959. His argument, based on historical facts and evidences, said: "All the various aspects of economic development – industrialization, urbanization, wealth and education – are so closely interrelated as to form one major factor which has the political correlate of democracy." Lipset added: "the more well-to-do a nation, the greater the chances that it will sustain democracy."[18]

Since the 1960s, several other studies have connected the per capita GDP level with the strength or weaknesses of democratic institutions. In its 2013 analysis of the countries transitioning from backwardness, the European Bank of Reconstruction and Development concluded: "There is an emerging consensus that economic development indeed had a causal effect on democracy." This connection is not automatic and is also highly contingent on several domestic and international factors. Moreover, the Bank added, the connection is not direct, but delayed: "the impact of economic development on democracy may take between 10 and 20 years to materialize."[19] The delay is evident, but the given time seems to be over-optimistically short.

Another factual survey also clearly reflects the connection between GDP levels and the existence of democratic institutions:

> In 1999, 94 percent of countries with average per capita income of more than US$10,000 (in constant 1996 prices) held free and competitive elections, while only 18 percent of those with average per capita income of less than US $2,000 did so.[20]

Nobel laureate economist Amartya Sen expressed this connection by underlining the fact that economic development also means more *freedom*. The first sentence of the introduction of his book, *Development as Freedom,* states: "[d]evelopment can be seen, it is argued here, as a process of expanding the real freedoms that people enjoy," the liberation of people from imprisonment in poverty, social deprivation, political tyranny and cultural authoritarianism.[21]

The social-cultural factors that are closely connected to the income level, play, of course, crucially important role in these connections. As will be discussed in Chapter 3, low-income levels in connection to social-cultural factors, play a central role in reproducing backwardness.

A connected question in need of clarification is the danger of *generalizing* a certain level of peripheral backwardness. Some historians implicitly or explicitly question this possibility and maintain the uniqueness of each case. In his excellent *Peaceful Conquest*, Sidney Pollard discusses separate national cases of peripheral backwardness without any categorization and generalization.[22] Joel Mokyr flatly denied the possibility of categorization of countries that economically "failed." Paraphrasing Lev Tolstoy's famous first sentence of his classic novel *Anna Karenina* – "All happy families are alike, each unhappy is unhappy in its own way" – Mokyr maintained that "all rich and successful economies are alike, every economic failure fails in its own way."[23] I disagree, and by grouping countries into advanced and backward regions, I generalize development levels among various countries and attempt to explain the reasons for their successes and relative failures in Chapters 3 to 7.

Finally, what about the use of the term of *backwardness* itself? As I speak about the backwardness of countries and regions it is always *relative* to more successful and richer countries and regions. Still, there is considerable resistance to the term "backwardness." Some find it derogatory and unfair, while some others reject making value judgements at all. Regarding South Italian early-20th-century backwardness, one author preferred to avoid this term in favor of "difficult modernization."[24] According to another, Maria Todorova, using the term of "Balkan backwardness" reflects a "frozen Western image" on the Balkans to create a positive, "self-congratulatory" counter-image of the West, and, instead of backwardness, prefers to speak about "social-cultural differences" and the "different civilization" of the Balkans.[25]

Today there is a plethora of literature on the modern Balkans that displays sensitive resistance to the term "backwardness." In their edited volume of Christian Promitzer, Sevasti Trubeta, and Marius Turda state that "Southeastern Europe was frequently viewed as a 'backward' region."[26] They use the term "backwardness" in quotation marks and maintain that late-19th- and early-20th-century development transformed the region from a backwater of Europe composed of premodern societies into modern states. Similar to Maria Todorova, Mary Neuberger in her 2004 study discusses the "caricature" of "Western progress and Eastern backwardness."[27] Timothy Snyder's preface to his and Katherine Younger's edited volume reiterates the same point: "The Balkans are commonly associated with backwardness. Why not with forwardness? There are good reasons to see the region and its constituent states as precursors of events in western Europe."[28] He goes so far as to state that the "first genuine nation-states"[29] were invented in the Balkans and became paradigms that were eventually echoed further west: "Balkan models contributed to the emergence of a new world order."[30] Snyder concludes: "One way to write European or global history, after all, is to begin from a region such as the Balkans … where important concepts were invented."[31]

Ulf Brunnbauer's book *Globalizing Southeastern Europe: Emigrants, America, and the State since the Late Nineteenth Century* (2016) describes the dramatic waves of emigration from the Balkans that occurred throughout modern history. He summarizes the relationship between this trend and the region's stalled economic progress in the book's preface: "I sensed that one of the things that Southeastern European history could contribute to a general European debate would be highlighting the importance of emigration from the perspective of sending countries."[32] He concludes: the "economies of the region have remained much less productive than the most advanced European countries."[33] Without Slovenia, which is on the westernmost edge of the region and was formerly part of Austria, the average (purchasing power parity) income level of the modern southeastern European countries equals about half of that of the West. Maria Todorova, however, enthusiastically welcomes Brunnbauer's conclusion that "no other part of Europe displayed such a high level of migration activity"[34] as the Balkans did as a positive denial of "the usual stereotype of the static and isolated Balkans."[35]

In my view, based on my very personal experience, backwardness is a harsh reality and is not a cultural prejudice or bias. It means, due to the level of backwardness, moderately or sharply less income for food and clothing, thus a different consumption pattern. It also means crowded, often substandard housing, lower-quality or nonexistent health care, and lower life expectancy. While Swiss, Norwegian, and French average life expectancy at birth is 82–83 years, in Bulgaria, Latvia, and Hungary it is 75–76 years, and in Russia, Ukraine, and Moldova it is only 71–72 years.

It is also connected to lower standard of everyday culture and entertainment. It also means less or virtually no traveling, lower level of education thus lower qualifications and less satisfactory work. During the 2010s, an average Norwegian, French, Swiss and German, older than 15 years, has spent about 11–12 years in schools, while a Slovak or Hungarian has spent about 9 years, Portuguese 6 years, and Turk 5 years. These are ways in which I analyze backwardness as I use the term in this book.[36]

Regional differences and the future of Europe

In the 21st century, Europe still exhibits sharp regional differences. These differences visibly resurfaced in the wake of the 2008 financial-economic crises, after two-thirds of a century of European integration and homogenization. The crisis revealed the drastic disparities and changed the relations between advanced and less developed regions. It became evident that Europe, in spite of its relatively long history of integration, is much divided. After 2008, the disparities between Europe's four markedly different regions and their opposing interests threatened the collapse of the entire integration process.

This latter possibility was often discussed between 2009 and 2011 when the financial market reacted hysterically to the deep financial and economic troubles of several peripheral member countries of the European Union. The demise of these countries not only endangered the common currency and heralded its collapse but also posed the possibility of some countries' exits from the EU, the beginning of disintegration. The so-called Grexit, Greece's collapse and exit from the EU, became an everyday possibility. On the other end of the spectrum, leaders of some rich countries including Britain and Finland began to speak about leaving the EU. A referendum in Britain was held to determine whether or not to leave the Union (known as Brexit). The official program of the right-wing populist Dutch and French oppositions to the EU included stepping out from the euro zone and even from the Union itself. Newspapers, including the *New York Times,* published series of articles about an "approaching endgame for Europe." The Dutch and French populist critics of the EU suddenly discovered that the EU and its common currency were an "artificial" creation and said that the "euro's time runs short" and its "inherent flaws undermine the project." One of *The Economist*'s cover pages showed a euro coin, depicted as a comet plunging to its elimination and asked the question: "Is it the end?"[37]

Although Britain voted to leave the European Union in June 2016, no other element of those dark forecasts was realized; moreover, the European Union responded to the challenge with further integration in the Euro zone. Populist anti-EU parties suffered defeats in the Netherlands, France, and Germany, but became victorious in Hungary, Poland, Austria, and Italy. Sharp regional differences are additional ticking bombs that may explode and ruin integration.

Notes

1 See Ivan T. Berend, *A History of European Integration: A New Perspective*, London: Routledge, 2016.

2 www.cvce.eu/obj/the_manifesto_of_ventotene_1941-en-316aa96c-e7ff-4b9e-b43a-958e96afbecc.html, accessed February 12, 2013.

3 See Walter Lipgens, *Europa-Föderationspläne der Wiederstandbewegungen 1940–1945*, München: R. Oldenburg Verlag, 1968.

4 *Winston Churchill, His Complete Speeches 1896–1949*, edited by R. Rhodes James, London: Chelsea House, 1974.

5 See note 1.

6 *International Churchill Society, Winston Churchill*, The "Sinews of Peace" (Iron Courtain Speech), https://winstonchurchill.org/resources/speeches/1946-1963-elder-statesman/, accessed January 16, 2020.

7 *Gazdaság*, "Why Are East-Europeans Dying Earlier than Westerners?," September 21, 2018.

8 About the micro-regional approach, see Edward Anthony Wrigley, *Industrial Growth and Population Change*, Cambridge: Cambridge University Press, 1962; Sidney Pollard, *Peaceful Conquest: The Industrialization of Europe, 1760–1970,* Oxford: Oxford University Press, 1981.

9 See detailed Eurostat data at: https://ec.europa.eu/eurostat/statistics-explained/index.php/Education_and_training_in_the_EU_-_facts_and_figures, accessed January 16, 2020.

10 Ken Jowitt, *New World Disorder: The Leninist Extinction*, Berkeley: University of California Press, 1992, p. 283.

11 Jody LaPorte and Danielle N. Lussier, "What Is the Leninist Legacy? Assessing Twenty Years of Scholarship," *Slavic Review* 70, no. 3 (Fall 2011): 637, 654.

12 Fernand Braudel, "History of the Social Science: The Longue Durée," *Review* 32, no. 2 (2009): 171–203, esp. 182.

13 See on the World Bank and IMF classification: Lynge Nielsen, *Classifications of Countries Based on Their Level of Development: How It Is Done and How It Could Be Done*, February 1, 2011, www.imf.org/external/pubs/ft/wp/2011/wp1131.pdf accessed December 31, 2016.

14 The World Bank uses the GNI (gross national income) figures that contain the GDP and all other incomes obtained from other countries. In its "high-income" category from 2014 are all the countries that have average incomes higher than $12,736; "middle-income" means an income level between $ 1,045 and $12,736. "Low-income" countries have less than $ 1,045 per capita income. In Europe, there is no country with lower than $ 1,045 income. The European cluster I introduced in this book is different. High income belongs to the upper 20 percent of the world's 190 countries with more than $20,000 per capita income. Middle-income

means higher than the world average of 190 countries, that is $10,562, while low-income level is below the world average, thus below $10,562 per capita.

15 The freshly published GDP figures for 2018 reflects some minor changes compared to 2016. The North-West European core countries increased their average per capita GDP from 49,317 to 57,344 by 16 percent; the Mediterranean-Irish region from $31,198 to $38,206, by 23 percent; the Central European region from $15,635 to $20,479, by 31 percent; while the Russian-Balkan-Turkish region from $5,516 to $6,379, by almost 16 percent. Those years were the period of postrecession prosperity and most of the less developed areas regained their somewhat faster growth rate. The catching up process, strongly assisted by the European Union's aid program for the less developed regions, thus characterizes the European integration process, returned. As a consequence, northwestern Europe approached the level of the United States from 86 percent to 92 percent. Within Europe, the Mediterranean-Irish and Central European regions somewhat strengthened their positions compared to the North-West. The former from 63.3 percent to 67 percent, the latter from 31.7 percent to 36 percent. The Russian-Balkan-Turkish region did not grow faster than the northwest, remaining at 11.2 percent. Nevertheless, while in 2016 that region's per capita income level reached 35 percent of Central Europe, in 2018, only 31 percent.

16 The calculations were made on the basis of: statisticstimes.com/economy/countries-by-projected-gdp-capita.php, accessed June 7, 2017.

17 Jon Clifton. "The Happiest and Unhappiest Countries in the World," Gallup, https://news.gallup.com/opinion/gallup/206468/happiest-unhappiest-countries-world.aspx, accessed March 20, 2017.

18 Seymour Lipset, *Political Man: The Social Bases of Politics* (New York: Doubleday, 1960), 41; and Seymour Lipset, "Some Social Requisites of Democracy: Economic Development and Political Development," *American Social Science Review* 53 (March 1959): 69–105, esp. 75.

19 European Bank of Reconstruction and Development, *Stuck in Transition?*, Transition ReportLondon: EBRD, 2013, p. 24.

20 Ibid., p. 25.

21 Amartya Sen, *Development as Freedom*, Oxford: Oxford University Press, 1999, p. 1. The connection between development and freedom is, of course, not a given. History offers several examples when authoritarian regimes were introduced in relatively high-income level countries. After World War I, the defeated and humiliated Germany, because of fear of decline and widespread feelings of defeat, led to Hitler, in spite of the relatively high income level of the country. The international situation also contributed because the lack of a benevolent dominating power created a political vacuum.

22 Pollard, *Peaceful Conquest*.

23 Joel Mokyr, "Preface: Successful Small Open Economies and the Importance of Good Institutions," in Jari Ojala, Jari Floranta and Jukka Jalava (eds.), *The Road to Prosperity: An Economic History of Finland*, Helsinki: Suomalaisen Kirjallisuuden Seura, 2006, p. 12.

24 Nelson Moe, *The View from Vesuvius: Italian Culture and the Southern Question*, Berkeley: University of California Press, 2002.

25 See Maria Todorova, *Imagining the Balkans*, Oxford: Oxford University Press, 1997.

26 Christian Promitzer, Sevasti Trubeta, and Marius Turda (eds.), *Health, Hygiene and Eugenics in Southeastern Europe to 1945*, Budapest: Central European University Press, 2011, p. 3.
27 Mary Neuburger, *The Orient Within: Muslim Minorities and the Negotiation of Nationhood in Modern Bulgaria*, Ithaca, NY: Cornell University Press, 2004, p. 1.
28 Timothy Snyder and Katherine Younger (eds.), *The Balkans as Europe, 1821–1914*, Rochester: University of Rochester Press, 2018, p. 1.
29 Ibid.
30 Ibid., p. 7.
31 Ibid., p. 9.
32 Ulf Brunnbauer, *Globalizing Southeastern Europe: Emigrants, America, and the State since the Late Nineteenth Century*, Lanham, MD: Lexington Books, 2016, p. xiii.
33 Ibid., p. 317.
34 Ibid., p. 7.
35 See Maria Todorova's Endorsement on the back cover of Ulf Brunnbauer's book cited in note 32.
36 I repeat in abbreviated form these debates from my *An Economic History of Nineteenth Century Europe: Diversity and Industrialization*, Cambridge: Cambridge University Press, 2013, pp. 10, 11.
37 See *New York Times*, November 11, November 16, November 25, and November 28, 2011; there are many articles on this topic on those dates. See also the November 2011 issue of *The Economist*.

1 Long historical roads toward regional differences within Europe

Four regions in 1913

Everybody knows that countries are highly different in the world, that some countries are rich, others are poor. There are countries in the world such as Luxembourg and Qatar with more than $100,000 per capita income and others such as Congo, Niger, or Malawi at the $300–400 income level. The difference between North and South America, between Europe and sub-Saharan Africa, as well as between Australia and Pakistan or Bangladesh are extreme. This is a major world problem with catastrophic consequences.

Within Europe the physical distance between the two capital cities of Luxembourg and Moldova (Chişinău), or Luxembourg and Ukraine (Kiev) is hardly more than 1,700 kilometers (about 1,100 miles) but the per capita income of Luxembourg ($102,000) and Moldova ($2,100) or Ukraine (less than $2,300) are light-year distances from each other. This is extreme as well, but one may think that these two East European states are brand new formations and the comparison is not really fair. Let's use another example: that of the two neighboring countries of Sweden and Russia, physically very near to each other. Two old states, two great powers in early modern times that shared a long border until 1809 (when Finland, part of Sweden that time, was occupied by Russia). Sweden is at the border of the super-rich zone ($49,824 per capita income in 2016) and Russia is just at the border between the low- and medium-income zones ($10,885). Russia has hardly more than one-fifth income level of Sweden. The distance in income and development levels that separates the two countries is tremendous.

However, the gap between rich and poor countries within Europe in general is somewhat less catastrophically huge than among countries in the whole world, but still huge enough. In a quite consistent way, the richest countries have at least four to five times more income than the poorest ones. That was the case in the early 20th century. By the start of the early 21st century, this gap became wider: the income level of the poorest regions (Russia-Turkey-Balkans) is only 13 percent of that of the richest group of European countries (the northwest). This is quite a central problem for Europe and the source of dangerous conflicts, including the ones that frightening the unity of the European Union. What are the origins of these differences within Europe?

Explanatory theories and the reality

Regional differences are the topic of various theories for a century. Trade connections between advanced industrialized and less developed agricultural countries were already under discussion in the early 19th century. Relations among advanced and backward regions has been examined in scholarly literature since the early 20th century. The impact of good institutional arrangements or the lack of good institutions as cause of advancement or backwardness is a topic of theories for half a century. The so-called core-periphery relations are in the interest of most of the analytical studies about international economic relations and interactions among rich and poor countries and regions. There are economic explanations from David Ricardo's early-19th-century "comparative advantage" theory to the late-20th-century concept of Douglas North's institutional economics.

Let me offer a short summary about the widespread theoretical explanations of the relationship between advanced and backward regions. One of the oldest was delivered by one of the giants of classical economics, David Ricardo. In his *Principles of Political Economy and Taxation* (1817), Ricardo developed his theory of "*comparative advantage*" about the mutual benefit of free trade between industrial and agricultural countries, or as he differentiated them, between countries of "different specialization." In his famous example, free trade between Portugal and England (established by the Methuen Treaty of 1703, the world first free trade agreement) was advantageous for both countries since England produced cloth cheaper with its higher labor productivity than Portugal, while Portugal produced wine cheaper than England. At last both countries could win from exchanging their products. This means that advanced industrialized and less developed agricultural countries are both winners from free trade.[1] Less than a century later, Ricardo's exemplary free trade connections between Portugal and Britain miserably failed to prove his theory of mutual advantage. England emerged as the world richest economic leader while Portugal, in spite of its colonial empire, declined and became one of the poorest countries of Europe. This does not mean that Ricardo was totally mistaken because modern economic history presents several examples when the less developed country also profited from the free trade. I will return to this issue later in this book. However, it showed that he was one-sided not to see the ambiguity and the negative effects of this connection.

Nearly a century later, from the early 20th century, non-Marxist, Marxist, and neo-Marxist theories interpreted the relations between highly developed and less developed regions as exploitation of the latter by the former. The theory of "imperialist dominance," the existence of "metropolis and countryside" relations, and more often "core and periphery" dichotomy is present in investigations for a whole century.

These theories unveil several crucial characteristics of the connection between advanced and backward countries, most of all the uneven thus exploitative character of trade relations. This connection is presented as a system that reproduces itself. The exploited peripheries remain backward because the uneven connection with the core.

The British economist John A. Hobson published his *Imperialism: A Study* (1902) and explained – in contrast with Ricardo – that the rich industrialized countries subordinate the poor agricultural countries. "Imperialism is the natural product of the economic pressure of a sudden advance of capitalism which cannot find occupation at home and needs foreign markets for goods and for investments."[2] To achieve this goal, the most advanced European powers, first of all Britain and France, built up huge colonial empires. By 1800, one-third of the world belonged to a few West European colonial empires, but before World War I half of the world became colony of a few Western countries. To their colonial empires, the leading powers of the West also added an "informal empire" to their sphere of influence in countries and regions, including the countries of the European peripheries, that remained formally and legally independent but essentially dependent in their trade, capital, technological and market relations.

All of these connections well served the advanced countries that robbed the colonies, sold people as slaves, and destroyed the existing handicraft industry by their deadly competition of marketing their industrial product in those regions. There was, however, another side of the same coin, dependent countries often profited from the empires' investments and technology export and the market they offered for their raw materials and agricultural products.

The relationship between advanced industrialized and backward agricultural countries was analyzed by a group of Marxist theoreticians in the 1910s. The Polish-German Rosa Luxemburg in her 1913 book, *The Accumulation of Capital,* correcting Marx, maintained that the society is not consists of only two classes, bourgeois and proletarian, but also has a huge layer of "Third Persons." This layer is neither bourgeois nor proletarian but a precapitalist layer of the society and precapitalist regions of the world around the advanced capitalist countries within and outside Europe. According to Luxemburg, capitalism cannot exist without this "Third Person," or as it was later called in the second half of the 20th century, "Third World," because they are serving as expanded market and new, cheap source of material and food as well as labor force for the advanced core.[3]

A few years later in 1915,[4] the Vienna trained Russian Marxist economist, Nikolai Bukharin introduced the metaphor of "town and country." Today, he noted, entire countries, the advanced industrialized ones, appear as "towns," whereas entire agrarian territories appear to be "country." The general international division of labor between them as producers of high-value industrial products versus lower value raw materials serves the interests of the advanced countries.[5]

Vladimir Lenin in his popular work on *Imperialism* (1917) spoke about the highest and last stage of the history of capitalism when the leading capitalist countries already distributed the world among them and then turned against each other to redistribute it. The world revolution, he prophesized, would end this conflict. Lenin harshly criticized Karl Kautsky, the leading theoretician of the German Social Democratic Party who considered imperialism and colonialism not as an organic higher stage of capitalism but as a *policy*, similarly to "low wage policy" in early capitalism, that may change. The capitalist system, Kautsky concluded, can exist without it and replacing it by other policies in the age of "ultra-imperialism."[6]

Theories on imperialism from Hobson via Luxemburg and Bukharin to Kautsky described and analyzed the turn of the 20th-century world system, the dominance of the advanced Western countries. However, while most of the theorists presented the system as unchanged and unchangeable without total revolutionary destruction, Kautsky turned to be right that the advanced countries could replace imperialist policy as replaced early capitalist low-wage policy and find other way to dominate.

On that theoretical base, after World War II when the colonial system was gradually dissolved various versions of dependency theories explained the *core-periphery* (or "center-periphery") dichotomy. According to these explanations, underdeveloped countries, even if they are legally independent, are not simply more traditional and backward (agricultural, not industrialized), but continued be dependent from and exploited by the core. The advanced core is using military, political, and trade power to extract economic surplus from the subordinated peripheral countries by an unequal division of labor and the inequality between wage-levels. The advanced countries are producing high value (with higher labor content) and more sophisticated products, while the backward, nonindustrialized countries are producing primary products (raw materials and food). The latter contains less labor thus lower value. (David Ricardo's generally accepted theory maintains that value is produced by labor. Less labor investment means less value.) The exchange of the sophisticated high-value industrial and the low-value primary products makes possible for the core countries to extract profit from the peripheries.

The Marxist Stanford economist Paul Baran, in his *On the Political Economy of Backwardness* (1952), summed up the argument of this school:

> Germany and Austria, Britain and France, some smaller countries in Western Europe, and the United States and Canada occupied places in the neighborhood of the sun. The ... multitude of inhabitants of Eastern Europe, Spain and Portugal, Italy and the Balkans, Latin America and Asia, not to speak of Africa, remained in the deep shadow of backwardness and squalor, of stagnation and misery. ... [Their economic and trade relations with the advanced countries] reoriented the partly or wholly self-sufficient economies of agricultural countries toward the production of marketable commodities. It linked their economic fate with the vagaries of the world market and connected it with ... international price movements. This superimposition of business mores ... resulted in compounded exploitation, more outrageous corruption, and more glaring injustice.[7]

He also argued that the imperialist powers in the core, as they penetrated underdeveloped countries, had destroyed earlier social formations and distorted the development of those areas. That situation created lasting conditions and *permanent reproduction* of dependency.[8]

The base of argumentation of the dependency theory after World War II was presented by two theorists, Hans W. Singer and Raúl Prebisch, both of whom in 1950 described the situation of backward countries in the same way: the "terms of trade," (the ratio of a country's export prices to its import prices) is disadvantageous for less developed countries as the latter exports raw materials and food product with relatively little work and value and buy processed industrial products with high work and value content. Consequently, the less developed peripheries are exploited by the core.[9]

Immanuel Wallerstein's *world-systems theory* criticized dependency theory from certain aspects but also spoke on a class system or positions in the world economy that similarly resulting in unequal distribution of rewards or resources. The core regions receive the greatest share of surplus production, while the peripheries the smallest. One of the most important differences compared to other core-periphery explanation that Wallerstein introduced an intermedia category between core and periphery, the so-called *semi-periphery*. In his model, the capitalist world system emerged from the 16th century when outside the northwestern core, the greatest part of Europe belonged to the peripheries, but later, in the later 19th and 20th centuries, most backward regions of Europe elevated to the level of semi-periphery. They progressed toward industrialization. Their level, however, remained on a lower stage and remained less sophisticated than the core's thus the semi-peripheries still remained dependent on the core's technology and finances. The unequal structure of the world and the European economy thus remained based on unequal exchange, leading to exploitation. Nevertheless, Wallerstein, unlike most of the core-periphery theorists, recognized the possibility of positive effects of the connection for the peripheries and even the elevation from peripheral positions.[10]

Realities proved the ambiguity of core-periphery connection and the one-sidedness of most of the theories that analyzed it. Not only was Ricardo's theory of comparative advantage and the mutual benefits from free trade for both advanced industrialized and backward agricultural countries one-sided, but the various core-periphery theories from Paul Baran to Raúl Prebisch were even more so.

Long-term analyses of modern development clearly prove that exporting their raw materials and agricultural products to the core, if appropriate domestic circumstances make it possible – infrastructural and educational development among them – may help capital accumulation in peripheral countries. Furthermore, the core's investment to develop raw material extraction and food production at the peripheries and finance railroad constructions for trade connections may also generate economic growth and stimulate the beginning of industrialization on the peripheries. This actually really happened in various countries and regions in modern times (and will be discussed in Chapter 2).

Another weakness of all core-periphery, dependency, and imperialism theories that they consider backwardness as the outcome of the structural core-periphery and uneven trade relation what is producing and permanently reproducing backwardness on the peripheries.[11] They don't ask the question of why certain regions emerged and became advanced and other not, why certain countries became colonial empires and others colonies.[12] What, therefore, are the *historical origins of* backwardness and major regional differences?

More recent theories turned to rather different explanation of advancement and backwardness. They stressed the role of political, social and economic institutions and laws, the direct and indirect role of the state. These factors were stressed by economic historians such as Max Hartwell and Barry Supple in the early 1970s, and gained a central role by Douglas North and the so-called institutional economics in the 1980s. Hartwell stressed the central role of the unique English law in Britain's economic elevation that was created by the world's first parliamentary system.[13] Two years later, in his new study, "The State and the Industrial Revolution," Barry Supple emphasized the role of indirect state activities in economic development by creating laws and institutions.[14]

Douglas North, alone and with coauthors, in a series of works between the early 1970s and 1990s created the theory about the central role of institutions in economic development. Good and stable institutions, he stated in 1990, are "the rule of the game in a society … the humanly devised constraints that shape human action," led to economic development while the lack of them are the major cause of backwardness. "It is clear," he announced in 1989:

> that the institutional changes of the Glorious Revolution [in 1688] permitted the drive toward British hegemony and dominance of the world. … Would there have been a first Industrial Revolution in England? One could tell a plausible counterfactual story that put more weight on the fundamental strength of English property rights and the common law … that … ultimately forced responsible government. … There exists neither a definitive theory of economic growth which would define for us the necessary and sufficient conditions nor the evidence to reconstruct the necessary counterfactual story. But we are convinced from the widespread contemporary Third World and historical evidence that one necessary condition for the creation of modem economies dependent on specialization and division of labor … is the ability to engage in secure contracting across time and space.

This was the kind of institutional transformation, he already underlined in 1971: "that brought about the prevalence of market relations and the Industrial Revolution in Northern Europe."[15] In other words, good and stable institutions are the base of advancement and the lack of them led to backwardness.

This theory was broadly criticized. The evident question of "what led to the introduction of strong institutions and laws in one country and not in others," was often asked.[16] Others pointed to the narrowness of approach toward institutions. Gérard Roland opinioned that there are two sets of institutions, the fast moving political ones that "can change more quickly – sometimes nearly overnight," and the slow-moving "cultural" institutions "including values, beliefs, and social norms," – many of them are embedded in religion that hardly changed for millennia. He also argues that there is an "interaction between slow-moving and fast-moving institutions" and the slow-moving ones may block the realization of the latter.[17] These are basic ideas for a better understanding of reality, and I will return to them in Chapter 3.

Others argue that not only the lack of good institutions may hinder development but also in certain dictatorial power situations the minority may introduce harmful "predatory" institutions.[18] This also reflects the reality of backward regions outside and within Europe.

All of these theories offer some realistic explanations about the unequal relations between more- and less developed countries as well as the characteristics of the system to reproduce inequalities among countries and regions. However, they do not try and cannot answer this question: What was the *genuine cause* of inequality among various regions and countries? All of these theories thus generate further questions.

Let me underline the central questions again: If an advance core, by unequal division of labor and trade, as several theories maintain, generate the backwardness of the dependent peripheries; if imperial powers subordinate and exploit other parts of the world in an imperialist world system, what are the forces that elevated some countries to be empires and colonize or/and indirectly subordinate others? Why some countries and regions emerged as the core and others as peripheries, some as colonial powers, others as colonies? What led regions to be dependent on others? If superior institutions and stable laws generate successful development while their lack is the cause of backwardness than what was the genuine cause of the introduction of superior and stable institutions in some countries and regions and the lack of them in others?

Johann Wolfgang Goethe said, "All theory, dear friend, is gray, but the golden tree of life springs ever green." Instead of "gray theories," we have to turn to the "golden tree of life," the long historical development that diversified countries and regions in the world, and also within Europe, the continent we are focusing in this book. Without history, as one of the greatest economists of the 20th century, Joseph Schumpeter, opinioned, scientific economic analyses are impossible.[19] Indeed, various and diverse long historical developmental roads created different regions within Europe and made some of them advanced and dominant, others less developed and dependent. Millennial development led to the rise of northwestern Europe as the most advance part of Europe and separated it from three less developed and more dependent regions.

One of the latter, surrounding the northwest in a croissant shape from the North to the South is the region what I call the Mediterranean-Irish region. Another and less developed region was Central Europe together with the Baltic area, and the third and least developed region became Russian Eastern Europe together with the Balkans and Turkey (see Figure 1.1). Some of those countries

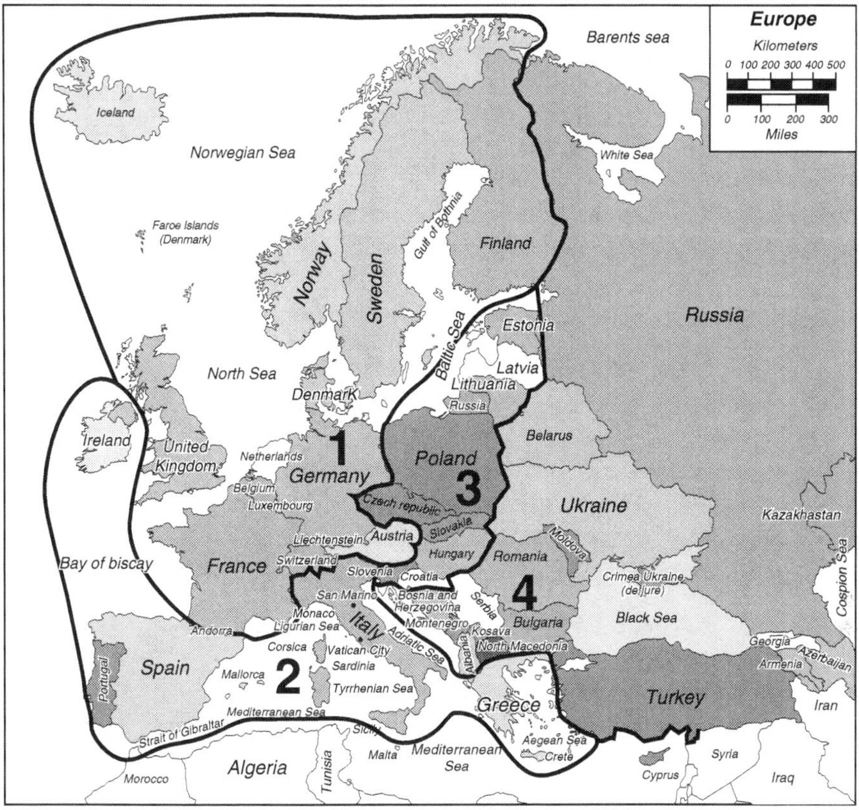

Figure 1.1 Four regions of Europe.

Note: Region 1: Northwestern Europe; Region 2: Irish-Mediterranean zone; Region 3: Central Europe and the Baltics; Region 4: East-South-East Europe.

are transcontinental; for example, the Russian empire and Turkey contain huge sections in Asia, not Europe.

The road toward a high level of advancement: Northwest Europe

Although the regions' modern development has its roots in the Roman empire, the early introduction of agricultural production and social-institutional arrangements, the real rise started in late medieval times when northern Italy (the area, in contrast with southern Italy, from that time on was an organic part of Western Europe) and Flanders played central roles in long-distance trade, early banking, and craftsmanship, and they became the prime forces behind an early European expansion.

The location of the countries next to the Atlantic Ocean had a tremendous advantage compared the others. In the 15th and 16th centuries, Portuguese and Spanish conquistadors crossed the Atlantic Ocean and the Indian Ocean. When the Iberian countries declined, the Dutch and the English assumed the leading role in ocean shipping and conquest in the 17th century, joined by the French, Swedes, and Danes in the 18th.

The Low Countries (today Belgium and the Netherlands) and Britain enjoyed easy access to the Atlantic trade route, as no part of those countries lay very far from the ocean. Both regions capitalized on this advantage by building canals (mostly in the 17th and 18th centuries) and creating the most extensive water transportation systems in the world. In the eighteenth century, each kilometer of navigable Dutch river and canal served seven square kilometers of land area. It was easy to reach the oceans from any part of the country. This transportation network density was not surpassed even two centuries later by the railroads.

England, located in the middle of the international trade routes, also had a huge navigable river and canal network. Canal building from the mid-16th century led to a navigable waterway system of nearly 7,000 kilometers, thus each kilometer waterway served 33 square kilometers of land by 1815.[20] The cost of water transportation in the northwestern region dropped to one-quarter of the cost of ground transportation, giving a unique advantage to the region.

The Netherlands and England soon emerged as commercial empires with settlements on various continents. Consequently, "the Northwestern littoral was the only region able to escape from prolonged economic stagnation."[21] Northwestern Europe had unmistakably transformed from the late Middle Ages. In the Low Countries, feudal class structures either did not exist at all or had been abolished from the 13th century on in Flanders and Brabant: "Serfdom, where it had existed at all, had by 1500 ceased to [exist and] … in the 'maritime provinces' … [a] basically free peasantry … functioned in a relatively individualistic society."[22] By the early 1500s, the Low Countries had a remarkably modern society and economy. Wage labor was dominant at a time when it was only marginal across the continent. Urbanization began in the 11th century in the southern provinces of the Low Countries and the 13th in the northern provinces. Unparalleled transformations took place between 1300 and 1500. To attract new settlers ready to reclaim the land, dig peat and cultivate the soil, that became predominant by the mid-14th century, the authorities sanctioned mass private ownership affecting two-thirds of peasant land. The urban population made up one-quarter of the population by the 14th century and had risen to nearly half of the population in the United Provinces by 1500. The urban elite attained political dominance over the nobility by 1572. In certain regions they began buying land and soon owned a third of it: "[The] adaptation of an urban-bourgeois practice to the larger stage of the territorial state is often seen as a key Dutch innovation."[23]

In an unparalleled unique way, in the 15th century, less than one-quarter of the population worked in agriculture in the region that contributed to the income by less than one-fifth of the region's income level. Industry, trade, and transportation employed 60 percent of the population, and these sectors contribution to the GDP was almost 70 percent. Such a modern socioeconomic structure was not achieved until several centuries later in other parts of Europe.[24]

The Netherlands achieved independence from Spain in 1648 that led to the formation of the Republic of the United Provinces. The Dutch Revolt was one of the earliest bourgeois revolutions that introduced constitutional rule, free markets for land and labor, modern property rights, and relative religious freedom. Taxation was based on expenditure, not on income, strengthening modern attitudes toward thrift and investment. The property tax on land and houses was a fixed percentage of the assessed value. The excise tax on the sale of wine, beer, meat, grain, soap, cloth, and later several other consumption goods provided two-thirds of the state's tax income. Inheritance and stamp taxes, and tolls for using canals, bridges, ports, and roads provided additional state revenue. Beginning in the 1720s, the Low Countries also collected wealth taxes.

These social transformations lay the groundwork for a new ethic, embodied in Protestantism that soon emerged in the United Provinces. An ethos of hard work, thrift, self-discipline, and a rejection of luxury as sin, was the essence of the Calvinist value system that created a new way of life.

Britain emerged on a similar road and also adapted most of these Dutch inventions. Some other Western countries, a few Swiss cantons, and parts of Germany followed soon. An interesting urban-merchant development, led by Lübeck, Hamburg and Bremen emerged in German lands between the 14th and 17th centuries. In those centuries, 70 to 170 cities united in a special guild of the Hansaetic League that became a merchant great power with its own Diet (parliament), army, and colonists in the Baltics.

The Low Countries developed a new social pattern fundamentally different from other parts of the continent: prestige and autonomy for merchants and financiers, and free rein for economic and technological innovation. A need for revenue for an almost permanent state of war led to the invention and introduction of a public debt system to finance state expenditures. Based on the earlier practices of certain areas from the 13th century on, the state consolidated public debt with short-term promissory notes and issued long-term self-amortizing life annuity bonds. The growth of savings – Amsterdam merchants increased their savings by nearly 13 percent per year around the turn of the 17th century – enabled the state to maintain a huge debt, soon twice exceeded the gross domestic product in the early 18th century, and it became the foundation of economic growth by replacing expensive short-term credit with cheaper long-term debt. Dutch debt increased by more than five times during the first half of that century.[25]

The Low Countries, based on its extensive trade, attained early economic specialization. The importation of grain from France enabled the Flemish to begin producing butter and cheese in the 13th and 14th centuries. Grain production was replaced by imports and highly specialized, market-oriented domestic agriculture between the mid-14th and mid-15th centuries. Windmills began to be built in 1407, and by the beginning of the 16th century about 200 mills were in operation providing energy for draining land. A flexible merchant class emerged during Holland's Golden Age.

The advanced shipbuilding industry produced 1,000 cargo ships per year and created the world's strongest navy and merchant marine. The 20,000 units in Holland's fleet were four times larger than its nearest competitor Britain's and 30 times larger than France's. Via *Der fliegende Holländer* the Netherlands emerged as the world's strongest maritime power. In the late 17th century, the Dutch merchant fleet's carrying capacity was almost equal to the combined capacity of the British, French, Spanish, Portuguese, and Italian merchant fleets.

In 1602, the Dutch *Vereenigde Oostindische Compagnie* (United East India, or Dutch East India Company) was founded, and it secured a monopoly of Asian colonial trade. At the end of the century, it was the wealthiest company in the world, with 150 merchant ships, 50,000 employees, 40 warships, and a private army of 10,000 soldiers. Dutch middlemen became the masters of Baltic, Russian, and distant overseas trade. Originally, the United Provinces imported high unit value goods from the Indies and the Levant, but, already by the 17th century, they had dominated the bulk trade of grain and herring from the Baltic region and the North Sea as well. First Antwerp and then Amsterdam emerged as the most important international trade centers that dictated market prices, and they became the home of the first stock exchanges. Shipping and long-distance trade promoted the growth of domestic agriculture and handicrafts industry. Dutch artisans soon began processing and reselling various kinds of imported goods: they wove raw silk, refined sugar, and cut and wrapped tobacco. From imported copper, Amsterdam's and Rotterdam's foundries manufactured guns. Heat-intensive industries, including brewing, salt-refining, distilling, bleaching, textile-dyeing, printing, and brick- and tile-making, sprang forth in the 14th century. Half of the beer and 30 percent of textile output were exported. Contemporary Dutch paintings present a highly realistic picture of the Dutch handicraft industry that was flourishing at that time.

The prosperity of the northern Low Countries was essentially a continuation of late medieval northern Italian and Flemish economic development. François Crouzet summed up this concept in the following way:

> Holland … was an entrepôt, like Venice had been … there was more imitation and transfer than mutation. … Eighteenth century [Netherlands] was rather the zenith of old-regime economies than the dawn of a new era.[26]

The Dutch Golden Age was the cradle of modern European transformation, and regions in the Netherlands became "the first areas of Western Europe to escape Malthusian checks,"[27] as well as the "first country to achieve sustained economic growth."[28] However, the Netherlands's advanced organic economy exhausted its potential, proving incapable of advancing further or competing with Britain's expanding, innovative, mineral-based economy. Additionally, the country fought and then mostly lost several devastating wars. The fourth

Dutch–British war effectively eliminated the faltering Dutch naval power in a final confrontation with British navy, which was nearly eight times as large. The United Provinces were powerless to defend their merchant fleet and colonies and lost a third of their fleet and their trade monopoly in East India to Britain.

British military victories over a 200-year-time span eliminated Britain's main rivals and established its leading position in the world. Expanded sea and military power represented the real comparative advantage of modernizing Britain, which took over global leadership.

Britain was far behind the United Provinces during the Dutch Golden Age of the 16th and 17th centuries, but merchant capitalism based on shipping and colonization soon emerged in Britain as well. Britain invested one-third to one-half of its enormous profits from the British–African-American slave trade "triangle" in domestic industries. Half to three-quarters of British industrial production was exported. The empire-generated income covered more than half of the domestic fixed capital formation. Exploited and looted Indian wealth helped pay down Britain's foreign debt.

The early start of the enclosure system created a special agricultural and social environment. Unlike in Holland, the system eliminated the peasant economy in half of the country until its climax in the mid-18th century, when the rapidly capitalizing system of big estates owned and cultivated 80 percent of the land. Britain introduced crop rotation, borrowing from the Flemish "intensive husbandry" that had eliminated fallow land. During the first two-thirds of the 18th century, a large part of the land that had been previously cultivated by small estates was appropriated as pastureland by the newly enlarged big estates. Agricultural productivity increased by three times between 1700 and 1850. As agriculture was the largest sector of the economy until 1840, "the key feature of the British economy was its (virtually) complete conversion to capitalist farming."[29] Smallholders lost their land, millions of people were uprooted, and large part of the countryside was depopulated. People migrated to the growing urban centers, providing an unlimited labor force for industry. Urbanization became the country's universal trend: the number of towns with 5,000 to 10,000 inhabitants doubled, and London emerged as the largest city in Europe. Several new cities emerged, including Manchester, Liverpool, Birmingham, Leeds, and Sheffield. Throughout the 18th century, the bulk of Europe's urban development took place in Britain.[30]

During the early modern centuries, the old feudal institution of serfdom was gradually replaced by free labor. A flourishing woolen industry emerged, and the amount of exported woolen fabric surpassed that of raw wool as early as the mid-15th century. One century later, wool represented 80 percent of British exports. Britain's real industrial breakthrough began in the mid-16th century with the development of iron, lead, and other manufacturing sectors. In 1790, the per capita iron output reached 15 kilograms, a level not attained in continental Europe until around 1870. Cotton consumption was also unparalleled: early-19th-century Britain's 2 kilograms per capita amount was only achieved on the continent in 1885. England pioneered a new energy source, coal, "the soul of all English industries." By 1800 Britain produced 15 million tons a year. As Anthony Wrigley observed, Britain's unlimited coal resources and their early extraction enabled the country to become the first in the world to advance from a high-level organic economy to a mineral-based energy economy. While the more advanced Dutch economy – which had attained an income level 50 percent higher than Britain's – was unable to enter the age of industrialization in the late 17th and 18th centuries, Britain pioneered industrialization in the 18th century.

The centralized British state emulated and reinvented the modern Dutch fiscal system. State finances were gradually modernized after Britain's Civil War (1642–1651). Excise consumer taxes and direct taxation (poll and property taxes) provided huge revenues for the state. In 1799, income tax was introduced. Britain also adopted the Dutch public debt system. When the Dutch William of Orange – Stadtholder of Holland, Zeeland, Utrecht, Gelderland, and Overijssel in the Dutch Republic from 1672 – was elevated to the English throne in 1689, he "introduced well-tried financial techniques from the Dutch Republic."[31] This act was linked to the issuing of Parliament-guaranteed securities, which had begun to be traded in the 1660s. The establishment of the Bank of England was a significant turning point, and public debt financing reached its height during the Napoleonic wars. Debts comprised 220 percent of the GDP by 1815. Fiscal centralization and revolution were century-long processes that were completed during the Napoleonic wars.[32]

Britain's superior naval strength emerged out of this sound financial system. The Royal Navy safeguarded the commercial network. In the early eighteenth century the British government established a permanent active armed service during times of war and peace, and naval bases in Gibraltar, Port Mahon, Jamaica, and Antigua. By 1780 the British merchant fleet, with its capacity of one million tons, became more than twice as large as the Dutch fleet, and nearly the same size as the Spanish, Portuguese, Italian, Norwegian, Swedish, and Danish fleets combined. By 1850, the carrying capacity of the British fleet surpassed 4,000 tons – nearly one-third of the world's fleets' total shipping capacity.

Like Holland, England also developed a modern society and a genuine market economy, which translated into merchant and maritime power. Also, like Holland, England dominated the emergent "modern trade." English merchants transported vast quantities of mass consumption goods. The rise of northwestern Europe exhibited both continuity and discontinuity in terms of European development. While the Netherlands fortified and continued Flanders's late medieval path toward development, Britain appropriated the economic innovations of the Low Countries and amplified them. As Amsterdam had replaced Antwerp, London replaced Amsterdam. Britain continued and also expanded upon the Flemish and Dutch agricultural revolution. Based on this inheritance and the spectacular rise of industry, however, Britain's development explosion led to a dramatic discontinuity that opened a new chapter of economic history.

All the gradual but revolutionary socioeconomic transformations of the early modern period affected the customs and habits of the emerging new societies in northwestern Europe. The increasingly affluent upper and middle classes, the upwardly mobile peasant families working in proto-industrial enterprises, and even the lower wage-earning workers were able to consume much more than they had ever before. Proto-industrial peasants, realistically presented by Dutch paintings, increased labor input by using female and child labor in family businesses to boost income and consumption even more. Jan de Vries documented the impact of the "*industrious* revolution," a change in the structure and behavior of households that reallocated productive resources and expanded both supply and demand on the market (my italics).[33] Improvements were augmented by the rapid spread of colonial luxuries such as coffee, tea, sugar, cocoa, and distilled spirits. European watch production jumped from a few thousand to 400,000 per year in the late 17th century. Expensive furniture, tapestries, and tiles adorned more and more homes.

Toward the end of the 18th century, Dutch consumption was two to four times larger than the European average, and British consumption surpassed this amount several times. As Abeé G. Raynal described in 1770, the "taste for luxuries and commodities has induced a love of work, which is today the principal source of [life style]."[34] Such a high level of consumption sharply stimulated demand for extensive economic growth, provided an increasingly sophisticated consumer market, and set the stage for the Industrial Revolution.[35]

These socioeconomic transformations also generated a new value system that began to take root – one that was strengthened and institutionalized by Henry VIII's Act of Supremacy in 1534, which established the English monarch as the head of the Church of England and paved the way for a Reformation from above. The Protestant ethic – the notions of thrift and hard work – coupled with the elevated social status of traders and merchants, assured British society's increasingly favorable attitude toward business and wealth. As had previously happened in Holland, religious tolerance led to rising immigration from the continent.[36]

Other than the Netherlands and Britain, no other country in the world had such a free, self-organizing society. Large groups of people founded clubs and associations to initiate and promote artistic, scholarly, technological, and economic progress by offering a host of awards and bonuses; this created open fora on burning scientific and practical questions. The sociopolitical transformation created an educational boom that was unique at that time in Europe. "Basic mathematical skills diffused earlier than literacy." Around the mid-17th century, in Western Europe it reached about 70 percent, and by 1800, 80–90 percent. The skill of calculations was a basic human capital in the period of rising capitalism.[37] By the late 17th century, 75–85 percent of the upper and middle classes were also literate, while literacy among the working classes reached 35–40 percent. At the end of the 18th century, more than half of newlyweds and nearly 70 percent of the grooms were literate.[38] Numeracy and literacy provided an exceptional advantage for northwestern countries. In comparison, the literacy rate in Eastern Europe at the turn of the 19th century was only 10 percent.

However, France – the model state of absolutism in the 17th and 18th centuries – also emerged as a modernizing and powerful European country. Its population was nearly 27 million in 1788, surpassing Britain's by nearly three times. The per capita national income was higher in France than in Britain, and France was more powerful during the 18th century. Under the 72-year rule of *roi soleil*, Louis XIV, France also possessed the strongest military force and became one of the largest colonial powers, and the military leader on the continent.

Together with Britain, France was the pioneer of modern colonialism and dynamic expansion. The founding of the French Indian Company in 1664 to promote trade with India and the establishment of trading posts in 1671 and 1688 signaled this development. During the first half of the 18th century, French colonial trade quadrupled and France's Indian trade increased tenfold. France emerged as the third European power to compete for primacy; in the 18th century, France significantly bolstered its leading position in world trade. In 1715, the French share of international trade hardly amounted to half of Britain's; by the mid-1780s, however, the value of French trade had surpassed Britain's.

Absolutist France established its economy through strong state interventionism, and, along with Britain, became one of the pioneers of mercantilism. Jean-Baptiste Colbert, the powerful minister of Louis XIV, introduced strict state regulations. The government administered a number of foreign trade companies, supervised the construction of ports and roads, and established preeminent state-owned manufacturing firms. In the 18th century, Lyon emerged as the center of the silk industry. Paris, with its large population and booming markets, became one of the most prominent hubs of artisan work: in the early 1790s, 350,000 Parisians worked in handicrafts.

At the beginning of the 18th century, the province of Languedoc became the world's largest textile center, producing high-quality, expensive woolen broadcloth that was sold on France's Mediterranean trade routes. Coal production increased eightfold during the 18th century. The French iron industry, which employed the old charcoal technology used in blast furnaces in the big estates, produced more iron than Britain. The royal cannon factory in the Loire Valley was an important player in the iron industry. Fifty years after the invention of coke smelting in Britain, France built the world's most modern blast furnace in Le Creusot. Along with original French innovations, "most of the British innovations in the textile manufacture were adapted in France in considerably less than a decade."[39]

Nevertheless, France preserved its feudal institutions and land ownership until the end of the 18th century. Political and economic freedoms were sharply restricted in the absolute state, and noble society stubbornly retained its anti-capitalist prejudices. Insecure property rights prevented investments. Agriculture remained hopelessly behind. Land reclamation through drainage, irrigation, and canal building was a rare occurrence in the French countryside. Crop cultivation mostly preserved the medieval three rotation system and yields remained traditionally low. Productivity stagnated. Feudal rents, including payments to the Catholic Church, consumed roughly one-third of the peasants' income. Population growth languished and reflected medieval norms. As a large and partly landlocked country, and despite its extensive road construction over the 18th century, France lacked the dense waterway system and shipping capability that had characterized the Netherlands and Britain. French feudal institutions prevented the development of modern state financing. Despite its much larger population and income, France lacked the modern taxation and debt financing systems found in the Low Countries and Britain. Tax revenue dwindled thanks to motley of personal and regional privileges and the absence of a national tax collecting body. In 1788 tax revenue was less than 7 percent of the GDP, barely more than half of Britain's. With its "privilege shaped" society and its obsolete institutional system, France was unable to generate higher state revenues and lacked an efficient debt-financing system.[40]

The absolute state, frozen in the *ancien régime,* very slowly emerged on the road to reform, but "the Revolution [in 1789 elevated] France into the modern world."[41] The revolution destroyed the noble society, introduced freedom of enterprise, and created a modern legal system. Although after 1791 the Revolution lost control and declined into terror, the Napoleonic era consolidated the achievements of the Revolution and the Napoleonic Code made property sacred. Social transformations that had been gradually gaining ground were now institutionalized. The Dutch, British, and French rivalry for economic primacy strongly contributed to the rise of northwestern Europe.

The groundbreaking historical transformation described earlier, however, was not a peaceful process at all. As Carlo Cipolla already noted, "It was the gun-carrying oceangoing sailing ship developed by Atlantic Europe during the fifteenth, sixteenth, and seventeenth centuries that made the European saga possible."[42] Ronald Findlay and Kevin O' Rourke, somewhat similarly to the imperialism and core-periphery theories, have called the attention to the central role of the colonial and informal empires:

> Purely domestic accounts of the "Rise of the West," emphasizing Western institutions, cultural attributes, or endowments, are hopelessly inadequate, since they ignore the vast web of interrelationship between Western Europe and the rest of the world that … was crucially important for the breakthrough to modern economic growth.[43]

The rise of the West, the birth of modern and advanced Western Europe, indeed, happened amidst terrible bloodshed and violence. The attempts to eliminate rivals in war – the British-Spanish, British-Hansaetic, British-Dutch, British-French, French-Dutch conflicts, not to mention "all-European wars" such as the Spanish and then Austrian succession wars, the Thirty Years' War, the Seven Years' War, and several others – accompanied and in several senses paved the way for Europe's transformation. The last 400 years of modern transformation were accompanied by 200 years of permanent warfare primarily by the Western powers. The "gun-carrying" ships were used for "gun-ship diplomacy" as well as trade, and the conquest of other continents created the forced establishment of Dutch, British, and French trade monopolies around the globe. The Western powers subordinated other countries and regions, climaxing in the occupation of most of the world through the creation of huge colonial empires. The "interrelationship between Western Europe and the rest of the world" indeed is the key element of the tremendous success and the rise of the West. This "interrelationship," however, not only describes peaceful trade connections but also conquest and bloodshed; the selling of African people as slaves; and robbing India, Sumatra, Indochina, black Africa, and half of the world. Building advanced northwest Europe was not solely a peaceful economic rise through economic development and industrialization. It involved not only "coal and iron" but indeed "blood and iron" as well.[44]

The revolutionary transformation of the Western mind from the Renaissance via Reformation to Scientific Revolution and Enlightenment

The rise of this region during the 17th and 18th centuries was also driven by a revolution in science and philosophy, which evolved into a new zeitgeist. This development had roots in several West European countries including the Netherlands, England, France, Germany, Italy, and Switzerland, and goes back at least to the Renaissance. Universities became hotbeds of rational thinking and fostered the cultivation of mathematics and philosophy. The flow of ideas crossed national borders with ease. A new conception of human society and indeed the universe, a new value system and a new way of thinking, all began to spread throughout the West. Secularized science and political theory replaced religion, and thus became the basis for the most fundamental intellectual transformation of the modern world. This process of radically changing ways of thinking, together with the spread of a commercial spirit that gradually appeared in Europe's late medieval centers, was closely connected with the Renaissance.

The reclaiming of ancient arts and scholarship was a tacit challenge to medieval religious bigotry. Men became fascinated by the human body and began to establish a new materialistic and rationalistic society. Renaissance individualism and *joie de vivre* created an intellectual fermentation that became a forerunner to the Reformation.

I am naturally not going to discuss in this book the glorious process of the centuries-long spiritual renewal and revolution of thinking about nature, people, society, state, and the entire world. Instead, I seek only to remind the reader of the crucial importance of this unstoppable intellectual revolution that occurred in Western Europe.

The Renaissance was followed by the Reformation in the 16th century, which represented the "triumph of the commercial spirit over the traditional social ethics of Christendom. ... Trade and tolerance flourished together."[45] The Reformation paved the way for the Scientific Revolution. The titans of this scientific and ideological cataclysm between the mid-16th and 17th centuries – Copernicus, Pascal, Kepler, Galileo, Descartes, and Newton – effectively revolutionized human awareness. An entirely new comprehension came to light in astronomy, physics, and anatomy. The proliferation of scientific societies under royal patronage in the 1660s – including the Royal Society, the Académie Royale des Sciences, and others – engendered a "monumental change in the realm of learning," a "seismic shift in understandings of the natural world" that led to the "crucial transition in the formation of the modern West."[46]

The Renaissance prepared the ground for the Protestant Reformation in Germany, Switzerland, the Netherlands, and Britain, which in turn paved the way for the scientific revolution, which ushered in the Enlightenment. The four countries swept up into Protestantism were united in their commitment to change and modernization. This centuries-long process was genuinely West European in origin. The forerunners included Joost Lips (Justus Lipsius) and René Descartes, who presented the first modern concept of the universe operating under mathematical laws in 1637. Descartes and his disciple Benedict (Baruch) Spinoza emerged as the philosophers of rationalism and natural law. Spinoza developed influential concepts regarding social contracts, majority rule, and individual freedom, and rejected religion as the product of human fear of nature's unknown forces.

The philosophy of the Enlightenment emerging from Holland paved the way for a revolution of thought in Britain. Isaac Newton published *Philosophiae Naturalis Principia Mathematica* in 1687, the "capstone of the Scientific Revolution of the sixteenth and seventeenth centuries."[47] In his early-18th-century works, Newton utilized rigorous experimentation and scholarly methodology to explain the laws of the physical world. "He [also] provided a rational mechanics for the operations of machines on earth."[48] The Newtonian scientific *Weltanschauung* transformed the way people thought about nature and society. It was the foundation of both Enlightenment scholarship and civil engineering. Mathematics became a practical tool for artisans in the early 17th century. A number of inexpensive textbooks became available, further widening access. The newly founded Royal Society "was actively concerned with the practical applications of natural philosophy" such as improvements in construction, metal smithing, shipbuilding, and agriculture.[49] A flourishing encyclopedic culture emerged, embodied in Diderot's *Encyclopédie*, which provided precise technological descriptions on everyday industrial practices.[50]

Modern political philosophy was also born. In *Leviathan* (1651), Thomas Hobbes challenged basic old concepts and replaced them with the notion of individualism: "The condition of man ... is a ... condition of war every one against every one... every one is governed by his own reason ... and every man has a right to everything, even one another's body."[51] John Locke, the most popular philosopher of the late 17th century, went even further. In his *Two Treatises of Government* he argued that laws are the most important guarantors of freedom and called for a social contract between kings and commoners to limit governmental power by making rulership constitutional:

> All men by nature are equal … [and] being born … with a title to perfect freedom and an uncontrolled enjoyment of all the rights and privileges of the law of Nature … It is evident that absolute monarchy … is indeed inconsistent with civil society, and so can be no form of civil-government.[52]

Locke also propagated the separation and mutual limitation of legislative and executive powers and became a most influential apostle of the modern *Rechtsstaat* and parliamentary system. Members of the English Enlightenment, especially Francis Bacon, envisioned the creation of research universities for basic and applied science. Bacon also advocated experimentation. As one researcher noted, "there is no doubt that it was an organic part of a complex package of social, intellectual, cultural, political, and economic factors that transformed the world in the nineteenth century."[53]

Special attention should be given to the rise of the modern political economy, which emerged in the second half of the 18th century with the work of François Quesnay, Richard Cantillon, Anne-Robert-Jacques Turgot, Sir James Stuart, and most of all Adam Smith. Smith published his *Wealth of Nations*, a thousand-page "crowning peak of the early development of economic theory,"[54] in 1776. In Smith's view, the preordained harmony of the market, governed by an "invisible hand" of market forces, ruled the economic world in the same way as harmony ruled Newton's universe. Human interventions (such as tariffs) only blocked this harmony and were thus harmful. Trade and exchange were natural characteristics of human beings, and market capitalism a genuine product of human nature. Smith formulated his free trade theory as a natural law that applied universally across the globe. Specialization and the division of labor were the primary instruments for increasing productivity and economic growth. Based on Smith's economic theory, David Ricardo established the theory of comparative advantage: free trade, he posited, is advantageous for both parties, as each party sells what it can most efficiently produce and buys what it cannot. Trade between industrial and agrarian countries, therefore, is not a zero-sum game in which one party wins and the other loses. The third member of the founding trio of modern economics, John Stuart Mill, introduced the notion of unrestricted private property and the free market as the sole bases of freedom and human rights. In this way, a laissez-faire economy, personal liberty, and democracy were seen as prerequisites for one another.

British philosophy had a strong impact on the French Enlightenment. François-Marie Arouet – or, as he called himself, Voltaire – in his *English Letters* (1734) expressed admiration for Britain's intellectual environment. He became one of the most powerful proponents of both natural law, "the instinct which makes us feel justice,"[55] and tolerance, as "intolerance is absurd and barbaric, it is the right of the tiger." He therefore passionately called for an intellectual revolt against an antiquated Church and State.[56]

The French Enlightenment produced a great number of influential thinkers. Charles-Louis de Secondat, baron de Montesquieu, idealized the British parliamentary system and attacked absolute power. Political liberty, he insisted, cannot exist "when the legislative and executive powers are united in the same person, or in the same body. ... [T]here is no liberty, if the judiciary power [is] not separated from the legislative and executive."[57] Here, the ideas of a revolutionary social and political system were clearly germinating. The Geneva-born Jean-Jacques Rousseau, who moved to Paris, expressed the aura of revolution most eloquently. The very first sentence of his *Social Contract* reads like a declaration of war against the ancient régime: "Man is born free and everywhere he is in chains." He defined a new concept of legitimate power: "Each, while uniting himself with all, may still obey himself alone, and remain as free as before. ... [Only the] State that is governed by laws ... [and] the public interest ... [has a] legitimate government."[58]

The Enlightenment was a fundamentally West European phenomenon. Its German giants were Immanuel Kant, a professor at Königsberg University, and Georg Wilhelm Friedrich Hegel. Hegel eagerly welcomed the arrival of the new world order, the end of history embodied in the *Weltseele* (Absolute Spirit) and "Reason" of Napoleon, "who ... reaches out over the world and masters it."[59] The new and liberating values of the Enlightenment held tremendous appeal for the elite and the educated throughout the region. "The religion of liberty took hold on the European continent ... England, France, and Germany exemplified the evolution of the religion of liberty in Europe."[60]

This "religion" made liberalism the dominant political trend in the 19th century. It was genuinely cosmopolitan and internationalist. The values of the Enlightenment became institutionalized by newly created legal systems and became the norms of modern society.

Northwest Europe at the top

Despite their significantly different trajectories and long histories of conflict with each other, the countries of Northwest Europe emerged from their millennial history shockingly similar and quite homogenous. The leading thinkers of the French Enlightenment – Mirabeau, Voltaire, and Rousseau – recognized the similarities between Britain, France, Belgium, and the Netherlands and spoke about the region as a "single republic." When writing about the uniqueness of the French Revolution in the 1850s, Alexis de Tocqueville also noted that he had studied the medieval political institutions of France, England, and Germany and:

> was struck by the remarkable similarity between the laws and institutions in all three countries. ... From the Polish frontier to the Irish Sea we find the same institutions ... and, more surprising still, behind all these ... was the same ideology. ... [I]n the fourteenth century the political, social, administrative, judicial, and financial institutions – and even the literary

productions – of the various European countries had more resemblance to each other than they have even in our time.[61]

Millennia-long historical development elevated the northwest to the most advanced region in Europe and also in the world. This region went through a series of successful agricultural revolutions, including science-based innovations and the mechanization of procedures. One significant advancement was the replacement of grazing with fodder production and stall-feed animal husbandry, which occurred from the 17th and 18th centuries to the late 19th century. Output increased two to three times or even more, and animal stocks doubled and quadrupled. Meanwhile agriculture employed many less people. For example, while German agricultural output tripled (measured by constant prices) between the mid-19th and early 20th centuries, employment dropped from one-third of the gainfully employed population to 18 percent.[62]

The region went through two industrial revolutions from the late 18th to the early 20th century as well, and all the countries became highly industrialized. A new energy system, first based on coal and the steam engine and then electric energy, served as the base of modern economy. This development clearly signals the West's rapid industrialization: the coal output of five countries of the region increased from 28 million metric tons in 1825–1829 to 629 million tons in 1910–1913 (over 22 times as much coal). At the same time and in same five countries, iron production jumped from 1 million to more than 34 million tons. Textile industry increased its cotton consumption from 150 to 1,900 million tons, nearly thirteen times as much.[63] Britain, the birthplace of the First Industrial Revolution, was the absolute leader until the last third of the 19th century; the other West European countries reached only three-quarters of the per capita income level of Britain.

As a result of the Second Industrial Revolution, led by Germany, steel output increased between 1875–1879 and 1910–1913 by 27 times in the five countries. Engineering industry increased its production by 5.7 percent per year and increased its output by more than six times in the West. A new chemical industry boomed; its output increased by 5.1 percent a year (increasing by five-fold in the last third of the 19th century). Germany and Switzerland became the world leaders in newly rising chemical production.[64] Paris declared itself to be the *capitale électrique* in 1891. New industries were born, including – primarily in France, northern Italy, and Germany – car manufacturing.

Parallel developing transportation revolutions decreased transportation costs by 80 percent between 1820 and 1910, further connecting the world – but most of all Europe. In the middle of this change, the railroads played a central role. Between 1830 and 1910, more than 362,000 kilometers of railroad lines were built in Europe. Until 1870, almost 90 percent of this construction was located in northwestern Europe, but around the turn of the centuries, the peripheries were also connected with the West (these lines were mostly financed by the West). Before World War I, in six Western countries there were more than 10 square kilometers of land per one kilometer railroad. Steam shipping, partly on the oceans and partly on a dense network of canal and navigable river systems, became dominant, pushing out sailboats and representing 90 percent of shipping capacities. Before the war, 79 percent of the world's shipping capacity was concentrated in European hands.[65]

An impressive demographic revolution accompanied all these developments, beginning in the Netherlands and Britain. After millennia of virtual stagnation, the populations of these two countries increased by 225 percent between 1700 and 1820, while the populations of other Western countries only increased by 54 percent. Altogether, northwestern Europe experienced a population explosion: its population swelled from 45 million in 1800 to 162 million by 1910.

In the northwest an ever-increasing segment of the population (from one-half to three-quarters throughout the 18th and 19th centuries) moved to urban settlements, in contrast to the rural peripheries' relative population stasis. All these significantly increased living standards during the last half century before the war. The caloric intake of the people grew by 50 percent on average, and its composition improved due to the sharp increase in animal product intake (from about 10 to 35 percent). The three-meal diet became the norm, and the region's population became, on average, between 4 and 10 centimeters taller than that of other European regions.

By 1913 all of northwestern Europe was industrialized and closely connected and enjoyed roughly similar economic standards. The other Western European countries advanced quickly in the second half of the 19th century, rapidly closing the distance that had separated them from Britain in early part of the century. While in 1870, the average income level in northwestern Europe reached only 69 percent of Britain's, by 1913, they became virtually equal (93 percent of Britain's).[66]

In spite of these facts, Western Europe was not fully homogenized: within the macro-regions quite important micro-regional differences were long preserved. Even in leading Britain, around the most advanced industrial zones less developed agricultural regions survived as backwaters for the industrial centers. France was much more uneven, with several backward areas in the south and east (especially when compared to northwestern France). Even before World War I, Germany clearly exhibited huge regional differences inherited from the major preunification variances among the German states. Bavaria remained more agricultural; the former East Prussian areas were closer to Polish and Hungarian economic models than to the rather different West German Ruhr area, the most industrialized part of the united country. However, all these micro-regional differences, which I will not discuss in this book, did not modify the basic features of the northwestern macro-region.

In the northwest, the countries basically exhibited similar advanced social-economic characteristics; however, the case of the Scandinavian region requires some additional explanation. Until the last third of the 19th century, that area did not belong to the industrialized, advanced part of Europe. Nevertheless, the Scandinavian countries performed the fastest and most spectacular catch-up to the West. This case offers the most important lessons for historical analysis. As late as the mid-19th century, the Scandinavian economy exhibited characteristically peripheral features. In the half century before 1870, the Scandinavian economy increased its income level by only 18 percent, in contrast to Western Europe's 55 percent growth rate. By 1870, the region's per capita GDP was only 69 percent of that of Western Europe. In Sweden and Norway, 72 and 60 percent of gainfully employed people worked in the primary sectors, respectively. Denmark remained totally agricultural and exported grain and livestock: altogether 80 percent of its exports were food products. Half of Norway's exports were fish. Both Sweden and Norway exported unprocessed wood to Britain. Scandinavian labor productivity was half of that of Britain's. Instead of big industry, small-scale handicraft industry dominated. In other words, the Scandinavian countries exhibited classical peripheral economic characteristics. They were predominantly agricultural and raw material producers and exporters. Processing industries were lacking. Karl-Gustav Hildebrand evaluated Sweden as "a peripheral country that builds on her natural assets, exporting … forests and minerals, [and] semi manufactures."[67] Until 1860–1870, Scandinavia was somewhat behind the Mediterranean region, and reflected certain similarities with Central Europe in most of its economic indexes.

Nevertheless, in sharp contrast to these economic indicators, Scandinavian society's Protestant culture, the early dissolution of serfdom, gradual but radical sociopolitical and institutional changes, increasing levels of education, and the radical elimination of the ancient regime made the sociocultural features of Scandinavia similar to northwestern Europe in the 19th century, despite its peripheral economic characteristics. The region thus gained the ability to exploit its virtually unlimited export possibilities and adopt modern technology and management.

In the half century before World War I, Scandinavia went through a miraculous economic transformation. According to certain calculations, it reached more than 80 percent of the British-Continental northwestern European per capita GDP; by other calculations Scandinavia achieved 90 percent.[68] Scandinavia, because of its historical sociocultural development, soon became similar to the West and an equal part of the core region.

Dead-end roads and relative backwardness in the peripheries

Millennial differences in historical development separated this northwestern core region from other parts of Europe. Around this emerging core – from Ireland to the Southern European or Mediterranean region, and to the Central and Eastern European half of the continent (including the Baltic area and Finland, as well as the Balkans) – different historical roads were followed that ended in rather different levels of development.

Compared to the northwestern core, these peripheral regions marched on a very bumpy historical road with potholes and long detours, and sometimes on ones that ended in dead ends. They did not lead to successful modernization, high levels of economic development, or radical modern social transformations. The peripheries, compared with the West, remained backward.

The entire history of development was behind their backwardness, starting with the age of the Roman empire. A huge part of the later peripheries namely remained outside the empire, which existed for a millennium (between 753 BC and AD 476). The empire incorporated the southern and western parts of the continent. But at its eastern borders, boarder lines divided the empire from the "barbarian" world beyond the River Danube, essentially separating the western and eastern parts of the continent in the middle of modern Hungary. The eastern half of the continent, including the Balkans, remained outside.

In the ninth century, the feudal, Christian, and agricultural Carolingian empire united the greatest parts of Western and Central Europe. The eastern border of the empire, this time, was the River Elbe, which separated the West; again the "barbarian" East was excluded.

The peripheral regions, of course, also had different geographical locations. At the eastern and southern edges of the continent, they remained open for the last waves of the Great Migration. For centuries, people arrived but moved farther or disappeared. Some parts of this peripheral ring were thus settled permanently much later. Consequently, the Central and Eastern half of the continent and a great part of the Mediterranean region joined Europe half a millennium later than the northwest.

Moreover, the regions at the edge of Europe remained vulnerable to non-European attacks and experienced more sustained "barbarian" dominance. Indeed, Asian and African attacks led to the conquest of a large part of the Mediterranean, Eastern Europe, and the Balkans. The Arabs attacked and occupied areas in the south of the European continent. For example, Sicily was occupied and ruled by the Abbasid Caliphate; Arab attacks led to the occupation of Malta, Sardinia, and Corsica as well. Attacks were launched against Rome and even northern Italy from the early ninth century to the late eleventh century. Spain was invaded in 711, and during the next seven years the peninsula was occupied (except the northwestern parts of Asturias and the Basque region). Although Muslim rule flourished most prominently in the 10th and 11th centuries during the Caliphate of Cordoba, it remained dominant in the south until the end of the 15th century. Consequently, a great part of the Iberian Peninsula was separated from Europe from the eighth until the 15th centuries.

In the 13th century, the Mongols invaded and occupied huge parts of the East. Russia, Poland, and Hungary became victims of successful Mongol offensives. The first invasion in 1221 occupied the Caucasus and small parts of Russia, but a second successful invasion in 1237 against Russia proper (first against Suzdal and Novgorod) led to the capture of Russia entirely by 1242. The area remained under Mongol rule until 1480 when Ivan III liberated Russia. These regions thus were separated from Europe from the mid-13th to the late 15th century.

The longest-lasting outside occupation of a European area occurred in the Balkans. The Ottoman occupation from the 14th to the late 19th century detached this region from Europe for nearly four centuries. All in all, Arab, Mongol, and Ottoman conquests separated the south and east from Europe until the 15th century (and in some areas, until the 19th century).

Other than the foreign (and, for a long time, non-European) attacks and occupations, a major natural catastrophe – geological shifts – hit the southern peripheries, especially the Mediterranean and Balkan regions. This happened partly in the 1300s and 1400s, but mostly from the 16th century onward, when the so-called Little Ice Age occurred. This major environmental cool-down led to very harsh, long winters; caused devastating flooding in the spring in lowlands; and ushered in the return of severe droughts. Cultivation moved to hills and mountain valleys while coastal regions became malarial wetlands. Wheat cultivation was replaced by maize and potatoes, and sheep and goat herding. Devastating famines and diseases decimated the population. The Mediterranean, the embodiment of wealth and power in medieval times, became an economic disaster and laggard after 1500.[69]

When the peripheries at last joined Europe and became an integrated part of it, their modern history continued to be characterized by devastating wars, bitter revolts, defeats, and continued backwardness. While of course war, devastation, and occupations happened throughout Europe and some of the northwestern countries also had troubled periods in their histories, they did not experience these calamities in such continuous and virtually permanent ways as the peripheries did.

In the modern centuries, most of Central and Eastern Europe, the Baltic area, and the Balkans remained under foreign occupation or lost their independence (such as Hungary, Italy, the Baltics, and tripartitioned as Poland). Most importantly, the peripheries did not experience the social development that led to the Protestant revolution and the whole set of resultant transformations in the West. When the northwest's modern transformation occurred and merchant capitalism elevated the region to the top, several peripheral regions declined back into a so-called "second serfdom" and remained frozen in the *ancien régime* until the late 19th century. The Protestant revolution was either defeated by Austrian Counter-Reformation or never even happened in the Russian East and the Balkan peripheries. Enlightenment was also excluded: the peripheral countries did not modernize prevailing ways of thinking, and thus these cultures did not generate scientific revolutions.

Instead, Romanticism arrived from the West: a revolt against the Enlightenment that generated passionate nationalism in the early 19th century, and also sparked several revolts against occupation and the rigid, unchanged *ancien régime*. Revolts and revolutions, however, were defeated; dependence on occupying or "only" dominating advanced countries characterized the entire history of these regions. During the 18th and 19th centuries this definitely aggravated backwardness by exacerbating the unequal, exploitative economic connections in which these regions became unprocessed food and raw material exporters who bought processed industrial products.

Nevertheless, certain layers of the societies in those areas looked to the northwest as a model and tried to sweep away the unchanged old regimes, but they were not strong enough to win. Revolutions struggling to create radical sociopolitical change were soundly defeated. In Hungary, the 1848 revolution partly succeeded in liberating the serfs and abolishing noble privileges and feudal institutions, but it completely failed to achieve independence from Austria and radically eliminate the old social structures. The retribution that followed created severe impediments to the country's development. Modern sociolegal and institutional systems were not established before the Austro-Hungarian Compromise of 1867. Half a century later, two revolutions followed the lost war in 1918–1919, a democratic one and then a communist one, but both were defeated.

In Spain, five revolutions in six decades of the 19th century attacked the *ancien régime*, but all were crushed. Modern institutions were sorely lacking. Liberal constitutions were rescinded and feudal fees and noble privileges, along with internal tariffs, were reposed. An all-powerful Catholic Church that oppressed science and the big entailed estate class in the south prevailed for a long time. A medieval mining law impeded the extraction of Spain's highly abundant natural resources. Moreover, the mining law of 1825 deemed that all of the country's natural resources belonged to the Crown – thus assuring no interest to explore. However, the Vicálvaro Revolution of 1854 and the La Gloriosa Revolution of 1868, at last abolished the *ancien régime* in Spain. A new liberal constitution in 1869 ushered in a return to reform that made modernization possible.

Portugal was on a similar trajectory. Political instability and permanent conflict between liberal forces and the *ancien régime*, together with wars, insurrections, and two civil wars in the 1830s and 1840s, paralyzed the country throughout the 19th century. Finally, the assassination of King Carlos (1908) assured the victory of a military-backed republican revolution in 1910.

Revolutions did not even occur in most parts of the peripheral regions. Nation- building and reform from above led to the gradual and partial abolition of feudal institutions, and a half-hearted introduction of modern ones, mostly from the 1860s onward. The Italian *Risorgimento*, the unification of the country, established modern institutions between 1860 and 1870. But it was a *rivoluzione mancata* (a failed revolution), as Antonio Gramsci opined – a missed opportunity for social and political renewal, as it was based on a compromise between the Piedmontese monarchy, the military elite, and the southern landowning nobility. The new reforms, as happened in most of the cases in the periphery, were enacted by the old *classe dirigente*. The Italian political dictionary created the term *gattopardismo* for the mentality of the painfully partially reformed old nobility, as was brilliantly described by Giuseppe Tomasi di Lampedusa's classic novel *Il Gattopardo* (The Leopard). The practice of pseudo-reforms and spurious societal change preserved the ingrained privileges of the old elite.

Until the early 20th century Russia remained frozen in Tsarist autocracy, with no semblance of parliamentarianism. (That was, however, even that time only a very short-lived episode.) Serfs were tied to the land and sold as appendages of private property. This archaic state of affairs remained unchanged for a very long time. Three waves of moderate reform over an entire century ushered in piecemeal gradual change. The first reform in 1832 under Tsar Nicholas I improved the conditions of "state peasants," some 40 percent of the Russian peasantry, who became "free rural dwellers" who lived on state land but gained freedom of movement and the ability to own private property. A second reform 30 years later officially abolished serfdom (1861). The peasants, however, had to pay large sums to compensate the landlords, and they lost the personal parcels they had previously cultivated. Above all, both reforms left intact the ancient structure of the village community. The peasants' land was not privately owned but belonged to the entire community, the *obshchina* (or *mir*), which was responsible for paying taxes and remuneration collectively. Leaving the community or obtaining a passport for domestic travel required the *obschina*'s permission. The peasants thus remained bound to the land, and their mobility was strictly limited. A third reform, which was not enacted until 1906, finally emancipated the peasants and abolished the ancient village communities. About 38 million acres of communal lands, or nearly one-third of total private peasant land, was privatized. The aims of this reform were not fulfilled until 1917.

That year two consecutive revolutions occurred. The first, a democratic revolt, was defeated by the second, the Bolshevik revolution, but a deformed socialism followed and thus that revolution, after only roughly three-quarters of a century, also failed.

In Poland, three failed uprisings by the Polish nobility against Russia paralyzed the partitioned country between the late 18th century and the early 1860s. The Polish nobility refused to liberate the serfs who, paradoxically, were emancipated by the Russian tsar in 1863 in spite of rebellious resistance by the Polish nobility. Reunification of the country happened one and half centuries later, after World War I.

Thus, modern economic and social transformations were badly delayed and incomplete during the entire 19th and 20th centuries. It took several decades to abolish serfdom and carry out agrarian reforms in the peripheral regions. With some differences in various localities, the process was strikingly similar throughout the peripheries. First, the former feudal aristocracy took charge of the reforms and "became their chief beneficiary. … The peasantry emerged weakened … they lost as a rule one-third or one-half of their land."[70] In the Balkans in the half-millennium of Ottoman bureaucratic and military rule, the land belonged to the Sultan, and the peasants paid taxes to the Sultan's military governors. When they emerged as owners of their lands, their parcels were insufficiently small to produce goods for the market, and they were bound to the village community (*zadruga*) until the 20th century. Consequently, Balkan agriculture remained confined to subsistence farming.

Modernization was not only delayed but also the surviving elements of the *ancien régime* infiltrated the new institutions. Pre-modern elements and other remnants of the past blocked the way of the new, and this hybrid status quo remained the essence of these partially modernized societies. The noble landowning elite continued to monopolize large swaths of land and to hold most of the wealth of several peripheral countries, even after the abolition of their feudal privileges. In the best case, the landowning aristocracy invested in their own estates, but, as Vilfredo Pareto concluded from the south Italian experience, they usually became parasitic, transforming from *classes dirigantes* to *classes digerantes* (digesting classes).

Unlike in the modernizing northwest where modern agriculture emerged, on the peripheries the "Malthusian check" remained the reality. Backward agriculture was unable to feed the fast-growing population, and famine decimated the people and cut back population growth time and time again. The last two major food crises of the 19th century affected Europe's peripheral regions. The best-known and most tragic was the Irish potato famine of 1846–1848. A series of climatic disasters destroyed a large part of the crop in consecutive years in the 1840s. Mass starvation and devastating diseases killed more than one million people between 1846 and 1851. Another one million emigrated. Emigration continued for the rest of the century and by 1911, Ireland had a population only 4.4 million compared to 8 million in 1841.

One of the last major famines in 19th century Europe nearly decimated Finland's population in the "years of the great hunger" in 1866–1868. Floods, frost, and consecutive crop failures killed nearly 8 percent of the country's population. Spain suffered famines in 1857, 1868, 1879, and 1898. Russia's situation is well expressed by the regular outbreaks of starvation and cholera, as well as the eruption of thousands of local peasant uprisings, throughout the 19th century. (Starvation killed millions of people even in the 1930s during Stalin's collectivization and "de-kulakization" drive.)

These peripheries did not have traditions of democratic political structures and institutions either. In modern times they were under foreign rule or local nationalist autocratic-authoritarian dictatorial systems.

Stimulating influence by the connection with the advanced core

The peripheral regions, nevertheless, were part of Europe geographically, and were influenced by the advanced northwestern core. A part of the elite on the peripheries looked to the West with envy and wanted to follow it. The Western influence thus belongs to the history of these peripheries, from the very beginning of their European saga until today. The connections are multifaceted. Christian priests were sent by the Church from the West to baptize the pagans of the East. Western princes were invited to the thrones, and noble soldiers to the royal courts of these countries. Indeed, these regions embraced Christianity (with several centuries of delay) beginning in the ninth and tenth centuries, and by the 13th century Europe as a whole was Christian.[71] The regions that were occupied by non-Christian powers remained or returned to Christianity after their liberation from non-European rule. Similarly, with a long historical delay the peripheral regions with permanent settlements and limited pastureland gave up their nomadic pastoral economies and turned to cultivating the land. (In the Balkans, this was the positive impact of early Ottoman rule.) Agriculture slowly developed and the sociopolitical structures were also transformed along the Western pattern. Tribal, blood-related social structures were reorganized according to territorial principles of the West. Centralized states and kingdoms were established, and private ownership of land and noble-serf relationships were copied as well.

For quite a long time after their "transplants," the imitative structures and institutions remained more superficial, rather than deeply rooted or mixed with old structures and customs.[72] They did not have an inner dynamism for organic further development. The peripheries of Europe remained much more stagnant compared to the northwest. When the gradual but spectacular transformation of the northwest gained momentum and started to transform the core by the closely connected chain of revolutions – the Protestant revolution, the scientific revolution, the Enlightenment, and the establishment of constitutional rule – the peripheries remained silent and could not follow in the footsteps of the West.

Modern society failed to materialize in the peripheries. In Spain, south Italy, Hungary, Poland, and Russia, a modern Western *burger* society with entrepreneurial business elite, a rising middle class, and an urban industrial proletariat remained in an embryonic state. Instead, a "dual society" emerged, with dominant and only somewhat modernized feudal elite and an emancipated peasantry on the one hand, and a small, modern, urban society on the other. The noble landowner elite and the gentry-based, bureaucratic and military middle class monopolized political power in these societies. The emancipated but still socially excluded mass of peasants – landless or dwarf-subsistence plots owners – remained at the bottom of the social hierarchy.

However, contact with and influence by the northwestern core also had positive impacts on the peripheries. This influence did not affect all peripheral regions equally. It had a stronger impact on the countries and areas that were geographically next to the core such as Ireland, Finland, the Baltic region, Hungary, and Poland; Russia, Spain, Portugal, and the Balkans were much less affected. The nearby peripheral regions enjoyed the gift of proximity and the rapidly industrializing West, which offered a huge market for their agricultural and even processed food products. They easily adopted new Western inventions such as vaccinations to cope with medieval illnesses and bolster demographic growth. Later, skilled Western workers and industrialists settled and transmitted their knowledge to establish banks, promote mining, and even found industrial companies in modern economic sectors.

Beside personal contacts and influence, the late-starter regions and countries that were several centuries behind looked to the more advanced West, duplicating their institutions and laws, and trying to follow their military structures and customs. They copied the modern agricultural system and some elements of the social organization as well.

The modern urban elements of the slowly transforming peripheries, especially those proximal to the core, gradually formed a parallel society comprised of entrepreneurial business elites that lacked political power and, in several countries, were considered non-indigenous foreigners – Greeks, Germans, and Jews. This emerging modern middle class was extremely weak, both in number and in social standing. Moreover, the new industrial working class represented only seven to seventeen percent of the population before World War I. The modern elements of these dual societies were subordinated to the traditional formerly noble elite.

A similar phenomenon of "parallel elites" characterized Spanish society. The political class was formed from the traditional provincial elite and the "Spanish government and bureaucracy were still being recruited via clientage and patronage."[73] Unlike in Central and Eastern Europe, the sharp ethnic-religious division did not exist between the two elites in Spain, and they "had a great deal in common. They shared a tendency toward 'aristocratic' values, similar provincial origins, and similar family trajectories ... similarities in behavior."[74] The peripheral countries' incomplete modernization enabled them to retain their old political systems in a somewhat modernized form. Autocratic power was only moderated by authoritarian regimes that introduced a veneer of formal parliamentary system; brutal oppression and entrenched corruption were also preserved.

Incomplete nation-building in much of the peripheral regions actually strengthened and legitimized the unquestioned rule of authoritarian monarchs, landowning oligarchies, and the gentry. They were now embraced as the embodiments of "national interest" and "saviors of the nation" in the fight against the "enemies of the nation," including foreign oppressors, hostile minorities, and rival neighbors. As the Hungarian sociologist István Bibó brilliantly summarized, "Deformed, interrupted national development led both to chauvinism and autocratic, authoritarian regimes and policies."[75]

In the Balkans "all power was concentrated in the hands of those who managed the government. ... Centralized autocracies dominated by narrowly recruited bureaucracy."[76] Russia did not even go this "far" and remained autocratic without even a semblance of formal democracy. The tsarist regime remained strictly centralized and the "service nobility," subordinated to the tsar, comprised the government bureaucracy.[77]

In the most backward peripheral regions, the state turned against its own population. The aristocratic military-bureaucratic elite ran corrupt, "kleptocratic" regimes. The Balkans and Russian predatory ruling elites turned against their own peasant populations. The prominent Romanian historian Nicolae Iorga characterized the Romanian state in a similar way around the turn of the 20th century, calling it a "*stat de pradă*," or predatory state. Both William McNeill, in his two celebrated works speaks about the fundamentally Asian culture of steppe nomads in the Balkans, and Samuel Huntington, similarly describe the existence of distinctly "Euro-Asiatic" civilizations in 70–90 percent of Greek Orthodox East European societies.[78] In these countries, closed social networks, patronage, and subordination were the rule, as was a culture in which people did not take their destiny into their own hands and did not organize to improve their social standing.

In the late 18th century, Adam Fergusson contrasted civil society with "barbarous" ones, where no law governs and "corruption … tends to political slavery." The uncivil society was a highly disadvantageous social and institutional environment for modern transformation. Painful historical circumstances created a pervasive negativism and insouciance in the face of major challenges. From time to time, desperate helplessness would be suddenly replaced by quixotic heroism and the waging of ultimately hopeless battles, which led to even greater desperation and self-pity. (The Serbs celebrate their historical fiasco as a national holiday.) They nurtured the bitter feeling of being heroically isolated; of being the victims of history; and of being the pawns of stronger, luckier, and evil enemies. This demoralizing negativism led to a culture of complaint that eradicated any determination to win peaceful, quotidian battles through successful compromise in order to gain a better future. This was a 180-degree difference from the response of the Swedes and Danes after their historical military defeats and their loss of empire and national territory. For them, external setbacks had to be met with internal fortitude. Difficult circumstances created positive responses, and consequently led to recovery and progress.

Economic geography and historical studies both speak about the "proximity factor." The European Bank for Reconstruction and Development, based on the experience of Central Europe and the Baltics as well as Southern Europe around the turn of the millennium, concluded that

> being close to global centres of economic activity promotes productivity catch-up. This is in line with the experience of CEB and SEE countries [Central European and Baltic and South East European], whose proximity to Western Europe is widely viewed as having helped them to catch up. Likewise, [it noted] the "negative coefficient for economic remoteness."[79]

Three distinct peripheral macro-regions before World War I

The peripheries were far from being similar. Some areas close to the Western core had more advantages and began down the road of better advancement, while others remained almost frozen in the past (although some advanced pockets emerged, signaling elements of development). A third type of region virtually failed to progress and remained almost entirely dominated by the past. The three distinct peripheral regions are the following:

A. *Finland, Ireland, Central Europe (with the eastern provinces of Prussia), and the Baltic area.* Based on their location and somewhat better historical background, these countries became able to profit from the huge imperial markets they belonged to, went through successful agricultural revolutions, significantly increased their food exports, and invested capital in certain industrial sectors. Poland, the Baltic countries, and Finland emerged as the relatively most advanced industrial regions of the Russian empire. Ireland and Hungary (parts of the developed British and Habsburg empires, respectively) established an advanced food processing sector (beer and whisky, and flour milling, respectively) and also started establishing modern industrial branches, such as shipbuilding in Ireland and electric industry in Hungary.

This peripheral region entered the road toward modern transformation and developed an agrarian-industrial structure. Before World War I, about two-thirds of gainfully occupied people still worked in agriculture, but one-third in industry and services. Their GDP tripled between 1820 and 1913. Although they were unable to catch up with the northwest, they did not lose much ground either. This half-modernized peripheral region had 62 percent of the per capita GDP of the core in 1820; their comparative economic level only declined to 57 percent by 1913.

B. *The Iberian Peninsula, Russia, and southern Italy* remained far behind. Their agricultural system remained basically traditional in these backward agricultural economies. However, some pockets of modernized islands signaled some very limited progress: in Catalonia and along the seashore in Spain and Portugal, in Siberia and some parts of the Don area in Russia, developing export-oriented agricultural in south Italy signaled minor development. Similarly, mineral extraction advanced fast, but industrialization did not start, except in some (mostly foreign owned) isolated industrial pockets in the Vizcaya area in Spain, and in Russia in St. Petersburg, the Donetsk area, and around Moscow. The per capita industrialization, however, reached only one-third of the Western level. Iron output (20 percent) and textile output (6 percent) were only small segments compared with the West. The region remained one-sidedly agricultural, with more than 70 percent of the active population working in this sector before the war. The Mediterranean and Russian regions increased their total national incomes only by 88 percent, less than half, between 1820 and 1913. They lost significant ground compared to the Northwest: in 1820 they represented 66 percent of the core's per capita GDP level, but by 1913 they were only responsible for 42 percent of it.

C. *The Balkans and the borderland of Austria-Hungary (Bosnia, Bukovina, Galicia, etc.)* hardly attracted any Western investments and remained entirely agricultural. Grain and animal production remained traditional. Unique to Europe, even the per capita output of the farm population declined between 1860 and 1913. The livestock production stagnated (Bulgaria) or sharply declined (Serbia and Montenegro). In the most traditional way, agriculture employed three-quarters of the population and produced 70 to 80 percent of the region's GDP. Industrialization virtually did not start. The embryonic industrial sector employed only 7–10 percent of the active population. In most of these countries, the entire industry employed fewer workers than one single major Western company. Two-thirds of the industrial employees worked in small-scale handicraft industries. Industry contributed to the region's GDP only by 10 percent. Although the region's per capita income level increased by 2.5 times between 1860 and 1913, ultimately the Balkan region failed to modernize. Its average per capita GDP was hardly more than one-third of the Western level, was 39 percent behind the Spanish GDP, and 8 percent behind the Russian level before the war.

Millennia of differences in historical development led to a severely divided Europe. At the dawn of the 20th century, although interconnections significantly increased, the northwestern region emerged as the most advanced area, while the peripheries remained far behind. Their level of economic development, measured by per capita GDP, represented only one-third to somewhat more than one-half that of the core.

Economic level, however, does not fully express the real differences among the regions. Economic structures were even farther from each other. Industrialization, agricultural structures, and up-to-date technology (or lack of it) distinguished the core and the peripheral regions to varying levels even more so. The most vital differences, however, that separated the regions were sociocultural and behavioral patterns: the contrast became so sharp that while some regions boasted modern 20th century societies, at the other extreme, some peripheral regions encapsulated societies at a near-medieval level of development.

The three distinct peripheral macro-regions exhibited major differences from each other (see Table 1.1). The relatively best-performing region reached 57 percent of the Western GDP level and started on the road toward industrialization, social modernization, and the adaptation of Western sociocultural features. The least advanced region represented only roughly one-third of Western income level, and its society was frozen in premodern times – it was collectivist, uneducated, anticapitalist, and had a deeply superstitious mentality. Between these two poles, the third region's GDP was 42 percent of the Northwest's, and was characterized by a mix of sociocultural features of the other two peripheral regions but was nearer to the Balkans than the Baltic Central European area.

Table 1.1 Per capita GDP in European regions, 1820 and 1913

Per capita GDP		
European regions	*1820*	*1913*
Northwestern Europe	100	100
Finnish-Irish-Baltic and Central European	62	57
Mediterranean, South Italian and Russian	66	42
Balkans and Habsburg Borderlands	–	33

Source: Based on Angus Maddison, *Monitoring the World Economy, 1820–1992*, Paris: OECD, 1995.

This was the base that 20th century Europe inherited, and where the early 21st century's Europe has the deepest roots. This is the past that strongly influences and in many ways determines the future of 21st century Europe. Moreover, historical roads continued to diverge in the 20th century, leading to further elevation of the Northwest, the spectacular rise of a few former peripheral countries that started catching up with the West, and, most of all, the continued relative decline of most of the peripheral regions.

Notes

1 David Ricardo, *Principles of Political Economy and Taxation*, London: John Murray, 1817.
2 John A. Hobson, *Imperialism: A Study*, London: James Nisbet, 1902.
3 Rosa Luxemburg, *The Accumulation of Capital*, London: Routledge, [1913] 2003.
4 Hobson, *Imperialism: A Study*, p. 85.
5 Nikolai Bukharin, *Imperialism and World Economy*, New York: International Publisher, [1915] 1929.
6 Vladimir I. Lenin, *Imperialism. The Highest Stage of Capitalism*, Moscow: Progress Publishers, [1917] 1963; Karl Kautsky, "Ultra-Imperialism," *Die Neue Zeit*, September 1914.
7 Paul A. Baran, "On the Political Economy of Backwardness," *The Manchester School of Economy and Social Studies* 20, no. 1 (January 1952): 66–84, here pp. 66–67.
8 Paul A. Baran, *The Political Economy of Growth*, New York: Monthly Review Press, 1957.
9 This idea is known as the Prebisch–Singer thesis, established by Raúl Prebisch, an Argentine economist and Hans W. Singer, a German-born British economist who independent and parallel (in the same month) published works with the same conclusion. See Raúl Prebisch, *The Economic Development of Latin America and Its Principal Problems*, New York: United Nations, 1950); and "Commercial Policy in the Underdeveloped Countries," *American Economic Review* 49 (1959): 251–273; Hans W. Singer, "The Distribution of Gains between Investing and Borrowing Countries," *American Economic Review*, 40 (January 1950).
10 Immanuel Wallerstein, *The Modern World System, Vol. I: Capitalist Agriculture and the Origins of the European World Economy in the Sixteenth Century*, New York: Academic Press, 1974; Immanuel Wallerstein, *The Modern World System, Vol. III: The Second Era of Great Expansion of the Capitalist World Economy, 1730–1840*, San Diego: Academic Press, 1989.
11 See *A Dictionary of Sociology*, Oxford: Oxford University Press, 1998, www.encyclopedia.com/social-sciences/dictionaries-thesauruses-pictures-and-press-releases/centre-periphery-model (accessed January 19, 2017).
12 We asked this question in our book, Ivan T. Berend and György Ránki, *The Peripheries and Industrialization*, Cambridge: Cambridge University Press, 1982.
13 Max Hartwell, *The Industrial Revolution and Economic Growth*, London: Methuen, 1971, p. 252.
14 Barry Supple, "The State and the Industrial Revolution," in Carlo Cipolla (ed.), *Fontana Economic History of Europe, Vol. III: The Industrial Revolution*, London: Fontana, 1973.

15 Lance E. Davis and Douglas C. North, *Institutional Change and American Economic Growth*, New York: Cambridge University Press, 1971; Douglas C. North and Barry Weingast, "Constitutions and Commitments: The Evolutions of Institutions Governing Public Choice in Seventeenth Century Britain," *Journal of Economic History* 49, no. 4 (1989): 832; 803; Douglas C. North, *Institutions, Institutional Change and Economic Performance*, Cambridge: Cambridge University Press, 1990, p. 3.

16 Sheilagh Ogilvie, "Whatever Is, Is Right? Economic Institutions in Pre-Industrial Europe," *Economic History Review* 60, no. 4 (2007).

17 Gérard Roland, "Understanding Institutional Change: Fast-Moving and Slow-Moving Institutions, pp. 3, 12, 16, eml.berkeley.edu/~groland/pubs/gr3.pdf, accessed February 3, 2017.

18 Peter B. Evans, "Predatory, Developmental and Other Apparatuses: A Comparative Political Economy Perspective on the Third World State," *Sociological Forum* 4, no. 4 (1989): 561–587.

19 The Austrian-born Harvard economist Joseph Schumpeter named three factors as key for scientific economic analysis: economic theory, statistics, and history. The latter two play central role in this economic history book. See Schumpeter, *History of Economic Analysis*, London: Allen & Unwin, 1954, p. 1260.

20 Peter Mathias, *The First Industrial Nation: An Economic History of Britain, 1700–1914*, London: Methuen, 1969, pp. 110–112.

21 David Ormrod, *The Rise of Commercial Empires: England and the Netherlands in the Age of Mercantilism, 1650–1770*, Cambridge: Cambridge University Press, 2003, pp. 335, 339, 343, 345, 350.

22 Jan de Vries, "The Netherlands in the New World: Legacy of European Fiscal, Monetary and Trading Institutions for New World Development from the 17th to the 19th Centuries," in Michael Bordo and Roberto Cortés-Conde (eds.), *Transferring Wealth and Power from the Old to the New World: Monetary and Fiscal Institutions through the 19th Centuries*, Cambridge: Cambridge University Press, 2001, p. 75.

23 Ibid., p. 109.

24 Jan Luiten Van Zanden, "The Revolt of the 'Early Modernists' and the 'First Modern Economy': An Assessment," *Economic History Review* 55, no. 4 (2002): 634.

25 Jan de Vries, "The Netherlands in the New World," pp. 105–106, 109–111; Oscar Gelderblom and Joost Jonker, "Public Finance and Economic Growth: The Case of Holland in the Seventeenth Century," *Journal of Economic History* 71, no. 1 (2011): 1–39, 1, 7, 10.

26 Françóis Crouzet, *A History of the European Economy, 1000–2000*, Charlottesville: University of Virginia Press, 2001, pp. 74, 97.

27 Thomas Malthus, in his *Essay on the Principle of Population (1798)*, developed the theory that human populations grow exponentially (i.e., 2, 4, 6), doubling with each cycle, while food production grows at an arithmetic rate (1, 2, 3, 4). Thus, food production creates an unbreakable obstacle for population growth.

28 Douglas C. North and Robert P. Thomas, *The Rise of the Western World: A New Economic History*, Cambridge: Cambridge University Press, 1973, pp. 132, 145.

29 Nicholas Crafts and C. Knick Harley, "Precocious British Industrialization: A General Equilibrium Perspective," in Leandro Prados de la Escosura (ed.), *Exceptionalism and Industrialization: Britain and Its European Rivals, 1688–1815*, Cambridge: Cambridge University Press, 2004, pp. 104, 107.

30 Edward Anthony Wrigley, *Continuity, Chance and Change: The Character of the Industrial Revolution in England*, Cambridge: Cambridge University Press, 1988, pp. 13, 15.

31 Oscar Gelderblom and Joost Jonker, "Completing a Financial Revolution: The Finance of the Dutch East India Trade and the Rise of the Amsterdam Capital Market, 1595–1612," *Journal of Economic History* 64, no. 3 (September 2004): 641–672, 642.

32 Forest Capie, "The Origins and Development of Stable Fiscal and Monetary Institutions in England," in Bordo and Cortés-Conde (eds.), *Transferring Wealth and Power from the Old to the New World*, pp. 26, 28, 38; David Stasavage, *Public Debt and the Birth of the Democratic State: France and Great Britain, 1688–1789*, Cambridge: Cambridge University Press, 2003; and Mark Dincecco, "Fiscal Centralization, Limited Government, and Public Revenues in Europe, 1650–1913, *Journal of Economic History* 69, no. 1 (March 2009): 70–80.

33 Jan de Vries, *The Industrious Revolution: Consumer Behavior and the Household Economy, 1650 to the Present*, Cambridge: Cambridge University Press, 2008.

34 Quoted in Emma Rothschild, "The English Kopf," in Patrick K. O'Brian and Donald Winch (eds.), *The Political Economy of British Historical Experience, 1688–1914*, Oxford: Oxford University Press, 2002, p. 31.

35 de Vries, *Industrious Revolution*, pp. 3, 9, 10, 55, 71, 134, 139, 161, 180.

36 Nigel Goose and Lien Luu, *Immigrants in Tudor and Early Stuart England*, Brighton: Sussex Academic Press, 2005.

37 Brian A'Hearn, Jörg Baten, and Dorothee Crayen, "Quantifying Quantitative Literacy: Age Heaping and the History of Human Capital," *Journal of Economic History* 69, no. 3 (2009): 804, 806.

38 Max Hartwell, *The Industrial Revolution and Economic Growth*, London: Methuen, 1971, pp. 237–239.

39 Alan Milward and S.B. Saul, *The Economic Development of Continental Europe, 1780–1870*, London: Allen & Unwin, 1973, p. 97.

40 Eugene N. White, "France and the Failure to Modernize Macroeconomic Institutions," in Bordo and Cortés-Conde (eds.), *Transferring Wealth and Power from the Old to the New World*, p. 96.

41 Jean-Laurent Rosenthal, *The Fruits of Revolution: Property Rights, Litigation, and French Agriculture, 1700–1860*, Cambridge: Cambridge University Press, 1992, p. 173.

42 Carlo Cipolla, *Before the Industrial Revolution: European Society and Economy, 1000–1700*, 3rd ed., New York: W.W. Norton, 1994, p. 212.

43 Ronald Findley and Kevin O'Rourke, *Power and Plenty: Trade, War, and the World Economy in the Second Millennium*, Princeton, NJ: Princeton University Press, 2007, p. xx.

44 Otto von Bismarck, prime minister of Germany, said in an 1862 speech that Germany (the united German state) was built by "Blut und Eisen," blood and iron. John Maynard Keynes later wittily corrected him by saying that Germany was built more by "coal and iron," (a reference to the country's tremendous economic development).

45 R.H. Tawney, *Religion and the Rise of Capitalism: A Historical Study, Holland Memorial Lecture*, New York: Mentor, 1954, pp. 17, 75.

46 Peter Harrison, "Was There a Scientific Revolution?," *European Review* 15, no. 4 (2007): 446, 450.

47 Betty Jo Teeter Dobbs and Margaret C. Jacob, *Newton and the Culture of Newtonianism*, Atlantic Highland, NJ: Humanities Press, 1995, p. 10.
48 Ibid., pp. 38, 44.
49 Albert Eduard Musson and Eric Robinson, *Science and Technology in the Industrial Revolution*, Manchester: Manchester University Press, 1969, pp. 12–25.
50 Joel Mokyr, *The Gift of Athena: Historical Origins of the Knowledge Economy*, Princeton, NJ: Princeton University Press, 2002, pp. 68–69.
51 Thomas Hobbes, *Leviathan*, Chicago: Gateway, [1651] 1956, pp. 122–123.
52 John Locke, *Two Treaties of Government*, New York: Hafner, [1690] 1947, p. 801.
53 See Mokyr, *Gift of Athena*, pp. 35–37, 39, 297; and Joel Mokyr, "The Intellectual Origins of Modern Economic Growth," *Journal of Economic History* 65, no. 2 (June 2005): 287, 290.
54 Eduard Heimann, *History of Economic Doctrines*, Oxford: Oxford University Press, 1964, pp. 63–64.
55 Voltaire (François-Marie Arouet), "Philosophical Dictionary," in *Introduction to Contemporary Civilization in the West*, p. 833.
56 Voltaire (François-Marie Arouet), "Treatise on Tolerance on the Occasion of the Death of Jean Calas from the Judgment Rendered in Toulouse" in *Introduction to Contemporary Civilization in the West*, p. 841.
57 Charles-Louis Montesquieu, "The Spirit of the Law," in *Introduction to Contemporary Civilization in the West*, pp. 936, 938.
58 Jean-Jacques Rousseau, "The Social Contract," in *Introduction to Contemporary Civilization in the West*, pp. 957, 965.
59 George W.F. Hegel, *The Letters*, trans. Clark Butler and Christine Seiler, Bloomington: Indiana University Press, [1806] 2005.
60 George L. Mosse, *The Culture of Western Europe: The Nineteenth and Twentieth Centuries*, 3rd ed., Boulder, CO: Westview Press, 1988, pp. 119, 130.
61 Alexis de Tocqueville, *The Old Regime and the French Revolution*, New York: Doubleday and Random House, [1856] 1983, pp. 15–16.
62 For the similar German and French development, see R.C. Mitchell, "Statistical Appendix," in Carlo Cipolla (ed.), *Fontana Economic History of Europe*, Vol. 6, Part II London: Fontana, 1973, pp. 766, 811.
63 Ibid., pp. 770, 773, 780.
64 Ibid., p. 775. The capacity of power machines in the industry increased from 178,000 horsepower to 3.6 million horsepower between 1860 and 1913.
65 See Paul Bairoch, "Europe's Gross National Product: 1800–1975," *Journal of European Economic History* 5 (1976): 273–340, 306; W.S. Wojtinsky, *Die Welt in Zahlen* (Berlin: Rudolf Mosse, 1927), pp. 34–35; Ivan T. Berend and György Ránki, *The European Periphery and Industrialization*, Cambridge: Cambridge University Press, 1982, p. 100.
66 Angus Maddison, *The World Economy: A Millennial Perspective*, Paris: OECD, 2001, p. 85.
67 Karl-Gustav Hildebrand, *Swedish Iron in the Seventeenth and Eighteenth Centuries: Export Industry before Industrialization*, Skriftserie 29, Södertälje: Jernkontorests Berghistorika, 1992, pp. 11, 13.
68 Paul Bairoch, "How and Not Why? Economic Inequalities between 1800 and 1913: Some Background Figures," in Jean Batou (ed.), *Between Development and Underdevelopment: The Precocious Attempts at Industrialization of the Preiphery,*

1800–1870, Geneva: Libairie Droz, 1991, p. 3; and Angus Maddison, *Monitoring the World Economy, 1820–1992*, Paris: OECD, 1995.

69 See Faruk Tabak, *The Waning of the Mediterranean, 1550–1870: A Geohistorical Approach*, Baltimore: Johns Hopkins University Press, 2008.

70 Werner Conze, "The Effects of Nineteenth Century Liberal Agrarian Reforms on Social Structure in Central Europe," in François Crouzet, William H. Chaloner, and Walter M. Stern (eds.), *Essays in European Economic History, 1789–1914*, New York: St. Martin's Press, 1969, pp. 55, 65–66.

71 Nora Berend (ed.), *Christianization and the Rise of Christian Monarchs. Scandinavia, Central Europe and Rus' c. 900–1200*, Cambridge: Cambridge University Press, 2007.

72 Jenő Szűcs, "Vázlat Európa három történeti régiójáról," *Történelmi Szemle* no. 3 (1981).

73 David R. Ringrose, *Spain, Europe and the "Spanish Miracle," 1700–1900*, Cambridge: Cambridge University Press, 1996, pp. 362–363, 367.

74 Ibid., p. 364.

75 István Bíbó, *Válogatott Tanulmányok*, Vol. II, Budapest: Magvetö Könyvkiadó, 1986, p. 343.

76 Peter Sugar, *East European Nationalism, Politics and Religion*, Aldershot: Ashgate, 1999, pp. 13–14.

77 Thomas S. Pearson, *Russian Officialdom in Crisis: Autocracy and Local Self-Government, 1861–1900*, Cambridge: Cambridge University Press, 1989, p. 257.

78 William H. McNeill, *The Rise of the West: A History of Human Community*, Chicago: University of Chicago Press, 1963; William H. McNeill, *Europe's Steppe Frontiers 1500–1800: A Study of the Eastward Movement of Europe*, Chicago: University of Chicago Press, 1964; Samuel Huntington, *The Clash of Civilization: The Remaking of the World Order*, New York: Simon & Schuster, 1996.

79 *Stuck in Transition?*, EBRD Transition Report 2013, London: European Bank of Reconstruction and Development, May 14, 2014, p. 19.

2 A radically changed world, yet unchanged regional division

Four regions in early-21st-century Europe

The 21st century: a dramatically changed world and Europe

Long and diverse historical developments resulted in huge modern regional differences. At the beginning of the 20th century, as I presented in Chapter 1, four distinct regions existed within Europe. One century later, drastic shifts in international relations, the global economy, and the technological environment had dramatically transformed the world. According to the well-based opinion of Robert Gilpin, "The world economic and political system is experiencing its most profound transformation since the emergence of the international economy in the seventeenth and eighteenth centuries."[1]

In summing up Gilpin's analysis, let me list the most outstanding elements of these dramatic changes. Around the millennium a new communication–industrial revolution ended the oil and electricity age and sparked a new computer age: the biotechnological, microelectronic, and telecommunication age. "More new knowledge has been produced over the last thirty years than in the previous five thousand. … The cost of storing and transmitting knowledge fell at the rate of about 20 percent a year for forty years." Process control, automation, and automatic data processing are revolutionizing both manufacturing and services in every industrial economy. The role of knowledge and education also became dominant. "Demand for low-skilled and unskilled labor … declined" and the "technological life cycle of both products and production processes … dramatically shortened."[2] Communication and transportation were revolutionized: a three-minute telephone call from New York to London was $293 in 1931 (roughly $4,500 today) and $1 in 2000. Transportation costs dropped by 90 percent during the twentieth century. That made the world small and global.

Virtually parallel to the technological revolution, the world's political system also dramatically changed. The Cold War determined the entire world system during the second half of the 20th century. After the first decade of the Cold War, when the world was at the edge of the third world war, the dangerous conflicts of the bipolar world system established, oddly enough, global stability. The United States and Western Europe, along with several other allies, created a Western-dominated world through strong political, military, and economic cooperation. "For the first time in world history the dominant capitalist powers cooperated with one another as the exigencies of survival necessitated that they subordinate parochial interests to alliance unity."[3] The outcome was rapid economic growth and prosperity. Western Europe increased its income by about 5 percent per year for two decades between the mid-1950s and the early 1970s.

Globalization started on the very foundations of the new technological revolution and the strongly integrated Western world. It gained elemental strength after the end of the Cold War. Capitalism triumphantly emerged and became global. Trade became unrestricted. Average tariffs dropped from 40 percent to 6 percent. International trade, which increased by only 0.5 percent per year between 1913 and 1948, shifted gears and increased by 7 percent in the second half of the 20th century. The value of trade increased from $57 billion in 1947 to $6 trillion by the 1990s. The volume of foreign exchange trade jumped eightfold in the few years between 1986 and 1990. The global export volume of goods and services elevated to $25 billion per day, reaching $6.6 trillion in 1997.[4]

Foreign investment flooded the world; the number of multinational firms mushroomed from 7,000 to 80,000 and spread throughout the entire world. Some of these firms developed assets equal to the GDP of a relatively smaller European country:

> Between 1985 and 1990, FDI grew at an average rate of 30 percent a year, an amount four times the growth of world output and three times the growth rate of trade. … [FDI] doubled from 1992 to nearly $350 billion in the late 1990s. … In 1994, intrafirm trade … accounted for one-third of U.S. exports and two-fifths of U.S. imported goods. … FDI in less-developed countries (LDCs) [grew] at about 15 percent annually.[5]

Earlier horizontal investments to establish self-sufficient subsidiaries were replaced by pluralistic vertical systems, creating an extensive network of local subsidiaries that produced parts and components. Technology and communication made it possible to organize global business and distribution systems.

While this process flourished around the turn of the millennium, it generated doubts, criticism, and resistance in the early 21st century. Globalization that had seemingly served Western interests became a double-edged sword. With their cheap labor and strong educational progress, several Asian countries emerged as competitors. Jobs started moving from highly developed to developing countries, generating harsh opposition to globalization and catalyzing the rise of populist political movements in rich countries. In its January 2017 issue, *The Economist* published two articles: "The Multinational Company Is in Trouble" and "The Retreat of the Global Company." The latter ended with the following sentence:

> The result will be a more fragmented and parochial kind of capitalism, and quite possibly a less efficient one – but also, perhaps, one with wider public

> support. And the infatuation with global companies will come to be seen as a passing episode in business history, rather than its end.[6]

Meanwhile, the world system also changed. The almost monolithic Western dominance was challenged. The subordination of narrow national interests during the Cold War was replaced by competition and conflicts. American world leadership was replaced by a multipolar world, with China, Germany, and the European Union as main powers. This trend was strengthened by the gradual turn of the United States toward national priorities. Gilpin, in 2000, spoke about "a shift in American policy [that] had already become evident during the Reagan and Bush Administrations";[7] this was the emergence of a new era in which economic security displaced military security. This trend culminated in the election of Donald J. Trump as president in 2017. His "America First!" policy openly challenged the North Atlantic Treaty Organization (NATO) and the postwar alliance system. Priorities changed for Europe and Japan as well:

> Both became willing to follow American leadership, much less tolerant of America's disregard of their economic and political interests, and more likely to emphasize their own national priorities. … During the 1990s, regional concerns began to take precedence over North American, Trans-Atlantic, and Trans-Pacific issues.[8]
>
> As the twenty-first century opens, the decline of American leadership, fraying economic cooperation between the United States and its Cold War allies, and increasing disillusionment with economic globalization … has weakened the underlying political support for an open world economy. Economic regionalism, financial instability, and trade protectionism all seriously threaten the stability and the integration of the global economy.[9]

In this new world order, Gilpin rightly stressed that:

> globalization [is not] irreversible; globalization rests on a political foundation that could disintegrate if the major powers fail to strengthen their economic and political ties. … Although the technology leading to increased globalization may be irreversible, the national policies responsible for the process of globalization have been reversed in the past and could be again in the future. … An open world economy will inevitably produce more losers than winners … unleashing market and other economic forces could result in an immense struggle among individual nations, economic classes and powerful groups.[10]

International conflict between capitalism and communism "has been replaced by conflict among rival forms of capitalism," and, as predicted by political scientist Samuel Huntington in 1991, "intra-civilizational conflicts will dominate the agenda of world politics well into the twenty-first century."[11]

In addition to these macro-changes, several further micro-elements related to changes in the human environment and everyday life also drove this process forward. In the century between 1913 and 2013, virtually everything changed in these spheres of life as well. Industrialization and economic development transformed the physical environment of peoples' lives in the advanced parts of the world. Hundreds of millions of people moved from villages to urban centers and from traditional peasant work to industrial and service employments.

Big, sometimes trigenerational, families that commonly had four to six children were replaced by smaller families that often had just one or two children, if any. The growth of Europe's population slowed dramatically in the late 20th century, as the number of children per families dropped below reproduction level, from 2.1 children to 1.4–1.8 children. The basic institution of family also dramatically changed and became more fragile; it was no longer the solid and fundamental societal institution that it had been before. In several European countries, nearly one-third of the people never marry; for those who do, nearly half of all marriages end in divorce. A growing number of children are born outside of marriage.

All of these shifts were closely connected to a dramatic demographic change. Although in the 18th and 19th centuries a reproductive boom increased the population of northwestern Europe by three to four times, in the 20th century this trend shifted to the developing world; the developed world faced a sharp population decrease. The wars of the 20th century contributed to this change. In this "age of extreme," as Eric Hobsbawm called the period in the title of his 1996 book, Europe was decimated by the two world wars and numerous civil wars, and tens of millions were killed as a result. Millions more migrated to other parts of the continent and the world, changed citizenships, learned other languages, and settled into their new homes. In contrast, millions migrated to Europe from other continents, and this rising trend eventually exploded into the migration crisis of the early 21st century.

People also had to adjust to rapidly changing regimes with different, often opposing ideologies and behavioral requirements. Historically speaking, during the 20th century regimes changed at a surprising speed: Europe was dominated by fascism, Nazism, and communism, and then all of these regimes disappeared and democratization followed. In some countries, this latter development – democratization – is happening for virtually the first time in their histories. These different regimes all required people to identify themselves to the government (not to do so was dangerous) and these requirements sometimes changed two or three times within a lifetime.

Until the early 20th century, women did not have voting rights and their position in society was subordinated, but from the end of the same century they were emancipated. People also became much more educated. Illiteracy, a mass phenomenon at the beginning of the 19th century, totally disappeared. A century later, basic education consisted not of studying for four or six years in elementary school; rather, it included secondary education as well, and – for an increasing part of the population – university training. Women gained the right to equal education from the second half of the 20th century, closing the historic gender gap in basic education.

In parts of Europe, and in most of the peripheral parts of the continent, communist regimes brutally destroyed the old aristocratic or peasant societies. Even though caste-like social divisions and the old elite were eliminated, new ones took their place. In the areas of Europe that were previously less and least educated, communist governments also carried out educational revolutions that greatly homogenized literacy levels on the continent.

One of the greatest and most striking changes that influenced everyday human life was the transformation of the technological environment. People had to learn the everyday use of rather different technologies. People who travelled in horse-driven coaches at the beginning of the century were driving their own cars by the end of it. Before World War I, hundreds of millions of people had never used a telephone. Now their grandchildren and great-grandchildren are checking their smartphones and making calls while walking down the street. Tourism and travelling abroad was rare and limited to an exclusive elite, but both are now mass phenomena. In the late 19th century, the train was still a shockingly new method of travel; a little more than a century later, flying on a plane is now routine. According to the United Nations Worldwide Tourism Statistics,[12] in 2008, 924 million international tourists travelled globally, and 503 million arrived in Europe. The annual revenue from tourism had risen to a striking figure: $2.1 trillion annually. In several countries, among them Greece and Spain, tourism became the biggest, or one of the biggest, business sectors. Sending messages and keeping in permanent contact with others, including people on other continents, was no longer accomplished through handwritten letters but by computer; instead of taking weeks and months to arrive, messages are received within minutes. In 1913, some households were nearly self-sufficient and shopping was limited. By 2013, shopping had transformed into mass consumerism and became a form of entertainment in and of itself. Shopping increasingly occurred in malls and through online means rather than in familiar, homey corner-shops.

The regionalization of the enlarged European Union

As the world changed, Europe changed as well. In addition to all of the previously mentioned changes, after a half-century of hostility and wars among the European nations, the nation-state and the idea of national identity were somewhat weakened by wartime devastation. Integration in Europe started occurring. The first step was the foundation of the European Coal and Steel Community, established in the 1950s by six Western European countries such as France, Belgium, the Netherland, Luxembourg, Germany, and Italy.[13] The level of integration reached a new turning point in 1957 with the Treaty of Rome, which led to the foundation of the European Economic Community (EEC). The Inner Six, or the founding member states of the European Community (EC), soon (beginning in 1973, and then in 1995) attracted Britain, Ireland,

Sweden, Denmark, Finland, and Austria to join – most of the northwestern countries.

Europe arrived at a new stage of integration between 1990 and 2000, when the EEC became the European Union (EU) with its single market and common currency. Integrating Europe was built on the values and achievements of the founding countries of Europe. Nevertheless, the common currency was not adopted by all of the EU member countries, for example, Britain, Denmark, Sweden, and some of the central European countries.

Globalization hit Europe hard. American and Japanese multinationals, which were far ahead in terms of technological development and represented cutthroat competition, occupied huge parts of the European markets. This trend began as early as the 1960s; indeed, the sensational 1967 book of French writer and journalist Jean-Jacques Servan-Schreiber, *Le Défi Américain* (The American Challenge), acted as an early wake-up call, spurring on Europe to defend itself from economic "occupation." Europe answered the challenge of globalization, which arose not only from growing competition with the United States and Japan but also from rising Asian competitors such as Hong Kong, South Korea, Taiwan, and Singapore. The first, the so-called "Small Asian Tigers," was later succeeded by China and India. Beginning in the mid-1980s, as a result of successful regionalization a "fortress Europe" was in the making, which elevated Europe to the level of an economic superpower. That also required a significant expansion in integration by accepting more new members and homogenizing the sharply divided European continent.

The nonmember peripheral countries of the Continent looked to the European Community as their future home and savior. That was their desire from the late 19th century, because the outcome of the earlier Scientific Revolution and to two Industrial Revolutions had led to the spectacular elevation of Western Europe. Due to their success the backward peripheral countries wanted to follow the example of the more advanced West. Although those countries had some success, and industrialization and modernization started spreading to nearby areas, for the most part those attempts were at best ambiguous and largely unsuccessful.

However, from the late 20th century a new, institutionalized, and very promising opportunity arose for the peripheries to join the West: European Union membership.

Around the turn of the millennium, most of the peripheral countries gradually started applying for membership. The EU was open to accepting new members who were ready and able to share the values and rules of the Community. In 1973 Ireland became the first peripheral, relatively backward country to join. The Mediterranean periphery – Greece, Spain, and Portugal – followed in the 1980s. After the collapse of communism, eight Central European, three Baltic, and two Balkan countries joined in three waves between 2004 and 2013.

In the early 21st century, European integration – the outcome of progressive developments that spanned two-thirds of a century – culminated in the foundation of the European Union. The institution had 28 member countries, and

19 of them were also members of a monetary union that boasted a common currency and the common European Central Bank.

Although not members, another four countries – Switzerland, Norway, Iceland, and Liechtenstein – joined the EU Single Market. The latter three are also part of the European Economic Area and are thus closely connected to the EU. They follow its rules and regulations and also contribute to its budget. Another five countries in the Balkans – Albania, Macedonia, Montenegro, Serbia, and Turkey – are candidates for membership and have started adjusting in order to meet the full membership requirements. Ultimately more than 70 percent of the 50 European states are, in some form or another, part of an impressive integration process. This share is even higher if one considers that four nonmember countries (Andorra, Monaco, San Marino, and the Vatican City) are mini-states, while five others countries (Turkey, Georgia, Azerbaijan, Kazakhstan, and Russia) are "transcontinental" and thus are only partly European and partly, or even mostly, Asian. Taking these factors into account, more than 80 percent of Europe is part of a progressing integration process.

Following the 1993 Copenhagen Agreement, the new peripheral member countries had to accept the so-called Copenhagen criteria of "stable institutions guaranteeing democracy, the rule of law, human rights and respect for and protection of minorities, the existence of a functioning market economy and the capacity to cope with competition and market forces in the EU." A candidate country must also have "the ability to take on and implement effectively the obligations of membership including adherence to the aims of political, economic and monetary union."[14]

To be accepted, the candidate countries worked toward realizing the norms, laws, and institutions of the Northwest by adopting the standards listed in the roughly 80,000–100,000-page *Acquis Communautaire*. This basic document contained the political, economic, and institutional criteria for membership. Beginning in 1998, the European Commission monitored and evaluated the progress of the candidates as they implemented the requirements via national legislation.

From the mid-1990s almost all of the Central European countries were involved, but to pave the way for further enlargement, the EU initiated a Stabilization Pact to establish greater solidity in the troubled Balkans. As the European Bank of Reconstruction and Development reported in 2003, "The EU aimed to bring south-eastern Europe toward full integration with EU structures, including eventual full membership." At the same time, between 2001 and 2003 the EU also introduced the Stabilization and Association Process:

> for the five south-east European countries that were not yet part of the EU accession process – Albania, Bosnia-Herzegovina, FYR Macedonia and Serbia and Montenegro. ... The EU summit for the western Balkans ... in June 2003 reaffirmed that EU accession remained the ultimate aim of the Stabilisation and Association Process.[15]

A great part of the eastern peripheries remained just outside the entrance to the European Union.

Member countries opened their borders and became part of a huge Single European Market, which at its zenith encapsulated 500 million people. Even as associates, new members could export freely to this large market; during a transitory period they were allowed to defend their own domestic markets at the same time. Already by the mid-1970s, three-quarters of Community member countries' foreign trade was exported to and imported from other member countries. While in the 1920s foreign trade had stagnated in Europe and the 1930s had even declined by 4 percent, during the second half of the 20th century European trade skyrocketed, increasing more than 14-fold. Between 1950 and 2012, the share of merchandise exports in several European countries jumped from 6–12 percent to 30–50 percent of their GDPs.[16]

Beside increased trade possibilities, member countries also benefitted from the EU's agricultural subsidies. Beginning in 1975 a Regional Development Fund was also created, and a Community program automatically offered assistance to less-developed regions. Consequently, those regions and countries that had an average income level of less than 75 percent of the EU's received billions in aid. In the final two decades of the 20th century, billions of ECUs (the fore-runner to and basic equivalent of the euro) – 7 billion in 1987 and 27 billion in 1999 – were already being sent to assist relatively backward regions of the Union. During the 1980s and 1990s, Greece and Portugal received Community assistance that equaled more than 3 percent of their Gross Domestic Product; Ireland and Spain received roughly 2 percent of their income.[17] Between 2000 and 2006 and then again between 2007 and 2013, the European Union assisted backward regions, including virtually most of the former communist transition countries, spending €729 billion altogether. In several cases involving new Central and Eastern European member countries, this assistance equaled about 5 percent of their GDPs. Between 2014 and 2020, Poland alone will receive nearly $27 billion per year; in the same budgetary period Hungary will receive $40 billion altogether. EU aid became a major driving force in these countries' economic development.

Most importantly, the free flow of capital on the common market generated a huge investment boom in countries with weak domestic accumulation and scarce investments. Between 1989 and 2004 – before the Central and Easter European region was accepted by the EU – eight Central European and Baltic countries had already received more than $161 billion in foreign investments. Seven Balkan countries received another $42 billion combined, mostly from the northwestern member countries of the EU.[18] The huge inflow of FDI amounted to between $15–30 billion per year, which was equal to 3 percent of the region's GDP. In certain periods the Czech Republic, Estonia, and Hungary got so much investment from abroad that it equaled 10–15 percent of their GDPs. Before the EU acceptance of some Balkan countries, FDI also flowed into the area: in 2003 Croatia received assistance equal to an unparalleled

49 percent of its GDP; Bulgaria and Romania received assistance equal to 20 and 23 percent, respectively.

Foreign, mostly West European corporations established modern high-tech and semi-high-tech industrial sectors in areas that had previously lacked new technologies. New foreign-founded high-tech companies became the most important exporters in several peripheral countries. In Hungary, they employed 47 percent of manufacturing workers, covered 82 percent of manufacturing investments, produced 73 per cent of purchased goods, and were responsible for 89 percent of exports. In the Czech Republic, 53 percent of investments and 61 percent of exports were produced by subsidiaries of foreign multinationals. Almost 60 percent of Poland's exports were delivered by foreign-established companies.[19]

West European investors also established modern banking sectors in less-developed member countries. In Ireland, 53 percent of banking assets were in foreign (mostly Western European) hands. This was true of 96–97 percent of assets in the Czech Republic, Slovakia, and Estonia; and 87 percent of assets in Central and Eastern Europe, on average.[20]

Foreign investment stock trading between European Union member countries increased by 167 times between 1970 and 2007. Already during the 1990s, 72 percent of total inward investments in Europe originated from other European countries.[21] Jobs were created in the millions. Cheap credit flooded the relatively backward regions and generated high prosperity. The credit-based consumption of the population increased beyond its disposable income. In a few years, car density equaled that of the core countries. The rate of home ownership in Greece, Spain, Portugal, and Ireland – around 80 percent – even surpassed levels in Switzerland, Germany, and America, which ranged between 50 to 67 percent. (An exaggerated construction boom actually led to skyrocketing home prices and a real estate bubble that soon burst and ended in economic crisis. Households accumulated a debt burden that reached 100–300 percent of families' disposable incomes. Foreign indebtedness in several peripheral countries surpassed between 170 percent [Greece and Hungary] and 115–131 percent [Latvia and Estonia] of their GDPs).[22]

The investments and aid assistance of the rich European core to peripheral countries were not self-sacrificing actions, but instead strategic capitalist business endeavors. Those who speak about Western EU countries' "unprecedented generosity" in assisting the less-developed peripheries – as Nobel laureate Joseph Stiglitz did[23] – are as one-sided and wrong as those who – like Perry Anderson[24] – condemned this connection as neoliberal exploitation of poor countries. The northwestern traders and retail chains – including France's Carrefour, Britain's Tesco, Germany's Metro, Sweden's IKEA, and Belgium's Delhaize Group – "invaded" the retail markets and occupied huge parts of it. Investors who established banks (such as the French BNP Paribas; the German Deutsche Bank; and several Austria, Italian, and Swedish banks) and industrial subsidiaries and value chains in these regions (Germany's Volkswagen and BMW, France's Peugeot, the Italian Fiat, and other corporations) profited from their business tremendously. They were able to create a backyard for their corporations and enjoy cheap labor sources that made them more competitive on the world market.

The rich and advanced countries that gained huge markets for their products were also able to exploit larger markets. The scale and scope of larger production not only increased their profits but also made possible further specialization and thus lower production costs. Producing large series and huge quantities of products helped to concentrate the production to certain product parts, while the production of other parts was concentrated into subsidiary or cooperating companies. And ultimately, the entire product was assembled at another separate plant. Each of the producers specialized more and consequently produced goods more cheaply.

While these possibilities served the interests of advanced countries in the Community, integration benefitted all EC members, including the less-developed ones. Large West European multinational corporations certainly profited a lot, but less-developed countries – if their domestic socioeconomic environment and infrastructure were prepared, and if they prioritized education enough to ensure a well-educated populace – also became able to start elevating toward a higher level of development. These possibilities were already emerging during the late 19th century, but very few countries were able to exploit it. The European Union expanded these possibilities and made it easier to take advantage of them.

The other side of core-periphery relations: the road to catch up

The economic and sociocultural differences between the European core and the peripheries that emerged during the dissimilar millennial historical development were unquestionably exploited in modern times by rich, dominant, advanced countries. One of the early historians of Western capital export to peripheral Europe, Herbert Feis, was certainly right when, with bitter sarcasm, he stated that some of the foreign capital recipient countries were finally able to buy enough rope to hang themselves.[25]

The emphasis of various core-periphery theories (discussed in Chapter 1) on the core's uneven trade policies and exploitation of raw material, food resources, and cheap labor sources only represent one side of this highly complex story. In many respects, theories analyzing core-periphery relations, did not answer – and actually did not even ask – why certain regions and countries had elevated to the advanced core, while others had declined into a backward peripheral state. The answer, as I suggested in Chapter 1, lies in the long and diverse historical developments that concluded with high regional differences within Europe. At this point, however, I have to add a new element to the core-periphery theory debate: the one-sidedness of their analysis.

The advanced core countries served their own profit interests and also provided factors of production (the other side of the same coin) to the subordinate, dependent and exploited peripheral regions. This impact was already clearly present in the late 19th century, from the 1860s–1870s onward, during what is often called the period of "first globalization." Since advanced countries needed food and raw materials from less-developed areas, they were ready to invest there to create cheap transportation connections, lend credit to increase agricultural output and raw material extraction, open mines, and even establish some kinds of manufacturing. While these investments were rather lucrative for investors, they also galvanized modern economic transformation in the peripheries.

Before World War I, the northwestern core invested huge amounts abroad. 26 percent of the $46,000 million total was channeled into the European peripheries. Taking inflation into account (the yearly average inflation rate of the US dollar between 1913 and 2017 was 3.14 percent), in 2017 USD, the European peripheries received nearly $3 trillion of Western capital before World War I.[26]

In poor peripheral regions, domestic capital accumulation was very low. During the last two decades of the 19th century, invested domestic Russian accumulation reached only 18 percent of foreign investments in the country. The huge inflow of capital financed the creation of the railroad system in the peripheries. Half of the Irish railroad system was financed by England. In Russia, 75 percent of railroad investments came from Western Europe; in Spain, 60 percent, mostly from France; in Hungary, 70 percent from Austria and Germany. Virtually the entire Balkan railroad was represented by the lines of the Orient Express (*Orientalische Eisenbahnen*), which was financed by the Deutsche Bank. The railroad density (measured in track length per 100,000 inhabitants) in the European peripheries represented two-thirds of the average Western level. Railroad transportation was thus the most advanced part of peripheral economy. That was the outcome of investments and technology exports from the core countries.

Western capital founded the nucleus – and in some countries the entire banking systems – in most of the backward countries. Germany played a crucial role in founding the banking industries in Spain, Romania, Austria-Hungary, and Russia. Western companies invested in mineral extractions (iron ore and copper in Spain; and oil in Russia, Galicia, and Romania) and even certain sectors of manufacturing industries. In Russia, 50 percent of industrial investments originated from abroad; in Greece, 65 percent of total economic investments came from the West. In Romania this share rose to 92 percent.

Because of rapidly increasing trade with the core, a segment of domestic merchants (mostly minority entrepreneurs), Germans, and Jews, also accumulated capital and started investing it. In Hungary, for example, grain merchants focused and invested in food processing industry, establishing one of the world's leading flourmill centers. Instead of unprocessed wheat, 60 percent of grain exports were processed by a highly developed and export-oriented flourmill industry. In Ireland, while the flourishing textile cottage industry was destroyed by English textile deliveries, the country specialized in beer and whisky production for the English market. In the Vizcaya region in Spain and the Donetsk area in Russia, iron and steel industrial bases were founded by foreign groups.

Capital inflow into the peripheries was rather uneven among peripheral regions. This influence was pretty significant in areas with bigger domestic potential, mostly next or very near to Western countries, while it was mostly insignificant in faraway and very backward territories. Nevertheless, in the places it went, it played a central role in generating the first steps of modern transformation. One of the most important positive outcomes was the exportation of Western transportation and agricultural revolutions to the peripheries, and the beginning of industrialization in certain areas.

The peripheral ring of Europe was not only different from the northwestern core but also exhibited regional differences within the ring. Some regions had better domestic socioeconomic sources, were nearer to the core, and received more foreign capital investments. They also had nearby transportation possibilities, which enabled them to deliver their export products to the large Western markets; consequently, these regions made more progress than others. Some of them – such as Finland, Ireland, the Baltic area, Hungary, and Poland – started on the road to industrialization, while others remained almost entirely agrarian.

The millennial road of historical development that led to backwardness compared with the Northwest also led to differences between peripheral regions. They exhibited rather different levels of backwardness and different potentials of elevating from it. The history of the 19th and 20th centuries presents interesting examples of catching up and elevation to the level of the advanced core. The most telling examples of peripheral economies that caught up and joined the advanced core include Scandinavia, Finland, and Ireland; in some respects, Italy and Spain belong to that group as well.

Until the 1870s, Sweden, Norway, and Denmark were nonindustrialized, relatively low-income countries that primarily produced and exported goods. Their transportation networks were undeveloped. Sweden produced and exported unprocessed wood and iron ore, Norway's export market was dominated by fish and unprocessed wood, and Denmark exported mostly grain. In 1870, the average per capita income level of the three Scandinavian countries was $1,631 – only 57 percent of the British, Dutch, and Belgian average of $2,847 (and only 15 percent higher than the estimated per capita income average of $1,411 for Hungary, the Czech Land, and Poland).[27]

Based on the income from exported primary products and foreign investments, especially in infrastructure, the Scandinavian countries started investing and industrializing by processing their own raw materials. During the half-century before World War I, the Scandinavian countries turned to processing wood into pulp and paper. These industrial sectors increased their output by 11 percent per year. Sweden, instead of exporting iron ore, also established its modern iron and steel industry. Before the war, 20 percent of the Swedish export market already consisted of iron, steel, and engineering products. Denmark stopped its grain economy and imported cheap grain, while developing its animal stocks in an extremely fast pace. Danish farmers processed milk and meat that was exported to the British breakfast table. The Danish food processing industry became a leading export sector, producing nearly 40 percent of the total industrial output. Between 1870 and 1913, the Scandinavian countries nearly doubled their per capita GDP. Sweden's economic growth was three times faster than Europe's. By the war, Denmark reached the West European average income level (98 percent), while Sweden neared it (84 percent). This catching-up process was accomplished after the war, and the region became an equal part of the core.

Finland belonged to Sweden's agricultural periphery until the end of the 18th century, when Russia occupied it beginning in 1809. Although part of autocratic Russia, Finland gained significant autonomy within the empire. Its strong Protestant culture had been formed during the long Swedish chapter in the country's history, and as a result it was able to build up a parliamentary democracy.

Finland also skillfully exploited the opportunities offered by the very backward Russian market by following the Scandinavian model. After gaining independence at the end of World War I, in the early 20th century unprocessed timber and wood represented more than 40 percent of Finnish export (and this trend actually continued until 1950). But in two decades this number declined to 18 percent. Processing developed by leaps and bounds until nearly half of the country's paper production was exported. Finland continued exploiting the opportunity of exporting to Russia. As a neutral "Finlandized" country, and after two lost wars with Russia during World War II, it did not join any Western institutions. It instead cultivated its special relations with the Soviet Union, which remained its most important export market. Meanwhile, Swedish investments and the lower labor costs in Finland helped its rapid industrialization. First engineering and other modern industries, and later electronics became leading export sectors in the highly educated country. Their share in exports jumped from 13 to 34 percent; by the 1970s, a few decades after the Scandinavian miracle, Finland's stable democracy and strong, modern, Westernized institutions increased its competitiveness. By 2014, Finland was the world's fourth most competitive country, before Germany and the Netherlands. The country's income level equaled Norway's and reached 80 percent of the Swedish and Danish level. In the mid-1870s, Finland's per capita GDP was close to Poland and Hungary's; six decades later, it elevated to almost 90 percent of the West European average and became part of the European core.

Unlike other peripheral regions in Europe that produced agricultural and raw materials, the Scandinavian countries and Finland were socially and culturally very similar to the advanced Northwest, even as they exhibited peripheral economic characteristics. This resemblance is certainly the "secret" behind their success. Social structures and freedom, frugality and Protestant work ethics, and proximity to Britain and Western Europe all differentiated this region from other peripheries. These factors definitely played the central role in the region's unparalleled elevation and catching up.

A few decades later, after joining the European Union in 1973 Ireland reproduced and even overdid Scandinavia and Finland's successes. Ireland was the poorest country in Western Europe in the 19th century. It was a cheap labor supplier to Britain and a country of mass emigration. By the 2010s the country of 4.5 million inhabitants had an immense émigré population all over the world. In the United States 40 million people consider themselves to be Irish descents. Ireland before World War I was on a similar middle-income peripheral economic level than Finland, Poland, and Hungary. After gaining independence in the early 1920s, the country's situation did not change much until the late 1980s. In the 1980s, one-fifth of the workforce was unemployed and the country's GDP per capita reached only somewhat more than 60 percent of Britain's. In 1987, after the EU's Mediterranean enlargement that included poorer countries like Greece, Portugal, and Spain that lowered the average income level of the European Community, Ireland's GDP still stood at only 69 percent of the EU's average.

Ireland's economic elevation started between one and one-and-half decades after the country joined the EU. It urged the organization to launch an aid program for less-developed regions. As a result, Ireland gained €43 billion in aid from the Community, or nearly 5 percent of its GDP, which generated an average of 0.5 percent in additional annual growth. In the first half of the 1990s, Ireland had a yearly growth rate of 5 percent, and in the latter half of the decade it reached 10 percent.

By 2000 the unemployment rate had dropped to 4.5 percent. In an unprecedented way in 2015, the growth rate again elevated to 7.8 percent. The international media started speaking about an "Irish economic miracle" and the "Celtic Tiger." Not without reason: the country's economic growth, as the *Financial Post* phrased it in 2016, rivaled that of China and India. By 2013, Ireland's per capita GDP stood high, at 136 percent above the EU average. It was higher than the per capita GDP of Britain, Germany, and most of the old Northwest countries.

Ireland did not copy others. Its sudden elevation resulted from its EU membership and low corporate tax rates (12.5 percent), its proximity to Britain and the European continent, its stable institutions, and a well-educated English-speaking population that became the central attraction for American and Asian investors. Ireland became a launching pad to the entire European Union. The biggest overseas multinational corporations, including high-tech industries, ran to establish business in the country. Seven out of the ten largest companies in Ireland currently are foreign or jointly owned. The country's exceptional growth was based on the inflow of huge amounts of foreign capital. Until 2000 this amount was not high, varying between $1 and 19 billion. Between 2000 and 2004 it increased to $30 billion per year, and between 2005 and 2009 it reached $50 to 60 billion. In 2013 and 2014, $50 billion and then almost $90 billion in capital investment flew into Ireland, respectively. In other words, economic growth was based on foreign capital investments and export-led development. More than half of Irish exports are produced by foreign companies. By the beginning of the 21st century, Ireland had risen to be the third richest country in Europe, behind only Switzerland and Norway.[28]

History has proved that in the integrated continent, exploiting the free movement of goods, capital, and the large EU market; and gaining investments from advanced countries made gradual development and a catching-up process possible. Beside Ireland, Italy and Spain also may be mentioned as examples. Although the development path in these latter countries has been burdened for a relatively longer time by the remnants of their peripheral pasts, especially in the slowly changing sociocultural arena, gradual changes are also progressing with time.

Similar signs also appeared in some well-performing former communist Central European countries. Before the 2008 financial and economic crisis that hit the region hard, three Baltic countries had exhibited the most promising signs. Despite the recession they produced a spectacular recovery afterwards. The window to catching up thus remained open but required a stable further integration progress; methodological, everyday adjustments and improvements; further reform; and accomplished transformation. The integration process started and progressed in peacefully allied Europe, as it never had before in the history of the continent.

The adjustment of the Mediterranean and Irish peripheries was a real success story. Italy was a founding country of the European Economic Community in the 1950s; Ireland joined in the 1970s, followed by Greece, Spain, and Portugal in the 1980s. Similar to Scandinavia – which elevated earlier, during the last third of the 19th century – the Mediterranean region began catching up with the Northwest in the second half of the 20th century. This is the only former middle-income-level peripheral region that has significantly improved its relative position. The region's Human Development Index – which beside GDP level, also measures life expectancy (reflecting health level) and the number of years an average citizen spends becoming educated – is only 4 percent lower than that of the West. Similarly, the Economic Freedom Index – which is based on trade freedom, business investments, and the regulation of property rights – is 9 percent lower than that of the West. An important major exception is the percentage of Internet users, which is still at only 24 percent and thus far below usage levels in the West.

The unique boom in the Mediterranean region was mostly the result of European Union membership and the adoption of the common currency. As Eduard Gracia argued:

> They benefited from their lower cost base while the single currency made capital available to them at unprecedented low interest rates. At the time, this was widely regarded as a sign of the new times, with the formerly "weaker" countries growing faster than the rest of the Union, whilst Germany, the traditional front-runner, was forced to undertake painful reforms.[29]

Until World War I, Italy (at least the south), Greece, and the Iberian peninsula belonged to the much-less-developed periphery, which (together with Russia) only had small islands of modernity in an ocean of a traditional backward peasant agricultural economy. Even in the first half of the 20th century this hardly changed. Indeed, in the aftermath of the war (1950) these countries' average per capita GDP had even dropped, from 47 to 39 percent of the Northwest's GDP. By the 2010s, however, their income level had elevated to nearly two-thirds of the northwestern core.

Even in troubled Central Europe and the Baltic area, despite the miserable interwar decades and then half a century of failed communist experiments, made significant economic progress in industrialization. Nevertheless, although income levels increased, the countries reproduced obsolete economic structures and technological standards. They had a stormy transformation period after the fall of communism in1989–1991, with a huge decline in production and income and a dramatic increase in poverty.

After the turn of the millennium in Russia and the Balkans, transformation and economic modernization gained speed only two decades after the collapse of communism. Some of the best-performing countries in the region elevated to 63 percent of the Western level by the early 2000s. Compared to the Northwest their backwardness was marked, but they ranked far above the deeply backward non-European regions of the world. That was clearly reflected by their relatively good Human Development Index ranking (only 6 percent below the Western level) – which takes GDP, health, and education into account. Relatedly, their Economic Freedom Index figure was only 8 percent below that of the West. However, the number of Internet users is 17 percent lower than the West's, and unemployment is 40 percent higher. Ultimately, almost all of the countries and regions that became part of integrating Europe became closely connected to the most advanced parts of core and made economic progress (some of them significantly so).

On the other hand, European regions that remained outside the integration process, Russia, other independent former Soviet republics (such as Ukraine, Belarus, Moldova, etc.), the Western Balkans (Bosnia, Serbia, Albania, etc.), and Turkey remained deeply and increasingly behind. While this region was also industrialized and socially modernized, the region's Human Development Index stands on average at 84 percent of the West's, and the number of Internet users is at 60 percent of the West's. The Economic Freedom Index is also low, standing at 80 percent of that of the Northwest.[30]

Four regions in the early 21st century

After comparing the economic indexes of European countries between 1913 and 2013–2016, there is no doubt that each region made significant advancements. Northwestern Europe increased its per capita GDP by more than 12 times. Together with Ireland, the Mediterranean region achieved an even faster pace of modernization by increasing its income level by more than 16 times, thus elevating from the middle-income to the high-income zone. Although this region did not elevate to the same level as the Northwest, its catching-up process was the most successful, and the distance between the Northwest and the Mediterranean-Irish region significantly narrowed.

The third region – Central Europe, together with the Baltic countries – increased its per capita income level by somewhat less than nine times. Russia (together with the other successor states of the Soviet Union), the Balkans, and Turkey were able to increase their income level by eight times. Thus, both regions modernized somewhat slower than the Northwest. In comparative terms, in spite of their significant progress, the relative economic backwardness of these two peripheral regions actually became somewhat worse than a century before.

Consequently, at the beginning of the 21st century and after the long progress of integration, we still can clearly differentiate *four* European macro-regions, basically similar to a century before.

As Table 2.1 clearly shows, most of this exceptional growth happened after 1950. In the interwar decades economic growth was very moderate, except during the Bolshevik Soviet Union, which created a nonmarket system and launched a forced accumulation and industrialization drive. As a result of its isolation, Russia was not hit by the Great Depression and increased its income level by nearly 80 percent.

In most of the regions, the spectacular economic development happened during the second half of the century. In slightly more than half a century Northwestern Europe's per capita GDP jumped by nearly 9 times; GDP in the Mediterranean-Irish region skyrocketed by more than 14 times. The two peripheral regions also achieved the bulk of their growth by increasing their per capita GDP by 5.4 and 4.7 times, respectively.

The Mediterranean region was thus the only area that achieved a higher growth than the northwest and elevated to the high-income level. The other two middle-income peripheral regions were unable to keep pace with the

Table 2.1 Increase of per capita GDP in the four European regions, 1913–2016

Year	*Northwestern Europe*	*Mediterranean Europe and Ireland*	*Central Europe and Baltics*	*Russia-Turkey-Balkans*[a]
1913	100	100	100	100
1950	138	115	156	142
2013	12,163	16,413	8,471	3,667

Sources: Based on Maddison, *Monitoring the World Economy*, Paris: OECD, 1985, for the 1913 and 1950 figures; and *The Economist, Pocket World in Figures 2017*, London: Profile Books, 2017, for the 2013 figures.

Note:

a The Russian-Turkey-Balkans region is based on the territory of the former Soviet Union and its Western successor states as of 2013: Russia, Ukraine, Belarus, Moldova, Serbia, Bosnia-Herzegovina, Macedonia, Montenegro, Bulgaria, and Romania.

Table 2.2 Per capita GDP in three low- and middle-income (relatively backward) European regions compared to northwestern Europe, 1913–2013

Year	*Northwestern Europe*	*Mediterranean Europe and Ireland*	*Central Europe and the Baltic*	*Russia-Turkey-Balkans*[a]
1913	100	47	45	30
1950	100	39	51	39
2013	100	64	32	13

Sources: Based on Maddison, *Monitoring the World Economy*, Paris: OECD, 1985, for the 1913 and 1950 figures; and *The Economist, Pocket World in Figures 2017*, London: Profile Books, 2017, for the 2013 figures.

Note:
a The Russian-Turkey-Balkans region includes the countries described in Table 2.1 note.

exceptional development of northwestern Europe and remained trapped in medium-level development state.

Compared with northwestern Europe, the Mediterranean region started catching up while the Central European-Baltic and Russian-Turkish-Balkan regions, in spite of their economic progress, became relatively even more backward than a century ago (see Table 2.2).

The changing position of some countries in an unchanged regional divide

In the early 21st century, after 100 years of dramatic change, the four regions remain as they existed in the 1910s. However, one must add that they are not exactly the same as they were. Although the overall regions remained basically the same, a couple of countries changed positions, either because they made exceptional progress, or because they lagged even further behind. During this century the most outstanding progress occurred in Ireland and Finland. As presented before, before World War I they were virtually on the same economic level as the middle-income, relatively backward peripheral group of Central Europe and the Baltics. While overall these countries lagged behind, relatively speaking they were already performing better than the other peripheries and were making further progress in industrialization. One century later, they joined the high-income northwestern core, as changes in their per capita GDPs show. Ireland and Finland's income levels surpassed the average northwestern level by 21–22 percent in 2012, signaling a historical turning point. By contrast, during the 20th century the Czech lands exhibited the opposite trend as Ireland and Finland. A century before, together with Austria, this area (the Bohemian part of Austria-Hungary) belonged to the edge of the advanced industrialized West, but then declined into the Central European periphery. Russia also relatively declined, shifting further downward.

Greece is a special case. In 1913, it was a typical backward Balkan country. In the 20th century, especially during the second half, it became "part of the

Table 2.3 Human Development Index, world in 2016 (maximum level is 1,000)

World average	717
Developing countries, average	670
Latin America, average	751
Sub-Saharan Africa, average	523
Northwestern Europe, average	915
Mediterranean-Irish, average	881
Central Europe and Baltic, average	856
Russia-Turkey-Balkans, average	771

Source: *Human Development Report 2016: Human Development for Everyone* (New York City: United Nations Development Programme), http://hdr.undp.org/sites/default/files/2016_human_development_report.pdf, accessed January 21, 2017.

West" politically and improved its position in the world. Although at the lower end of the group, this country was legitimately categorized as part of the rapidly rising Mediterranean-Irish zone. This was quite a spectacular elevation. Inner weaknesses, however, were much, much stronger than in Ireland, Italy, or Spain. In the early 21st century, Greece's relative position started to shift downward to a level similar to that of the Czech Republic, Slovakia, or Estonia, but still better than that of Poland, Hungary, Croatia, or Latvia. Ultimately, Greece became virtually nearer to the Central European–Baltic average than to the Mediterranean level.

Europe's divided regions' position in the world

To understand better the relative backwardness of these European peripheral regions, one must put them into a larger international context. The United Nations Development Program calculated the world's Human Development Index for 2016. It clearly shows that Europe belongs to the best category of the global standard for combined income, health, and educational levels. Northwestern Europe ranks at the top. The Mediterranean-Irish region is only 4 percent lower than the Northwest, and the Central Europe-Baltic region is 7 percent behind the Northwest. The Russia-Turkey-Balkans average, however, is 16 percent lower than the West, and only 15 percent higher than the developing countries' average. In the World Bank categorization, most of the European countries (except Ukraine, Moldova, and some Balkan countries) are in the "high-income" zone, because they are above or at the border of the world's average per capita income level (somewhat more than $10,000) and also above the world average Human Development Index of 717 points.

In other words, in spite of the huge regional divide within Europe, even the less-developed Russian-Turkish-Balkan region is above the world average and is better than the averages for developing countries, Africa, and Latin America.

Nevertheless, the sharp differences within Europe from the early 20th century are still present in the early 21st century. After the tremendous changes in the world and the long and successful progress of European integration, it legitimate to ask: What were the main factors that contributed to the conservation of regional divisions? In this chapter, I discussed what radically changed in the world and Europe in terms of socioeconomic and political environment. In the next chapter, I turn to the slowly changing factors in human life, and the unchanged or only partially changed mentalities and customs.

Notes

1 Robert Gilpin, *The Challenge of Global Capitalism. The World Economy in the 21st Century*, Princeton, NJ: Princeton University Press, 2000, p. 15. His description and analyses serve as a basis for the following paragraphs.
2 Ibid., p. 32.
3 Ibid., p. 52.
4 Ibid., pp. 20–22.
5 Ibid., p. 169.
6 "The Retreat of the Global Company," *The Economist*, January 28, 2017. www.economist.com/briefing/2017/01/28/the-retreat-of-the-global-company, accessed February 1, 2017.
7 Ibid., p. 17.
8 Ibid.
9 Gilpin, *Challenge of Global Capitalism* p. 357.
10 Ibid., p. 294.
11 Ibid., p. 29.
12 *International Recommendations for Tourism Statistics 2008*, Studies in Methods, New York: United Nations, https://unstats.un.org/unsd/publication/seriesm/seriesm_83rev1e.pdf, accessed January 29, 2017.
13 Italy was among the founders, thus joined the northwest region. Italy itself was a sharply divided country. Italy had been divided into several small, highly different countries for centuries. As one author put it, the country was "accidentally united" in the last third of the 19th century. Northern Italy was on par with countries in the northwest of Europe, while southern Italy and Sicily were not as advanced or developed. In this book, Italy is not categorized as belonging to the same group as the northwestern European countries but instead as part of the Mediterranean-Irish region.
14 "Copenhagen European Council Presidency Conclusions – 21–22 June 1993," European Parliament, June 21, 1993, www.europarl.europa.eu/enlargement/ec/cop_en.htm, accessed February 3, 2017.
15 *Transition Report 2003: Integration and Regional Cooperation*, Transition Report, European Bank, October 1, 2003, pp. 7–8, www.ebrd.com/downloads/research/transition/TR03.pdf, accessed February 21, 2017.
16 Maddison Angus, *The World Economy: A Millennial Perspective* (Paris: OECD Publishing, 2001), p. 363; *Pocket World in Figures 2015* London: *The Economist*, 2015.
17 Loukas Tsoukalis, *The New European Economy Revisited*, Oxford: Oxford University Press, 1997, pp. 203–205.

18 "Berlin European Council 24–25 March 1999: Presidency Conclusions," European Parliament, March 24, 1999, www.europarl.europa.eu/summits/ber1_en.htm, accessed March 1, 2017; *Transition Report 2005: Business in Transition*, Transition Report, London: European Bank, October 10, 2005, www.ebrd.com/downloads/research/transition/TR05.pdf, 19, accessed February 20, 2017.

19 "Missions Economiques: Revue Regionale," *Regions Magazine* 248, no. 1 (November 1, 2003): 6–8, https://doi.org/10.1080/714042091. *World Investment Report: The Shift Towards Services* (United Nations, 2004), https://unctad.org/en/Docs/wir2004_en.pdf, accessed February 20, 2017.

20 Nicole Lindstrom and Dóra Piroska, "The Politics of Privatization and Europeanization in Europe's Periphery: Slovenian Banks and Breweries for Sale?," *Competition & Change* 11, no. 2 (June 1, 2007): 117–135; 118–119, 125, https://doi.org/10.1179/102452907X181938, accessed February 21, 2017.

21 Roberto Basile, Davide Castellani, and Antonello Zanfei, "Location Choices of Multinational Firms in Europe: The Role of EU Cohesion Policy," *Journal of International Economics* 74, no. 2 (March 1, 2008): 328–340, https://doi.org/10.1016/j.jinteco.2007.08.006.

22 *Pocket World in Figures 2015*, pp. 42–43.

23 Joseph E. Stiglitz, *Globalization and Its Discontents*, New York: W.W. Norton, 2003.

24 Perry Anderson, "Why the System Will Still Win," *Le Monde Diplomatique*, March 1, 2017, https://mondediplo.com/2017/03/02brexit, accessed March 3, 2017.

25 Herbert Feis, *Europe the World's Banker, 1870–1914: An Account of European Foreign Investment and the Connection of World Finance with Diplomacy before World War I*, New York: W.W. Norton, 1965, p. 263.

26 A.G. Kenwood and Allen L. Lougheed, *The Growth of the International Economy, 1820–1960*, London: Allen & Unwin, 1971, p. 43.

27 Maddison, *The World Economy*.

28 John Shmuel, "How Ireland Pulled off an Economic Miracle That Rivals China, India," *The Financial Post*, May 16, 2016, https://financialpost.com/investing/global-investor/how-ireland-pulled-off-an-economic-miracle-that-rivals-china-india, accessed January 12, 2017.

29 Eduard Gracia, "The Curse of Geography and the Dilemma of Europe's Periphery," 2017, www.westga.edu/~bquest/2017/geography2017.pdf, accessed March 1, 2017. Nevertheless, Gracia rejects the role of sociocultural factors in the weakness of the Mediterranean region:

> Throughout the intense debate on the causes of the crisis many explanations have been put forward: corruption and low institutional quality; democratic deficits; bureaucratic obstacles; small average company size; educational and human capital shortfalls; social inequality; unproductive and uncooperative local cultures; and long naps and late dinner. It is in fact remarkable how quickly the discussion drifts from objective analysis to moral indictment even when the evidence supporting this causal link is … questionable.

30 All of the quoted indexes are based on *The Economist*, *Pocket World in Figures 2008*, London: Profile Books, 2007.

3 What preserves regional differences?

The social, economic, and cultural factors

The dialectic of change and continuity

As the world and Europe have changed, several basics of human life and human mind-set also have changed, but these transformations have occurred at a much slower rate and in a more partial way, and even have left certain elements nearly untouched. History, in an endless chain, exhibits both changes and continuities, but their interrelation is quite mysterious. Yet within the chain, the links fashioned from social-cultural-behavioral customs resist breaking more than do those related to the economic level of a society. Has the radical socioeconomic and technological progress of the 19th and 20th centuries changed human morals, habits, reflexes, customs and behaviors? Of course, it definitely has. The generation of the great-grandchildren certainly does not have the habits and behavioral patterns of its great-grandfathers. But has progress eliminated all of the old habits and ways of thinking and created totally new ones? It definitely has not.

The persistence of old ways manifests itself in multiple areas and ways. If four generations before the present people did not identify with the state where they lived because it was an oppressor, an alien state imposed by an occupying power or by a predatory, autocratic elite, then even as those types of state have been replaced by radically different ones, people still have tended to distrust the state and its institutions, as their forebears had done for generations. If they want to arrange something, they still have a nearly instinctual impulse to turn for help to friends that is to influential patrons, in this way avoiding as much as possible the self-serving bureaucrats in state offices. Yes, today, a man of the generation of the great-grandchildren probably uses email or a cellphone to make appointments, but he still relies on influential friends-patrons to broker relations with bureaucrats. He probably still avoids paying sales tax on car repairs by taking his car to a family-owned shop where the owner usually does not give a receipt. He rents out his apartment to tourists, without registering at the city. Some families continue to devalue education and to direct their children into jobs at a young age, which consequently causes "lost" years of schooling. They may not want their children to go to college for a higher education because they distrust educated "eggheads." Even people better educated than their grandparents retain some old suspicions automatically learned as children. If a man wants to arrange a delicate deal with a city official to get permission to build his family villa in a restricted city-zone, he is still ready to slip an envelope filled with money into the official's pocket. He does the same for the tax official. Yes, in very new circumstances very old habits survive in broad layers of the society. Changes most certainly do not eliminate continuity; moreover, in certain situations they revitalize some of the habits learned at the family table from a father who learned the same habits from his father. Old habits and attitudes developed for centuries in backward environments in peripheral countries and passed from parents to children in continued chains, thus smolder in peoples' minds and produce automatic actions even in changed historical situations.

When historians and sociologists began speaking about "path-dependence," the impact of the past on the present, they gave a name to a phenomenon well-known long before the birth of modern historiography in the late 19th century. Alexis de Tocqueville, the congenial French political thinker, described this phenomenon in a beautiful way in the foreword to his mid-19th-century book, *The Old Regime and the French Revolution*. The revolutionaries of the late 18th century, he stated, created:

> all sorts of restrictions in order to differentiate themselves in every possible way from the previous generation. … They were far less successful in this curious attempt than is generally supposed. … Though they had no inkling of this, they took over from the old regime not only most of its customs, conventions, and modes of thought, but even those very ideas which prompted our revolutionaries to destroy it. … They used the debris of the old order for building the new. … The peculiarities of our modern social system are deeply rooted in the ancient soil of France. … [Things suppressed in 1789, reappeared] as some rivers after going underground re-emerge at another point, in new surroundings.[1]

Survival of micro-regional peripheral backwardness in advanced countries

One also must not forget that just as "inherited" habits and behavioral patterns persist, so too, the old peripheral environment with all of its backward features and influences on human behavior does not entirely disappear in the now more advanced country. Even in already high-income-level countries such as Italy and Spain, just a few especially advanced regions, the north in Italy or the Basque Land and Catalonia in Spain, are the most important areas and sources of high income, while other areas within the same countries remain in a rather backward, rural state, scarcely different from the past. In several parts of these countries a very large part of the population still lives in rural areas in peripheral circumstances.

In this book, I am dealing with countries and group of countries or macro-regions, but not with small micro-regions within countries. At this point, however, I have to make some remarks about those micro-regions. The Assembly of European Regions, established in 1985, divided 33 countries into 270 regions. The European Union categorizes the member countries with three different groups: "more developed" regions with GDP per capita over 90 percent of the EU average; "transition" regions, between 75 and 90 percent; and "less developed" regions with less than 75 percent of EU average income level. The current Nomenclature of Territorial Units for Statistics (NUTS) recognizes even smaller micro-regions.[2]

In several micro-regions in relatively more developed countries, old peripheral backwardness is a present reality. In 2015, 175 regions had an income level below the EU average, 85 regions had less than 75 percent of that average, and among them 22 regions had less than half that average. Regions in the last category are mostly found within former communist Central European and Balkan countries, but three of them are Greek, although Greece as a whole has a higher middle-income average level.[3] Similarly, in high-income level Italy and Spain, some regions remained behind at middle-income levels.

After 150 years of Italian unification, the country's south remains a peripheral region, with lower income levels. It has only half the per capita GDP level of the north and much higher unemployment rates. In the north, for example, unemployment was 6 percent in 1997, in the south 23 percent. In the north, 50 percent of women now are participating in the labor force, but in the south only 37 percent. In the 2010s, foreign direct investments created 50,000 jobs in the north, but only 400 in a south that attracted only 10 percent of foreign investment to the country. The employment rate in the same decade in the north was 64.2 percent, in the south 42 percent. In 2011, 48 percent of the residents of the south were at risk of poverty. Southern peripheral status haunts southerners even when they have moved northwards by the millions to take up industrial work. Between 1951 and 1965, alone, about 1.5 million people moved every year. Not only have these new arrivals in the north tended to retain their traditional ways of thinking, but northerners have held on to their old prejudices against them, calling them *terroni* (peasant in a pejorative sense) or accusing them of ignorance, lack of desire to work, laziness, rude manners and contempt of civil norms. In other words, in micro-regions, as elsewhere, peripheral habits and traditions persist even as people move into more advanced parts of their countries.[4]

A similar phenomenon characterizes Spain. The post-Franco 1978 constitution created 17 *Communidad Autónoma,* autonomous communities with limited self-government, but these exhibit glaring economic disparities. Five of them (including Madrid) produce 65 percent of Spanish GDP, with the Basque country in the northwest, Catalonia in the northeast, and some coastal regions of Valencia contributing the greatest part and reaching the high income level. The Basque country's income level is on a par with Germany and Catalonia is on a par with France, but Extremadura's and Andalusia's levels are closer to middle-income Argentina and Poland, respectively. The Basque unemployment rate of 14 percent is similar to Slovakia's rate, but Andalusia's and Extremadura's 32–33 percent is closer to Macedonia's and Yemen's rate.

The Basque country and Catalonia have strong and even sophisticated industries, while several inner Spanish regions are frozen in agricultural production and related social-cultural habits. The Basque country's per capita GDP is $32,600 while Extremadura's is less than half that, $15,133. Catalonia's 7.5 million inhabitants represent 16 percent of Spain's total population, but they produce nearly 20 percent of Spain's GDP, own 23 percent of the country's industry, locate half of their manufacturing in Spain itself, and deliver one-quarter of the country's exports. Catalonia has 22 percent of the country's innovative firms, 21 percent of investment in R&D, and 34 percent of the country's patents. This region's per capita GDP is almost 40 percent higher than Spain's total. In contrast, the largely agricultural communities of the Extremadura, Asturia, Castille-La Mancha, and Castilla y León regions still lag far behind, with their societies mired in a quasi-peripheral, middle-income status, life-style and general social-cultural practices.[5] Extremadura's per capita income level is only 28 percent of the Catalonian level.

In this chapter, I will present the social-cultural-behavioral characteristics typical of peripheral, low- and middle-income countries. I am going to explore these peripheral characteristics without differentiating according to level of backwardness. Thus I am going to present them wherever they exist today, whether in countries that already have risen from the middle-income to high-income level (Ireland, Italy, and Spain), or in those that are trapped at the middle-income level (Hungary and Croatia), or that stand just at the borderline between the low- and middle-income level (Russia and Turkey), or even that remain in the low-income category (Ukraine, Moldova, Albania, or Macedonia). I am not suggesting that all of these weaknesses and behavioral characteristics of peripheral condition have the same impact everywhere. There are major differences between Italy and Ukraine, Spain and Hungary, Poland and Turkey, in the deep-rootedness and impact of these weaknesses. I will discuss these differences in subsequent chapters: Chapter 5 (the Mediterranean-Irish region), Chapter 6 (the Central European-Baltic area), and Chapter 7 (the Russian-Turkish-Balkan region).

Social-economic structural weaknesses of peripheral countries

I call attention first to the Mediterranean-Irish region, the region of the so-called PIIGS countries (Portugal, Italy, Ireland, Greece, Spain), a former periphery now in the high-income zone, but exhibiting important social and economic weaknesses inherited from a peripheral past.[6] When the economic crisis hit Europe in 2008, the boom of this region not only stopped but – unlike in the northwest – caused a financial collapse and a deep, long-lasting recession. Between 2009 and 2013 the GDP level of the Mediterranean countries, for example, dropped by 6–8 percent. During the crisis, these countries could not pay their government obligations or rescue and refinance their failing banks. They all fell into bankruptcy (except Italy, which stood for a long time at the brink) and needed bailouts from the European Union and the International Monetary Fund (IMF). They all had to introduce severe austerity measures including cuts of nearly one-quarter to wages, pensions, healthcare and educational expenditures, in order to put their financial households in order. Their collective unemployment rate, almost a decade after 2008, was still nearly three times (271 percent) higher than in the northwest. In Greece and Spain one-quarter of the total workforce became unemployed during the crisis, including half of working-age youth. The collapse and struggle to return to financial health has made it clear that the Mediterranean-Irish region did not really belong to the European core because they had "neither institutional nor human capital, religious conditioning, racial heritage, cultural baggage nor even climatology… [in common with] the economic and industrial core of Europe."[7]

In spite of the successful catching-up process and in spite of the high level of per capita GDP (that in the case of Ireland is higher than in old core countries), they exhibited structural-economic and social weaknesses. The PIIGS countries have lower level of capital accumulation and domestic investments. The rapid economic growth was thus mostly generated by massive foreign capital inflow and investments, in great part from the core region. Foreign corporations established large networks of branches and subsidiaries in these countries. In some cases, a significant part of the economy is in foreign hands.

In all the PIIGS small- and middle-sized companies have a larger than usual role in the economy. Companies employing less than 500 people represent about 95 percent of existing enterprises. Their share in employment in Spain, Portugal, and Ireland is 30–45 percent, in Greece and Italy over 50 percent, in Turkey 77 percent; by contrast in the northwestern countries their share is about 20 percent. The role of small enterprises is especially large in nonmanufacturing sectors where 90 percent of firms have fewer than 100 employees; in manufacturing such firms represent 50 percent.

A great part of small- and medium-sized firms are in family ownership. This phenomenon is very widespread across all of Europe, but in former peripheral countries such as Italy and Greece, it is much more dominant than in the core region and carries with it the characteristics of traditional kinship relations. For Greece, Malcolm Chapman and Christos Antoniou have provided an excellent description:

> The family was and is important in Greek society. The great majority of Greek companies is family-owned and managed. … [The companies] belong to the figures … that founded the company. … Greek society until recently retained many traditional features. … Contacts were local. … Self-sufficiency could largely achieve with this narrow circle, and contacts with anonymous strangers were unusual. … Outsiders were mistrusted and largely avoided. … In this new environment of change, [the companies] sought to maintain the friendly security of the old system. … A company … looks rather like an extension of the family, rather than an entity with its own autonomy.[8]

Across the Adriatic, in Italy, nearly 800,000 firms are family businesses, 85 percent of the total number of firms; 43 percent are in the manufacturing sector and 28 percent in commerce. Two-thirds are fully managed by family members and nearly half of the owners plan to pass management on to the next generation of the family. Some studies maintain that 75 percent of the senior executives are family members. In comparison, family members manage only 26 percent of French and 10 percent of British family-owned companies.[9]

Although several leading world firms mostly in the United States and Asia – but among them the German Volkswagen, the Swiss Novartis (Sandoz-Ciba-Geigy) or the Belgian Anheuser-Busch corporations in the European core – are in family ownership, according to a 2015 report of Credit Suisse, this phenomenon takes a rather different form in peripheral or formerly peripheral countries.[10] Here these firms are often extremely conservative and do not want capitalization from outside, from foreign investors or the stock exchange. Old-fashioned, even obsolete management practices are common, and owners frequently draw their managers from among relatives lacking in expertise. Often the company seeks not to grow but rather to keep the tight family circle in control and collective family decision making in place. Although such family businesses can be modern and competitive, a great many represent an earlier stage in the evolution of the business world. They may be closely connected to big firms, either in value-chains or as parts producers, but in some sectors they are independent producers or service providers, and in several cases, they produce only for the domestic market.[11] In other words, some elements of a dual economy are present in these regions. Competitive, partly foreign-owned, large-scale, advanced-technology export sectors coexist with noncompetitive, mostly smaller-scale domestic enterprises producing to the domestic market.

Unlike in the northwestern core, Mediterranean welfare regimes also exhibit some dualism, with northwestern-type healthcare systems and traditional family services operating in parallel. Private healthcare flourishes alongside a particular clientelist form of welfare state. Neither the state nor the workplace but rather the extended family plays the central role as welfare provider. Social traditions are strong in the region. Extended family obligations and solidarity, along with the traditional sentiment that care-work is a family responsibility, have major importance and support a more traditional form of elder care to this day. In lower-income families female family members provide home care for the elderly; in more well-to-do families, home care is also the rule but is provided by hired female immigrant labor.[12]

What lies behind the underperformance and the virtual collapse of this best-performing, nearly caught up former Mediterranean-Irish periphery after the 2008 financial-economic crisis? And what lies behind the increased relative backwardness of other middle-income peripheries in Central Europe? Why has the Russian-Turkish-Balkan region fallen into what is, in the European sense, the low-income zone? In reply, let me sum up in advance the conclusion of the detailed analysis below: economic progress and transformation from middle-income toward high-income (core) level occurs at much faster rates than the movement of social-cultural characteristics, habits and behavioral patterns away from peripheral patterns. Social and cultural remnants of the peripheral economic past, whether recurring or persistent, have contributed to complicating and hindering countries undergoing modern forms of capitalist transformation. To the extent they affect a country, whether as partial characteristics in otherwise more economically flourishing countries, or as dominant characteristics in countries struggling to capture some of the benefits of the 21st-century economy, they join with specifically economic factors to produce poorer economic outcomes. In other words, economic performance does not depend merely on economic factors. Social-cultural features also belong to the center of this problem. In what follows I am going to discuss the contributions of these features to the preservation of relative backwardness and to the trap of mediocracy.

Preserved peripheral social-cultural characteristics

What are these surviving and still dominant peripheral social-cultural features? In my interpretation the idea "social-cultural characteristics" encompasses the entire social and income structure, lifestyle, and behavior of the people together with their underlying principles. The idea thus contains values and norms as well as internalized behavioral patterns, interpersonal relations and attitudes expressed in social situations or in interactions with the state and its institutions. Together these characteristics of the behavior of a society strongly influence economic developments and the features of the state, governments and political systems.

In the middle-income and lower-income countries and regions of Europe, people are socialized and encultured in families and small communities according to the dominant, traditional, peripheral social-cultural norms, values and behavioral patterns. Their shared morals and ethics are in many ways different from those predominating in the northwest. They are deeply rooted in history, change very slowly. They are relatively independent from the faster changing economy, and also resistant to legal, regulatory and institutional innovations introduced by new regimes and governments. In other words, developed social-cultural characteristics have a rather stable and long-lasting independent life, and this may explain the often surprising neglect of modern institutions and the attempt to replace them by old kinship and patron-client networks in the peripheries. This is also often behind the suspicious and even hostile behavior of citizens toward their own states; they do not yet feel these new states to be theirs. In all of the peripheries including those former ones economically nearly caught up, the social-cultural characteristics defined above distinguish their citizens from their counterparts in advanced core countries where centuries-long development gradually has transformed habitual ways.

Anti-capitalist mentalities, sharply divided societies, and lower levels of education

In low- and middle-income level, relatively backward peripheries the combination of low education levels and traditional values and social behaviors has always characterized most of the population. In Spain, for example, an aristocratic feudal mentality known as the *hidalgo* attitude, the idea that industry and commerce are activities incompatible with noble status, survived the collapse of feudalism, then fused with a suppression of secular and scientific thinking, and persisted as a strong obstacle to modernization even during the 18th and 19th centuries. In Gabriel Tortella's words:

> Practicing industry or commerce still seems incompatible with the status of nobility ... the ideal of aristocratic life impregnated the mentality of all strata of Spanish society in the Old Regime and was solidly rooted in the lower layers, so much so that work on some trades was socially rejected.[13]

The social traits that were "responsible for backwardness," Tortella concluded, were the "old aristocratic prejudice against work ... the traditional Catholic distrust of capitalism ... intellectual passivity and respect for orthodoxy ... [and a] long mercantilist tradition supporting state intervention."[14]

Throughout the peripheries, as in Spain, elites and the large parts of the population emulating them have looked down on business as "ungentlemanly," as an undertaking alien for a Pole, Hungarian, or Russian, or Italian. Testimony to this attitude abounds, for example in Slavic writing from the later 19th and early 20th centuries. Anton Chekhov had one of the heroes in the *Cherry Orchard* (1904) declare:

> The human race [is] progressing ... Meanwhile in Russia a very few of us work. The vast majority ... [of the elite] seek for nothing, do nothing, and ... [are] incapable of hard work ... they treat the peasants like animals. ... Only dirt, vulgarity, and Asiatic plagues really exist.[15]

Nobel laureate Bolesław Prus described the Polish aristocratic ethic in these words: "He who makes a fortune is called a miser, a skinflint, a parvenu, he who wastes money is called generous, disinterested, open-handed. ... Simplicity is eccentric, economy is shameful."[16] And an anonymous pamphlet of 1880, *Glos szlachcica polskiego* (The Voice of a Polish Gentleman), similarly claimed that noble men live according

> to the customs of their forebears and not the customs of shopkeepers ... [reject] the worship of the golden calf and utilitarianism. ... [They are] the exclusive heir to the entire historic national past. ... Religion, Motherland, Family and Tradition.[17]

In non-Slavic peripheral nations writers evaluating their cultures have seen much the same set of attitudes. In 1920, for example, Gyula Szekfű, the leading Hungarian historian of the interwar period, described Hungarians as a "race" with "anti-commercial and anti-capitalist talents." He claimed that "the principle of trading and producing for profit disagreed with the Hungarian nature"; that "bourgeois characteristics were quite far from the mental habit of Hungarians, nobility and peasantry alike"; and that "undoubtedly, the Hungarians may be listed among those peoples that have the least inclination to develop in a capitalist direction."[18] And Giorgio Mori, writing in the late 20th century, noted the "radical anti-industrialism, latent or explicit, of a large part of economic thought and of the culture of the ruling classes of the Italian states."[19]

Peripheral and former peripheral regions historically also have had more *divided societies* than in the north and west, with more extreme degrees of income inequality. A small layer of society has enjoyed great wealth while a larger section of landless peasants or holders of tiny plots, either has lived in poverty or at least at a very low standard of living. Pronounced social stratification and forms of social exclusion (structurally produced confinement to a kind of underclass status) were the norm until well into modern times. In countries where hereditary nobility dominated, the bulk of the population was denied political and legal rights and real opportunities to participate in profitable business, economic and social life. The masses remained poor, uneducated and superstitious, essentially pushed into passivity.

The extreme income inequality of the past remains a central social problem today. This fact requires a somewhat more detailed explanation. The GINI coefficient, a good way to reflect on the problem, measures inequality on a scale between 0 and 1. Zero reflects absolute equality while1 means that one member of the society has all the income. As the French economist, Thomas Piketty has proven with rich statistical evidence, income inequality, which decreased during the second half of the 20th century, started increasing again in the last third of the century. This phenomenon challenges the so-called Kuznetz-curve, the broadly shared concept that inequality "automatically decreases in advance phases of capitalist development," eventually stabilizing at an acceptable level. Piketty found that income distribution follows a bell-shape curve, wide at the beginning but narrowing at the top of high development level, and that in reality, "since [the] 1970s, income inequality has increased significantly … [and] in the first decade of the twenty-first century regained … the level attained in the second decade of the previous century."[20] Piketty focuses on the most advanced countries but nevertheless also documents worldwide inequality, divisions among European countries, and the existence within the advanced "Western World" of "highly unequal sub-regions: a hyper-developed core and a less developed periphery." He differentiates among the West and Sub-Saharan Africa, the Western core, and the Eastern European or even Russian-Ukrainian bloc, countries with monthly income of more than €3,000, around €1,000 and only €150, respectively.[21]

Table 3.1 Income inequality (GINI Index), 2010

Scandinavia	0.26–0.27
Northwestern Europe	0.30–0.35
Former communist countries with low level inequality	0.25–0.26
Mediterranean countries	0.35–0.36
Former communist countries with higher level inequality	0.29–0.35
Russia and Turkey[a]	0.40–0.42
Africa and Latin America	0.53–0.64

Source: World Bank, "GINI Index Calculations," 2010, www.indexmundi.com/facts/Indicators/51.POV.GINI/rankings, accessed April 2, 2017.

Note:
a Chapter 7 will discuss further details about sharp Russian and Turkish income inequality.

Table 3.1 shows income distributions worldwide. African and Latin American peripheral countries have the most unequal distribution. Europe has a relatively well-balanced, more equal income level, especially in the Nordic countries (Finland and Scandinavia). Western European income distribution has changed in recent decades, shifting away from the Nordic level toward a greater but still not large degree of inequality. The Mediterranean countries are somewhat more inegalitarian. The post–World War II communist countries, announcing their break with the past, introduced an overly egalitarian income distribution, but after the collapse of the Soviet regime the former Soviet Bloc countries began falling into several different distribution groups. Especially Russia, but also Bulgaria, Estonia, Bosnia and Latvia, jumped into a rather unequal category, while other former Soviet republics and Balkan countries, including Ukraine, Belarus, Slovenia, the Czech Republic, and Slovakia, kept their more egalitarian systems. In between these two groups, Hungary, Poland, and Croatia increased inequality to the Western European level. Hungary's GINI coefficient, 0.24 in 2007, jumped to 0.31 by 2013.

The long-surviving *ancien régime* in the peripheral regions was accompanied by lower levels of education, even by mass illiteracy, unlike in the northwest, where numeracy and literacy were quite developed long before the introduction of compulsory education. In the late 19th century, 75 percent of Spaniards, for example, were still illiterate. According to Tortella, "the heavy hand of the Inquisition, the interference of the Church with learning was at its worst in Spain."[22] In Portugal, only one-quarter of the population could read and write as late as 1911. Illiteracy of 75–80 percent in Italy in the mid-19th century dropped, on average, to 25 percent by 1914, but it was much higher still in the South where more than half of children did not, or did not regularly attend school. In 1880, in Warsaw, the "city of illiterates" as it was called, only 20 percent of school-age children attended primary schools, and this rate actually increased to 25 percent at the beginning of World War I. In Galicia in 1910, 59 percent of the population was still illiterate and nearly 70 percent of school-age children did not attend school.[23] In Dalmatia, only 1 percent of conscripts could sign their names in 1870. Until the late decades of the 19th century, roughly 80 percent of Russians and 90 percent of the Balkan populace remained illiterate and this share did not drop to less than 70–75 percent until just before World War I.

In these societies vast swaths of the population were excluded from the possibility of adequate education, in part because economic necessity required people to begin working at a young age, or because they did not have the financial means and even less the ambition to dedicate years to study. Those who received good education and who were highly talented often could not find appropriate places to work, and therefore their talents could not be put to use. Many of them looked for opportunities in rich foreign countries and the resulting brain drain only worsened the situation in their home countries.

Even today, although with several exceptions, a huge skills-gap in reading, mathematics and science separates the peripheral countries from the core, and peripheral countries from each other. According to the OECD world education ranking, among the 35 relatively advanced member countries of the organization, Finland, the Netherlands, Belgium, Norway, and Switzerland are among the top ten countries, while Hungary, Portugal, Italy, Slovenia, Greece, Spain, the Czech Republic, Slovakia, and Turkey belong to lowest group, between 21st and 32nd. In 2015, OECD ranked 76 countries of the world by educational level. Asia came out the best, a result that surely contributes to explaining the unparalleled economic success of the region. Among the top ten, one still can find four northwestern countries. The Mediterranean and Central East European countries, including Italy, are mostly found between 26th and 37th. The Balkan countries together with Turkey occupy 40th to 44th, while some of them, such as Albania, Macedonia, and Greece, together with some Soviet successor states, rank between 50th and 65th.[24]

OECD studies for Italy and Greece add some depth to the portrait. The "Education at Glance" report of 2016 found that Italy's educational system is weak compared to the 35 OECD countries average: expenditure for education is 9 percent lower than the OECD average. Teachers' salaries have decreased by 7 percent in real terms between 2010 and 2014 and reach only somewhat more than three-quarters of the OECD average. Teaching is an overwhelmingly female profession and poorly regarded, unlike in Finland where teachers enjoy one of the highest reputations. The teachers' corps is also getting old and requires "rejuvenation." Only 37 percent of young Italians apply to universities, against the 59 percent OECD average. The employment rate for 25- to 34-year-olds with a university degree is only 62 percent, significantly lower than the 83 percent OECD average. In Italy, over one-third of the people aged 20 to 24 are neither working nor studying; their share increased by 10 percent between 2005 and 2015.[25] Another OECD report found that Greece lagged behind even that level. At the turn of the millennium, only 56 percent of the population between the ages of 24 and 64 had completed upper secondary school education and 13 percent, tertiary education. The state budget for education is only 3.5 percent of the GDP, instead of the OECD average of 5 percent, and expenditure per students stands at 71 percent of the European Union average.[26]

If the least-developed peripheries exhibit the worst educational systems, as all the facts above indicate, these peripheries also have populations and governments favoring antimodern, obsolete attitudes toward education. In Hungary, for example, the far-right authoritarian Horthy regime's injection of nationalist and religious education into the curriculum persists today. Thus, in the 2010s, when Hungarian students at international competitions regularly were failing tests and placing at low levels in the OECD analyses, Prime Minister Viktor Orbán stated that studying at high schools and universities as the main road to a life career is obsolete. One of his closest subordinates, head of the Prime Minister's Office, János Lázár added in December 2016:

> The most that education can give to a student is that it educate him to become a good Christian and as a Christian a good Hungarian. Everything beyond that is debatable and questionable and one cannot know whether it will be valid for centuries.[27]

Nationalist populism has deformed the attitude toward education and in this way reinforces the traditional nationalist mentality.

Weaknesses in entrepreneurship

In connection with these social-cultural and educational characteristics, including the anti-business mentality, an indigenous entrepreneurial class was barely present in these regions. Rigid social division blocked both downward and upward social mobility. The nobility, including its lower stratum, the already often landless gentry, did not move toward business but rather looked to careers in the army, state, and local bureaucracy. Peasants, including the richest among them, were excluded from the society, and it was almost impossible for them to elevate to higher social standing. Modern sectors of the economy, finance, trade, and manufacturing were disparaged by the noble elite and gentry middle class and virtually unattainable for peasants.

Consequently most of the early entrepreneurs belonged either to native-born ethnic and religious minorities who were largely considered alien to the dominant culture, or to groups who had recently arrived from abroad: "There were hardly any Poles among [the] industrialists, bankers or traders," and "educated Romanians have shown a tendency to avoid following a commercial career, leaving this field of activity to alien elements."[28] Foreign entrepreneurs, mostly from France and Britain, established the entire banking and mining industry in Spain, where "a society that was frozen in orthodoxy," to quote Gabriel Tortella again, "found itself three centuries later without a competitive and inventive entrepreneurial class."[29] Portugal, according to Jorge Miguel, lacked an exclusively industrial-entrepreneurial class; its merchants, industrialists and entrepreneurs preferred to engage in the lucrative colonial trade, tax farming and other monopolistic endeavors.[30] William Blackwell notes that "religious outcasts, such as the Old Believers and Jews, were among the earliest of industrial capitalists and bankers in the tsarist empire," and Dittmar Dahlmann has found that 40 percent of entrepreneurs in Moscow and 30 percent in Saint Petersburg were "German-speaking foreigners" in 1869–1870.[31] In Belarus at the end of the 19th century, 90 percent of merchants were Jewish, in Vilna 98 percent, and in Vitebsk 85 percent.[32] In Łódź, the "Polish Manchester," the most advanced textile center of the country, 67 percent of inhabitants were German, and another nearly 20 percent Jewish in 1864.[33] The majority of the Hungarian and Romanian business elite were also Germans and Jews who occupied, as Karl Marx opined, the "Lücken Positionen," or position gaps. The capital cities of these countries, in which the bulk of modern economic sectors were concentrated, were strongly Jewish. In fact, while Jews comprised just 5 percent of the total population of both countries, they made up one-quarter of Budapest's, and one-third of Bucharest's inhabitants and half of Romania's urban population in the early 20th century.[34]

Frozen in rigid autocratic traditionalism, an immobile and uneducated Russian society did not long for the rise of modern business and entrepreneurial attitudes and modernization. Religious fatalism, fear of innovation and resistance to monetized market relations were deeply embedded in Russia's peasant society. Aleksandr Nikolaevich Engelgardt's *Letters from the Country,* published in a journal in the 1870s and 1880s, illuminated these attitudes most authentically. In one of his letters he described an incident that happened at his inherited landed estate after he returned there from St. Petersburg. He wanted to repair a bridge and a road by hiring peasants to do it. It did not work. A local friend cleared up the mystery for him:

> Why do you have to hire them? Just call them to help you, everyone'll come out of respect for you, and they will repair both the road and the bridge. Of course, give them a glass of vodka. … As neighbors, we shouldn't take your money. … Hire for money means you don't want to live as a neighbor, it means you're going to do everything the German way, with money.

Indeed, Engelgardt acted as the friend suggested and it worked.[35]

Nineteenth-century political movements defended these social values and economic ways. For example, the Russian populist movement *Narodnaya Volya* (People's Will), which emerged in the 1870s, idealized "uncorrupted peasant virtue" and rejected industrialization because it destroys the natural egalitarian values of peasant life. The conservative and nationalist Slavophils celebrated the unspoiled Russian values of common ownership and "real and concrete equality." Nikolai Danilevski rejected the Western ("Germano-Roman") culture, the religious "anarchy of Protestantism" and the political "anarchy of democracy" and praised the superior traits of the Russian communal society and orderly tsarist autocracy.[36]

Autocratic political rule has accompanied Russian history for centuries, and it has left a strong and decisive imprint on the relations between the state and the economy. In communist times, the state owned and ran the economy directly, and the state still plays a quite central role in the Russian-type capitalism of the post-Soviet era. In 1991, when the Soviet Union collapsed, 91 percent of fixed assets were state-owned. The decade of transformation and extremely corrupt privatization, which followed the collapse, did not destroy the state role. In 2001, still 42 percent of fixed assets remained in the hand of the Russian state, and in 2008, the public sector produced 40 percent of the GDP. Renationalization increased the state sector. In the crucial oil industry its ownership share grew between 2005 and 2008 from 32 percent to 47 percent and, instead of 10 percent in the 1990s, in 2011 it controlled 52 percent of production.[37] President Vladimir Putin summed up this legacy as a leading ideological principle: "For us, the state, its institutions … have always played an exceptionally important role. … [It is] the initiator and main driving force of change."[38]

The dominant role of the state, although exceptional in Russia, was a quite widespread phenomenon in backward regions in Europe and strongly present in the earliest years of the 21st century in Central and Eastern Europe. The Viktor Orbán government in Hungary shared the idea of the special role of the state in the economy as an already tested, successful Asian characteristic and also renationalized certain sectors and companies. In Turkey, where bourgeoisie did not emerge during the 19th and first half of the 20th century, the autocratic Ottoman legacy is still present: "Turkish social and management culture is deeply rooted in its Ottoman heritage."[39] Thus the state and government still dominate business, and the society has been called a "network society," that is one "in which trust-based relations and longstanding connections are highly valued."[40] In the late 20th century just a few groups closely connected with governments controlled 80 percent of total industrial output. Alenka Kuhelj and Bojan Bugarič speak about the "state-catch" in Central and Eastern Europe: "The capture of the state by various political and informal groups has progressed to such a dramatic extent that it is undermining the independence and credibility of almost all rule-of-law institutions in the country."[41]

State dominance is partly the consequence of the weak entrepreneurial element and lack of business orientation in modernization in the peripheries, again with significant differences among the regions and countries. Lack of entrepreneurship has combined with the long tradition of illiterate peasant masses in Russia, the Balkans, Turkey, south Italy, and Spain to preserve preindustrial behavioral patterns. If their income was sufficient to meet their usual consumption needs, people opted to spend more time engaging in leisure rather than to work still harder to earn more in order to climb up on the social ladder.[42] Mass illiteracy, deep poverty, superstition and extremely traditional ways of thinking rendered the peripheral societies "uncreative"; that is, not oriented toward modern technics and not ready to apply modern methods. In other words, the level of human ability necessary to adopt the new technology was very high, indeed missing in these countries. The consequences of these phenomena went beyond blocking the transfer of technology or the spread of innovation, to also obstructing capitalist transformation, economic modernization and basic institution-building in the region.[43] This cultural burden was carried even in modern times and strongly influenced peoples' mind-set and behavior.

Another investment behavioral difference was discovered by a group of German economists, led by Armin Falk of Bonn University, after analyzing 76 countries and concluded that investment behavior is highly contingent on national culture. Their study compared two factors: *patience* and *risk taking*. Patience was defined as a willingness to wait a year or more for a higher return on their investments, as opposed to a desire for an immediate return. While a patient approach to investment requires sacrifices in the present, it most often results in much higher income later. The economists found that the most patient peoples are Swedes, Dutch, and North Americans, followed by Germans, Austrians, Finns, and British, who are willing to wait 0.5–1.0 year for a higher return on their investments. The least patient groups of people whose priorities are receiving immediate returns on their investment are the Latvians, Croats, Romanians, Portuguese, Greeks, and Hungarians. Beyond Europe, the least patient peoples are the Georgians, Rwandans, and Nicaraguans.

As for the second factor, Dutch, Croats, Swedes, and British people proved to be the most *risk-taking* groups in Europe, while the most *risk-averse* investors are Greeks, Spaniards, Romanians, Finns, Estonians, and, chief among these, Hungarians and Portuguese.

What factors contribute to such diverse investment attitudes? Certainly, the richness of one's country of origin plays a major role in shaping an approach to investment. In rich countries, people can much more easily afford to be patient and take greater risks. Moreover, we cannot deny the role of history: in countries where regimes change too often – such as in Hungary ten times in 150 years – and the future is rather unpredictable, people become impatient and much more averse to risk than in countries where stability ensures faith in the future. The variance of approaches to investment is also closely connected to education levels. Investment attitudes of people from better educated Western-northwest European countries are much better calculated and have a broader and more far-seeing characteristic than less educated investors from peripheral countries.[44]

Peripheral attitude toward the state and institutions

One important element of this attitude is the relation of citizens to the state. Suspicion about and fear from the state was natural in times when the state was in the hands of either foreign hostile occupants or oppressive and autocratic local elites that excluded, suppressed and robbed the majority of inhabitants.

The state thus was a traditional enemy of the people; in several countries, parts of the citizenry did not feel that the state was theirs. That was the case when the state was alien, as with the Ottoman state in the Balkans, the Habsburg state in Central Europe, the English state in Ireland, the Russian state in Poland and the Baltics, the Czech-dominated Czechoslovak state for the Slovaks and the Serb-dominated Yugoslav state for the Croats. The European Bank of Reconstruction and Development, for example, recognized that the "Ottoman rule, in particular, has had persistent negative effects on … social norms relating to trust in south-eastern Europe."[45]

The state was also considered to be an enemy if an extremely autocratic, oppressive and exclusive rule, serving a small, dominant elite, characterized it, as, for example, in the tsarist Russian state or the traditional Polish *szlachta* (nobility) state. The list is long and also contains the French and Austrian rules in Italy, military dictatorships in Turkey and Greece, Franco and Salazar's dictatorial rule on the Iberian Peninsula. People, and most of all the peasant majority, had their own institutions, the village community (*obshchina* or *mir* in Russia, *zadruga* on the Balkans) and the extended large family. The result was a real, visible community that created its own rules and provided mutual assistance for members. Village communities dissolved in most of the West in the late middle ages, and in the Habsburg Empire in the late 18th century, but they survived in Slavic lands until the early 20th century.

From the communal perspective of the village it was natural not to turn to the state and its institutions to arrange something, and a virtue to cheat and disobey state orders and rules. Anything that was ordered by the state was perceived as hurtful, alien, including useful neutral regulations such as traffic rules. Not to observe these rules became an instinctive behavioral practice. This was the situation most of the time in the peripheries in the past and preserved by many as feelings and attitudes in a rather different present. People do not identify with the state even long after liberation from foreign powers or from autocratic-dictatorial regimes. The state, in their mind, was not and still is not the guarantor of safety and freedom. The political elite is considered to be self-serving and politics to be a road to enrichment. The state and its representatives are hostile corrupt bureaucrats.

Thus for example, a Slovak antigovernment teenager in the 2010s could say, "In politics, there is no place for people who want to change things, only for those who want to steal."[46] Or an Italian novel *Suburra* (the name of a district of Rome) – and its film version, too – depicting the deformed, corrupt state and the connection of organized crime (mafia) to politics, could portray the political institutions of the country as rotten and self-serving.[47] Or Joseph LaPalombara could write, "When it comes to the systematic use of state power for the benefit of a handful of powerful families in the private sector, Italy looks more like a Third World country than a modern industrial democracy." It is quite evident that people follow an old path, as well-expressed in the Italian saying: "Fatta la legge, trovata l'inganno" (There is a loophole to be exploited in every law). A "good deal of the time, Italians are at war with the state …

this attitude has deep historical roots," in Italian experience with arbitrary and capricious governments. People interpret democracy to "include the right of the individual to ignore those laws s/he considers unjust. In the Italian context, the argument makes sense."[48]

This behavior is not, however, only an outcome of the preserved old mindset but also, often, of weaknesses affecting institutions copied from the West. In core countries, with centuries-long social-economic progress and strong, stable political structures, administrative and legal institutions became strong, stable and well-working too. That made the rule of law dominant in life. Institutions and the constitutional-legal system thus gained central importance, while stable, merit-based civil service systems guaranteed expertise and neutrality in operation.

In most cases the same institutions do not function well in peripheral environments. Modern institutions and legal systems grew over hundreds of years in northwestern Europe. When peripheral nations have copied the Western institutions, they have introduced them into social-political environments not yet ready to adopt and absorb their norms and values and modes of operation. A great many people have not adjusted to them. Instead, they have continued their old habits and remained loyal to informal "institutions" reliant on patron-client, family, and friend relations. In Italy, in earlier times, for example, peasants were:

> forever in search of political patrons who might provide protection and livelihood. But always with an opportunistic eye peeled for new changes in the political climate and the possible arrival of a stronger, more reliable patron. … Patrons and clients are still a prominent feature of the Italian political landscape. … Clientelism is an efficient and effective way through which the political allegiances, preferences, and demands of citizens are brought to weight on public policies. … The modern political party or interest group does not necessarily destroy or replace such relationship; instead, as is the case in Italy, it may incorporate them. … The Italian who wants real help in this Kafkaesque world will, more often than not, go to his "patron", that is, to a person, trade union, political party, or church group … that can bring real pressure to bear on the public officials … the approach is indirect.[49]

And in Slovenia, for another example, "East Central Europe's democratic consolidation is better viewed as having always been somewhat illusory. … Its liberal institutions have been merged with … ethnic nationalism and social conservativism." Alenka Kuhelj and Bojan Bugarič speak of a "shallow Europeanization of EU norms" and a "Potemkin harmonization" of EU rules. Only the executive, the political parties and Parliament are less respected than judiciary. "… The most politicized civil services are found in Slovakia and Poland, followed by Hungary, the Czech Republic and Slovenia." Independent media is absent.[50]

People in these countries – albeit to different degrees – did not and do not trust in law and institutions. They had and still have good reasons for their attitudes. In the case of Italy, "public servants are completely misnamed," LaPalombara has noted.

> They serve essentially their own interests and convenience. Their demeanor toward the public varies between annoyance and arrogance. … It crosses no one's mind to file a complaint about this kind of treatment; it would only make things worse. Franz Kafka would understand.[51]

Indeed, bureaucrats were not civil servants in a modern Western sense but arrogant self-serving employees, many times even thieves. They were often removed and replaced, over-politicized and corrupt. To arrange something outside was often easier and better in the old way. Governments came and went frequently, and they altered the workings of administration as well. In postwar Italy until the late 1980s, 45 governments followed one after the other, with an average lifetime of ten months. In some cases – Russia is an outstanding example – authoritarian governments have tried to establish an everlasting rule and to subordinate the administrative apparatus to their political interests. A *Quora* contributor compares the situation of the European South to the North and connects traditional cultural features and ineffective institutions to the alienation from the state:

> In a society in which corruption is prevalent you are a member of a clan first, and a citizen a distant second. Weak state, inefficient public institutions … and an unproductive bureaucracy breed corruption. For example if you know that the state is unable to make everyone pay their taxes fairly you will be tempted not to pay yours. But isn't the state weak because of corruption, i.e. isn't corruption the cause not the effect? No, because what we call "corruption" was just the normal way of doing things in pre-modern societies, when social relationships were largely tribal, familial and feudal and the state was just a distant, abstract entity that had little relevance in everyday life. Hence the prevalence of corruption is a sign of weak institutions and the prevalence of traditional/pre-modern social structures.[52]

The OECD 2013 Economic Survey on Italy, one of the most advanced countries among former peripheries, noted that policy implementation appears to be a weakness. Effective policy implementation needs effective public administration (ranging from prompt introduction of implementing regulations to effective enforcement of their specific provisions) and an efficient legal system to back up enforcement and prevent corruption. "An inefficient public administration can be a barrier to effective implementation of reforms," the report argues. "Weaknesses in the Italian public administration have included absenteeism, low skills, mismatch, lack of transparency and cronyism. Past reforms have tackled many of these areas [in Italy], though progress has been slow."[53] At a survey, Italians were asked whether they contacted with officials if they had some problem. This is a normal question in the United States or North Europe,

> but it may be completely off the mark in the kind of patron and client society, and system of "making contact" with public officials that prevails in Italy. ... When it comes to resistance against taxes, the evasion of other laws or regulations considered unacceptable, or the shunning of contact with public authorities. ... As a fundamental operational rule, they consider it highly preferable to keep encounters with officialdom to the barest possible minimum.[54]

The World Economic Forum's Global Competitiveness Report for 2010/2011 ranked Italy 43rd out of 139 countries in terms of competitiveness. The country's competitiveness is held back by its weak institutional environment. Regarding the working of its institutions, Italy ranked 92nd in the world, thus far away from the European standard. Institutional effectiveness is also connected with weaknesses in the labor market where Italy ranked 118th and weak public finances (ranked 131st on public indebtedness). Italy also dropped four spots in the World Bank's 2012 "Doing Business Report" to place 87th out of 183 countries. It fell ten places in the category of ease in "starting a business." In this respect, Italy is in 77th place.[55] None of these rankings reflect European qualities and efficiencies. Italy is not ranked among the 50 European countries.

Among other countries of the peripheries, Hungary declined from 33rd to 63rd in the 2015 Global Competitiveness Index. The low quality of institutions and business ethics are among the causes of the decline. Of the 140 countries ranked in this index on the quality of their institutions, Hungary came in at 97th, and on business ethics at 99th.[56] In Turkey government efficiency has ranked 59th among 121 countries of the world. On the index that reflects ease of starting a business, this country is 71st among 183 countries and in competitiveness its place is 59th among 133 countries. None of these indexes reflect purely European standards.[57]

People who are unable to realize their needs through efficient institutions and the rule of law look instead for solutions to personal connections, kinship, nepotism, and friendship. In more traditional societies, a kind of "tribal" connections or their remnants survived. To arrange something, one has to turn to patrons, friends, or relatives who can help you, to noninstitutionalized solutions in other words. Or, as it is said in various forms and languages: "Beside each (closed) big gate there is an (open) small gate or loophole" ("Minden nagy kapu mellett van egy kis kapu" in Hungarian.)

At this point, however, I have to call attention to the danger of contrasting the different regions. The act of comparing the peripheries with the northwest can create a distorted point of view, sometimes even seeming to be an idealization of the latter. But the human behaviors so evident in the peripheries, and the weaknesses, are present everywhere. All of the described peripheral social phenomena sporadically appear, disappear and reappear in advanced societies as well. There are relatively marginalized people, let us say, at the peripheries of advanced societies. Oppositions may emerge to express dissatisfactions with aspects of the status quo and social conflicts sometimes unite the populists, whether their political orientation is right or left. In the sections to follow in this chapter, I describe some of the most typical negative features that characterize peripheral social behavior, the relative significance of the black (or shadow) economy and of widespread corruption. These phenomena are not exclusively "peripheral" at all. They are also present in the most advanced societies. Nevertheless, while black market and corruption are peripheral in the northwestern core, they are the core characteristic in the Southern and Eastern peripheries. Since both phenomena are relatively measurable, we will see the major difference between their presence in the core countries and the peripheries.

The black (or shadow) economy

Lack of stable and well-working institutions, the weakness of the rule of law and, the derivative popular distrust in the state and its institutions together deform both market economies and the democratic political systems. If market rules and institutions are inefficient, then a virulent black economy shadows the official system.[58] The form of economy contributes to the national product but is neither registered nor taxed, since the associated trade of goods, currencies and services takes place outside government-sanctioned channels. Black markets exist everywhere in the world in economically difficult situations – war, severe shortages, excessive state regulation – that impinge on daily life. In the financial context, black markets flourish when strict currency controls exist. In troubled situations there is no other choice but to turn to black markets to be able to buy otherwise unavailable goods. That was the situation in post–World War I Germany or in post–World War II Hungary, where the inflation rate at the peak was 12 percent per hour and no one accepted official currency.

In developed countries with well-functioning institutions black markets are an exception and play an unimportant role. Their average contribution to GDP in the 35 most advanced OECD countries was 17 percent around the turn of the millennium. In Europe's Nordic countries, the black economy represented 9–15 percent of GDP in the 2010s. In Austria the share of "illicit work" in car repairs and renovating jobs was 19 percent and 23 percent, respectively, of the total GDP, followed by beautician and hairdresser work (14 percent) and electronic appliance repair (13 percent). In Germany, nearly half of illicit work in that decade occurred in the building, renovating, and repairing trades.[59]

In low- and medium-income countries with weak institutions and uncertain rule of law, black economies are a permanent but illegal institution. This sector is perversely large in Third World countries. At the turn of the century, Gambia ranked at the top in this respect with 80 percent of the domestic labor force working outside the official economy. In Africa, Thailand, and the

Philippines in the early 21st century 68–76 percent of market transactions and services took place in the shadow economy. In Latin America, the share ranges from 25 percent to 60 percent. Black economy as an institution is also prevalent in the European peripheries and even in former peripheries such as the more advanced Mediterranean region where its share is still 24–26 percent. In Central Europe and the Baltic area, the contribution is 20–27 percent, in Turkey more than 29 percent, and in Bulgaria and Romania 33 percent and 30 percent, respectively.[60]

In Europe,

> the biggest shadow economies belong to some of the transition countries of the former Soviet Union. About a decade after the collapse of the Soviet Union, Armenia had the largest illicit labor force, equal with 76 percent of the official labor force. In the early 21st century market transactions in the shadow economy represent between 28 percent and 43 percent of GDP in Georgia, Ukraine and Belarus.[61]

In Ukraine the blackmarket share of GDP of 30 percent in 2007 jumped to 50 percent by 2015.[62]

In these cases, causes are less connected with shortage than with tax evasion. Shopkeepers and service providers ask clients whether they want a receipt or not. Without receipt, the good or service may be somewhat cheaper since the buyer does not pay the tax and provider also do not pay taxes after the income.

> In principle, if the car-repair shop asks: "Do you require an invoice?" more than half of the people asked would not expect one and would thus save at least the value added tax. More than half would at least think about hiring an illicit worker to renovate their house. However, in the "well-behaved" group [of the rich northwest countries], less than 16 percent would demand illicit work.[63]

As calculations show, just under two-thirds of work in the shadow economy is done by males and a little more than a third by females. Surprisingly enough, the share attributable to the unemployed is not significant (only 6 percent), while pensioners perform one-fifth of the work.[64]

Labor market and work ethic weaknesses

Another major market weakness, the percentage of working-age people actually working, characterizes the labor market in the peripheries. The European Union aims at achieving a 75 percent participation among people aged 20–64, by 2020. The reality, three years before that deadline, suggests the goals will not be met, especially in the peripheries. In the northwest, in several countries the participation is about 70 percent. The participating ratio in Moldova is 40 percent, in Croatia, Greece, Turkey, Romania, and Bulgaria, 51–53 percent.[65]

Participation in the work force in peripheral countries is sometimes 20–25 percent lower than in advanced countries.

One of the main reasons for these low percentages, other than the fact that many people work in the black economies and are not registered as workers at all, is the low rate of participation by women and the elderly. In the EU-28 in the 2010s, female participation in the labor force was 55 percent, in contrast to 73 percent among males. The overall figure is determined in large part by the situation in peripheral countries. The lowest rates of female participation are found in the peripheries. In Slovakia, Croatia and Greece, among women and the older generations (people 55–64) labor participation is below 30 percent. In Turkey it also is extremely low, only 27 percent of the labor force.

It pays to note that in the core countries part-time employment is institutionalized for women with children or other family responsibilities. In Germany and Austria, 40 percent of women work on a part-time base. In several peripheral countries, the possibility of working part-time is limited, and the institutions that would support it do not exist. In Bulgaria, Slovakia, Croatia, and the Czech Republic, part-time employment among females in less than 5 percent of the total; less than 10 percent in Hungary, in all three Baltic countries, and in Romania, Slovakia, Greece, and Portugal.[66]

In peripheral countries, the traditional social role assigned to women, particularly the strong belief that women's place is at home in the household, joins with institutional weaknesses as a main cause. Other factors, such as unequal wages for men and women, and the workplace sexual harassment by male bosses and co-workers that goes unpunished, contribute to keeping women out of the labor market. So does the responsibility for caring for children or older family members at home. Unlike in the West, less than a quarter of children up to three years old are using childcare facilities. The OECD average is one-third. About 8 percent of women withdraw from the labor market for family care reasons.[67]

An OECD report on Italy presents a telling example. Although participation in the labor market significantly increased in Italy during the crisis years of the 2010s, it nevertheless lags far behind the advanced countries: the participation of 55- to 64-year-olds, between 2008 and 2013, rose from 46 percent to 57 percent but still remains below the rate in the northwest. Moreover, the female labor force participation rate is among the lowest in the OECD: 54 percent against the OECD average of nearly 63 percent in 2013.[68]

The question of the work ethic in these countries is also controversial. In the rich and mostly Protestant northwest where hard work traditionally has produced benefits for families, work that makes people really independent and that causes the feeling of self-fulfillment, has a high value in itself. That was certainly behind the work ethic that has been associated with the emergence of Protestantism. Following Max Weber's pioneering idea, Brigitte Berger has concluded that Protestant ethic and a rising new economy "required and emphasized hard work, frugality, individual accountability … [and] rationally balancing defendable risk [taking] against mere adventurism." Prosperity in this life was interpreted by Calvinism as a sign of salvation. Protestantism changed the work ethic and caused a

> shift in the attitude toward work … transformed [work] from a technic of survival and crude profit-making into a tool for "salvation". … In this shift, individuals became dislodged from their embeddedness in family and kinship and received a new autonomy. While the activity of work was "sacralized," it [later] became secularized and eventually developed into an end in itself.[69]

In the peripheries work did not have a value in itself. In those countries, free labor has not existed for as long as in the West; it emerged sometime after the middle to late 19th century when serfdom was at last abolished. People's relation to work is different than in countries with a most fortunate and successful past. In these societies the painful tradition of working for others without the beneficial outcome of work survived the past for decades and even centuries and work traditionally was considered to be a burden. Bad payment, low wages, and incomes contributed to lack of interest in work in a relatively large part of the population. Already in the 19th century, Western travelers in Spain, the Balkans, or Hungary were often shocked by what they saw as the "laziness" in those countries. (They also recognized and spoke about extremely low levels of education and widespread illiteracy.) Path-dependence led to survive major elements of the past including different relations to work.

Epidemic corruption and tax evasion

One of the most devastating social, market and political deformations, however, is caused by an epidemic corruption that penetrates every sphere of life. Among the ten least corrupt countries of the world, as the Corruption Perceptions Index reflects, seven are European, all from northwest Europe: Denmark, Luxembourg, the Netherlands, Sweden, Norway, Switzerland, and Finland, followed by Britain.[70] Corruption in Denmark, Finland, and Sweden registered in 2015 at the 89–91 mark on a scale in which 100 means no corruption at all. The EU average the same year was 66. An investigation revealed that "in terms of law enforcement, political stability, government effectiveness, rule of law, control of corruption as well as … accountability," the Scandinavian countries rank at the top. "We find," the researchers said, "that all three Scandinavian countries can be characterized as 'small worlds' in which trust, information diffusion and reputation mechanisms are active governance mechanisms."[71]

In contrast several of the European peripheral countries – in Central Europe, the Balkans, Turkey, Russia, Ukraine, and other backward, now independent, former Soviet republics – have a non-European level of corruption substituting for good institutions and the rule of law. To arrange something, to get the required permission from state office, to get good health service or a job, to find an important product not freely available, to ensure a fair decision in a court or acceptance by a university or just a university diploma without studying, or to avoid some punishment for violation rules, people have to bribe and corrupt public officials, tax collectors, medical doctors, judges, shop clerks, university officers, and even inspectors of parking meters. Corruption penetrates everyday life, becomes a routine habit, a form of "help" aimed at keeping the administrative machine working, but it also eliminates fairness, justice and equality. And it fuels the black market. There is "a statistically significant relationship between the various measures of bribery or corruption and the shadow economy: *ceteris paribus*, a one-point improvement in the corruption index leads to an eight to eleven percentage point decline in the shadow economy."[72]

Corruption somewhat paralyzes normal life in Central Europe, but is absolutely devastating in the Balkans, Turkey, Russia, Ukraine, and other backward, now independent, former Soviet republics. Turkey belongs among the worst in this respect. In 2015, in Transparency International's rankings of 177 countries, Turkey had slid downward since 2005 by 21 levels, to 122nd place. The episodes behind this slide cast bright light on the unprecedentedly deep penetration of corruption into everyday Turkish life. In connection with ongoing bank privatization (in the case of the Türk Ticaret Bankasi), it was discovered that Prime Minister Mesut Yilmaz and the minister responsible for economic affairs were personally involved in a huge corruption scheme. That scandal led to the resignation of the entire government in early 1999.

When the new Erdoğan government took over in 2002, it announced, as a centerpiece of its program, the fight against corruption. A book by Turkish author Digdem Soyaltin provides detailed information. It discusses the series of legal and institutional measures introduced between 1999 and 2017. At the beginning of those years, the fight against corruption was a major governmental program. Erdoğan stated: "When we came into power … there were corruption, there was poverty and there were restrictions. We promised to fight against these three" (the so-called fight against the 3Y – Yolsuzluk, Yoksulluk, Yasaklar). "Yet," Soyaltin noted, "a decisive anti-corruption policy was formulated only after the 2001 financial crisis … the worst economic recession in the history of the Republic." The change was closely connected with the IMF requirements for international financial assistance. The effective forces behind the anticorruption campaign were outside forces: the IMF and also the European Union. The EU decision at the Helsinki Summit in 1999, which officially accepted Turkey as a candidate country, required "Europeanization" including, "a massive amount of reforms to fight against corruption." This effort met with strong popular support as well. "Between 2002 and 2005, the AKP government introduced a rather impressive amount of legal and institutional changes." Soltayin's book convincingly proves that those laws were "neither explicitly codified nor externally enforced … [and] remained largely ineffective." As a public officer underscored in 2004, "we turned into a country where no civil servant would do anything without a bribe." In 2006, a new anticorruption program "was put on the shelf." Less than a decade later, it had virtually disappeared.[73]

The fact of its disappearance became evident after the exposure in December 2013 of a massive new public corruption scandal. The appeal of EU membership, with its requirements for internal reform, had soured, and the government had turned toward more autocratic rule. This new scandal deeply compromised several members of the government, including the inner circle of Erdoğan. High-level state bureaucrats were involved in connection with public tenders, contracts for land development and money laundering from Iran. The Istanbul and Ankara police detained dozens of people, and the subsequent investigations opened up one of the most serious corruption cases in its modern history. Cengiz Aktar of the Istanbul Policy Group stated that this investigation is "revolutionary; nothing of the kind happened in this country before. Of course, corruptions always existed ... but the scale and the persons involved, indicted – it's unique."[74]

Nevertheless, Prime Minister Recep Tayyip Erdoğan, earlier the crusader against corruption, stopped the investigation stating that "there is a very dirty operation here. Some circles inside and outside of Turkey are seeking to hinder Turkey from its rapid growth." He accused an influential émigré, the opposition cleric Fethullah Gulen, of being behind the conspiracy against the government. Istanbul's police chief and several others (judges and prosecutors who took part in the corruption investigation) were dismissed, and the Turkish parliament in early January 2015 vetoed sending four former cabinet ministers to trial.[75] In effect, Turkey, together with most of the countries of the neighboring region (Russia, Ukraine, Moldova and the Balkans), has legitimized corruption and the backward economic environment that is its hotbed.

Such corruption, however, is not directly connected to backward economic situations. It is also flourishing today in those former peripheral countries – Italy and Spain – that before the 2008 recession had joined the ranks of the more advanced European nations. In the 1980s, Italian Prime Minister Bettino Craxi declared "that as much as one-fourth of Italy's real gross national product might be in the 'hidden' ... non reported economy"; that translated in 1987 into tax evasion amounting to $60 billion.[76] As if in a grotesque historical farce, former Prime Minister Craxi himself was later indicted by corruption and tax evasion, then escaped from Italy and lived in exile until his death. His friend Silvio Berlusconi, elected three times as prime minister, a few years later also ended his political career after being indicted on corruption charges.

Tax evasion in Greece is extreme and costs the country about $20 billion per year. About one-third of the value added tax (VAT) owed, roughly 7–8 percent of the country's GDP, is never paid. In 2012, the government published a long list of leading tax evaders. Two financiers alone had stolen $19 billion from the state. In Italy 22 percent of the annual VAT goes unpaid, and only 76,000 persons declare annual income over €200,000 in a country where every year 210,000 luxury cars are sold.[77]

Tax evasion and the practice of bribing corrupt officials work together. Joseph LaPalombara has reported that in Italy, "where the value-added tax is concerned, both sellers and buyers enter into unspoken agreement to evade it." In 1984, it was estimated that 45 percent of value added tax was evaded, an amount equal to one-fourth of the government's deficit. The Ministry of Finance released a list of prominent Italians who regularly report only fractions of their income: movie stars "who claim to make less than your postal carrier, or industrial magnates who report little more than is now paid school administrators." LaPalombara also found that medical doctors, dentists and lawyers often report, "on average, less income than is paid to skilled industrial workers. The owners of leading restaurants and bars … regularly report less income than they pay to the chefs, waiters, and dishwashers in their employ." A similar pattern held for pharmacists, car rental and travel agency owners, jewelers, butchers, bakers, and so on. The real problem, however, is not that this tax evasion exists: "It is rather, that like the rampant violation of traffic laws or building codes and zoning ordinances, the situation is tolerated and, indeed, accepted as quite normal."[78]

Victor Lapuente Giné, a Spanish political scientist, published an article in the popular Spanish newspaper, *El País*, in March 2009 with the title "Why is Spain so corrupt?" The World Economic Forum, in its report for 2013–2014, placed Portugal at 51st place on its Global Competitiveness Index. This ranking is partly connected with the level of corruption. According to the 2012 Corruption Perceptions Index, the country belongs to the bottom group of European countries. Some cases are well known and were widely reported in the media, such as the affairs in several municipalities involving local town hall officials and businesspersons, as well as a number of politicians with wider responsibilities and power.[79]

History matters, corruption is a pervasive disease on the peripheries, fed by the centuries of practice. In the Balkans, the new ruling elites in countries liberated late in the 19th century inherited the Ottoman culture of corruption that had oiled the rusty machine of the central and local bureaucracies. Old Ottoman habits lived on as natural, everyday phenomenon in the independent Balkans. Two British travelers in the 1860s reported:

> In former days … the Christians had only to bribe [the Ottoman governor] in order to secure [a] certain amount of protection. Now-a-days, the governor must still be bribed, but … all the *medjilis* [local town councils] must be bribed too.[80]

In Transparency International's annual surveys, Italy consistently ranks as the most corrupt country in the euro-zone. Corruption costs the country a reported €60 billion a year, 4 percent of its GDP. On the 2016 Corruption Perceptions Index, Italy stood at 61st place among the world's 174 reported countries, equal with Senegal, Montenegro, and South Africa. Political corruption remains a major problem particularly in the South, in Calabria, Campania, and Sicily. Political parties are ranked as the most corrupt institution in Italy, closely followed by public officials and parliament.

In its handling of corruption cases, Italy also stands out. For example, Gianstefano Frigerio, a Christian Democrat parliamentarian, faced four trials between 1992 and 1994, and in three cases he was found guilty. His six-year prison sentence, however, was reduced to community service and his public service in the parliament was accepted as community service. He was reelected to parliament in 2001 and arrested again in 2014 for participation in the massive corruption scheme surrounding the Expo in Milan. In connection with this case, seven officials were arrested as of April 2015. The mayor of Venice and over 30 other public officials also were arrested in 2015 for accepting bribes in exchange for building contracts. In the same year, several businessmen were taken into custody on charges of belonging to "a gang involved in kickbacks and dodgy contracts" for high-speed rail lines, Expo 2015, a flood barrier in Venice, and other large-scale projects. Among those who had received kickbacks was Infrastructure and Transport Minister Maurizio Lupi, who was forced to resign.[81]

Greece is especially penetrated by corruption. Because the state bureaucracy is highly inefficient and deliberately slow, the implementation of a commercial contract or the administrative arrangement to establish a new company takes four years because several ministries have to give permissions. To get permissions state officials are regularly bribed. The World Bank's Ease of Doing Business Index ranked Greece 61st in the world, behind Rwanda. Bribing is so naturally a part of life in Greece that its price is virtually fixed and stable for various state services, ranging from tax auditing to getting a driver's license. It is common knowledge that a driver's license, for example, requires a bribe of €1,400. Corruption and cronyism penetrate the highest echelon of state administration. The International Corruption Perceptions Index ranked Greece eightieth among 185 countries. Papandreou, formerly prime minister, stated: "Greece was riddled with corruption [that] was the main reason for its economic woes." His minister of finance added: "tax collection … collapsed almost entirely" because of corruption. Direct and indirect taxes should on average contribute €50 billion a year to the state coffer, but between €10 to 20 billion of that amount is regularly lost. The deputy chief of the tax collection office declared, if tax collection worked "there would be no debt problem."[82]

Other Balkan countries and the Central European region resemble Greece in being very corrupt. Power, almost as a rule, is misused, and even at the highest levels of government. Adrian Nastase and Ivo Sanader, former prime ministers of Romania and Croatia, respectively, were arrested for corruption in 2012. Between 2006 and 2012 alone, no fewer than 4,700 people were tried in Romania on corruption charges, including 15 ministers and secretaries of state, 23 members of parliament, and more than 500 police officers. The British *Independent* has reported that Romania, Bulgaria and Croatia are the most corrupt countries in the EU. A recent European parliament study reveals that corruption throughout Europe is costing almost £800 billion a year.[83] This new estimate of the total annual loss exceeds previous calculations by more than eight times, largely because it measures the full cost of the problem, ranging from indirect effects such as companies postponing investing, to direct impacts including money lost from tax revenues.

As all of these examples reveal, the culture of corruption produces a wide range of behaviors and involves officials at all levels of government, and the cost to a country is not just financial. There are also significant social and political costs, such as greater inequality, higher levels of organized crime, and a weaker rule of law.[84] The staggering sum for EU losses, quoted earlier, which equates to 6.3 per cent of overall EU-28 GDP, has prompted calls for the creation of a European Public Prosecutors' Office as part of a crackdown on corrupt practices.

In the article "How Corruption Is Driving Eastern Europe's Brain Drain," based on several interviews and an IMF analysis, the *Washington Post* called attention to the connection between corruption and emigration from the region. Since the Berlin Wall was torn down in November 1989, nearly 20 million people, 5.5 percent of the population, have left Central, Eastern, and Southeastern Europe because of the lack of opportunities and high corruption. An analysis from the IMF, asserts that together with the poor situation and lack of opportunities, "the pervasive corruption perpetuated by the political elites and the local oligarchs, especially in the Western Balkan and South Eastern countries" belongs to the push effect for young people to escape. It argues that the weaker the institutions in their home countries, the more likely the young and educated are motivated to seek better opportunities abroad. "This brain drain has a debilitating effect on the economy. It is the best and brightest who often bolt, leaving behind an unskilled and an ageing population."[85] The same is true in Slovakia where two teenagers organized an anticorruption movement and "want to take their country back." As they see it, they have to decide to stay or go abroad "where we have a good life without so much corruption." The problem with staying is that in politics there is room only for those who want to steal.[86]

In 2016, Romania registered on Transparency International's Corruption Perceptions Index as the fifth most corrupt country in the European Union, after Bulgaria, Greece, and Italy, and at the same level with Hungary. In response to European Union requirements, Romanian laws and regulations sought to prevent corruption, but enforcement was weak. In 2012, 2015, and 2017, major demonstrations and social unrest signaled the population's reaction to the almost unbearable level of corruption. In 2014, the ambitious head of the National Anticorruption Directorate (the Romanian acronym is DNA) investigated and prosecuted 1,138 leading public figures, including top politicians, businessmen, judges and prosecutors. This activity, however, soon slowed down and 80 percent of indicted persons received only suspended sentences. Nevertheless, in 2015, the DNA indicted an additional 1,250 individuals, including Prime Minister Victor Ponta, five ministers, and 21 parliamentarians. Despite the fact that the prime minister resigned after his indictment, other indicted ministers remained in office, and so did parliamentarians, even those with final convictions for corruption.[87] Moreover, the new Social Democratic government of Sorin

Grindeanu issued a new emergency ordinance decriminalizing certain cases of corruption if the amount does not surpass 200,000 lei ($47,600). This "emergency ordinance" generated a quasi-revolt with several hundreds of thousands of people flooding the streets of all of the cities of the country for days, even after the government withdrew the ordinance. *The New York Times* interviewed several demonstrators. One of the respondents, Christina Iftode, 62 years old, stated: "I've paid a lot of money – the equivalent of 5,000 euros – in the hospital from the doorman to nurses, assistants, residents, doctors and for medicine for my husband. … Generally you have to give to get anything done." Monica Vlad, a 43-year-old university professor at Sibiu stated: "My colleagues took huge amounts of money from selling graduation papers and grades."[88] With these protests, corruption levels that had caused the Ponta government to resign finally came to the fore in political debate.[89]

The situation is rather similar in neighboring Bulgaria and Hungary. In Bulgaria, a new report has found that around 158,000 corrupt transactions are carried out each month. The research, by the Center for the Study for Democracy, a Sofia-based think tank, found that the number of people participating in corruption is now the highest in 15 years, and that it has increased despite significant pressure from Brussels to accelerate the fight against it. "The very high levels of corruption involvement of the Bulgarian population make criminal law enforcement initiatives ineffective and inadequate," the report said. Bulgaria's struggle with corruption is judged inefficient because of chronic political instability and the country's weak economy and high rate of poverty.[90]

Hungary's public procurement system suffers from endemic corruption and therefore poses high risks for foreign investors. Two-thirds to three-quarters of public tenders are believed to involve corrupt transactions. The government has channeled significant public funds to people with close ties to the ruling political elite. More than half of companies expect to give "gifts" to procurement officials to secure government contracts. Local-level public procurement is particularly corrupt because of the lack of transparency and the strong informal relations linking local businesses with political actors. More than a third of business respondents believe that corruption has prevented their company from winning a public tender in Hungary. Corruption within the sector may add 20–25 percent to the costs of government procurement. The Public Procurement Act allows procedures to be initiated without holding open public tender if the project does not exceed US$647,000. The law leaves a large opening for corruption because government officers have broken down large projects into smaller units in order to avoid holding a public tender.[91]

To consolidate his power, *Der Spiegel* reports, Prime Minister Viktor Orbán is creating a corrupt oligarchy in Hungary, and he is letting his family and friends in on the lucrative action.[92] Felcsút, Orbán's small home-township, offers an outstanding example. A childhood schoolmate and friend, Lörinc Mészáros, became the mayor of the township and soon also became the richest men in Hungary. Only six years earlier, he barely had been making a living as a heating contractor. When Orbán became prime minister Mészáros's company was flooded by various kinds of contracts. It received the contract to build a soccer stadium in Felcsút – the people of the country regard it as symbolic – with 3,800 seats in the township of 1,812 inhabitants. Today the company runs a hotel chain and owns holdings in various companies. Mészáros openly admits that, he owes this tremendous business success to Viktor Orbán, rather than to God. Most importantly, *Der Spiegel* concludes, Orbán surrounds himself with oligarchs who are not only enriching themselves, but also reinforcing his own power. It is a declared goal of his Fidesz party to form a "domestic entrepreneurial class." Orbán decides who gets rich in Hungary, and who does not.

The government's promotional policies benefit Orbán's family, including his son-in-law, István Tiborcz. After studying law, Tiborcz founded a small electronics company. Since his father-in-law became prime minister in 2010, things have been looking up. In 2014 and 2015, the company was awarded contracts for about 65 million euros to produce LED streetlights for cities and towns throughout the country, run by Fidesz mayors. Because the projects also received EU funding, the European anti-fraud office (OLAF) launched an investigation. In 2015, the Hungarian *Forbes Magazine* estimated the assets of the Orbán clan at about more than €22 million.[93] The family has little to fear, control bodies, such as the audit office and most courts, are already filled by Orbán's clients.[94]

The Economist's article "From Bolshevism to backhanders, corruption has replaced communism as the scourge of eastern Europe" focused on aspects of the failure of anticorruption fights. Firms not willing to pay bribes lose out to those competitors that are. Businesses fear that taking a stand will bring retribution: bureaucratic harassment, arbitrary tax demands or missing out on public contracts. Companies, politicians and officials collude to rig tenders, usually with impunity. Legal scrutiny is weak, and voters seem apathetic and cynical. Even starry-eyed outsiders who win elections on anticorruption tickets seem to be captured by the system within months. Anticorruption efforts have failed to engage the wider public, so activists quickly become dispirited. Mentioning the case of Juta Strike, Latvia's best-known anticorruption official, who had to leave the country for her own safety, *The Economist* analysis emphasized the troubles, even dangers, facing those who try to tackle the problem. Leverage from the European Union loses its force once countries have joined.[95]

Corruption is devastating in various peripheral countries, but nowhere more than in Russia, Ukraine, Moldova, and other former Soviet republics that became independent states after 1991. Countries covered by the anticorruption clauses of the Eastern Partnership agreement with the European Union, such as Moldova and Ukraine, deserve case studies of the cancerous spread of corruption and the faked "fight" against it. Moldova, a small place that had never been an independent country before 1991, is ruled by two oligarchs. One of them, former Prime Minister Pavel Filip, "hasn't just control [of] the country, he owns it."[96] The other, Vadim Filat, was in jail. In one year, three governments failed. A third oligarch, Vlad Plahotniuk, organized a unique action and with vast corruption, including bribes to banks, the government, prosecutors and judges, stole $1 billion, 12 percent of the country's GDP, from three major commercial banks. The IMF discovered that the operation had been nearly effortless: oligarchs bought majority control stakes in those banks, arranged loans for faked companies and the money disappeared offshore. On the 2015 corruption scale, Moldova stands at 103rd place among 168 countries.[97]

The *Guardian*, in 2015, published an article "Welcome to Ukraine, the most corrupt nation in Europe." Indeed, between 2007 and 2015, Transparency International's Corruption Perceptions Index rated Ukraine among the worst: sometimes 142nd in the world, alongside Uganda, and even behind Nigeria.[98] On other occasions Ukraine ranked 130th of the 167 countries investigated, tied with Paraguay and the Comoros. In 2012, Ukraine was ranked among the three most corrupted nations of the world together with Colombia and Brazil.

Officials from the general prosecutor's office of Ukraine who were interviewed by Reuters claimed that between 2010 and 2014, government officers stole a fifth of the country's national output every year. The theft has crippled the country. The country's economy was as large as Poland's at independence; now it is a third of the size. In 2009, a report exposed how businessmen use offshore shell companies to conspire with corrupt officials, rig state tenders and jack up prices. Within weeks of the Reuters report being completed, an assailant threw a grenade at the operative who had written it, as he got out of his car on Tatarska Street in central Kiev.

Ukraine often is called a kleptocracy. Bribes to secure public services belong to life and their amounts have reached as high as $1 million. According to a 2008 Management Systems International (MSI) survey, the highest corruption levels (between 44 percent and 58 percent) were to be found in vehicle inspection, police, health care, the courts and higher education.[99] President Yanukovich estimated that 10–15 percent of the state budget, thus $7 billion in revenues annually, was being siphoned off into the pockets of officials. In the late 2000s and early 2010s, around two-thirds of Ukrainians who had dealt with government said that they had been directly involved in corrupt transactions. Prior to 2010 there was a "gentleman's agreement" in Ukrainian politics not to accuse members of the outgoing government, but in that year and the next, "criminal charges were brought against 78 members of the former government; and more than 500 criminal cases have been opened against sitting officials." About 400 politicians have faced criminal charges in connection with corruption since 2010, and judges have been arrested while taking bribes.[100] Their number includes the highest state officials, the president, speaker of the parliament, prime minister, prosecutor general, several cabinet ministers and other top civil servants. In 2015, *The Economist* used the strongest language to describe the situation: "The Ukrainian state … still resemble a giant mafia … Oligarchs and their political cronies still dominate Ukrainian life. Should the government do too much to fight corruption the oligarchs may use their private armies to stage a coup."[101]

Russia, although much more centrally organized than chaotic Ukraine, exhibits basic similarities. Transparency International ranked Russia 133rd out of 176 countries on its Corruption Perceptions Index in 2012 (in joint position with Kazakhstan). The World Bank's Ease of Doing Business Index also ranked the country 112th out of 185. The reason for that place was the persistent abuse of foreign companies by local authorities who demanded bribes in return for undisturbed work possibilities.[102]

The report of the Transparency International Secretariat of July 2, 2015, "The State of Corruption: Armenia, Azerbaijan, Georgia, Moldova and Ukraine," concluded that corruption remained endemic in these nations. Although more than 60 institutions are responsible for preventing and fighting corruption, all of them are extremely weak due to political interference and a lack of independent oversight. All five countries have adopted anticorruption laws, but political and business elites still exert influence over important watchdog institutions, such as the judiciary and legislature, allowing their power to go unchecked and limiting the effectiveness of law enforcement. In some of these countries several judges have been convicted for receiving bribes. In sum, as the head of the Department of Transparency International has said: "Corrupt individuals – be they politicians or businesspersons – are often able to get away without worry of prosecution."[103]

Peripheral social-cultural characteristics, partly inherited from the long troubled past and in various forms are still present, and they heavily burden economic and social life in these regions. These features still are slowing down better integration into Europe.

Tendencies toward authoritarian-dictatorial power

Lower income level, as discussed in the Introduction to this book, influences political structures as well as other spheres of life. Higher income level with its social and educational connections creates the conditions for democratic power; in contrast, low income level, with all of its social-educational consequences, may be the hotbed of authoritarian and dictatorial rule. Again, this is by far not an automatic connection, but rather is influenced by several domestic and international factors. However, as also noted in the Introduction, at the turn of the millennium, most of the countries with $10,000 and higher per capita income level at least have democratic institutions and competitive elections while most of the very low-income countries of $2,000 per head, do not.

It is a well-known historical fact that before the 19th century democratic political structures virtually did not exist in Europe. The majority of people in these societies – women and the uneducated and low-income groups of the society – did not have voting rights. State and local institutions used different practices with different strata of the society. During the times of triumphant industrialization and urbanization, as societies transformed and the bourgeoisie became strong and dominant, pluralistic parliamentary systems and democracy gradually emerged as the dominant political power structure.

In countries of peripheral backwardness, where industrialization did not occur and the bourgeoisie remained a marginal social layer without political power, countries, in other words, where the obsolete nobility or bureaucratic military elite remained dominant, political democracy could not emerge. If basic democratic institutions such as the parliamentary system and pluralistic elections were introduced in the 20th century, they nevertheless remained formalities without essential democratic content.

This legacy hounded peripheral Europe even when specific countries became industrialized during the second half of the 20th century. Central Europe, the Baltic countries, the Balkans, Russia, and Turkey, thus most of the peripheries, remained under authoritarian rulers until the end of the century. Mediterranean countries such as Greece, Spain, and Portugal faced a similar situation until the last third of the century. In other words, democratization in all these countries started only around the turn of the millennium.

In several peripheral countries this process has been troubled. At the beginning of the post-communist transformation some of them, Slovakia and Croatia for example, were ruled by nationalist authoritarian governments. In others, such as Albania, Bulgaria, and Romania, communist remained in power for a while, and in still others, such as Poland and Hungary, authoritarian tendencies actually began to return early in the 21st century.

Some peripheral countries today openly reject liberal democracy. Vladimir Putin of Russia has announced that Russia will not be a "second edition" of the United States or Britain "where liberal values have deep historical roots." In Russia, "the state and its institutions ... have always played an exceptionally important role" and market economy and democracy have to adjust to "Russian realities."[104] This reality is an increasingly autocratic rule. In Hungary Prime Minister Viktor Orbán also rejects Western democracy and openly states his preference for "illiberal democracy":

> the current thinking is to glean systems that are not Western, nor liberal, nor liberal democracies, and perhaps not even democracies at all, but that are nonetheless enabling nations to succeed. Today, the stars of analysts around the world are Singapore, China, India, Turkey, Russia. ... [W]e are searching for, and we are doing our best to find, a way to part with West European dogmas, to free ourselves from them.[105]

Orbán is using the classical metaphor of the ship of state, observing that Hungary is sailing under Western flag when the "Eastern Wind" dominates the world.

In several less developed countries real pluralistic parliamentary systems with stable rule of law and strict divisions separating the executive, legislative and judiciary branches of government have not been and still are not the rule of the game. Authoritarian tendencies, degradation of democratic institutions, centralized, state-controlled media, the dominance of the executive branch of government, subordination of the courts to the executive branch essentially have remained in place or have returned from time to time to destroy or endanger essential democracy.

All in all, even in the early 21st century, relative backwardness in the Central European region, in the Balkans and especially in Turkey and Russia, has remained connected with authoritarian political tendencies. The pluralistic democracy of the northwest is fragile in Central Europe and may endanger further development. The peripheral areas, as their entire modern history proves, are strongly dependent on capital and technology imports. The lack of the rule of law and stable democratic institutions creates an uncertain economic environment for foreign investors. Nationalist authoritarian state interventionism, renationalization of companies or rules discriminating against foreign corporations often slow down or cause the withdrawal of foreign investments. Moreover, domestic political uncertainties sometimes even cause capital flight, the escape of significant amounts of money, potential domestic investments, into bank accounts abroad. Several examples of these phenomena have been seen in Russia or Turkey (see Chapter 7). Similarly major differences in FDI inflow, distinguish stable and promising Central European and Baltic countries from the politically unstable Balkans (see Chapter 6).

Nevertheless, regional differences, though deeply rooted and slowly changing, are not cemented into history forever. Slowly working international and domestic forces may contribute to changes and elevate countries and regions from middle- and low-income peripheral status toward the advanced high-income level. Membership in the European Union and closer integration with the West may contribute to the gradual economic rise of the peripheries and gradually weaken corruption, black market activity, authoritarian political tendencies and other economic-social-cultural and political characteristics of backwardness.

Notes

1 Alexis de Tocqueville, *The Old Regime and the French Revolution*, trans. Stuart Gilbert, New York: Doubleday of Random House, 1955, pp. vii, ix, x.

2 The Nomenclature of Territorial Units for Statistics (NUTS) divides the economic territory of the EU into 97 regions at NUTS 1 level, 270 regions at NUTS 2 level and 1294 regions at NUTS 3 level: ec.europa.eu/eurostat/documents/3859598/5916917/KS-RA-11-011-EN.PDF, accessed August 11, 2012.

3 Eurostat, "GDP at Regional Level," March 2017, ec.europa.eu/Eurostat/statistics-explained/index.php/GDP_at_regional_level, accessed March 30, 2017.

4 Directorate General for Internal Policies, Policy Department A: Economic and Scientific Policy, "The Social and Employment Situation in Italy," European Parliament, March 2014, www.europarl.europa.eu/RegData/etudes/note/join/2014/518757/IPOL-EMPL_NT(2014)518757_EN.pdf, accessed September 28, 2016.

5 OECD, "Catalonia," www.oecd.org/edu/lmhe/46827358.pdf, accessed March 4, 2017.

6 The literature of the crisis introduced the acronym "PIIGS" as a derogatory description of the Mediterranean region and Ireland (Portugal, Italy, Ireland, Greece, and Spain).

7 Eduard Gracia, "The Curse of Geography and the Dilemma of Europe's Periphery," www.westga.edu/~bquest/2017/geography2017.pdf, accessed March 5, 2017.

8 Malcolm Chapman and Christos Antoniou, "Uncertainty Avoidance in Greece: An Ethnographic Illustration," in Peter J. Buckley, Fred Burton, and Hafiz Mirza (eds.),

The Strategy of Organization of International Business, Houndmills: Macmillan, 1998, pp. 61–62.

9 Associazione Italiana delle Aziende Familiari (AIDAF), "Family Business in Italy," www.aidaf.it/en/aidaf-3/1650–2/, accessed March 15, 2017.

10 www.businessinsider.com/the-worlds-21-biggest-family-owned-businesses-2015–7, accessed, March 15, 2017.

11 Laurens-Jan Danen, "The Role of the Small and Middle-Sized Companies in the Policy of the European Union," Manuscript, UCLA, 2017, quoting "Job Creation in Small and Middle Sized Enterprises," EU Commission, Working Paper 5, pp. 151–153, 171, 211.

12 John Gal, "Is There an Extended Family of Mediterranean Welfare States?," *Journal of European Social Policy* 20, no. 4 (2010): 290–294.

13 Quoted by Gabriel Tortella, "Economic Entrepreneurship: A Scarce Factor in Spain: The Banking Sector 1782–1914," in Paul Klep and Eddy Van Cauwenberghe (eds.), *Entrepreneurship and the Transformation of the Economy: Essays in Honor of Herman Van der Wee*, Leuven: Leuven University Press, 1994, p. 190.

14 Gabriel Tortella, *The Development of Modern Spain. An Economic History of the Nineteenth and Twentieth Centuries*, Cambridge, MA: Harvard University Press, 2000, p. 224.

15 Anton P. Chekhov, *The Cherry Orchard*, trans. Julius West, New York: Scribner's, [1904] 1917.

16 Beth Holmgreen, *Rewriting Capitalism: Literature and the Market in Late Tsarist Russia and the Kingdom of Poland*, Pittsburgh: University of Pittsburgh Press, 1998, pp. 70–77.

17 Quoted by Jerzy Jedlicki, *A Suburb of Europe: Nineteenth Century Polish Approaches to Western Civilization*, Budapest: Central European University Press, 1999, pp. 218–219; Maria Bogucka, "Social Structures and Customs in Early Modern Poland," *Acta Poloniae Historica* 68 (1993): 110.

18 Gyula Szekfű, *Három nemzedék. Egy hanyatló kor törtenete*, Budapest: Királyi Magyar Egyetemi Nyomda, 1920, p. 291; Gyula Szekfű, *A Magyar bortermelő lelki alkata. Gazdaságtörténeti tanulmány*, Budapest: Minerva Társaság, 1922, pp. 81–82.

19 Giorgio Mori, "Industry without Industrialization: The Italian Peninsula from the End of French Domination to National Unification, 1815–1861," in Jean Batou (ed.), *Between Development and Underdevelopment: The Precocious Attempts at Industrialization of the Periphery, 1800–1870*, Genève: Librairie Droz, 1991, pp. 328–329.

20 Thomas Piketty, *Capital in the Twenty-First Century*, Cambridge, MA: Belknap Press, 2014, pp. 11, 15.

21 Ibid., pp. 61–63.

22 Tortella, *Development of Modern Spain*, p. 223.

23 Anna Zarnowska, "Education of Working-Class Women in the Polish Kingdom," *Acta Poloniae Historica* 74 (1996): 142, 144; John-Paul Himka, *Galician Villagers and the Ukrainian National Movement in the Nineteenth Century*, New York: St. Martin's Press, 1988, pp. 59–60, 64.

24 OECD Programme for International Student Assessment (PISA), 2015, www.oecd.org/pisa/pisa-2015-results-in-focus.pdf, accessed May 3, 2017.

25 OECD, "Education Policy Outlook: Italy," February, 2017, www.oecd.org/education/Education-Policy-Outlook-Country-Profile-Italy.pdf, accessed June 18, 2017.

26 *OECD Education at Glance, 2017 - Data and Methodology*, http://www.oecd.org/education/eag2017indicators.htm, accessed April 1, 2017.

27 See Lázár János, https://vastagbor.atlatszo.hu/2016/12/13/5-kormanyparti-politikus-az-oktatasrol/, accessed March 15, 2017.

28 Piotr S. Windycz, *The Land of Partitioned Poland, 1795–1918*, Seattle: University of Washington Press, 1974, p. 230; George Clenton Logio, *Rumania: Its History, Politics and Economics*, Manchester: Sherratt & Hughes, 1932, p. 115.

29 Tortella, "Economic Entrepreneurship," p. 192.

30 Jorge Miguel Pedreira, "The Obstacles of Early Industrialization in Portugal, 1800–1870," in Batou (ed.), *Between Development and Underdevelopment*, pp. 362–363.

31 William Blackwell, *The Industrialization of Russia: An Historical Perspective*, 2nd ed., Arlington Heights, IL: Harlan Davidson, 1982, pp. 21, 40–41; on Moscow and Saint Petersburg, Dittmar Dahlmann, "Religion und Gesellschaft. Deutsche Unternehmer in Moskau und St. Petersburg von der Mitte des 19. Jahrhunderts bis 1914," in Jörg Gebhard, Rainer Lindner and Bianca Pietrow-Ennker (eds.), *Unternehmer im Russische Reich. Sozialprofil, Symbolwelten, Integrationsstartegien in 19 und frühen 20 Jahrhundert*, Osnabrück: Fibre Verlag, 2006, p. 169.

32 Andrej Kištimau, "Jüdische Unternehmer in Weissrussland. Zeitgenössische Wahrnehmung, Sozialprofil und Wirtschaftsformen," in Gebhard, Lindner, and Pietrow-Ennker (eds.), *Unternehmer im Russische Reich*, p. 222.

33 Andreas Kossert, "Gelobte Land? Religiosität und Unternehmer in der Industriegesellschaft Lodz und Manchester in langen 19. Jahrhundert," in Gebhard, Lindner and Pietrow-Ennker (eds.), *Unternehmer im Russische Reich*, p. 234.

34 Ivan T. Berend, *History Derailed: Central and Eastern Europe in the Long Nineteenth Century*, Berkeley: University of California Press, 2003).

35 *Alexandr Nikolaevich Engelgardt's Letters from the Country, 1872–1877*, trans. Cathy A. Frierson, Oxford: Oxford University Press, 1993, pp. 64–71.

36 Nikolai Y. Danilevski, "Russia and Europe: A Look at the Cultural and Political Relations of the Slavic World to the Romano-German world," *Zarya* (1869).

37 Marina V. Klinova and Elena A. Sidorova, "Public Enterprise Sector in Russia in the 21st Century," www.ciriec.ulg.ac.be/wp-content/upload/2016/10/Reins-Klinova-Ru.pdf, accessed December 27, 2016.

38 Timothy J. Colton, "Paradoxes of Putinism," *Daedalus, Journal of the American Academy of Arts and Sciences* (Spring 2017): 8–18, p. 9.

39 Bryan Christiansen and M. Mustafa Erdoğdu (eds.), *Comparative Economics and Regional Development in Turkey*, Hershey, PA: IGI Global, 2016, p. 309.

40 Ibid., p. 346.

41 Alenka Kuhelj and Bojan Bugarič, "Slovenia in Crisis: From a Success Story to a Failed State?," in Frane Adam (ed.), *Slovenia: Social, Economic and Environmental Issues*, New York: Nova, 2017, p. 59.

42 Alexander V. Chayanov, *The Theory of Peasant Economy*, New York: R.D. Irwin, 1966.

43 See Joel Mokyr, *The Lever of Riches: Technological Creativity and Economic Progress*, Oxford: Oxford University Press, 1990, pp. 11, 76; David Landes, "Does It Pay To Be Late?," in Colin Holm and Alan Booth (eds.), *Economy and Society: European Industrialization and Its Social Consequences: Essays Presented to Sidney Pollard*, Leicester: Leicester University Press, 1991, p. 18.

44 Armin Falk, Anke Becker, Thomas Dohmen, David Huffman, and Uwe Sunde, *The Preference Survey Module: A Validated Instrument for Measuring Risk, Time, and Social Preferences*, IZA (Institute of Labor Economics) DP No. 9674, January 12, 2016, www.iza.org/publications/dp/9674/the-preference-survey-module-a-validated-instrument-for-measuring-risk-time-and-social-preferences, accessed June 18, 2018.

45 The European Bank of Reconstruction and Development, for example, recognized that the "Ottoman rule, in particular, has had persistent negative effects on … social norms relating to trust in south-eastern Europe": European Bank of Reconstruction and Development, *Transition Report 2013*, London: EBRD, 2013, p. 54.

46 "Young and Idealistic But Resolute: Slovak Teenagers Lead Anti-Corruption Crusade," *New York Times*, May 1, 2017.

47 Carlo Bonini and Giancarlo De Cataldo, *Suburra*, Rome: Einaudi, [2013] 2014. The eponymous film is by Stefano Sollima (2015).

48 Joseph LaPalombara, *Democracy Italian Type*, New Haven: Yale University Press, 1987, pp. 74, 50–51, in that order.

49 Ibid., pp. 58–59, 102.

50 Kuhelj and Bugarič, "Slovenia in Crisis," pp. 59–64.

51 LaPalombara, *Democracy Italian Type*, p. 99.

52 "Why Is Corruption More Prevalent in Southern European Countries than in the Northern Ones? Is This Due to a Difference in Culture?," *Quora*, December 15, 2015, www.quora.com/Why-is-corruption-more-prevalent-in-Southern-European-countries-than-in-the-Northern-ones-Is-this-due-to-a-difference-in-culture, accessed March 9, 2017.

53 *OECD Economic Surveys*, Italy, February 2015, pp. 14–15, www.oecd.org/eco/surveys/Overview_Italy_2015_ENG.pdf, accessed April 16, 2017.

54 LaPalombara, *Democracy Italian Type*, pp. 97–98. The author describes a case when his friend's car did not have a front bumper, had one headlight that did not work, one taillight missing and one door partly ripped off, and lacked a sticker indicating that the road tax was paid up and the owner insured. The car had a long-expired German license plate.

> When I remarked about all of these violations, my friend added that he did not have, nor had he ever applied for, a driver's license. … Listen, he said, 'if we are stopped by police, they will find me with at least fourteen different violations, some of them serious. This means … that they will have to spend at least three months with me in court if they write tickets. Instead they will give me a lecture and then let me go. … In this country, we all try to have as little contact as possible with the state.
>
> (ibid., p. 99)

55 www.oecd.org/italy, accessed February 7, 2017.

56 World Economic Forum, Reports, weforum.org/global-competitiveness – report-2014–2015, accessed September 3, 2014.

57 Christiansen and Erdoğdu, *Comparative Economics*, p. 349.

58 The black or shadow economy has a tremendous literature. Friedrich Schneider and Dominik H. Enste, *The Shadow Economy. An International Survey*, Cambridge: Cambridge University Press, 2002, used approximately 280–300 books and studies about the topic, listed in the Reference section of the book.

59 Ibid., pp. 13, 14.

60 Eugenia-Ramona Mara, "Causes and Consequences of Underground Economy," February 6, 2012, https://mpra.ub.uni-muenchen.de/36438/1/MPRA_paper_36438.pdf, accessed January 8, 2017; Christiansen and Erdoğdu, *Comparative Economics*, p. 85. There are several scholarly measurements of the size of the black economy. One of them is a direct method by surveys, others are indirect analysis via the discrepancy between income and expenditure of households, or monetary approach by cash velocity and cash demand, and also by physical input method by electricity consumption, and so on, and the combination of these methods. On the calculation methods, see Schneider and Enste, *Shadow Economy*, pp. 15–28.

61 Quotation from Friedrich Schneider and Dominik H. Enste, "Shadow Economies: Size, Causes, and Consequences," *Journal of Economic Literature*, 38 (March 2000): 81–82.

62 "Progress Ukraine," *The Economist*, September 26, 2015.

63 Ibid., 81.

64 Ibid., 82.

65 www.tradingeconomics.com/country-list/labor-force-participation-rate, accessed April 4, 2017.

66 European Commission, "Europe 2020. A European Strategy for Smart, Sustainable and Inclusive Growth," https://ec.europa.eu/eu2020/pdf/COMPLET%20EN%20BARROSO%20%20%20007%20-%20Europe%202020%20-%20EN%20version.pdf, accessed December 17, 2018.

67 *OECD Economic Surveys*, Italy, February 2015, p. 23, www.oecd.org/eco/surveys/Overview_Italy_2015_ENG.pdfOECD, accessed February 2, 2017.

68 Ibid.

69 Brigitte Berger (ed.), *The Culture of Entrepreneurship*, San Francisco: ICS Press, 1991, pp. 17, 19, 20. Berger also quoted Norbert Elias, who connected modern "book-keeping" business mentality to the religious requirement to give account daily to God on everything one did.

70 https://themysteriousworld.com/10-least-corrupt-countries-in-the-world/, accessed April 23, 2017.

71 "Corporate governance in Scandinavia: comparing networks and formal institutions," *European Management Review* 5 (March 2008): 27–40.

72 Ibid., 91.

73 Digdem Soyaltin, *Europeanization, Good Governance and Corruption in the Public Sector: The Case of Turkey*, London: Routledge, 2017, pp. 2, 72, 87, 117, 121.

74 www.globalsecurity.org/military/world/europe/tu-corruption.htm, accessed March 14, 2017.

75 Sukru Kucuksahin, Has Turkey Given Up Fighting Corruption?, June 8, 2016. https://www.al-monitor.com/pulse/originals/2016/06/turkey-akp-abandons-fighting-corruption.html, accessed March 16, 2017.

76 LaPalombara, *Democracy Italian Type*, p. 3.

77 "Greece Publishes List of 4,000 Tax Scofflaws," *New York Times*, January 24, 2012; Beppe Severgi, "If Only…," *World in 2012*, p. 97, www.economist.com/theworldin/2012; Stergios Babanasis, *Apo tēn stē viosimē anaptyxē*, Athens: Papasisi, 2011.

78 LaPalombara, *Democracy Italian Type*, pp. 48–49.

79 "Portugal's Economic Weaknesses: Country Report Portugal," Rabobank, April 24, 2014, https://economics.rabobank.com/publications/2014/april/country-report-portugal/, accessed December 17, 2016. Scandals include the cases of Face Oculta, the Oeiras Municipality Mayor Isaltino Morais, Apito Dourado and Saco Azul de Felgueiras.

80 Georgina M.M. Mackenzie and A.P. Irby, *Travels in the Slavonic Provinces of Turkey-in-Europe*, 3rd rev. ed., London: Bell and Daldy, [1867] 1877, p. 257.

81 "Global Corruption Barometer 2013," Transparency International, December 6, 2013; also *Independent*, March 22, 2016, www.independent.co.uk; Michael Day, "Corruption in Italy 'Worse than Ever' as Minister Quits over Links with Gang Accused of Bribery," *Independent*, March 20, 2015; Rosie Scammell, "Rubbish on the Streets, Corruption in the Air: Rome Looks for a Clean-up Candidate," *The Guardian*, June 11, 2016; Jonathan Webb, "Corruption in Italy Is Getting Worse, says Supreme Court Judge," *Forbes*, April 25, 2016.

82 Quotations from *The Economist*, November 21–27, 2009, pp. 53, 89; and from "Greece Struggles to Address Its Tax Evasion Problem," *The Guardian*, February 24, 2015.

83 The Cost of Corruption in Europe – Up to €990 Billion (£781.64 Billion) Lost Annually. Rand Corporation News Releases, March 22, 2016, https://www.rand.org/news/press/2016/03/22.html, accessed March 21, 2017.

84 *Independent*, March 22, 2016, www.independent.co.uk.

85 Judy Dempsey, "How Corruption Is Driving Eastern Europe's Brain Drain," *Washington Post*, September 9, 2016.

86 "Young and Idealistic But Resolute: Slovak Teenagers Lead Anticorruption Crusade," *New York Times*, May 1, 2017. Indeed, among countries (including several in Africa and Latin America) with the highest role of remittance by emigrant citizens are some former Soviet and Yugoslav, now independent, republics: remittances are equal with 42 percent of Tajikistan's GDP and 32 percent of Kyrgyzstan's, and they amount to 25 percent of Moldova's, 21 percent of Armenia's, and 16 percent and 13 percent of Kosovo's and Bosnia-Herzegovina's GDP, respectively. On this, see *CIA World Factbook*, www.cia.gov/library/publications/the-world-factbook/geos/md.html, accessed June 2, 2017.

87 Corruption Perceptions Index 2016, Transparency International, January 25, 2017; "Romania Anti-Sleaze Drive Reaches Elite," BBC News, February 19, 2015; "Raport de activitate 2015," National Anticorruption Directorate, January 25, 2017; "EU Commission Chides Romania over State Corruption," BBC News, July 18, 2012.

88 "Corruption in Romania," *The Economist*, February 11, 2017; "Across Romania, the Long Tentacles of Corruption Grip Everyday Life," *New York Times*, February 10, 2017.

89 "I'm handing in my mandate, I'm resigning, and implicitly my government too," Mr. Ponta said in a statement. In September, Mr. Ponta became the first sitting Romanian prime minister to go on trial charged with corruption. He faces allegations of fraud, tax evasion and money laundering. See BBC News, "Romania PM Ponta resigns over Bucharest nightclub fire," November 4, 2015, www.bbc.com/news/world-europe-34720183, accessed November 4, 2015.

90 "Bulgarian Corruption at 15-Year High," *The Telegraph*, Saturday, February 18, 2017.

91 www.business-anti-corruption.com/country-profiles/hungary, October 2015.

92 "A Whiff of Corruption in Orbán's Hungary," *Der Spiegel Online*, January 17, 2017.

93 www.forbes.com/sites/realspin/2014/11/14/continued-corruption-in-hungary/; www.spiegel.de.

94 "Whiff of Corruption," *Der Spiegel Online*.

95 "From Bolshevism to Backhanders, Corruption Has Replaced Communism as the Scourge of Eastern Europe," *The Economist*, April 14, 2011.

96 www.nytimes.com/2016/06/04/world/europe/moldova-vlad-plahotniuc.html, June 3, 2016, accessed December 8, 2016.

97 Corruption Index Reflects Moldova's Disappointing Response to Corruption. Issued by Transparency International Moldova. https://www.transparency.org/news/pressrelease/corruption_index_reflects_moldovas_disappointing_response_to_corruption, accessed November 28, 2016.

98 The Corruption Perception Index measures corruption on a scale between 0 and 100. 100 means no corruption at all, 0 signal the worst possible corruption.

99 The Director of the National Cancer Institute explained that the institute does not have a budget able to serve all the patients; thus, almost all of his doctors collect money from patients to maintain the equipment. These are the realities of being a doctor in Ukraine, he said. "We have total corruption – it couldn't be more total." Quotation from "Welcome to Ukraine, the Most Corrupt Nation in Europe," *The Guardian*, Friday, February 6, 2015.

100 Transparency International Interfax-Ukraine, December 3, 2014; Transparency International Corruption Perceptions Index 2007 Table; Transparency International Global Corruption Report 2008, chap. 7.4, p. 280; "Under Yanukovych, Ukraine Slides Deeper in Ranks of Corrupt Nations," *Kyiv Post*, December 1, 2011, June 2, 2009, February 7, 2011, January 10, 2010, December 8, 2009; "Global Corruption Barometer 2009 Report," Transparency International. June Barometer 2009 Report, published 30 November, 2009.

101 "Progress in Ukraine," *The Economist*, January 26, 2015.

102 "Is Russia Too Corrupt for International Business?," CNBC, June 11, 2013.

103 Transparency International Secretariat, "Corruption in Five Eastern European Countries Remains Endemic," July 2, 2015, p. 94, https://www.transparency.org/news/pressrelease/corruption_in_five_eastern_european_countries_remains_endemic, accessed March 21, 2017; Angus Maddison, *Monitoring the World Economy 1820–1992*, Paris: OECD, 1995, pp. 194, 198, 200.

104 Colton, "Paradoxes of Putinism," p. 9.

105 gatesofvienna.net/2016/03/the-full-text-of-viktor-orbans-speech/, March 19, 2016.

4 The most developed core of Europe

The northwest

Europe's superpower status and the northwest region

The integrated European continent is an economic superpower, with its European Union bloc figuring as the second largest economy in the world. The aggregate EU gross domestic product (GDP) of nearly €17 trillion in 2016 represented almost 23 percent of the global world economy for that year, while the common currency of the eurozone is the second largest traded currency, and reserve currency, after the American dollar. The European Union is by far the biggest trader in the world: its nearly $3.5 trillion export and import activity exceeds that of the United States and China combined. Moreover, its sectoral distribution resembles that of other advanced economies: the 73 percent of the EU's 233 million strong workforce employed in services accounts for roughly 73 percent of the aggregate GDP; the 22 percent working in industry produces 25 percent of GDP, while the 5 percent laboring in agriculture produces less than 2 percent. The still relatively high level of unemployment (21 million in early 2017) represents 8 percent of the entire workforce.

Among the 20 top economic powers of the world in 2016, as measured by per capita income, eight were Northwest European, both EU and non-EU: Switzerland, Norway, Denmark, Sweden, the Netherlands, Austria, Finland, and Germany. Belgium, Britain, and France ranked among the top 30, at 21st, 25th, and 26th, respectively. These countries sit at the top of the high-income level group. Their unweighted per capita income in 2016 was $49,317, approaching that of the group of super-rich countries. If the GDP of Switzerland, Norway, and Britain is added to that of the EU nations of this region, then the region's gross domestic product for the 2010s equals $15.4 trillion, or 90 percent of the EU's total.[1] In general then, Europe owes its enormous economic strength to these 11 Northwestern countries.

In addition to economic strength, these countries have some of the world's best welfare and educational systems and also a much more egalitarian income distribution (0.31 GINI coefficients, according to the World Bank calculations) than in most other countries, including the United States. (At present, the United States' GINI index is 0.46, Russia's is 0.42, and the world average is 0.68. The GINI coefficient measures income distribution on a scale of 0 to 1, where 0 is equal with absolute egalitarian income distribution and 1 means the most in-egalitarian level. Thus the higher the index number, the higher the inequality.) Among the world's top 11 countries in education, according to the World Economic Forum's evaluation, there are six from the north and west of Europe: the Netherlands, Belgium, Switzerland, Finland, Estonia, and Ireland.[2]

All these impressive figures and the international standing of the Northwest region of the continent reflect a spectacular progress, a stable economic growth, and up-to-date structural modernization. Often called the "European Metropolis" or "Europe's Backbone," on account of its concentration of economic, financial and industrial power, the Northwest region also embodies the values and social-political achievements of the European project.

The countries of the Northwest have climbed to this position over a millennium of history (discussed in Chapter 1). They dominated already in the early modern centuries and secured their 19th-century world economic leadership through a series of cultural, scientific, agricultural, and industrial revolutions. Today, although the region no longer is the top world economic leader, it still stands among the most thriving economic powers, enjoying definitive advantages and playing a leading role in the social-cultural and quality-of-life spheres.

Power within the region has shifted over the centuries. In early modern times the Low Countries acted as the engine of the Northwest, but Britain superseded them in the 18th century and kept its leading position during most of the 19th century. From the later part of that century, however, Germany took over as the locomotive of the region's train of development. In 1991, as the turn of the millennium approached, that role was strengthened by the reunification of the West German state (Federal Republic of Germany) and the former communist East Germany (German Democratic Republic).

Reunified Germany in the driver's seat

After the collapse of communism, all of Europe, from Gorbachev's Soviet Union to Mitterrand's France, Thatcher's Britain, and Andreotti's Italy, opposed the reunification of the two postwar German states. However, the leader of the Western world, the American president George H. W. Bush, accepted the idea and aided the process. So did the German people, including the millions of East Germans who immediately voted with their feet by resettling in the West, and of course German Chancellor Helmut Kohl, whose excellent diplomacy, strong commitment to anchoring a renewed Germany within an integrated Europe, and advocacy of political and monetary unification, assuaged concerns and brought the process to a successful conclusion. The Unification Treaty was signed in August 1990.

Despite this success, the actual reunification process was difficult. Former East Germany had 16.7 million inhabitants. It had the strongest economy in the Soviet Bloc, but, at the time of unification, it was producing only 10 percent of the West German GDP. Both the structure and the technological level of the

Eastern economy were obsolete. For example, while only 5 percent of the West German capital stock was older than 5 years, in the East, the figure was 21 percent. In agriculture, 11 percent of the workforce labored, and in manufacturing 47 percent, while in the West these percentages were less than 5 percent and 40 percent respectively. Eastern labor productivity was only one-third that of the West, but wage levels were 50 percent and 60 percent in manufacturing and services respectively. The soviet-type, centrally planned, and state-owned economic regime required transformation to function within a free, privately owned market system.[3]

In the former East Germany, a severe economic contraction followed quickly upon reunification, as domestic products were immediately replaced by Western products. GDP declined by 40 percent until the second half of 1991. The consumer goods market sank to 30–40 percent of its 1989 level, while machinery and other investment goods and export products also dropped to about 30 percent of previous levels. By the second half of the 1990s, agricultural output had been cut in half and employment stood at just 30 percent of the 1989 level.[4]

To incorporate the former East (now the new *Bundesländer* of the Federal Republic) into the overall economy of the country, West Germany invested €1.3 trillion ($1.6 trillion). Indeed, for years West Germany dedicated 4–5 percent of its GDP to reconstructing the region. Western growth consequently slowed down for a while, declining from more than 4 percent to less than 1 percent and overall German indebtedness rose from 42 percent to 64 percent of GDP. Instead of its earlier surplus the national budget now ran a 3 percent deficit.

In the first five years, however, as an outcome of Western investments, an economic boom not only reconstructed but also elevated the former East Germany: its GDP per capita rose from 49 percent to 66 percent of the West's between 1991 and 1995. In the mid-1990s, however, the Eastern economy stopped catching up: economic output per capita stagnated at 71 percent and productivity at 79 percent of the West. Export intensity (meaning the percentage of export turnover in total turnover) in the East is less than half, 32 percent, versus 69 percent of the West in the 2010s. United Germany's GDP surpassed DM3 trillion.[5]

As a consequence of unification, Germany, with its 82 million inhabitants, strong banking and European lending positions, internationally dominant export-oriented manufacturing sectors, and stable trade and budgetary surpluses, became by far the largest country and economy of the European Northwest and of the European Union. The country's culture of stability (*Stabilitätskultur*), based on a legacy of frugality associated with Protestant ethic, its strong welfare system, "social market" and social spending of 11 percent of the GDP, surpassed only by the Scandinavian countries, enhanced its position. Together with its unwavering commitment to the European Union and to further integration, the *Stabilitätskultur* elevated Germany to the leading position within the EU. As former President Richard von Weizsäcker stated in April 1992: "It is no exaggeration to say that our monetary concept becomes part of the European constitution and our social market economy the basic law of European economic policy."[6] Indeed, during and after the financial-economic crisis of the 2010s, the stabilization policy of the European Union, the bail outs of bankrupt member countries and the further integration steps in the banking and financial system aimed at strengthening the eurozone all were dictated by Germany. In order to ban deficit creation and indebtedness, Germany even demanded the insertion of the "Stability and Growth Pact" into member countries' constitutions.

The "German dictate" of austerity did not automatically bring praise from EU member nations. "For many observers," Franz-Josef Meiers opined:

> the euro crisis revealed another uncomfortable reality: Berlin's primacy. Germany as the continent's biggest economy has emerged from the crisis as the Union's undisputed economic and political powerhouse. Germany's preeminent role in the euro crisis management is again the subject of often deep and bitter contention in and outside of Europe … Reviving the German question in a new form not only reinforces old stereotypes, prejudices, and misconceptions about the role of Germany within the context of the euro-Atlantic institutions, but also leads to highly dubious and misleading conclusions that the Berlin Republic is drifting away from the "long road west" and that the German Uberpower can only be balanced by countervailing coalitions. These unfounded fears actually conceal the real challenges the Berlin Republic faces in putting the currency union on a lasting and stable foundation.[7]

The German-demanded policy of austerity provoked frequent sharp criticism. Several influential economists called it counterproductive and predicted that it would push the EU into long stagnation. Some populist politicians spoke about a new German "imperialism" and the exploitation of the poor member countries. Austerity, however, definitely was needed to stabilize countries that were using the common currency but were unable to keep their financial households in order. Their practices were endangering the euro.

"For Merkel," quoting Franz-Josef Meiers again, "the stabilization and preservation of the Eurozone was vital to German and European interests." Speaking to the German Bundestag in 2010, Merkel summarized her position this way:

> The euro which is together with the common market the foundation of growth and prosperity for Germany is in danger. If we do not avert this danger the consequences for Europe will be immense. … It is about much more than one currency. Monetary union is a common destiny. It is therefore no more and no less than the preservation and viability of the European idea. This is our historic task, for if the euro fails Europe fails.[8]

Deeply unpopular in many countries, nicknamed the "thrifty Swabian housewife" by some critics and represented in a Nazi uniform with a Hitler mustache in Greece, Merkel nevertheless was reelected in March 2018 to a fourth term as chancellor of Germany and consequently will continue to be part of European leadership.

What factors have helped the reproduction of Northwest's preeminence in the 21st century?

How has a Germany-led Northwestern Europe been able to reproduce its centuries-long economic preeminence in the present era? Several factors together explain the success. In the first place, the region's cultural-educational and innovative research position should be mentioned. The Northwest has the best developed educational system of the world. (Only some Asian countries, but not the United States, belong also to this category.) As a consequence, not only did several of its countries, even some of the smallest, contribute significantly to the scientific and communication revolution of the second half of the 20th century, but also some, most of all the four Nordic countries, continue to lead Europe in research and development. The so-called Research and Development (R&D) index represents the percentage of the region's GDP investment in research and development. It demonstrates the divide separating the Central European and Mediterranean countries from the Northwest. In the former pair of regions, figures for 2015 show that R&D investment amounted only to about 1 percent of GDP, and in seven of them, to less than 1 percent, while in Sweden the figure is 3.26 percent and in Denmark, 3.03 percent, placing both countries at the top world level. Finland and Austria had similarly high percentage levels that year.

Europe's universities, however, are still not producing enough graduates in mathematics, informatics, natural science and technology to compete with the current world leaders. Compared to China and Taiwan's 31 percent of students and to the United States' and South Korea's 29 percent, at the present only 17 percent of EU students take such courses.[9] The capacity to produce knowledge, once unilaterally concentrated in Europe, is increasingly more evenly distributed around the world. The EU is still a major knowledge center, but it is losing ground to Asia in technology development. Today 70 percent of knowledge creation takes place outside the EU, and around 50 percent of the world's human resources for research and innovation actually are to be found outside the triad of the United States, Japan, and Europe.[10]

Europe thus does not lead in research and development. As an average in the Northwest-led EU, such investment is 2.03 percent of the GDP, far below the examples of Japan and the United States (3.59 percent and 2.73 percent, respectively, in 2013–2014). In 2014, even China, with its 2.05 percent investment, somewhat surpassed the EU. The European Commission, however, has set an ambitious program to increase such investment. Between 2005 and 2015, as calculated in current prices, it increased by nearly 50 percent.[11] Since 1984, the EU has invested to support research in areas such as health, food and biotechnology, information technology, and nano and production technologies.[12]

In 2014, the new "Horizon 2020" program to strengthen innovations and develop key industrial technologies was launched. It has set an average 3 percent R&D investment as a 2020 target, in line with the United States but still lagging behind Japan.

The *Financial Times* reported in 2014 that only 9 of the world's top 100 information and communication companies worldwide have headquarters in Europe. Some, however, are highly competitive, such as the software giant SAP, semiconductor manufacturer STMicroelectronics, IT service providers Cap Gemini, T-Systems, and Atos, as well as communication equipment and services suppliers Ericsson, NSN, and Alcatel-Lucent. They number among the world leaders in their sectors. Europe also has world leaders in several smaller sectors or sub-sectors; for example, semiconductor equipment manufacturers ASML of the Netherlands and Aixtron of Germany, semiconductor makers Infineon, NXP, and ARM, communications services company Unify (known as Siemens Enterprise Communications prior to October 2013) and home communications firm Gigaset. Meanwhile, major conglomerates such as Siemens and Philips, which once dominated parts of high-tech, are gradually leaving that sector, offloading ICT divisions into joint ventures with other players.[13]

The huge common market of Europe attracts significant amounts of foreign investment into these sectors. The EU is still a main destination for investors. It receives one-quarter of worldwide foreign investment, twice the level of the United States or China. And even though it does not lead, the Northwest is still strong enough in research and its industrial applications.

Another major factor contributing to the strength of the Northwest region is its combination of stable and efficient institutions, rule of law and low corruption levels. The region's inherited and cultivated ethics and its citizens' customary behavioral patterns provide extremely strong assurance of smooth and efficient economic operation. The "best countries for business" index produced by *Forbes* clearly reflects this. It is a complex measurement reflecting the efficiency of a country, its institutional, administrative capacity and entire business environment. This index calculates 11 different factors – property rights, innovation, taxes, technology, corruption, freedom (personal, trade, and monetary), red tape, investor protection, and stock market performance – and equally weights each of them to produce its rankings of 139 countries around the world. Seven of the top ten countries are Northwest European while countries with top economies, such as Australia and the United States, are only 11th and 23rd, respectively.[14]

Business environment is influenced also by the proximity of economic centers to each other and by their connections. In this respect, Northwest Europe, with its highly developed transportation network, is an absolute winner, the best in the world. The network facilitates the movement of goods and people and serves as a powerful symbol of union. Europe started building its advanced high-speed train systems in the 1980s; the first of these systems, the French TGV, opened its first lines already in 1981. The EU, with its Council Decision 96/48/EC of July 23, 1996, organized and contributed to financing cross-border lines as part of the Single Market program. The trans-European high-speed rail network rapidly developed thereafter.

The construction of new rail tunnels and bridges was critical to the project. For a long time, the 20-kilometer Simplon Tunnel, built at the turn of the 20th century, was Europe's most important and longest railway tunnel, but toward the turn of the millennium it had to cede its place. First came the exceptional, more than 50-kilometer-long Channel Tunnel connecting Britain to the continent. It opened in 1994. Then, after the millennium turned, came several additional landmark tunnels and projects traversing the Alps and Pyrenees; for example, the 8.3-kilometer-long Pyrenees Tunnel, which opened in 2003 and the nearly 57-kilometer-long Gotthard Tunnel, opened in 2016. The Brenner Tunnel (55 kilometers) and the Lyon-Turin Tunnel (nearly 58 kilometers long) are slated to open in 2026 and 2030, respectively. With regard to bridges, the nearly 5-kilometer-long structure linking Denmark and Sweden (the Copenhagen-Malmo bridge), which opened in 2000, stands out.[15] As of this writing, European fast trains, operated since 2007 by the Railteam consortium, run at speeds of 200, and on some lines even at 360–400 kilometers per hour. With 78,000 kilometers of modern railway, complemented by 50,000 kilometers of high-quality autobahn, and more to come, and with travel distances shortened by tunnels and bridges, cross-European transportation is now faster, less costly and easier than ever before.[16]

The world's rail network has not increased as much as Europe's has. At 1 million kilometers in 1980, it had grown only to 1.05 million by 2015. The networks of the 35 advanced OECD countries increased from 555,000 to 558,000 kilometers, just 1 percent, while the United States network basically stagnated at 266,000 kilometers length and, moreover, mostly preserved its obsolete technology. In contrast, the European Union's network increased from 181,000 to 211,000 kilometers, or 14 percent, and the 19-member eurozone's network enlarged from 98,000 to 129,000 kilometers, 32 percent. Furthermore, as a detailed comparative analysis found, the total of train-kilometers is 1,233 million in the United States but 3,968 million in the European Economic Area. In the United States, train frequency is 22 trains per day, in Europe more than twice that, 54 trains per day, and furthermore, the "European network is constantly being upgraded with new technology to automate operations to reduce driver task loads and to reduce the chance of human error."[17]

The modern fast-rail network connects the Northwest region's countries not only to each other but also to the Mediterranean area and the Central European peripheries, in this way linking the important markets of the core countries to their subsidiaries and value-chains.[18] As a consequence, the Northwest European transportation infrastructure stands at the top level internationally. It connects each and every industrial center to ports and airports, as well as to each other.[19] These links provide an essential foundation for the integrated Single European Market, with its common standards and free licenses allowing banks and companies to operate without barriers in all EU member markets. The common currency contributes by making business cheaper and faster. All of these elements work together to offer companies the best business environment.

To the special regional magnetism associated with the high concentration of industries and services in the Northwest, as New Economic Geography emphasizes, must be added the benefits of the region's highly concentrated infrastructure, pools of skilled labor, and levels of cooperation. Paul Krugman, Masahisa Fujita and Anthony Venables have proved that the higher the concentration of industries and services in economic agglomerations, the more they attract investors seeking to enjoy the returns made possible by concentration.[20] Levels of affluence increase with this growth and over time these regions pull away from their poorer neighbors. *The Economist* has found that for places left behind "this geographical divergence has dramatic consequences." For example:

> A child, born in the bottom 20% in wealthy San Francisco has twice as much chance as a similar child in Detroit of ending up in the top 20% as an adult. Boys born in London's Chelsea can expect to live nearly nine years longer than those born in Blackpool. Opportunities are limited for those stuck in the wrong place. ... If all its citizens had lived in places of high productivity over the past 50 years, America's economy could have grown twice as fast as it did." Further examples were added: "American incomes. ... were a bit less than nine times those in the world's poorest countries in 1870, but nearly 50 times larger by 1990. ... Similarly, from 1997 to 2015 London's share of Britain's gross value added rose from 19% to 23%.[21]

Small wonder then that Northwestern Europe has significantly strengthened its position in Europe and the world. At the beginning of the 21st century, the region symbolizes "Europe," its economic standard, values, institutions and political system.

The economic strength of Northwest Europe

Postwar economic miracles in this region brought about surprisingly rapid reconstruction in the 1950s. The annual growth of 5–7 percent was based on an *extensive development model*, a reliance on expanding the labor force annually by about 1 percent and on using imported technology generously provided by the United States to strengthen its crucial Cold War allies. Reconstruction growth came to a halt in the late 1960s, however, as the economy reached the level predicted by its long-term growth-trend (the so-called Jánossy trend); the region in effect arrived at the economic level it likely would have reached anyway, had war not interrupted its peacetime trajectory.[22]

The 1970s and early 1980s became a period of crisis and decline. The causes were the devastating effects of two oil crises (1973 and 1979–1980), coupled with increasing globalization and consequent competition from deregulated overseas economies. The postwar European development model based on imported technology had been excellent for reconstruction, but it had kept

Europe in a *follower* status, disadvantaged seriously in international competition. Indeed, the region remained painfully behind the United States and Japan, the world's technology leaders, and, moreover, it was starting to be defenseless against the newly industrializing, cheap labor of Asian competitors. Not only international competitiveness was being lost, but also competitiveness in internal markets as overseas companies started occupying a huge slice of the European market. Europe paled in the realm of modern technology. "European cars" were produced by the American Ford and General Motors corporations in factories in Europe and computers were installed in Europe by the American IBM. French journalist-writer Jean-Jacques Servan-Schreiber recognized the dangers as early as 1967 and published an excellent description and a wake-up call in his *Le Défi Américain* (The American Challenge).

In the mid-1980s, but especially around the turn of the millennium, the European Union and its engine, Northwest Europe, opened a new chapter in its development. Responding to the challenge of globalization, the EU launched its Single Market program in 1985 and introduced a new *intensive development model* based on its own scientific input and R&D results. Europe started defending itself in the cutthroat global competition. It embarked on a massive drive of *regionalization*, further strengthened the integration process by creating a borderless more integrated economy with harmonized rules, unified various product standards, and opened the road for cross-national corporate mergers.

The EU clearly recognized the need to stimulate innovation with research and development programs and to this end instituted initiatives to concentrate fragmented and small national programs and to support and stimulate joint research. The European Strategic Programme for Research and Development in Information Technology (ESPIRIT), the Research in Advanced Communication for Europe (RACE), and also the Basic Research in Industrial Technologies in Europe were set up in 1985 and given €1.21 billion seed money with the goal of promoting a change of direction and orientation of the economy by 1992. In the end, the European Union invested more than €63 billion in various research and technology programs, which contributed by 5 percent to the member countries rising R&D expenditures.[23]

As part and parcel of regionalization, a huge wave of mergers and collaborative agreements started europeanizing national industries in the late 20th century. The defense industry has led this trend with the launch of seven cooperative weapons programs. The armaments industry was one of the pioneers of the europeanization of production, while collaboration in space technology replaced untenable national programs. As early as the 1960s, the European Space Research Organization was founded, and the European Launcher Development Organization, with its Ariane Program, launched the first jointly produced rocket in 1979. They conquered half of the international market for commercial satellite launchers. In 2004, six countries established the European Defense Agency to rationalize weapons production by introducing cooperation. Four companies, meanwhile, formed the Eurofighter Program to build new fighter planes.

Although several major mergers of French, German, British, and Dutch companies occurred in the 1970s, in the next decade the pace increased significantly. Between 1985 and 1987, after the start of the Single Market project, 57 mergers occurred and 43 joint venture agreements were signed, while various national corporations initiated joint research and production. Between 1983 and 1990, 1,654 mergers were launched among the 1,000 largest European companies and 396 joint venture agreements were also accomplished. Between 1990 and 2011, 4,400 mergers and acquisitions crowned this process. In 2005, while 26 giant cross-border mergers (with more than $1 billion value each) happened in America and Asia, in Europe their number was 107. The size of the European companies increased so that the largest among them equaled the biggest American corporations.[24]

One of the most important and most successful signature agreements was the creation of leading French, British, German and Dutch (and later Spanish) aircraft manufacturers. The resulting Groupement d'Intérêt Économique started the Airbus program with the joint production of the A-300 Airbus for 250–270 passengers. These planes started flying in 1973 and have been followed by the A-320 and A-380, the world's largest airliners. By 2013, more than seven-thousand Airbuses were in operation and the joint venture received half of all world orders, consequently sharing the market 50–50 with the previously solely dominant American Boeing.[25]

The "merger-mania" has continued to create an all-European industry in the 2010s. In 2016, Finnish Nokia merged with French Alcatel-Lucent, a telecommunications equipment maker. One of the most sensational mergers was announced in September 2017, when Europe's two giant train producers, German Siemens and French Alstom, of legendary TVG fast train fame, both iconic representatives of national industries, merged to become Siemens-Alstom. As Joe Kaeser, chief executive of Siemens declared, "The message of this merger is that the European spirit is alive. That's a powerful message in times that are marked by populism and nationalism and social and political divides." Foreign competition, in this case the giant Chinese Railway Rolling Stock (CRRC), endlessly pushes forward the mergers and the europeanization of the European economy. It is an interesting sign of the times that in the early 1980s, France was the model country for creating "national champion" companies, but in the late 2010s, French President Emmanuel Macron is one of the main advocates of strengthening the European Union so that it can be "a power that can face the United States and China."[26]

Meanwhile, an aggressive enlargement strategy launched in 1973, then continued in the 1980s, 1990s, and 2000s, resulted in a European Union with 28 member countries and a market of 500 million people. The enlargement toward the less developed peripheries, a first in Northwest European history, not only accounted for 170 million of that 500-million figure, but also created a cheap labor backwater for the Northwest , which made it competitive against its overseas rivals. Integration also made possible the reorganization of formerly national industries. A European Central Bank study in 2013, strongly underlined the importance of this change: "Internationalization of production and, more specifically, a higher degree of vertical integration into global value-chains provided in recent years critical stimulus to the European economy."[27]

Economic growth is basically the result of five main factors: increases in labor participation, discovery of new resources, increases in labor specialization, new technology and increases in trade. Around the turn of the millennium, the EU began emphasizing the last three factors with a new, integration-based, development model. The superb European educational systems and high levels of joint investment in research and development enabled European technological inventions to reach the market, while the Single Market offered the greatest possibility for increased trade. The latter, in turn, supported even greater production in the mostly export-oriented Northwest countries. Larger-scale production inspired and made possible further labor specialization. The outcome, economic growth, was most impressive.

One of the major strengths of the region was its high level of savings. A well-known truth is that the richer a country the lower the share of income people must spend for basics. Consequently, they can spend more for luxuries and also save and invest if they so wish. From the late 19th to the mid-20th century the countries of the Northwest accumulated on average about 12–14 percent of their GDP. During the second half of the 20th century, this level increased steeply, until around the turn of the millennium it stood at 20–25 percent of the GDP. The stock of fixed nonresidential capital, the stock of assets of the economy, increased by leaps and bounds. Instead of the 40 percent of the United States level in 1950, it now not only equaled the American level, even though the American stock meanwhile increased by fourfold but even surpassed it at the beginning of the 21st century. The stock of the region's machinery and equipment has increased by 13 times and average age has declined by nearly seven years.[28]

Technological revolution, the renewed energy system, and deindustrialization

Western Europe became a strong participant in the ongoing technological-communication revolution, with its affected sectors reaching new heights at the turn of the 21st century. Here the transformation of the region's energy system, which began in the 1970–1980s provided an essential support. Coal, which had dominated energy production (75 percent in the postwar decades), began losing its decisive role to alternative sources of energy. Nuclear energy already was supplying 28 percent of the electric energy in the region with major differences among countries. In Sweden and France, for example, 60 percent and 78 percent of electricity production was nuclear-based, while in Germany and Finland the percentage was much smaller, a little more than a quarter, and in Britain only 10 percent.[29] Around the turn of the millennium, however, when the European Union defined as major targets, not only energy efficiency and independence (reducing reliance on imported oil and natural gas), but also defense of the environment by carbon emissions decreases, Northwest Europe radically increased the production of renewable energy.

Today coal production, which created the conditions for industrial revolution and Western European economic dominance from early modern times through the 19th century, is coming to an end. It is more than symbolic that Britain, once the largest coal producer in Europe by far, has shut down its last deep coal mine, and that Belgium, where coal used to employ 10 percent of the workforce and produce 12 percent of industrial output, has closed down its entire industry. Meanwhile, although coal mining still exists in Poland, Romania, and some other East European countries, it is struggling to survive. News organizations have taken note with reports in 2016, for example, bearing titles such as "Europe's last coal mines struggle for lifelines," or "The way things are going, Europe is going to lose its coal industry."[30] Northwest Europe, again in the avant-garde of modern world economies, has entered yet another period of historic change, this time with the rise of a new energy age.

Since the turn of the millennium, various national directives and crucial EU's decisions have led to a fast increase – 73 percent between 2004 and 2014 – in renewable energy production. Wind, solar, hydroelectric, geothermal, biofuel, and waste-based energy production have become significant. In gross energy consumption renewables already have a 26 percent share in Denmark, and 29, 30, 35, and 45 percent in Finland, Austria, Sweden, and Norway, respectively. Renewable sources provide 70 and 63 percent of electricity production in Sweden and Austria. The European Union's ambitious, so-called 20-20-20 target envisions the reduction of greenhouse gas emissions to at least 20 percent of 1990 levels, an increase of 20 percent in the share of renewable energy in final energy consumption, and a 20 percent increase in energy efficiency, all by 2020.[31]

The Northwest closely has followed the modern structural transformation of the advanced world economy in other areas as well as energy. With technological advances and rapidly increasing productivity, many fewer workers are needed in traditional sectors. In agriculture, productivity had been increasing by 3–5 percent per year for decades before the turn of the millennium. Now, in the 2010s only about 10 million people (in full-time terms), a mere 5 percent of the EU labor force, work in agriculture, compared to 20–30 percent half a century before. However, the peripheral countries still employ between 10 percent and 30 percent of their total working population in agriculture (Romania 31 percent, Bulgaria 19 percent, Poland 13 percent, Greece 11 percent, Portugal 10 percent). In contrast, in the Northwest, the average of nine countries is only 2.3 percent. Even in countries with important food output, such as France, Denmark and the Netherlands, this employment is not higher than 2.5 percent of the total.[32] Meanwhile, instead of importing food as in the past, Western Europe actually has become an agricultural exporter.

A similar transformation has taken place in the industrial sector. Productivity increased tremendously in the 20th century: the \$3–\$5 value produced in an hour at mid-century by a West European worker increased by century's end three- to sixfold in various countries, on average in Western Europe 4.3-fold. Thus, at the turn of the millennium a Northwest European worker produced \$25–\$28 value in an hour, measured by constant prices. Between 1999 and 2010, productivity continued to improve, increasing at an annual rate of 1.1–1.7 percent in Finland, Germany, the Netherlands, and Austria. This trend has produced a sharp decline in the employed industrial labor force in the Northwest as it has across the entire, advanced, industrialized world.

In the middle to late 19th century, a high development level was equal with industrialization, with the industrial labor force in the most advanced economic powers reaching about 40–45 percent of total employment, but this situation has changed radically. As early as 1974, Daniel Bell recognized the new development trend and popularized the term "postindustrial society" to describe its probable consequence.[33] Indeed, by the end of the 20th century, in the United States, the leading economic power of the time, industrial employment had declined from 28 percent to 18 percent of total employment. Similarly, in the EU-15 countries (the Northwestern countries plus three Mediterranean nations), industrial employment had dropped from 30 percent to 20 percent. In Britain, the "first industrial nation" in the world, manufacturing employment alone dropped from 48 percent to 19 percent in the second half of the 20th century. Now, in the 2010s, only 11 percent of British GDP is being produced by this sector. In Sweden the decline of industrial employment has been quite similar, from 45 percent to 18 percent, with the contribution of manufacturing to GDP dropping to 16 percent; in the Netherlands the share of industrial workers decreased from 40 percent to 18 percent and the contribution of manufacturing to the GDP declined to 12 percent. The drop was strong although less dramatic in Germany, the real economic engine of the region, which preserved more of its export-oriented industry. In the 2010s, German industry still employed 28 percent of workers, and manufacturing produced 23 percent of the GDP.[34]

Several interpretations connect this trend with globalization and the import of industrial products from newly industrializing, mostly Asian countries. Populist politicians are loudly complaining about the jobs "stolen" by China and other nations and are advocating economic nationalism to defend domestic markets. More reasonable experts reject this interpretation and maintain that deindustrialization is a positive outcome of technological development, including the robotization of production.

The service revolution and the financial sector

Deindustrialization has marched hand-in-hand with a service revolution, including the sharp increase of various personal services, a consequence of increasing living standards and the dramatic drops of expenditure for food and basics in family budgets. At the beginning of the 20th century, even in the richest countries such as Switzerland, families spent about 60 percent of their income for basics, but a century later only about 10–15 percent. Consequently, expenditure for various kinds of services, education, traveling, leisure, health care, and fitness, now consume the biggest share of family budgets.

Other, and even more important, independent service branches have developed in an organic connection with agricultural and industrial production (see Table 4.1). Service companies for agriculture employ two to three times more people than agriculture itself and perform work previously done within peasant estates or agrobusinesses. Specialized service companies offer, for example, transportation of farm products, field fertilization and pesticide spraying. Similarly, tasks such as accounting, production design, and marketing, for example, which previously were the responsibility of industrial company employees, are being outsourced to specialized service companies. Service content now accounts for a greater percentage of the value of manufactured goods, and a large percentage of service employees work for the manufacturing sector. By 2012, the service sector as a whole in the EU-15 countries was contributing 75 percent of total value, in contrast to its 52 percent share in the early 1970s.[35]

Parallel with this development, the financial sector has emerged as the most significant branch of services in Western Europe in the early 21st century. This phenomenon is often described as the financialization, or even overfinancialization of the advanced economies. It owes its existence in part to the combination of the Northwest region's high-income level and the frugality of the region's Protestant population. Great Britain, the first country in the world to financialize, is an outstanding example. The trend actually started

Table 4.1 Sectoral share in the production of the GDP in percentage, 2010s

Country	*Agriculture*	*Industry*	*Manufacturing within industry*	*Services*
Austria	1	28	18	71
Belgium	1	22	14	77
Denmark	1	22	14	76
Finland	3	27	17	71
France	2	19	11	79
Germany	1	30	23	69
Netherland	2	21	12	77
Norway	2	38	8	60
Sweden	1	26	16	73
Switzerland	1	26	19	73
United Kingdom	1	21	11	78
United States	1	21	12	78
Japan	1	26	18	73

Source: *The Economist*, Pocket World in Figures 2017, 1 September 2016, London: The Economist.

there in the last third of the 19th century, but in 1970 the value of bank assets was still roughly equal with only half of GDP. By 2007, however, in connection with deregulated globalization, that value had become five times greater than the GDP of the country.[36]

Financial transactions in the world jumped from $15 billion per day in the early 1970s to $1.3 trillion by 2000. In 2007, they surpassed the world's aggregate GDP by 66 times. Foreign exchange transactions skyrocketed to $1.5–$2.0 trillion by 2006, an amount equaling 50 to 60 times the value of total world trade. But in the early 21st century, only a small portion of these transactions could be attributed to trade or investment. The bulk was connected to speculation, whether in currency or in arbitrage actions, the simultaneous buying and selling of assets to exploit price differences on various markets.[37] Cross-border claims in Europe elevated from a small, $20 billion business in the preglobalization era to $3.1 trillion already in the late 20th century.[38] The stock of banks and their loans jumped from 10 percent to 48 percent of the world's GDP between 1980 and 2006. Global capital flow trebled between 1996 and 2006 to reach $7.2 trillion. The flow of direct investment in West European countries, $62.4 billion inflow and $71.4 billion outflow in Britain and $25.1 and 37.2 billion in France in 2012, reflected the extensive financialization of the economy.[39]

Pan-European finance institutions made banking and so-called shadow banking by far the strongest sector of the Northwest European economies. Regionalization of the banking sector was a new development associated with European integration. In 1966, a detailed 380-page report issued by the European Commission declared that capital markets are fragmented and "the common market for capital is at present little more than a preliminary plan"; additionally, that capital movement is not free yet and "new laws and regulations of various types will be needed to speed the establishment of an integrated European capital market." A group of experts urged the banks to establish branches and subsidiaries in other member countries.[40] Based on the 1979 decision of the European Court of Justice, the European Council regulation of 1999 and then Community regulation No.764/2008 made it compulsory to accept other member countries laws and rules. That opened the borders for unrestricted business activity with other member countries' banks and corporations. The EU issued the Single Passport for banks as a license for their all-European activities. The introduction of the common currency eliminated the problems and risks of multiple European currencies and opened the door for the rise of an all-European banking sector.

Banking mergers skyrocketed. Deutsche Bank started aggressively expanding and acquiring financial institutions in Britain, Italy, and other EU countries. The French Crédit Lyonnais followed this example. By 2007, almost half of cross-border mergers in the EU happened in the banking sector. After the collapse of communism, the West European banks took over the transformation of Central European countries' financial sectors. They established branches and subsidiary banks, eventually coming to own 87 percent of the Central European and Baltic banking industry. In Estonia, the Czech Republic and Slovakia this share was nearly 100 percent. The leading Northwestern banks became giant all-European institutions. The Deutsche Bank Annual Report in 2013 proudly announced that the bank had more than €2 trillion assets, nearly 3,000 branches and close to 100,000 employees all over Europe. Only 45 percent was in German lands, the rest mostly in other European countries. The French BNP Paribas also became an all-European bank with nearly €2 trillion assets, which elevated it to fourth place among the world's leading banks. Of its 200,000 employees 145,000 worked outside France in other European countries. Its business activity was greater in other EU countries than in France (46 percent, compared to 31 percent in France).

The British banking industry, centered in "The City" in London, one of the world's leading financial centers, rose to a leading position in Europe. The largest British bank, HSBC Holding, had $2.67 trillion assets, 6,200 offices and 95 million customers worldwide. The strength of its European business is clearly expressed by its 1,136 branches in just two countries, France and Turkey. A second British banking giant, the Royal Bank of Scotland, held assets of $2.3 trillion, while the two other institutions that belong to the dominant British banking sector, Barclays Bank ($1.5 trillion) and Lloyds Banking Group ($1 trillion) joined with other British banks to create the strongest banking sector in Europe.

The European Banking Federation reported in 2011 that its 8,878 banking entities owned €46.34 trillion in assets, an amount four times the value of the EU-28 countries aggregate GDP. About 72 percent of these assets were concentrated in the eurozone. The banking industry's loans and deposits accounted for 144 and 135 percent of the EU's aggregate GDP.[41] The exceptional rise of the financial sector and its leading role in the European economy was one of that economy's most important structural changes at the turn of the millennium.

The strength of modern industries

Beside the elevation of the Northwestern financial sector to exceptional strength and role, the other most important structural change of the region's economy came with the rise of the high-tech and semi-high-tech sectors, in particular the electrical and electronic industry (EEI), the information and communication industries (ICT), the automotive industry and electrical engineering. The EEI sector provides an example of this effect. Although after the turn of the millennium the share of the EU's GDP attributable to manufacturing declined overall, from 19 percent to 15 percent, the EEI share in gross output actually grew. It increased at an average annual rate of 2.7 percent after 1998, so that by 2012, its value added in constant prices averaged €212.4 billion annually. Today this sector accounts for more than 11 percent of manufacturing and employs 3.4 million people. This development was driven above all by the electrical industry which employs 65 percent of the labor force of the total EEI sector.

The range of electricity products is broad, covering the categories of capital goods, durable consumer goods and intermediary products, such as those delivered to companies that construct power generation plants and electricity grids. One of its major products, the electric motor, is used by airplanes, locomotives, commuter trains, and cars. It is also an essential component in industrial automation and process control, building automation, and heating and air conditioning, as well as in household equipment and appliances.

Among the most famous corporations in the EEI sector are Alstom, the Siemens Group and the ThyssenKrupp Group. Alstom (the company adopted this name in 1999), a French company, is a global player in rail transportation, especially for passengers, and in signaling and locomotive production. Its most famous products are the AGV, TGV, Eurostar, and Pendolino high-speed trains. The Siemens Group began expanding rapidly in 1985, acquiring virtually one additional company in every subsequent year until 2012. In its four divisions, industry, health care, energy, and infrastructure, it employs 360,000 people (its R&D section alone employs 28,000). The company works in 190 countries, but its main activity is in Europe. In 2008, it created the German-Finnish Nokia-Siemens Network, an end-to-end supply chain that increased installation engineering productivity by a factor of two to three.[42] And in 2017, as has been noted earlier, it merged with Alstom to form Siemens-Alstom. The ThyssenKrupp Group (the two traditionally leading companies merged in 1999) operates in nine business areas, owns 670 companies and employs 150,000 people. Like Siemens-Alstom, ThyssenKrupp is a worldwide enterprise, with most (more than 60 percent) of its business concentrated in Europe (one-third in Germany).[43] The EU's overall EEI production is mostly sold on the European markets, but it also gained share in international trade from 13 percent to 16 percent from the 1990s to the 2010s, while the United States and Japan suffered major losses in Asia.[44]

The EU's EEI sector regional distribution reflects the dominant role of the more developed Northwest. In 2012, the countries of this region possessed 33 percent of the EU's total manufacturing industry, 41 percent of total electrical and electronic engineering and 34 percent of components production. EEI, measured by workplaces, played and still plays an important role in manufacturing (in Finland 16.2 percent, Germany14.6 percent, and Austria 13.6 percent, followed by Sweden 12.3 percent and France 12.2 percent).[45]

Around the turn of the millennium, the information and communication technology (ICT) sector became one of the fastest growing branches of the EU economy with a 10–13 percent annual growth rate in Finland, France, Sweden, and Britain and a somewhat lower 7 percent in Germany. The share of the value added in total business kept pace with the American and Japanese shares of 10.5 percent and 8.1 percent, respectively. The share in employment was somewhat higher (about 8–9 percent) than the American and Japanese 6–8 percent.

The European semiconductor industry commands a strong global position in the development of advanced process technologies and products. Its vital nucleus consists of three clusters. The first is located around the cities of Nijmegen and Eindhoven in the Netherlands, Leuven in Belgium, and Aachen in Germany; the second in France around Grenoble; the third in Germany around Dresden. The Grenoble nanotech cluster is largely built around the Grenoble Institute of Technology (GIT), which is part of the Master Nanotech initiative. Besides the GIT, this cluster includes two other institutes, the École Polytechnique Fédérale de Lausanne (Switzerland) and the Politecnico di Torino (Italy). An important business player in the field of micro- and nano-electronics, also active in the Grenoble nanotech cluster, is STMicroelectronics. Around Dresden is located the high-tech cluster nicknamed "Silicon Saxony."[46]

The countries of the Northwest region are competitive regarding ICT expenditure per resident as a percentage of GDP. In 2000 the figure in Sweden was 7.4 percent, in Britain 6.5 percent, while Germany, Finland, and France each had around 6 percent, as compared to 6.8 percent and 4.3 percent in the United States and Japan. The spread of high-tech instruments in Western Europe, expressed as PCs/100 households, was already high around the millennium's turn, 60 in Sweden, 47 in Germany, Finland, and Britain. This was on par with the technology leaders: 51 in the United States, 38 in Japan. Only France remained somewhat behind at 27. In the use of e-commerce by enterprises, measured by a scale of 100, the United States was far ahead at 70; Sweden, Germany, and Britain, ranging from 47 to 53, were better than Japan at 40. In another important measure, Internet users/100 residents, the situation was similar. The United States was ahead at 61, surpassed only by Sweden at 63, while the average among other West European countries (Finland 56, Germany 33, and France 17) hovered around the Japanese level of 36.[47]

In the car industry Northwest Europe belongs at the top. The car was invented in Europe, in Germany in the late 19th century, while France quickly emerged as a leader in the young industry. Production began early in north Italy and Britain as well. Nevertheless, in the first half of the 20th century the United States assumed a dominant position in the industry. After World War II, Japan joined, followed soon by South Korea. These leading producers invaded the European market and conquered, even dominated, until the 1970s.

The European Commission began tackling this problem in that decade. Its analysis of the industry's situation in 1976, concluded that forward-looking investments in R&D, especially in developing electric cars, establishing assembly production in low-wage countries and, most of all, furthering transnational cooperation through the europeanization of production and concentration of leading companies, all were needed by European producers.[48] Returning in 1981 to the issue, the Commission called special attention to the huge productivity gap between Japan and Europe. At the time, the cost of car production in Japan was 20–30 percent lower than in Europe. Assembly of a car required twice as many hours in Europe as in Japan. Specialization was also far behind: 65–80 percent of parts were produced by subcontractors, subsidiaries and value-chains in Japan and only 50 percent in Europe. To be competitive, the Commission warned, European carmakers have "to think in Community rather than national terms. … [Only with cooperation] can economies of scale be fully exploited." Among the recommendations the Commission mentioned the need of all-European standards and harmonized regulations and taxation and ending the compartmentalization of markets.[49]

All these recommendations were gradually realized as the EU began pursuing its aggressive enlargement goals in 1973, and especially after it launched the Single Market project (1985). The European car industry rejuvenated. A strong concentration process created fewer but bigger companies, all-European standards replaced the former national standards and the big carmakers established subsidiaries in low-wage peripheral Europe, first in Ireland, then in Spain and Portugal, and after 1990, in Central and Eastern Europe.[50] Together these changes radically cut of the costs of production – in the Slovakian subsidiary of the VW, for example, the company paid $6/hour instead of $40 in Germany with benefits – and thus became competitive. By 2007 the companies all were producing for the entire European market: 83 percent of Volkswagen's output was sold outside Germany in Europe, 81 percent of BMW's and 78 percent of Peugeot's. From higher profits, the European carmakers invested 6 percent of their turnover income compared to 4 percent in Japan.

Northwest Europe thus regained the leading position it had lost in the first half of the 20th century. A great role was played in this achievement by an immense investment in R&D. Germany alone spent 33.3 billion for technological development. About 20 European car manufacturers were producing 9 percent of the total value of European manufacturing. Germany alone – the huge Volkswagen group, Daimler-Benz and BMW – produced 30 percent of the European car production, followed by France with 19 percent (Peugeot-Citroen) and Britain (10 percent). (Outside this region Spain also has emerged as a major producer, representing 17 percent of European car production.) Altogether Europe's car industry has become the world leader. Its output around the turn of the millennium amounted to 29 percent of world production in contrast to the 24 percent American and 21 percent Japanese shares.[51]

The chemical industry is another world-leading sector of Northwest European industry. It employs 1.15 million high-skilled workers, three times more than other industries, produces 7 percent of the EU's total industrial output and 1.1 percent of its GDP. It has a 17 percent share in global sales of chemical products, equal to NAFTA's share but far behind the Asian share of 57 percent. Pharmaceutical and chemical industries are #1 and #2 in producing added value per employee. Two-thirds of the sector's products are used by other sectors of European manufacturing.[52]

At the center of Europe's chemical industry stands Germany with 2,000 companies (90 percent of them small and medium size), nearly a half-million employees and €191 billion in revenue. The companies are mostly located in 30 German chemical parks with superb infrastructure and interconnected system of raw materials and energy supply. R&D spending in the chemical and pharmaceutical industries was €10.6 billion in 2015. Its result is embodied in its 18 percent share of the world's chemical patents (small Switzerland's share is 15 percent compared to the United States' 27 percent). The productivity of this industry has increased by 14 times in the last 50 years. Today it is the fourth largest chemical industry in the world, with the third largest market share (11 percent) after China and the United States. Although 60 percent of its products are sold on the European markets, it is still the second biggest exporter in the world behind the United States.[53]

The Northwest: the biggest service provider

As with to manufacturing and banking, other service sectors throughout Europe have been europeanized and now are dominated by Northwestern companies. The affected sectors included formerly national services, such as electricity. The European Community's "Electricity Directive" of 1996 opened the common market so that companies could operate and compete in all member countries. The same happened to the natural gas market and national airlines. Several airlines merged or signed agreements of cooperation.[54] One of the most important was the Air France–KLM Royal Dutch Airlines merger in 2004.

The strategy of building all-European networks spread to retail trade as well. The European Community's "Green Paper" of 1997 already registered that "retail chains are increasingly undertaking cross-border activities." The paper also reported that "three-quarters of the Community's food retailing was controlled by the corporations of just three countries, Germany, France and Britain." Intra-EU direct investments in services, it was reported in 1999, increased by more than 73 percent after the introduction of the Single Market.[55]

Western Europe is home to some of the world's biggest retail companies. The French Carrefour, the German Metro and the British Tesco are the 21st-century world's second, third, and fourth biggest retailers. The world's 30th, Swedish IKEA, and 33rd, Belgian Delhaize Group, have joined the top retailers in building all-European networks. Carrefour, established as a discount shop in Annecy, France in 1960, started its chain-building in that country, but from the 1970s already began spreading internationally, including to the Americas and Asia. During the 1990s and 2000s its hypermarket chains and malls appeared in Spain, Greece, Italy, Turkey, Poland, Portugal, Belgium, Romania, the Czech Republic, and Slovakia. It became the number one retailer in Spain, Portugal, and Greece. By 2015, it had 6,137 stores in 29 countries with 87 percent of its sales occurring within Europe.[56] TESCO started as a street stand in 1919, became a retail network after World War II in London and then a leading supermarket chain. Around the turn of the millennium, it gradually emerged as the world's third biggest retailer with 3,146 stores in 12 countries employing 330,000 people. After the collapse of communism, it conquered the Polish, Czech, Slovak, and Hungarian markets as well.[57] The German Metro Group, founded in 1996, immediately started doing business in other European countries as well. By 2000, 42 percent of its turnover originated abroad. The corporation focused on Central and Eastern Europe and established its network in Poland, Russia, Romania, Turkey, Greece, Serbia, Montenegro, and even in Ukraine and Kazakhstan. By 2004, the company employed 250,000 people in 32 countries (including Asia).[58]

The 2008 financial crisis in Northwest Europe

The years around the turn of the millennium belonged to the most prosperous in European history: the eurozone's GDP increased annually by 1.5 percent between 1992 and 1996, by 2.8 percent between 1997 and 2001, and by 1.7 percent between 2002 and 2007. Both the total GDP and the per capita income level have increased by more than 50 percent in advanced Europe between 1992 and 2005. Before 2008 neoliberal economists announced that business cycles and the possibility of crisis had come to an end. They talked as if "depression-prevention" was a task fully mastered and prophesied that fluctuation, oscillations between rapid and slower growth periods, were the future.[59] They were wrong.

In reality, the deregulated financial sector was becoming less and less controllable. The American mortgage bank, Lehman Brothers, with its mountain of subprime mortgages that could not be repaid, declared bankruptcy on September 15, 2008. The New York Stock Exchange, in the same month, twice suffered daily losses of 500 points and the Dow Jones dropped from its 2007 peak of 14,164 to 6,469 points. The 2008 financial crisis erupted and overwhelmed the world. European capitalism was shocked and European countries, like those elsewhere, were unable to escape the ensuing consequences.

Northwestern Europe, the model of stability and strength, was no exception. One may not forget that some of the countries of the region, Britain, France, Norway, Sweden, Finland, and Denmark, shared in a real estate boom with several peripheral countries and experienced a growing housing bubble between 2000 and 2007. House prices in those countries augmented by 80 percent, and in France and Britain, by 108 percent and 138 percent, respectively. Only Germany and the Netherlands avoided "the worldwide rise in house prices, the biggest bubble in history," as *The Economist* called it already in the summer of 2005.[60]

Financial panic swept throughout Europe. *Der Spiegel* reported in November 2008 that "trust has been essentially destroyed in the financial and credit markets, banks, companies and consumers are hoarding their money instead of lending or spending it."[61] A liquidity crisis, the lack of available money and credit, stopped the entire world economy. Since investments are strongly based on credits, and old credits, in modern economies, are paid back from new credits, the freezing up on credit caused economies to stop functioning. People and companies could not pay back their loans and banks suffered tremendous losses. British banks lost or wrote down about $300 billion, eurozone banks lost between $500 to 800 billion, 10 percent of the aggregate GDP. According to the IMF, in the spring of 2009, Britain and the eurozone jointly suffered $1.2 trillion in losses.[62]

The hard-hit banking sector of the Northwest region was paralyzed and needed to be rescued. In two weeks after the collapse of Lehman Brothers, the Netherlands, Belgium and Luxembourg stepped in to save the banking and insurance giant Forbis with €11.2 billion and within a couple of days they also bailed out Dexia with €6.4 billion. Britain nationalized the mortgage lender Bradford & Bingley with £50 billion and rescued the Royal Bank of Scotland and Lloyds TSB with £37 billion. Germany rescued Hypo Real Estate with €50 billion. The British Treasury announced a giant £500 billion bank rescue action. Among 29 endangered major banks worldwide, a Financial Stability Board of the G-20 countries included a score of leading European banks. Among them were the giants Banque Populaire, Barclays, BNP Paribas, Commerzbank, Credit Suisse, Deutsche Bank, Dexia, Royal Bank of Scotland, and Société Général. The European Union decided at its Paris meeting in October 2008 to prevent the meltdown of its banking system by means of coordinated measures. It succeeded, and in 2009, the European Commission was able to announce that bank collapse had been avoided.[63]

Nevertheless, financial panic and the paralysis of credit unavoidably spread to the real economy with "record speed," as the European Commission reported.[64] After years of impressive growth, already in the second and third quarters of 2008 a decline of the eurozone's GDP was being reported. In early 2009, the aggregate GDP declined by 1.5 percent and industrial output by 3.5 percent. Formal recession, defined as the decline of GDP in two consecutive quarters, arrived in Northwest Europe in the fall of 2008. British GDP declined by 6.15 percent for six consecutive quarters until January 2010. France and Germany had, in four quarters, a total decline of 3.9 percent and 6.6 percent, respectively. Sweden and Finland suffered 7.4 percent and 9.9 percent decline over seven and four quarters, respectively. Denmark and Norway had 8 percent (over six quarters) and 3.4 percent (over 11 quarters) decline, respectively. Switzerland's GDP shrank by 3.3 percent over four quarters.[65] Strong Germany was rattled. In late 2008 and early 2009, its domestic consumption declined by 60 percent, its signature electro industry and machine building by 19 percent and 40 percent and the country's car exports dropped by 39 percent. The government rushed to accept a €18 billion public investment and a €9 billion cut of income taxes, the so-called "Pakt für Beschäftigung und Stabilität in Deutschland zur Sicherung der Arbeitsplätze, Starkung der Wachstumkräfte und Mobilisierung des Landes," in January 2009.[66] Similar stimulus packages were introduced throughout Europe.

Dramatic as it was, the recession in the European core lasted only about a year; recovery in the Northwest actually began as early as 2009. (In contrast, several peripheral countries had double-dip recessions and even depressions, sustained, long-term downturns, for years.) Between 2009 and 2014, when the United States was celebrating the return to normalcy with a 2.1 per cent average annual growth rate, and the eurozone's 19 countries had a slow average of 0.7 percent, Sweden, Germany, and Britain, in contrast, had an impressive 2.4, 2.0 and 1.8 percent growth. The growth for Norway (1.5 percent), Austria

(1.2 percent), Belgium (1.1 percent), and France (1 percent) was slower, while for the Netherlands, Denmark, and Finland (just 0.5 percent in each country), near stagnation was the rule.[67] Despite the crisis, none of the core countries declined into bankruptcy, none of them had to be bailed out. They were able to recapitalize their banking systems and pump money into their economies with stimulus programs. The strong economy of the Northwest survived the trial well.

Moderate neoliberal turn: weakening the welfare state and workers' rights

Adjusting to global competition in early 21st century, before and during the crisis, several Northwest European governments loosened the signature welfare systems they had built in the postwar atmosphere of solidarity and in the time of sharp social competition with communism during the Cold War decades. During the postwar period income inequalities decreased and working people and their trade unions gained various privileges. These benefits became a burden on business competitiveness. One of the first and most successful neoliberal reforms was introduced, paradoxically enough, by the German left coalition of Social Democrats and Greens under Chancellor Gerhard Schröder. In 2000, the country was spending roughly one-third of its GDP for public social expenditures. In March 2003, in his speech at the Bundestag, Schröder argued that labor market reform was unavoidable. If we do not do it, he argued, it would be modernized through the brute forces of the global markets leaving barely room for social protection.

The institution of a series of changes started in 2003 under the aegis of Agenda 2010, with the last steps (Hartz Plan IV) being taken on January 1, 2005. These reforms radically reduced unemployment benefits, tightened job acceptance regulations and merged unemployment assistance with welfare. The long-term, working-age unemployed now would receive a €391 fixed payment regardless of previous salary. About 6 million people depended on it. The unemployed had to accept any kind of job within a certain short period, and the country developed the largest low-wage sector in Europe. In 2008, about 20 percent of the workforce (7 million people) worked in low-wage sectors (€9 per hour). The wage share dropped to 65 percent of the GDP, a 50-year low and poverty increased from 11 percent to 14 percent.

A huge boom followed. Between the last quarter of 2004 and the second quarter of 2008, production grew by 9.4 percent and manufacturing output by nearly 19 percent. Price competitiveness as compared to that in other eurozone countries improved by 10 percent. Profits, in real term, increased by 40 percent. The reforms helped employment: the number of unemployed declined from 5.2 million to 3.5 million, the lowest rate since 1990. Workers income level (in real terms), however, increased only by 4 percent.[68]

The other countries of Northwestern Europe joined Germany in seeking competitiveness by reforming or planning to reform their welfare states and labor markets. Even Sweden, the inventor and model welfare state, introduced modifications and cuts. In the domain of the labor market, the Swedish model is characterized by generous unemployment benefits through voluntary, state-subsidized unemployment insurances, combined with a long tradition of employment protection and active labor market policy (including free-of-charge extensive retraining programs). The Swedish postwar system of unemployment protection was put under enormous stress during the early 1990s, which might be considered a critical juncture for the general model. The country's GDP dropped by 5 percent and unemployment rose dramatically from 1.5 percent to almost 10 percent; consequently, the public deficit steeply increased. A center-right coalition (between 1991 and 1994) pursued an economic strategy of deregulation, structural reform, and austerity. The traditionally exceptional benefit generosity was curbed. Employers departed from the previous politics of compromise that long had characterized the Swedish model, taking instead, as the Confederation of Swedish Enterprise put it, an "aggressive neoliberal posture," which challenged the idea of the persistence of cross-class alliance. In the second half of the 1990s, welfare state restructuring, despite much resistance from organized labor, indicated an increasing rift between labor and capital. Benefit generosity was cut even further. At 2.8 percent of GDP, spending on active labor market policy peaked in the first half of the 1990s, dropping to 1.0 percent in 2009, despite an unemployment rate of more than 8 percent. Training and retraining practices (especially strong in Sweden) virtually collapsed and spending for such programs fell from 1.0 percent to 0.1 percent of GDP between the early 1990s and 2009.

These developments in labor market policy suggest a considerable decline in social solidarity in Sweden around the turn of the millennium. Increases in poverty have followed. From the mid-1990s to 2011, as the poverty rate in Sweden after taxes and transfers more than doubled to 17.4 percent, Sweden reached Britain's rate (17 percent) and exceeded Germany's (15 percent). Nevertheless, Sweden, with a GINI coefficient of 0.273 in 2011, still displays much less income inequality than Britain (0.344) or Germany (0.293). The Swedish welfare state retains some continuity with its past, and social democratic ideas still govern social policies during difficult times.

The Netherlands, traditionally the "European leader in the labor market field" also deregulated its labor market and restructured its unemployment protection (including reducing unemployment benefits and introducing stricter eligibility criteria). Neoliberal reforms had a huge impact on both Christian and social democratic political parties. Within the traditional postwar "social partnership," power resources were shifted toward business.[69]

France, also during a social democratic presidency (François Holland), tried to follow its neighboring countries' labor market reform. The country has probably the most generous labor regime with its signature 35-hour work week, rigid rules that make firing workers almost impossible and trade union dominance in labor affairs. The bill backed by Holland originally allowed for multinational companies to lay off workers if their worldwide revenues declined, even if they weren't necessarily sinking in France. Companies would have been allowed to lengthen the working day to a maximum daily ceiling of 10 hours, and to increase the limit on the work week from 44 to 46 hours in negotiation with the workers' unions. Local, company-specific deals would have taken precedence over industry-wide collective agreements. The main argument of the government was that such changes would decrease the more than 10 percent unemployment in France itself. Extremely strong workers' resistance, with violent demonstrations, followed and blocked the road for radical reforms for weeks. Although railroad infrastructure and high-speed Internet availability elevate France to the 22nd spot in overall international competitiveness, the country still definitely might benefit from a more flexible labor market as it ranks only 127th.[70]

The new centrist president, Emmanuel Macron, elected in the spring of 2017, has declared he will start again reforming the labor market. France must climb 50 places to reach the top three nations worldwide. It certainly cannot compete with a Britain which successfully has destroyed its welfare system and belongs to the top three countries among the 35 OECD countries in competitiveness according to OECD ranking. The race to the bottom regarding labor market freedom is questionable if one considers that the World Economic Forum's ranking of the most competitive countries includes Sweden, Norway, and Finland at the top, all of which have strong employment protections, similar to France, thereby showing that winning foreign investment and creating jobs is more complex than just introducing labor market flexibility.[71]

Northwestern Europe in the early 21st century definitely adjusted to the strong neoliberal turn taken by its main rivals, the United States and China, and consequently it has regained its competitive edge. The region belongs to the most advanced part of the world. However, it tries to keep some balance between the competitive market system and the social market principles. Its income distribution is still the least unequal among advanced countries and its welfare institutions – undoubtedly with some major exceptions – are still offering some social safety net to everyone.

Questionable stability of the Northwest

May we consider the stability and development level of the Northwest as a "God-given" reality that will last forever? There are several factors that cast serious doubt on the positive answer. One is the demographic crisis of the region, its rapidly aging and shrinking population; another, the partly related diminution of its labor force. For half a century the population consistently has failed to reproduce at a replacement rate. Moreover, the traditional retirement age has become obsolete in face of significantly increased lifespans. In the United States and Japan, people live on average about 10 years in retirement; in France 19, in Italy, Belgium, and the Netherlands, 17–18 years.

In the second half of the 20th century, immigration compensated for the decreasing domestic labor force, but during the 2010s, immigration itself became a major problem, generating strong resistance and political turmoil. Can Europe handle this problem well? Can it defend its borders and return to controlled and regulated immigration? The pressures coming from the 60 million people uprooted all over the world because of climatic change and local civil wars may exaggerate this problem, making it more acute and even more dangerous.

Several of the region's countries have numberless unsolved problems. Germany is overly dependent on exports while world competition is wildly increasing. France is suffering long-term slow development and high unemployment. Its labor market laws and regulations are too rigid and counterproductive. The country's market share sharply decreased, from 6.3 percent to 4.8 percent, in a single decade before the 2008 crisis. It has an oversized bureaucracy that consumes more than half of the governments' expenditures. Higher education throughout Europe is behind that in the United States. There is not a single university from the continent among the 50 best universities defined by international ranking of the world. The European integration process, especially the monetary unification, is unfinished and, as the 2008 crisis proved, creates severe obstacles to further development. Going ahead with further integration, however, is politically more and more questionable.

Political opposition against integration is strong. Even though the populist-nationalist parties failed to break through in the series of 2017 elections, in some countries, such as the Netherlands, France, and Germany, they nevertheless emerged stronger and are dangerously active everywhere. Brexit is clearly signaling still-existing potential appeal of the populists. The new trend of state-led economic development and policy, the revitalized authoritarian tendencies and attacks against democracy, the rise of a "post-truth" era, as the American elections in 2016 clearly have demonstrated, are together immense dangers for the entire Western world. Fareed Zakaria identified a new frightening political trend, "illiberal democracy" already in his 1997 essay in *Foreign Affairs*: "From Peru to the Palestinian Authority," he stated, "from Sierra Leone to Slovakia, from Pakistan to the Philippines, we see the rise of a disturbing phenomenon in international life – illiberal democracy."[72] This danger has become much more visible, more realistic and more frightening. It is already very present in Central and Eastern Europe, is trying to dominate in the United States and appeared – also only in opposition – in some West European countries during the 2010s. In other words, keeping stability and international standards requires unrelenting struggle, further reforms, actions, integration, thus everyday political success.

The Northwest region is the heart of Europe and the leader of integration. The dramatic 2008 economic crisis, which shocked the common currency and the entire integration process, fueled the rise of populist-nationalist attacks against free trade, free movement of people, and against European integration. The socio-economic factors that created the hot bed for the populist opposition and refueled nationalism are still present all over Europe.

The international political environment has also changed by the American presidential elections in November 2016 and the Donald J. Trump presidency.

During the early 2017 NATO and G-7 meetings, European leaders learned that a chapter of Western cooperation is closing and that they now must take their destiny into their own hands. With German leadership and – after the French elections in the spring of 2017 – strong French participation and even initiative, the renewal of the integration process has again become a realistic hope. The EU, already during the crisis years, started strengthening the eurozone's common institutions. The first step, correcting the mistake of monetary unification without fiscal unification, already has been progressing. The region's strong and stale leading countries are focusing now on banking union, energy union, capital union and even strengthening political and military ties, but still the Northwest EU members have far to go to incorporate the bitter lessons of crisis years into their current policy prescriptions. One cannot exclude important further steps, such as creating a stronger and deeper European self-defense plan to reduce reliance on United States-backed NATO.

The balance between the possibilities of disintegration or further integration, which was shifted toward disintegration during the early 2010s, now is starting to move toward further integration, at least within the eurozone. Integration played a central role in Northwestern Europe's stabilization and elevation already during the second half of the 20th century, and additional steps in this direction may further strengthen the region. The leading role of the region in Europe thus may become stronger in the 21st century. Moreover, as already has been proven, a strengthening Northwest will produce further positive developments in other less or somewhat less developed EU regions.

Notes

1 Investopedia, "The World's Top 10 Economies," www.investopedia.com/articles/investing/022415/worlds-top-10-economies.asp#ixzz4hqXcTPr6, accessed June 27, 2016; The World Economic Forum, "The 4 Europes: The Competitiveness Divide in Europe," June 22, 2012, www.weforum.org/agenda/2012/06/ranking-the-top-most-competitive-economies-in-europe-2012/.

2 World Economic Forum report, www.businessinsider.com/wef-ranking-of-best-school-systems-in-the-world-2016–20, November 18, 2016.

3 Paul J.J. Welfens, "International Effects of German Unification," *Intereconomics* 26 (January/February 1991), p. 12, link.springer.com/article/10.1007/BF02928890.

4 Archive of European Integration, "The German Economy after Unification: Domestic and European Aspects," The Directorate-General for Economic and Financial Affairs, Commission of the European Communities, Economic Papers, Number 91, April 1, 1992, pp. 6, 11, 13–14, aei.pitt.edu/36998/1/A3033.pdf.

5 *Der Spiegel Online*, July 1, 2010; Jennifer Hunt, "The Economics of German Reunification", February 2006, www.rci.rutgers.edu/~jah357/Hunt/Transition_files/german_unification.pdf; Stephen Padgett, William E. Paterson, and Reimut Zohlnhöfer, *Developments in German Politics*, New York: Palgrave Macmillan, 2012; Simon Green, Dan Hough, and Alister Miskimmon, *The Politics of the New Germany*, London and New York, 2012; "Depopulation in Germany: Germany Is Running out of People, Starting in the East," *The Economist*, April 15, 2017.

6 Franz-Josef Meiers, *Germany's Role in the Euro Crisis: Berlin's Quest for a More Perfect Monetary Union*, Cham, Switzerland: Springer International Publishing, 2015, p. 15.
7 Ibid., pp. v–vi.
8 Ibid., p. 25.
9 Reported by the United States National Science Board. For this report, see European Union, "Europe's Competitive Technology Profile in the Globalised Knowledge Economy," Innovation Union, Competitiveness Papers, no. 3 (2013), https://ec.europa.eu/research/innovation-union/pdf/europe_competitive_technology_profile.pdf, accessed October 2, 2017.
10 Ibid.
11 EU, European Commission, "R & D Expenditure," ec.europa.eu/eurostat/statistics-explained/index.php/R_%26_D_expenditure, February 8, 2017,
12 https://ec.europa.eu/research/innovation-union/pdf/state-of-the-union/2012/innovation_union_progress_at_country_level_2013.pdf, July 1, 2011.
13 "Europe Loses Ground in Global High-Tech Race," *Financial Times*, February 19, 2014.
14 Badenhausen, Kurt, "Best Countries for Business 2019: Behind the Numbers," *Forbes*, December 19, 2018, www.forbes.com/sites/kurtbadenhausen/2018/12/19/best-countries-for-business-2019-behind-the-numbers/#6c674786161c, accessed July 20, 2019.
15 Donald McNeill, *New Europe: Imagined Spaces* (London: Routledge, 2014), p. 158.
16 Amber Engineering, "Engineering at Its Best. 50 Years, 800 Projects, 25 Countries, 5 Continents," https://ambergengineering.com/fileadmin/user_upload/amberg-engineering/brochures/001_COMPANY_BROCHURE_En.pdf, accessed January 7, 2018.
17 Association of American Railroads, "Rail Traffic Data," www.aar.org/data-center/rail-traffic-data/, accessed June 22, 2017.
18 data.worldbank.org/indicator/IS.RRS.TOTL.KM.
19 European Union, European Commission, "Road Safety: European Commission Sets Out Next Steps Towards "Vision Zero" Including Key Performance Indicators," June 19, 2019, ec.europa.eu; Oliver Heneric, Georg Licht, and Wolfgang Sofka (eds.), *Europe's Automotive Industry on the Move: Competitiveness in a Changing World*, Mannheim: Physica Verlag, 2004, p. 177.
20 Masahisa Fujita, Paul Krugman, and Anthony Venables, *The Spatial Economy: Cities, Regions, and International Trade*, Cambridge, MA: MIT Press, 1999.
21 "Globalization's Losers and Left-Behind Places," *The Economist*, October 21, 2017.
22 See Ferenc Jánossy, *The End of the Economic Miracle: Appearance and Reality in Economic Development*, London: Routledge, [1971] 2016.
23 Ivan T. Berend, *Europe since 1980*, Cambridge: Cambridge University Press, 2010, pp. 177–178; *OECD Factbook: Economic, Environmental and Social Statistics*, Paris: OECD, 2007, p. 149.
24 United Nations, *From the Common Market to EC92: Regional Economic Integration in the European Community and Transnational Corporations*. New York: UN, 1993, pp. 40, 41; Andrew Cox and Glyn Watson, "The European Community and the Restructuring of Europe's National Champions," in Jack Hayward (ed.), *Industrial Enterprise and European Integration: From National to International Champions in Western Europe*, Oxford: Oxford University Press, 1995, pp. 322, 324, 327; Neil Fligstein,

Euro-Clash, The EU, European Identity and the Future of Europe, Oxford: Oxford University Press, 2008, pp. 84–85.

25 Wayne Sandholtz, *High-Tech Europe: The Politics of International Cooperation*, Berkeley: University of California Press, 1992, pp. 100–102.

26 "Facing Threat from China, Europe's Two Largest Train Makers Will Merge," *New York Times*, September 28, 2017.

27 A recent study of the European economy since the collapse emphasizes the importance of integration to the postrecession European revival. See EBC Working Group of Global Value Chains, "The Impact of Global Value Chains on the Euro Area Economy," Occasional Papers, European Central Bank, April 2019, www.ecb.europa.eu/pub/pdf/scpops/ecb.op221~38185e6936.en.pdf, accessed January 5, 2018.

> Internationalization of production and, more specifically, a higher degree of vertical integration into global value chains provided in recent years critical stimulus to the European economy. First, it fostered an industrial restructuring both across the European economies … which allowed European firms to vertically specialize in those activities in which they have a comparative advantage.

28 Angus Maddison, *Explaining the Economic Performance of Nations: Essays in Time and Space*, Aldershot: Edward Elgar, 1995, pp. 144–149, 154–155, 185–186.

29 European Commission, "EU Energy in Figures. Statistical Pocketbook 2017," https://ec.europa.eu/energy/sites/ener/files/documents/pocketbook_energy_2017_web.pdf, accessed February 7, 2018..

30 "Europe's Last Coal Mines Struggle for Lifelines," *Politico*, May 10, 2016, www.politico.eu/article/europe-chokes-on-coal/; André Mommen, *The Belgian Economy in the Twentieth Century*, London: Routledge, 1994.

31 Eurostat, ec.europa.eu/eurostat/statistics-explained/index.php/Renewable_energy_statistics; European Union, European Commission, COM (2012) 271 Final, ec.europa.eu/energy/en/topics/renewable-energy, accessed July 31, 2014.

32 "How Many People Work in Agriculture in the European Union," EU Agricultural Economic Briefs, No. 8, July 2013, https://ec.europa.eu/info/sites/info/files/food-farming-fisheries/farming/documents/agri-economics-brief-08_en.pdf, accessed March 17, 2017.

33 Daniel Bell, *The Coming of Post-Industrial Society*, New York: Harper Colophon Books, 1974.

34 International Monetary Fund, "Deindustrialization – Its Causes and Implications," www.imf.org/external/pubs/ft/wp/wp9742.pdf; International Monetary Fund, www.imf.org/EXTERNAL/PUBS/FT/ISSUES10/INDEX.HTM; *The Economist, Pocket World in Figures 2017*, 1 September 2016, London: The Economist.

35 OECD, *Historical Statistics, 1970–1999*, Paris: OECD, 2000, p. 63; *The Economist, Pocket World in Figures 2015*, 1 September 2014, London: The Economist.

36 Tejvan Pettinger, "The Great Recession 2008–13," December 2, 2019, www.economicshelp.org.

37 See Zsolt Darvas and Jacob von Weizsäcker, "Financial Transaction Tax: Small Is Beautiful," *Society and Economy in Central and Eastern Europe* 33, no. 3 (December 2012): 452; Mark Rupert, *Ideologies of Globalization. Contending Visions of a New World Order*, London: Routledge, 2000, p. 79; Kevin Philips, *Bad Money, Reckless Finance,*

Failed Politics and the Global Crisis of American Capitalism, New York: Penguin Books, 2008.

38 Mervin Lewis and Kevin T. Davis, *Domestic and International Banking*, Boston: MIT Press, 1987, pp. 266, 269.

39 *The Economist: Pocket World in Figures 2015*, p. 64.

40 Archive of European Integration, "The Development of a European Capital Market: Report of a Group of Experts Appointed by the EEC Commission," November 1966, pp. 39, 46.

41 Deutsche Bank, *Annual Report*, 2013, www.db.com/ir/en/content/reports_2013.htm; www.bnparibas.com/en; *European Banking Sector: Facts and Figures*, 2012. London: The Economist, September 1, 2011.

42 *Supply Chain Standard Magazine* (December 2008), 46.

43 www.thyssenkrupp.com/.

44 ECSIP Consortium, "Study on the Competitiveness of the Electrical and Electronic Engineering Industry," Final Report. Munich, December 18, 2013.

45 The EU's overall EEI production as of 2013 was mostly sold on the European markets but had gained share in international trade, from 13 percent to 16 percent, between the 1990s and 2010s, while the United States and Japan had suffered major losses; see note 44.

46 See note 44.

47 *New Economy: The German Perspective*, *RWI Schriften*, Heft 70, Essen: Rheinisch-Westfalisches Institut für Wirtschaftsforschungen, 2003, pp. 60, 82–83.

48 Archive of European Integration, "Commission Statement on the European Automobile Industry, Structure and Prospects of the European Car Industry," 1981, pp. 4, 28, 29, 33, 39, 42–44, 50; Commission Communication to the Council, "COM (81) 317 Final," presented on June 16, 1981.

49 Archive of European Integration, "The Future of the Community's Car Industry," Commission of the European Communities, Brussels, SEC (76) 4407 Final, 17 December 1976.

50 Stefan Schmid and Philipp Grosche, "Managing the International Value Chain in the Automotive Industry," *Bertelsmann Stiftung*, 16, www.bertelsmann-stiftung.de/fileadmin/system/flexpaper/rsmbstpublications/download_file/3424/3424_1.pdf.

51 Leon R. Domansky, *Automobile Industry, Current Issues*, New York: Novinka Book, 2006, p. 51; European Commission, //ec.europa.eu/growth/sectors/chemicals_en.

52 The German Chemical Industry, www.gtai.de/GTAI/Content/EN/Invest/_SharedDocs/Download/GTA/branches//Industries/the-german-chemical.industry.pdf.2v=4, January 5, 2017.

53 Ibid.

54 Archive of European Integration, "Second Report from the Commission to the Council and the European Parliament on the State of Liberalization of the Energy Market," COM (99) 198 Final, May 4, 1999, pp. 3, 5.

55 Archive of European Integration, "Green Paper on Vertical Restrains in EC Competition Policy," COM (96) 721 Final, January 22, 1997; Archive of European Integration, "Economic Reform: Report on the Functioning of Community Product and Capital Market," presented by the Commission in response to the conclusions of the Cardiff European Council, COM (99) 10 Final, January 20, 1999.

56 www.carrefour.com/content/carrefour-stores-worldwide, accessed December 2015; "Carrefour of France in Deal to Buy 127 Malls," *New York Times*, December 17, 2013; Alan M. Rugman and Simon Collinson, "Multinational Empires in the New Europe: Are They Really Global?," https://core.ac.uk.download/files/153/7080947.PDF.

57 *BBC News Magazine*, September 9, 2013; *Telegraph*, January 1, 2015.

58 www.metrogroup.de/en/company/history.

59 Ivan T. Berend, *Europe in Crisis: Bolt from the Blue?* London: Routledge, 2013, 140; Martin Bronfenbrenner (ed.), *Is the Business Cycle Obsolete?*, New York: Wiley, 1969; Robert E. Lucas Jr., "Macroeconomic Priorities," Presidential address at the annual meeting of the American Economic Association, January 10, 2003, https://citeseerx.ist.psu.edu/viewdoc/summary?doi=10.1.1.366.2404&rank=1

60 *The Economist*, June 16, 2005. House prices increased only by 18 percent and 38 percent in Germany and the Netherlands, respectively.

61 *Spiegel Online*, November 4, 2008.

62 European Union, European Commission, Economic and Financial Affairs, *Economic Crisis in Europe: Causes, Consequences and Responses*, European Economy, 7/2009, Luxembourg: Office for Official Publications of the European Community, 2009, p. 14.

63 Ibid., p. 13.

64 European Commission, "Interim EPC-SPC, Joint Report on Pensions," Brussels, 31/05/2010, ARES save number(2010)221924 – REV, https://ec.europa.eu/social/main.jsp?catId=860&langId=en, accessed December 25, 2019.

65 OECD, "Quarterly National Accounts: Quarterly Growth Rates of Real GDP," http://states.oecd.org/index.aspx?queryid=350.

66 "Von der Krise in den Absturz? Stabilisierung, Umbau, Demokratisierung," Arbeitsgruppe Alternative Wirtschaftspolitik, Memorandum 2009, Köln: PapyRossa Verlag, 2009, pp. 16, 27–28.

67 *The Economist, Pocket World in Figures 2017*.

68 "Von der Krise in den Absturz?," pp. 25, 26, 75; Joachim Möller, "Hartz IV and the Consequences: Did the Labor Market Reform Destroy the German Model?" doku.iab.de/veranstaltungen/2014/ws_transformation_2014_moeller.pdf, February 14, 2014; Sebastian Dullien, "German Reforms as Blueprint for Europe?," www.ecfr.eu/publications/summary/a_german_model_for_europe210, July 1, 2013.

69 Timo Fleckenstein and Soohyun Christine Lee, "The Politics of Labor Market Reform in Coordinated Welfare Capitalism: Comparing Sweden, Germany and South Korea," London School of Economics Research Online, eprints.Ise.ac.uk/68210/1/Fleckenstein_Politics%20of%20labor%20market 2016.pdf.

70 "Labor Market Reform in France: Ideology vs. Efficiency," July 19, 2016, www.dw.com/en/labor-market-reform-in-france-ideology-vs-efficiency/a-19408362, accessed June 7, 2017.

71 "Why Have France's Labour Reforms Proved So Vontentious?," *The Guardian*, May 26, 2016; "France Opts for Big over Small with Its Labour Reforms," *Financial Times*, March 20, 2016.

72 Fareed Zakaria, "The Rise of Illiberal Democracy," *Foreign Affairs* (November/December 1997), pp. 22–43.

5 The Mediterranean-Irish region

Catching up with the West but burdened with remnants of a peripheral past

The half-circle of countries bounding the advanced Northwest – Ireland, Portugal, Spain, Italy, and Greece – together constitute a separate region, defined less by geography than by the similarities in the history of their economic development. These are countries which, in the early 21st century, enjoyed an average per capita income level ($31,198) that situated them among the top 20 percent of the world's countries; in other words, in the high-income zone, defined as average per capita income exceeding $20,000. From this point of view, it might seem that these countries should be categorized with the countries of the European Northwest. But there are several reasons that invalidate such a classification, not least the fact that the income level of these five countries in 2016 was only 63.3 percent of the West's $49,317 average. The most decisive reason for assigning them to a separate group is a history-grounded one.

Despite stark differences and eminent position in their pre-modern histories, all the countries of this region, unlike those of the Northwest, have the shared experience of being peripheral, relatively backward, middle-income places in the 18th, 19th and even first half of the 20th centuries. They did not cross over into the high-income category until the second half of the 20th century. Their relative catch-up with the Northwest, therefore, has been quite recent. This historical difference with respect to the Northwest, this *nouveau riche* status, means that the countries even today still are shouldering several of the social-cultural features and hidden economic weaknesses of their peripheral past.

Middle-income peripheral level until the mid-20th century

The countries of the peripheral ring around Northwestern Europe were unable to follow the path of their increasingly prosperous Northwestern neighbors in early modern times. Rather than experiencing revolutionary developments, for example, most of these countries (Greece excepted) remained under the arch-conservative dominance of the Roman Catholic Church. They adopted neither the new modes of behavior and thinking of the 16th-century Protestant Reformation nor the 18th-century enlightened concepts of society, state, science, and economy. Again, unlike the Northwest, they preserved the increasingly obsolete traditions of agrarian economies, along with their social structures, until well into the 20th century. The Industrial Revolution passed them by and only some scattered modernization elements slowly appeared. Meanwhile the needs of the nearby industrializing Northwest for imports of food and raw material, created a "pull effect," essentially discouraging these ring countries from developing new economic sectors or reforming old ones.

World trade increased 50-fold between 1850 and 1913 but, well before the impact of these increases could be experienced firsthand, the Italian Camille Cavour, prime minister of Piedmont and one of the initiators of Italian unification, recognized the potential for substantial change. In 1845 he stated:

> The commercial revolution which is now taking place in England … will have a mighty impact on the continent. By opening up the richest market in the world to foodstuffs, it will encourage their production. … The need to provide for regular foreign demand will arouse the energy of these agricultural industries. … Trade will then become an essential element in the prosperity of the agrarian classes who will then naturally tend to join the supporters of the liberal system. The producers of primary materials will come to hold the same position in relation to our monopolist manufacturers as the English industrial classes hold in relation to the landowners.[1]

Indeed, the West was ready to invest to develop agriculture and raw material extraction in the Mediterranean world, and also to build railways to deliver Mediterranean products to Western markets. The less-developed Mediterranean also offered cheap labor and huge markets for Western industrial products. The resulting exchanges sparked some industrial development in the Mediterranean countries, as well as the modernization of their transportation and agriculture during the later decades of the 19th century.

Ireland offers a good example. Part of Britain until 1922, Ireland lost half of its population in 19th-century Europe, due to a combination of crop failures, famines, and mass emigration. The country's cottage industry was destroyed by the arrival of the revolutionized-mechanized English textile industry. The Irish became the cheap labor force for rapidly industrializing England. The English financed modern rail transportation, which encouraged the mass export of food and the establishment of a food processing industry, especially for beer and whisky to be sold on the English market. An agricultural sector developed slowly, along with some industrialization, particularly ship building.

A radical mid-19th-century series of events changed the course of history in the Italian peninsula. Austrian and French occupation of several Northern and Central areas ended and then, between 1860 and 1870, a new political entity was created from the union of all the small, formerly sovereign states of the peninsula. Despite newfound unity, harsh social, cultural, and economic divisions persisted. The Italian North, bordering the heart of Western Europe and virtually a part of it for centuries, was, as always, the most developed Italian region. The mid-peninsula and especially the south and Sicily retained their traditional, deep-rooted, socioeconomic backwardness. The middle-income level of united

Italy was merely a statistical artifact, a meaningless *average*. (Statistics always work with averages, but the average, of course, is but an abstraction seldom existing in the real world.)

Spain in its early modern condition of backwardness had a few advanced economic pockets along its coasts. In the Basque region, a major, iron-based export sector developed. British investment increased the extraction of iron-ore from the resource-rich region, and even spawned a modern iron industry. In Valencia, on the Mediterranean coast, and soon in other coastal areas, modern export-oriented citrus, olive, and grape cultivation developed with the European Northwest as its target market. To the north and east, still on the Mediterranean coast, Catalonia added textile production to its wine and olive oil industries, all of which produced for the large Spanish domestic market. With the exception of these advanced pockets, most of the Spanish Iberian peninsula remained frozen in the past in a very backward state.

The weakest countries of the Mediterranean region, Greece and Portugal, remained far behind all the others. Industrialization did not start at all and income level, compared to Ireland, Italy, and Spain, remained at roughly two-thirds in Greece and half in Portugal.

In general, the Mediterranean-Irish region existed basically at a peripheral level, belonging to a similar category as Central Europe, although with country-by-country differences. Ireland and North Italy were more developed than the Central European region; South Italy, Greece, and Portugal, less so.

As Table 5.1 shows, by the early 20th century, slow and partial economic development had elevated this region to a middle-income level position, but with average income at just a little more than half the Western level, it still lagged far behind. This middle-income level hardly changed until the mid-20th century.

As Table 5.2 shows, by 1950 the Mediterranean-Irish region had increased its income level by 28 percent from its 1913 level, but not by as much as developed Northwestern Europe had, at 38 percent. Thus, despite income improvements, by comparison with Northwestern Europe the Mediterranean-Irish region had

Table 5.1 Income level of the region in 1913 (in constant 1990 Geary-Khamish $)

Country	*Per capita GDP*	*% of Western Europe*
Region's average	2,094	56.5
Ireland	2,733	74
Italy	2,507	67
Spain	2,255	61
Greece	1,621	44
Portugal	1,354	36
Western Europe	3,704	100

Source: Based on Angus Maddison, *Monitoring the World Economy, 1920–1992*, Paris: OECD, 1995.

Table 5.2 Income level of the region in 1950 (in constant 1990 Geary-Khamish $)

Country	*Per capita GDP*	*% increase since 1913*	*% of the West*
Ireland	3,518	29	68
Italy	3,425	36	67
Spain	2,397	−6	47
Greece	1,951	20	38
Portugal	2,132	57	41
Region's average	2,685	28	52.3
Western Europe	5,126	38	100

Source: Based on Angus Maddison, *Monitoring the World Economy, 1920–1992*, Paris: OECD, 1995.

Table 5.3 Income level of the region in 1973 (in constant 1990 Geary-Khamish $)

Country	*Per capita GDP*	*% increase since 1950*	*% of the West*
Ireland	7,023	199	35
Italy	10,409	304	52
Spain	8,739	364	44
Greece	7,799	399	39
Portugal	7,568	355	38
Region's average	8,307	309	42
Western Europe	19,837	387	100

Source: Based on Angus Maddison, *Monitoring the World Economy, 1920–1992*, Paris: OECD, 1995.

slipped further behind during the first half of the 20th century; its income level decreased from 56.5 percent of the Western average to 52.3 percent. Only Italy preserved its relative position. All of the other countries became more backward as compared to the West, especially Spain, which did not increase its income level at all.

After 1950, a new chapter in the history of the region opened and prosperous decades followed until 1973. All European countries significantly increased their income levels. As Table 5.3 demonstrates, the Mediterranean-Irish region broke with historical precedent during this period by more than trebling its average per capita income level. Yet this very impressive growth was slower than in Northwestern Europe, where the per capital income level nearly quadrupled (387 percent increase). Consequently, once again, the relative backwardness of the Mediterranean-Irish region increased: the five countries average per capita income dropped from more than 52 percent of the West's in 1950 to less than 42 percent in 1973.

These three tables clearly show that the income level of the Mediterranean-Irish region never fell but rather elevated for six decades after 1913. Growth in the Northwest, however, was much faster, and so, in comparison with that region relative backwardness in the Mediterranean-Irish area steadily increased. This relative decline was even more pronounced if we consider patterns of relative growth over the two hundred years of the entire modern era. Around the end of the first Industrial Revolution in the 1820s, when Britain had emerged as the first industrial nation but Northwestern Europe as a whole had not yet started down the road of rapid development, the Irish, Italian, and Spanish average per capita income level – data on Greece and Portugal are not available – was only about 20 percent lower than the West. Were an estimate to be made for Greece and Portugal and then combined with the data on Ireland, Italy, and Spain, the gap might be as great as 40–45 percent. Consequently, relative decline over 200 years would be even more tragic, with the Mediterranean-Irish region falling from a level of 65–80 percent of the Northwestern average per capita income to little more than 40 percent. In the 1980s, however, this long and persistent pattern began giving way to something new; for the first time in history, growth in this less-developed region surpassed that in the West. A promising catching-up process was underway.

The rise of Ireland and the Mediterranean

From the 1980s, and then even more strikingly in the 1990s, economic growth and the standard of living of the population started booming. The average growth in each of the region's five countries surpassed the West's between 1973 and 2014. Ireland spectacularly increased its per capita income level by nearly eightfold, all the others between nearly threefold and almost 3.5-fold. The region's average fourfold economic growth was twice as fast as the West's average of less than twofold.

On that foundation the level of consumption and the quality of life, expressed by the significant increase of the average lifespan, elevated to levels never before experienced in the Mediterranean-Irish region and a consumer society emerged. The change became evident between 1985 and 1990, when the region's consumption began to increase by 4.2 percent per year, much faster than the West's average 3.3 percent.[2] In contrast, between 1980 and 1984 the region's increase had been by a mere 0.7 percent per annum, roughly half of the West's 1.3 percent, and less than the 1.2 percent European average. In another key development, by 2006–2007, private home-ownership reached 80 percent in the formerly poor countries of Ireland, Spain, Portugal, and Greece, surpassing the levels in the United States (67 percent) and in Switzerland and Germany (50–60 percent). Car ownership became widespread. Using Italy's example: in 1950 every 1,000 families owned 7.5 cars, but around the end of the century, this number had increased by 40-fold and, on average, 1,000 inhabitants owned about 350 cars, one per family. Life expectancy at birth in 1950 was 4.5 years shorter in the Mediterranean (62.98 years) than in the Northwest (67.43 years), but by 2005 it was the same in both regions (approaching 80 years).[3] Not all countries shared an equally spectacular rise, but all of them elevated substantially.

Table 5.4 Increase of the per capita GDP, 1973–2014

Countries		*1973*	*1998*	*2014*
Ireland		6,867	18,867	53,648
	%	100	265	781
Italy		10,643	17,759	35,825
	%	100	167	336
Spain		8,739	14,227	29,908
	%	100	163	342
Portugal		7,343	12,929	22,157
	%	100	176	301
Greece		7,655	11,268	21,448
	%	100	147	280
The five countries together[a]		41,247	75,050	162,986
	%	100	182	395
Western Europe[b]		307,754	456,502	582,575
	%	100	155	189

Sources: Based on Angus Maddison, *Monitoring the World Economy, 1920–1992*, Paris: OECD, 1995; see also *The Economist: Pocket World in Figures 2017*, London: Profile Books, 2017.

Notes:
a 5 countries unweighted average.
b 11 countries unweighted average.

What caused this historic change? Why did a region, which consistently had lost ground in competition with the Northwest from the early 19th century until the last quarter of the 20th century, shift gears and start catching up with the West? What factors generated this new phenomenon?

While each of the region's countries had special and unique dynamics, they all operated within the general framework of the so-called "second globalization"; the resumption, that is, of trends of the late 19th and early 20th centuries that had been brought to a halt during the two world wars and the interwar period of economic nationalism. This renewed globalization took root along with the reconstruction of the free trade system, also after World War II. In the later 1940s, as the Cold War was beginning, the Bretton Woods Agreement established an international monetary system and its basic institutions, the International Monetary Fund (IMF) and the World Bank. The General Agreement of Trade and Tariffs (GATT) also contributed to this new international economy system. In the context of sharp Cold War divisions and unquestioned American leadership of the "free Western world," the political will to end national isolation, tariff wars, attempts at national self-sufficiency, and endless economic warfare in the "West" was uniquely strong.

The renewed commitment to globalization, accompanied by the destruction of tariff barriers and other road blocks inhibiting free trade and the free flow of capital, worked hand in hand with incipient West European integration: in the 1950s the creation by six West European countries of the European Coal and Steel Community and then the European Economic Community. Both forms of integration have been repeatedly altered and strengthened since the 1970s. Especially after the collapse of the Soviet Bloc and the Soviet Union itself in 1989–1991, globalization became dominant, helped along by deregulation, and the elimination of various restrictions and controls that stopped or at least significantly slowed down international trade, capital flows, and transnational business. Multinational companies mushroomed from 7,000 to about 80,000 in half a century.

A parallel revolution in communication and transportation technologies, which produced new communication networks, fast trains and larger, lighter-weight planes, plus new shipping containers and ways of managing them, supported the internationalization of business. The "computer age," robotization and new modes of energy production ended the age of coal and the dominance of the economies that had been established during the two industrial revolutions of the late 17th to early 20th centuries. Technological innovation joined with the 20th-century postwar political will to make globalization successful.

In the global competition the world technology and economic leaders, the United States and Japan not only overwhelmingly dominated non-European markets but also successfully occupied huge slices of the European market itself. Economic integration in Europe had been stagnating since the late 1960s, due to the end of the postwar construction boom and the onset of the crises of the 1970s (signaled by two oil crises in 1973 and 1979–1980). By the 1980s, however, in face of the ominous prospect of losing ground to the United States and Japan and of experiencing even more relative decline, Western European leaders renewed their efforts to advance integration. In 1985, the Single Europe, Single Market initiative opened a new phase, based on regionalization. This led to the creation of a 500-million-strong European domestic market, with free flow of goods, capital and people. From the turn of the millennium, integration received another boost with the introduction of a common currency, the euro, soon used by 19 of the countries of the EU. European trade flourished. Europe also followed the neoliberal turn by eliminating several regulations and rules in order to allow undisturbed economic growth, even though this introduced greater risk.

The expansion of the "European unit" by the addition of new member countries provided a strong impetus for growth. Stagnation ended, a new growth trend took hold, and Europe became competitive again. This is the broad framework in which the five countries of the Mediterranean-Irish region, although each in unique circumstances, entered a nevertheless common, new chapter of history, marked by fast growth, catching up to the West and arrival at the threshold of the high-income level enjoyed by the world's most advanced nations.

The Irish miracle

Ireland offers the most spectacular example of the process that unfolded across this region; in the early 21st century, the world was stunned by its sudden change.[4] "Fifteen years ago," *The Economist* wrote in 2004:

> Ireland was deemed an economic failure, a country that after years of mismanagement was suffering from an awful cocktail of high unemployment, slow growth, high inflation, heavy taxation and towering public debts. Yet within a few years it had become the "Celtic Tiger," a rare example of a developed country with a growth record to match East Asia's ... It goes to show how remarkable has been the transformation of a sleepy European backwater into a vibrant economy that in some years grew by as much as 10%.[5]

Two years later, a Heritage Foundation analysis added:

> In just over a generation, Ireland has evolved from one of the poorest countries in Western Europe to one of the most successful. ... As a result of sustained efforts over many years, the past of declining population, poor living standards, and economic stagnation has been left behind. Ireland now has the second highest gross domestic product (GDP) per capita within the European Union (after Luxembourg), one-third higher than the EU-25 average, and has achieved exceptional growth.[6]

The transformation of the country was indeed not less than miraculous. Ireland's 19th-century history had been disastrous, as I have noted earlier in this chapter. Next to, and actually politically part of, the world's fastest-rising and richest industrial power, Britain, the backward agricultural country had suffered devastating famine, mass death, and emigration. Ireland's most important export item was its people. In a century during which Europe's population trebled, Ireland's sharply declined. From 1922, the newly independent Irish Republic, as most other countries in the Europe of that era, turned to economic nationalism, even blocked investments from abroad. In 1928, the income level of the country was the same as in 1913, and by 1938, only 14 percent higher.

The destiny of the country did not change after independence. People continued to emigrate, *en masse*: in the single decade of the 1950s, 400,000 people, one-seventh of the population, moved out of the country. By 1960 the population had sunk to 2.8 million, from its high point of 8 million in 1840. The Heritage Foundation noted:

> the feeling of failure in the 1970s–80s was exacerbated by the waves of emigration of young people, just as in a generation earlier. Whole classes of university graduates would frequently leave the country. There was

> a disheartening drain of human capital. A net 200,000 people left from 1981 to 1990. In the worst years, more than 1 percent of the country's population fled.[7]

After decades of failed economic nationalism, a new Irish government embraced free trade and in 1965 signed its first such agreement with Britain. By 1970, the island country had become home to more than 350 foreign, mostly American, companies. The real turning point, however, must be dated to 1973, the year Ireland joined the European Economic Community. But, because Europe just then was entering a long period of economic crisis and stagnation, the positive potential of the Irish decision did not become apparent until the early 1990s. Between 1982 and 1987, economic growth in Ireland averaged only 0.2 percent per annum and in three years of that period GDP actually declined. Unemployment mounted to 18 percent of the workforce, and the national debt elevated to 125 percent of GDP.[8] A positive turn would not occur until the mid-1990s.

The road toward that change, however, had been paved even before the crises of the 1970s set in, when Ireland instituted the internal reforms, especially in education, which laid the groundwork for its later successes. These reforms began in 1967, when the state started covering all secondary schooling expenses, including transportation to school. The OECD educational report of 2013 summed up the results: 38 percent of 25- to 34-year-olds now had an upper secondary education as the highest level of attainment, and 47 percent had tertiary (university) qualifications. In contrast, in tertiary education, the OECD average was only 39 percent, and Ireland ranked only behind Canada, Japan, and South Korea.

Strong focusing to education became a permanent policy. Between 2005 and 2010 educational expenditure per student rose by 33 percent, nearly twice the OECD average of 17 percent. The total cumulative expenditure per student by educational institutions in 2010 reached nearly US$129,000, while the OECD average was $106,000. In this respect, only Denmark, Luxembourg, and Norway surpassed Ireland. By 2010, the number of students at tertiary level was 9 percent greater and expenditure 28 percent more than in 2005. The cumulative expenditure per student by tertiary educational institutions amounted to $52,000, approaching the OECD average and far above medium-income level countries such as Hungary ($29,000) or Slovenia ($31,000).[9]

Antoin Murphy used the metaphor of the "movement of tectonic plates" to explain what happened in Ireland:

> Ireland's transformation was primarily caused by multi-nationals, was facilitated by the phenomenon of globalization and in particular the shifting closer together of two economic tectonic plates that of the United States and the European Union. Ireland, at the geographic periphery of the latter, but, as the closest European ethnic partner of the former ... has flourished, rather than been crushed, by the inner shifts of these economic plates. ...

> Globalization enabled Ireland to move from the periphery towards the center of the new global economy. ... Europeanisation has been a key element in the transformation of the Irish economy.[10]

By the end of the 20th century, Ireland, together with the United States and seven Northwestern European countries, belonged to the top ten mostinternationalized economies of the world.[11] The chapter of Ireland's economic miracle, a period of sustained fast growth and increasing employment, had opened in 1994. That was the year the term "Celtic Tiger" first was used. GDP growth averaged 8.4 percent in the six years between 1994 and 1999, while employment increased by over 390,000 and unemployment fell to 6 percent. The public sector deficit was replaced by a substantial surplus and the national debt/GDP ratio dropped below 60 percent, half what it had been in 1987.[12] Rapid East Asian–type growth of 7.4 percent per year continued between 1995 and 2005.[13]

Ireland, indeed, became the example *par excellence* of the potentially positive impact of two partly overlapping but also antagonistic trends: globalization and European regionalization. The realization of the EU Single Market in 1992 and the introduction of the common currency announced soon thereafter motivated companies from overseas, especially American high-tech multinationals, to rush to get a foot in the door of this huge new market by establishing companies in the EU.

Ireland offered outstanding opportunities. Its familiar English-speaking culture and environment, and its highly educated population assured foreign corporations a pool of adequately trained employees, while radical tax reductions created an exceptional, enticing business climate. Ireland quickly became a tax haven, with tax exemptions for capital gains and for corporate profits remitted from an Irish branch to foreign headquarters. Banking and insurance services were even exempted from Value Added Taxation (VAT).[14]

The OECD reported in 1999 that "US investment in Ireland tripled from 1991 to 1993, just at the time the Single European Market programme was being implemented." American direct investments in Ireland averaged about 2.75 percent of the country's GDP in the second half of the 1990s, 50 percent higher per capita than in Britain and six times higher than in France or Germany. In 1997, Ireland "ranked fifth in the world as a destination for US direct investment outflows. For some Americans Ireland has become the fifty first state."[15] One may not forget that because the large Irish emigration over centuries about 40 million American citizens consider themselves of Irish extraction.

A large group of multinational corporations, several of them from the high-tech sectors, founded companies in Ireland as export platforms for the EU. Many of them represented the computer industry, pharmaceuticals, medical technology and international services. Small wonder that already in the 1980s and 1990s exports were growing by 8.5 percent per year and Ireland was exhibiting the second fastest export growth in the world behind Japan, or that the share of the high-tech and semi-high-tech sectors elevated to 48 percent, while the share of traditional export sectors declined to 34 percent.[16]

The list of the multinational companies that settled in Ireland is long. Among them are Amdahl, Baxter Travenol, Digital, Merck Sharpe, Wang, Warner Lambert, Boston Scientific, Coca Cola, 3 Com, Dell, Gateway, IBM, Intel, Hewlett Packard, Macintosh, Microsoft, Motorola, Northern Telecom, Pepsi, Pfizer, and Schering Plough. Together with other foreign-owned companies they controlled 77 percent of Ireland net manufacturing output already in 1996. Before the end of the first decade of the new millennium 53 percent of the shares of companies in the country were in foreign hands (in contrast to the EU's average of 29 percent).[17] Twelve of *Fortune* magazine's top 20 electronic companies and all of its top ten pharmaceutical companies had plants in Ireland exporting to the European market.[18] Ireland also had become the world's second largest exporter of computer software after the United States.[19] Between 1990 and 2005, 800,000 new jobs had been created and the one-and-half-century trend of permanent mass emigration had been replaced by immigration: from 1996 to 2005 the population actually increased by 15 percent.

As an important outcome of the massive inflow of foreign investments in the most modern sectors, the Irish manufacturing industry exhibited the characteristic typical of a dual economy: in contrast with the foreign-owned high productivity, export-oriented, modern sectors, traditional Irish manufacturing sectors did not change much; they were not competitively productive and sold their product only in the domestic markets. This feature of the Irish economy, clear already in the 1990s, started changing very slowly in later decades.[20] What rarely happens in economic history occurred: the poorest country of Western Europe became the richest one over the span of a single generation. In 2016, Ireland ranked as the world's seventh richest country with a per capita GDP of more than $62,000. In the rich European Northwest, only Switzerland and Norway were richer. Moreover, Ireland also surpassed the United States (United States income level was a little over $59,000).

Catching up on the Mediterranean

The Mediterranean countries shared the Irish experience, but to a lesser degree. Despite some differences distinguishing their development from patterns in Ireland, the commonalities, linked to the effects of globalization and regionalization, and to membership in the European Union, were significant. Italy was actually a founding member of both the European Coal and Steel Community and the European Economic Community already in the 1950s, but until the mid-1970s, Greece, Spain, and Portugal were political pariahs, excluded from EU membership on account of their extreme rightwing dictatorial regimes. The logic of the Cold War, however, made these countries military allies of the United States and recipients of that country's financial aid. Successive American governments pushed the European Community to accept them, first as associates with binding trade agreements and then, as soon as possible, as full members. This happened for Greece in 1981 and for Spain and Portugal in 1986. For all of these countries, association with the EU brought rates of growth higher than in the European Northwest. And thus began their process of catching up with that advanced region.

Before the Mediterranean countries – Italy excepted – could hope to exploit the opportunities coming their way, they had some major political obstacles to overcome. Spain, in particular, was a political pariah. From the late 1930s until the mid-1970s, dictator Francisco Franco, an ally of Mussolini and Hitler, ruled the country. Consequently, the country was excluded from the Marshall Aid program and its political culture clashed with the European Community's values of freedom and democracy. Portugal, under the similarly extreme autocratic regime of António Salazar, an ally of Franco who took power by coup in 1932, was not much better situated. Greece, after two civil wars in the 1940s, was mostly ruled by rightwing dictatorial military juntas.

Cold War confrontation and the construction of an American alliance system somewhat counterbalanced these disadvantages. From 1947 President Truman began to assist Greece financially and militarily, and he included both Greece and Portugal in the Marshall Aid program. The next president of the United States, Dwight D. Eisenhower, clearly distinguished between communist and anticommunist dictatorships. The classic rhetoric against communist regimes was not used against autocratic, oppressive, anticommunist systems. Eisenhower indicated an acceptance of antidemocratic rule in the Iberian peninsula by saying that "dictatorships of this type are something necessary in countries whose political institutions are not so advanced as ours."[21] In the 1970s, President Nixon and his foreign policy guru, the pragmatic Henry Kissinger, cynically declared their lack of concern about human rights and domestic affairs in countries important for American foreign policy interests.[22]

The strategic importance of the Mediterranean led to the inclusion of Franco's Spain, Salazar's Portugal and junta-ruled Greece in the Western alliance system. Greece and Portugal became members of NATO. In 1953 the United States signed military and defense cooperation agreements with Spain and Greece. Franco received $62.5 million in American aid as early as 1950. Between 1953, when the United States-Spanish military agreement was signed, and 1961, Spain received another $1.4 billion in aid from the United States. In the first half of the 1980s $8 billion flowed into the country. Greece received $649 million in Marshall Aid and together with Turkey, another $400 million through the framework of the Truman Doctrine.

As the Congressional Research Service retrospectively registered, successive US administrations and several members of the US Congress urged the European Community to stabilize the military and political alliance (NATO) by including rightwing anticommunist dictatorships in the European integration process.[23] Encouraged by the United States, Franco's Spain indeed applied for membership in 1962. The European Community followed the American advice but disguised the betrayal of democratic values entailed in the untimely acceptance of Hitler's ally, by quietly signing a Preferential Commercial Agreement with

Spain. The agreement immediately reduced the EC's tariffs by 60 percent and declared the goal of progressing toward totally free trade. Greece had applied for EC membership in 1959, and along with Portugal, joined the European Community in the 1960s with "external member" status.

Subsequent experience in Spain shows the effects of EU connections.[24] A World Bank development plan of March 1961 and $420 million in stabilization aid contributed to drawing Spain out of its previous economic isolation. Between 1950 and 1970, the Franco regime received $2.5 billion in Western assistance. Western tourists started "invading" the Mediterranean countries, stimulating growth in Spain and Greece. Over four decades, *El País* reported in 2015, Spain's foreign tourist industry grew to become the second-biggest and most competitive in the world.[25] Even during the crisis of the 2010s, the country remained the world's third most-sought-after destination, with more than 75 million visitors. From about €40 billion in 2006, the industry increased to about €77 billion in 2016, nearly 11 percent of the country's GDP. It employed about 2 million people.[26] Spain ended its isolationist policy and its state-dictated corporative economic system, which Franco had copied from Mussolini's fascist Italy. Subsequent economic liberalization led to an impressive growth rate of around 5 percent per annum. During the 1970s, industrial output increased by nearly two-thirds and productivity by 76 percent, surpassing the British level. In the same decade, mechanization of agriculture progressed and productivity increased 6.5 times: output from agriculture, formerly the leading sector of the country, increased by nearly four times.[27] Western companies began taking steps to exploit the Spain's lower wage levels and subcontracted textile and clothing works to "bloody Taylorist sweatshops."[28] Multinational companies started establishing modern export capacities throughout the Iberian peninsula as well. By 1978, 72 percent of Spanish industrial exports were being sold on the European Community's market.

Portugal had a somewhat similar history in those years. As a member of the British-initiated free trade organization (EFTA) from 1960, it gained access to duty-free markets and aid that covered 40 percent of investments. In 1973 the country – via an EFTA agreement with the European Community – became an external member of the European Community market and half of its products were then sold duty-free in the Community. In 1975–1977, the country received roughly $2 billion in Western aid and loans. Capital inflow by 1979 amounted to $6 billion and Portugal's economic growth increased by an annual 25 percent over the preceding year.

The catching-up process in the Mediterranean region began in the second half of the 1960s. Between 1966 and 1973, Portugal's annual growth rate was 10.3 percent, Greece's 8.3 percent and Spain's 5.8 percent, while the Northwest's was only 4.6 percent. The process was propelled by the rapid increase of exports. Portuguese merchandise exports, for example, grew during the period 1959–73 at a notable 11 percent per annum. In 1960 the bulk of exports consisted of products such as canned fish, raw and manufactured cork, cotton textiles and wine. By contrast, in the early 1970s (before the 1974 military coup), the country's export list already showed significant product diversification, including in both consumer and capital goods. Several branches of Portuguese industry became export-oriented, and in 1973 over one-fifth of Portuguese manufactured output was being sent out of the country.[29]

In spite of these successes, "the rapid growth of the 1960s and early 1970s," an OECD analysis of 1991 maintained,

> masked the five weaknesses of the southern European countries' economic and social structures. These weaknesses became more visible in the wake of the first oil shock. EC membership and the opening up of markets that it brought with it forced the pace of structural adjustment.[30]

Indeed, the region's socioeconomic infrastructure, including technological level and educational systems, remained backward. The overall structure of the economy was a stage behind the Northwest. In 1980, agriculture still employed 30 percent and 19 percent of Greek and Spanish workforces, respectively, while services, an undeveloped sector throughout the region, accounted for 45 percent in Spain, 39 percent in Greece, and in Portugal, 36 percent. Financial markets – quoting again the 1991 OECD report – were "in their infancy."[31] Also traditional policies aimed at defending domestic markets continued almost until the end of the 1980s. Despite having opened its markets to Mediterranean countries' products, the European Community, for a transitory period, had not required reciprocity. Consequently, during that period, protected Mediterranean domestic markets had not adjusted to competition from the rest of Europe. In Greece, for example, structures of production and trade specialization remained unchanged.

All these weaknesses came to the surface after the two oil crises of the 1970s. Between 1973 and 1985 economic growth came to a halt: in the period 1973–1979 in Spain it was only 1.4 percent and in the period 1979–1985 it was 0.1 percent, compared to Greece (2.9 percent and 0.8 percent) and Portugal (0.8 percent and 0.0 percent), slower than the slowed down Western growth of 2.3 percent and 1.0 percent.[32] The OECD reported in 1991 that macroeconomic imbalances worsened during the 1980s, with unemployment in Spain rising to over 20 percent in 1984–1985. In Greece and Portugal, the annual rate of inflation in the first half of the 1980s was 21 percent and 24 percent, respectively, while the general government borrowing requirement was more than 10 percent of GDP. The current account deficit in Portugal was also one of the highest among the OECD countries, nearly 13 percent of the GDP in 1981 and 1982.

Still, radical changes had been set in motion in the region. The collapse of the Greek military junta after its Cyprus adventure in 1974, the death of Salazar followed by the military coup that destroyed his successor's dictatorial regime in the same year, and the death of Franco in November 1975, ended the era of oppressive dictatorships. A real democratization process followed. In the 1980s, as has already been noted, the newly democratic countries all joined the European Community as full members, Greece in 1981, and Spain and Portugal in 1986. By the mid-1980s, per capita income level (with Ireland but without Italy) averaged $9,182, 60 percent of the Northwest level. With more developed Italy added in, the regional income already had reached $11,361 per capita, 75 percent of the Western level. During the 1980s and 1990s, as globalization was spreading and the introduction of the Single Market and the euro was advancing regionalization, the Mediterranean region continued catching up with the Northwestern core.

Economic restructuring, involving the introduction of multinational companies, the establishment of modern technology-based companies in sectors such as biotechnology and information technology, and the transformation of energy production, played a large role in the case of Portugal. The list of Portuguese subsidiaries of large multinational companies, mostly Northwestern European and founded after 1986, is very long. Most important and productive among them were Siemens Portugal, Volkswagen Autoeuropa, IKEA, Nestlé Portugal, Microsoft Portugal, Unilever/Jerónimo Martins, and Danone Portugal. Also on this list are SONAE, Amorim, Sogrape, EFACEC, Portugal Telecom, Cimpor, Unicer, Millennium BCP, Lactogal, Sumol + Compal, Delta Cafés, Derovo, Critical Software, Galp Energia, EDP, Grupo José de Mello, Sovena Group, Valouro, Renova, Teixeira Duarte, Soares da Costa, Portucel Soporcel, Simoldes, Iberomoldes, Logoplaste, and TAP Portugal. Modern, early-21st-century technology-based industries like biotechnology and information technology developed in Lisbon, Porto, Braga, Coimbra, and Aveiro. An aerospace industry was established in four locations around the country, led by the local branch of the Brazilian Embraer and by OGMA. Meanwhile Portugal was transforming its energy system to meet 21st-century requirements. By 2013, renewables (including 30 percent hydroelectric and 24 percent wind) accounted for nearly 62 percent of energy production. As a consequence, energy imports fell to 5 percent of total energy consumption.

Spain might be said to have been "occupied" by Northwestern multinationals, but SEAT, Telefonica, Ferrovial, and Banco Santander also played important roles in the country's economic modernization. Spain was the second largest destination after the United States for German investment, most of it directed toward the auto industry. Multinationals created a competitive export sector: by 1992, nine out of ten leading export companies were foreign-owned. By the 2010s, the foreign-established automotive industry had become a leading branch of Spanish manufacturing, generating nearly 9 percent of Spain's GDP and employing about 9 percent of the manufacturing workforce. In 2008, the automobile industry was Spain's second most export-oriented industry with about 80 percent of total production sold abroad.

From the 1990s on, the countries of the Mediterranean region adjusted to the principles of the European Community by abolishing their protectionist and state-run economic systems and establishing free market regimes.[33] After the years of stagnation in the 1970s, the economies of Portugal and Spain began growing rapidly again during the second half of the 1980s: by 6.6 percent and

5.4 percent per year, respectively. Both economies registered impressive, albeit slower, growth rates between 1995 and 2005: 3.5 percent per year in Spain with unemployment dropping from about 21 percent to 8 percent, and 2.1 percent per year in Portugal Neither country, however, matched the record 7.4 percent annual growth of the "Celtic Tiger."

Greece could not follow on the same road. The country was barely industrialized and joining the European Community as a full member actually caused deindustrialization. Foreign investors did not see their interests served in a country where neither industrial practice nor education levels offered the likelihood of positive returns. Economic growth consequently slowed down: agriculture, already less productive than elsewhere in Europe, as well as industry lost ground. Even tomatoes were imported – from the Netherlands. Between 1979 and 1985, average annual growth was only 0.8 percent, and between 1985 and 1989, when Spain and Portugal were enjoying quite exceptional rates of growth, it slowed further down in Greece to 0.4 percent per year.

Greece had a strange, even distorted economic structure: manufacturing produced less than 10 percent of the country's GDP (half of the euro-zone's average) while service industries produced 79 percent of GDP, shipping and tourism most of all. About 950 shipping companies headed by a handful of shipping magnates, the Vardinoyannis, Latsis, Niarchos, and others, owned more than 5,000 vessels, 33 percent of the world's tankers and altogether 23 percent of the world's merchant fleet, employing nearly 200,000 people. Between 2006 and 2009, the Greek merchant fleet ranked between third and fifth in the world in shipping capacity. Exceptional incomes accumulated in the hands of the owners, but this sector had a relatively loose connection with the domestic economy. Several major Greek shipping companies had headquarters in London and New York and even the employment in this sector was rather international.[34]

By the mid-1980s, Italy, a founding member of the European Community, had already reaped many of the benefits – economic stimulus and rapid growth – of European integration. The postwar *miracolo economico*, the reconstruction boom, had raised the country's per capita income level from $2,996 in 1848 to $5,789 in 1960 and then to $13,859 by 1985, an unprecedented increase of 463 percent. With income level having grown since the 1960s from just 58 percent of Western European levels to 91 percent, this period had been the real time of Italian catching up with Western Europe. After the 1980s, when most of the other Mediterranean countries were flourishing, Italy's growth was slow: between 1995 and 2007 only 1.3 percent annually, although unemployment still declined from more than 11 percent to 6 percent.

By the turn of the millennium Italy's economic structure had become obsolete. The dominant small and medium size companies, the backbone of the Italian economy, were mostly involved in production in low-wage sectors, including luxury goods: textiles, clothing, leather goods, furniture, machine tools, food processing, and white goods. Such companies needed a low-cost base to sustain competitiveness. This was secured by low-wage migrant labor moving from the South to the North, but this wave significantly slowed down around the turn of the millennium, wage levels started rising and the wage cost increased in Italy by almost 35 percent between 1999 and 2012.[35] The other weapon to sustain competitiveness was the devaluation of the Italian currency, the lira, which made products cheaper. This possibility was used several times but was lost as an option when Italy joined the eurozone at the turn of the millennium. The last straw came with the spectacular growth of some Asian countries and also of the transforming former communist East European countries. Their competition, with their unbeatably lower wages, destroyed the basis of the Italian growth model.[36]

Roberto Di Quirico has reported that several Italian firms tried to defend themselves by transferring production facilities to underdeveloped countries.[37] Some firms simply closed. Although experts of the early 1990s were conscious of the unsustainability of the traditional development model and of the need to move toward high-tech production, the dramatic political crisis of the Berlusconi years and the near bankruptcy of the Italian state blocked attempts to define a new model of development.

Additionally, in 1970 Italy introduced an administrative reform that transferred the main responsibility for urban affairs, regional planning, public works and economic development from the discredited and unpopular national government to a newly created set of elected regional governments. This innovation had a positive impact in the North, but, by contrast, in the southern regions of Puglia, Calabria, and Sicily, for the most part it transferred responsibility to local governments, which have remained unresponsive, crooked, and unable or unwilling to make positive changes.[38]

Most of the small and medium-size companies that formerly carried the country's economy were not sufficiently capitalized to compete. Their management remained in family hands or even in the control of founders who had been able to establish and consolidate the firms at a time when hard-working entrepreneurs, even if poorly educated, could manage businesses. However, they did not have the skills for managing the transition of their companies to more competitive or high-tech production, and they often obstructed company mergers because of their fear of being personally marginalized or excluded.

Over 20 years of political instability and economic inertia the Italian economic system deteriorated. According to Di Quirico:

> the circumstances responsible for Italy's decline and the avoidance of structural reforms have also prevented attempts to use the global crisis as a stimulus for rescuing the country and reforming the system. These circumstances are the long-term effects of the early 1990s collapse and the absence of new project for economic growth and thoroughgoing reform.[39]

Large firms such as Montedison, Parmalat, and ILVA have lost or are losing their leading roles in the Italian economy. Except for Fiat, which successfully has recovered after being brought to the brink of collapse by managerial mistakes, there are few major companies in the country. Certain medium-sized firms, such as Ferrero, Jacuzzi, and Ducati, have gained international success, and some smaller firms have gained leading positions even internationally in niche markets as the manufacturers of machinery for very specific production processes. This, however, has not been enough to establish a new model for development in the country.

One of the connected problems has been the lack of sufficient research of the type needed to move toward a high-tech economy. In Italy few industries fund university research and few industries or institutions have their own research laboratories. Several Italian firms work with foreign patents and rely on foreign research activities. Poor investments in R&D, lack of sufficient laboratories and advanced university infrastructure, and the almost bankrupt position of many universities and their inability to attract foreign researchers all worsen the problem.[40] This situation has discouraged foreign direct investments into Italy, slowing down rates of investment and decreasing amounts by comparison with the Western core countries.

An analysis by the Brussels-based think tank Bruegel summed up this situation in the following way:

> Italy has been technologically and physically aging for some decades. It has been unable to keep pace with the technological demands of a competitive global economy. The Italian technological lag reflects a falling behind in educational standards: low growth and weak investment in technology and human capital have reinforced each other. The aging population has made reversing these trends a formidable task.[41]

The World Economic Forum's Global Competitiveness Report for 2010/2011 ranked Italy 43rd out of 139 countries. Its competitiveness was held back by structural weaknesses in the labor market (ranked 118th on labor market efficiency), weak public finances (ranked 131st on public indebtedness) and a poor institutional environment (ranked 92nd). According to the World Bank's 2012 Doing Business Report, Italy occupied the 87th place out of 183 countries. In the matter of "starting a business," the country was also in a non-European position (77th).[42]

The Mediterranean-Irish 21st-century credit-fueled consumption bubble

Although the introduction of the euro removed the possibility of devaluing currency to protect competitiveness, it nevertheless contributed to increasing economic prosperity in the Mediterranean-Irish region. This happened largely because this new common currency stimulated domestic consumption by sharply reducing long-term interest rates. The integrated EU market encouraged cheap credit to flood the region and a new, credit-based domestic-demand-led development model to emerge in Spain, Greece and Portugal. Greece alone received $414 billion in credit. Mortgage lending surged more than fourfold between 2000 and 2010. Banks offered cheap mortgages and other forms of credit. An unprecedented housing boom exploded, financed in Spain, at least, mostly by regional savings banks (*cajas*) controlled by regional governments. At the height of the boom, Spain was building more houses than Germany, France and Britain combined. Home prices soared by 71 percent between 2003 and 2008 together with the credit explosion.[43] By 2007, construction had expanded to an incredible 16 percent of Spanish GDP, and the sector employed 12 percent of the workforce.

An even more extreme housing boom emerged in Ireland. There, 80 percent of investments in the early 2000s served residential construction, 12 percent of the workforce was employed in direct construction work, and altogether 20–30 percent was related to the real estate sector. The elimination of real estate taxes and introduction of tax deductions for mortgages amplified the effects of unlimited cheap credit. Residential mortgage lending increased by 25 percent per year in the 2000s, and from 2004 to 2007 jumped from 40 percent to 65 percent of the country's GDP. Out-of-control urban and suburban housing development followed: 23,000 newly constructed houses per year went on the market in the 1980s, 75,000 per year between 2000 and 2006, and at the climax of the housing boom, in 2006 alone, 93,000. Housing prices skyrocketed, increasing overall by 300 percent between 2000 and 2006, and in the capital city, Dublin, by 500 percent.[44]

In the *nouveau riche* Ireland and Mediterranean, people who were poor a generation earlier, began copying the envied Western lifestyle. Extreme consumerism became a contagious disease. By 2014, in the five countries of the region, every 1,000 inhabitants owned 584 cars, somewhat more than in traditionally rich West, where in five countries – Norway, Switzerland, France, Germany, and Austria – car ownership in the comparable period was 576 cars per 1,000 people.[45]

Runaway consumption, or "consumption mania," as Ralf Dahrendorf called it, led to higher spending than earning. During the Irish real estate boom, reckless spending and crediting increased household debts from 60 percent to 160 percent of the country's GDP, with 60 percent of this debt connected to real estate. Spain's level of personal and household debt in connection with real estate purchases trebled and by 2005 the median ratio of total household indebtedness to income had grown to 125 percent.

State spending in some of the countries was similarly reckless. Greece, which did not have a state-supported health care system before joining the European Community in 1981, built up a lavish healthcare and pension system, based on credit. Retirement age was fixed for most of the population at the exceptionally low age of 58 years and in some areas at 45. National social expenditures, 10.2 percent of GDP in 1980, jumped to 23 percent by 2005. Government expenditures altogether equaled 50 percent of the country's GDP by 2009. Spain and Italy together accumulated a $3.3 trillion (!) debt burden by the end of 2011. Spain also built up a massive trade deficit financed by capital inflows, which, however, were directed, not to manufacturing or other export industries but rather mostly to real estate, or to the commercial and finance sectors, or to privatized oligopoly sectors such as energy and communications where competition was not relevant. Between 2000 and 2007, the trade deficit mattered little as the Spanish economy was booming. Unemployment in 2007 was the lowest since 1975, even though the country had absorbed more than 4 million immigrants in a decade. Prime Minister Rodriguez Zapatero, elected in 2004, was so confident that he announced that in a few years Spain would overtake France. Nevertheless, the current account positions deteriorated in the country from balance to 10 percent deficit between 1995 and 2007. In Italy, similarly, account positions deteriorated from a 2.9 percent surplus to a 1.3 percent deficit. The combination of credit- and consumption-based prosperity, the long-standing peripheral habit of tax evasion and the *nouveau riche* tendency toward reckless spending slowly was creating the conditions for financial and economic collapse.

Financial-economic crisis hits the region hard

In 2008, that was what happened. It was not without a typical prehistory. Macro-economic imbalances had been accumulating from the turn of the millennium. The countries of the region had suffered huge losses of competitiveness and accumulated significant current account deficit. Their indebtedness had started to increase, and when the international liquidity crisis emerged, they were defenseless.[46]

Although there is neither space here nor need to repeat the details of the origins of the 2008 financial-economic crisis, it must be noted that the crisis started in the United States with a severe liquidity crunch caused by the collapse of a giant mortgage bank, Lehman Brothers, which was overburdened by toxic loans in arrears. Banks all over the world, worried about similar possibilities, soon stopped issuing new loans. Because the modern economy is based on credits, with old debts often being repaid by new loans, the entire international economy became paralyzed. Although well-established countries with solid economies and disciplined financial households were hit hard and suffered losses, they soon recovered, as we have seen in Chapter 4. In general, recession in those countries lasted less than a full year. Countries in peripheral regions, with weak financial systems and accumulated huge indebtedness, however, declined into deep and long crisis. That was the fate of the Mediterranean region and Ireland.

The crisis was uniformly serious but not exactly similar in every country of the region. In some, reckless state spending and overindebtedness led to state bankruptcy; debts could not be repaid. The classic example of this type in the region was Greece. Selling state bonds to finance existing debts became very expensive. At one point, instead of the usual 2–5 percent interest rates, Greek bonds with 37 percent interest returns were sold. As Franz-Josef Meiers has noted, Greece

> emerged as epicentre of the euro crisis. Greece's economic boom was propelled by large foreign-funded fiscal deficits which reached 13.6 percent at the end of 2009; the stock of debt accounted for 129 percent of GDP at the end of 2009 … 75 percent of the country's debt was held by foreign creditors.[47]

Greek national debt increased to 160 percent of the GDP in three years. This indebtedness level was nearly three times higher than the European Union's norm, which required keeping public debt below 60 percent of GDP.

If in Italy the situation was almost as bad as in Greece, with the national debt already 120 percent of GDP in the mid-1990s and increasing continually until 2009, in contrast, in Ireland and Spain financial households were in order. Irish and Greek government debts amounted to only 25 and 40 percent of GDP, respectively, much lower than the EU's requirement. State indebtedness thus was easily manageable. Banks, however, were overburdened with bad loans. The financial crisis actually destroyed Ireland's six biggest lenders, and Dublin declined from being the world's tenth most desirable financial center to its seventieth.[48]

Throughout the region, banking sectors were paralyzed and governments rushed to bail out their banks in order to save the real economy. The state's debt burden, consequently, increased to an intolerable level. In the case of Ireland, the government devoted 42 percent of national output to consolidating the banking sector, a policy which increased the government's debt burden to 112 per cent of the GDP by 2011. Experts started to call the Irish-Mediterranean countries the "misery belt":

> Government debt as a proportion of GDP rose across the euro area from 66% in 2007 to 95% at the end of 2013. The debts of the misery belt have increased by an average of 26% since 2010 to 131% of GDP, or 120% excluding Greece. By 2015, Spanish general government debt will be 101.4%, of GDP; Irish, 121.1%; Portuguese, 131.8%; Italian, 134.5%; and Greek, 177.2%. Even if the bond yields stay at record low level for years to come, nominal GDP must grow on average by 3% a year just to keep the public debt ratio stable; the misery belt economies need to grow by 5% indefinitely, to lower their debt burden to the 60% Maastricht debt criteria.[49]

The picture and the future were painted in dark colors. In the end – but for Italy – all of the region's states declared bankruptcy.

The crisis rapidly spread from the financial sector to the real economy. Greece led the way: in the four consecutive years between 2009 and 2012, the country's GDP declined between 2.0 and 6.0 percent annually. Between 2009 and 2014, the average annual decline was 4.9 percent. In Portugal, Spain and Italy, in those five years, the average yearly decline was 1.0–0.5 percent. Between 2009 and 2013, almost 230,000 companies collapsed in Spain and the country's GDP contracted by 9 percent. In Ireland, however, the decline after the first crisis years soon stopped and growth returned: in the end the average annual growth rate over five years registered at 1.9 percent.

The Economist published a dramatic report on the crisis in this region in the summer of 2011. It pays to quote it at length:

> With hindsight, it was no surprise that the debt crisis started in Greece. ... When its debt crisis flared up last year European leaders hoped to contain it at the Greek border, providing a bail-out worth €110 billion ($158 billion) over three years, of which €80 billion came from other euro-area members and €30 billion from the IMF. Any hope of containment was shattered when Ireland's banking difficulties forced a second rescue last November. After that a third bail-out became inevitable, for Portugal, as the cost of its government borrowing shot up and Portuguese banks were shut off from normal funding ... [in November 2011, the Portuguese government received a rescue package from Europe and the IMF, worth €78 billion.] What caused consternation was a new shock – from Greece, again – that the first package was insufficient and that the country needed more money for longer. [In the end, unlike in other countries, Greece needed a third bail-out as well.] Credit markets paid no heed to the risks that were building up from sustained big current-account deficits, which would have caused alarm in emerging economies. They smiled on Ireland's property boom, overlooked Portugal's slack growth and forgave Greece its poor public finances. Spain also benefited from dirt-cheap money even though it shared many of the same weaknesses, notably a housing-market bubble and a huge current-account deficit. ... The flood of easy money disguised the hard truth that the competitiveness of the peripheral economies, gauged by measures like unit labour costs, had steadily worsened after joining the euro. This deterioration came from a poor starting-point, for Greece in particular. As one senior negotiator in the bail-out talks laments, Greece is part of the single-currency area even though it has managed in effect to stay out of the single market. With the lowest exports-to-GDP ratio in the euro area, membership became a way to import cheap goods on the never-never rather than a means to foster higher productivity. Ireland, with exports now roughly equal to GDP, is quite different, but Portugal also has a lowish exports-to-GDP ratio for a small economy within a single-currency zone and, like Greece, has insulated much of its economy from the single market. Once the credit machine went into reverse as the financial crisis broke in the summer of 2007, the underlying weaknesses of the peripheral economies were exposed.[50]

Table 5.5 Nominal GDP for countries of the region (in billion US$)

	2010	*2011*	*2012*	*2013*	*2014*	*2015*	*2016*
Italy	2,129.021	2,278.376	2,073.972	2,130.997	2,141.937	1,815.759	1,852.636
Spain	1,434.257	1,489.381	1,340.689	1,369.690	1,383.537	1,199.715	1,252.163
Ireland	218.843	237.990	222.089	232.150	246.438	238.031	254.596
Portugal	238.748	245.120	216.488	224.983	230.012	199.077	205.085
Greece	300.156	289.068	249.663	242.306	238.023	195.320	194.594

With the disappearance of cheap credit, all the hidden economic weaknesses of the Mediterranean-Irish region came to the surface. More significantly the crisis was followed by an exceptionally strong resurgence of peripheral social-cultural characteristics (discussed in Chapter 3), which undermined and halted the fast economic growth of preceding decades. This was rather painful in Portugal, where even before the crash, GDP per capita had been falling (from 80 percent of the EU-25 average in 1999 to just over 70 percent in 2007). *The Economist* published an article on Portugal in April 2007 with the title "A New Sick Man of Europe."[51]

Table 5.5 clearly reflects an expanded economic recession in the region. All countries remained somewhat behind their pre-crisis levels even in 2016, Greece by a tragic measure: in 2016 its income level was more than one-third lower than in 2010. The decline was 13 percent in both Italy and Spain, and 14 percent in Portugal.

Reports from the spring of 2015, however, started to become more optimistic. The combination of austerity measures, budgetary deficit reductions, energy price declines, euro weakening, and skillful interventions by the European Central Bank all helped these countries to cope with the crisis. GDP started rising again. The euro area economy rose by 0.9 percent in 2014, while Spain's economy grew by 1.4 percent in 2013, and Portugal's by 0.9 percent. The Greek economy, in 2013, in contrast, suffered an additional 0.4 percent contraction while the mostly stagnant Italian economy declined 0.4 percent in 2014.

Despite signs of improvement the crisis was still not entirely over even in early 2017. In the summer of that year the European Commission approved the plans of the Italian government to provide €4.8 billion ($5.4 billion) in cash to two failing Italian banks, the Veneto Banca and the Banca Populare di Vicenza, and another €12 billion in guarantees to protect the depositors of these banks. Although these are relatively small local institutions, the still fragile Italian banking system could be endangered by their collapse. The amount is covered by a special fund, established by the Italian government to save the banking system if needed. In the same month the fifth largest Spanish bank, the Banco Popular, with over $100 billion loans, collapsed, despite having received $4 billion in emergency assistance from the Spanish National Bank just a few weeks before. This collapse is a late consequence of the earlier real estate boom and extreme mortgage expansion. The bank was not protected but rather quietly taken over by its rival, Banco Santander. "The root of the problem is the nonperforming loans on the books of European banks."[52]

By the middle of 2017, only Ireland had recovered its financial stability. In June of that year, just as the troubles of some Spanish and Italian banks were being reported by the international media, the news appeared that Ireland's biggest bank, the Allied Irish Bank, collapsed during the financial crisis, then bailed out and nationalized by the government in 2009–2010, had returned to private business with €12 billion share value.[53] Ireland was the only country in the region to begin growing as early as 2011 and to quickly surpass the precrisis level. *The Telegraph* asked rhetorically in the summer of 2017: "Is the Celtic Tiger really ready to roar again?" The journal gave a positive answer:

> Six years ago, the diagnosis for the Irish economy was terminal. The one-time roaring Celtic Tiger was on life support. The state was forced to bail out national banks, the construction sector imploded, public debt soared and Ireland hemorrhaged its well-educated labour force at an astonishing rate. Humiliating as it was, the economic lifeline, in the form of the €85bn (£60bn) bail-out from the European Central Bank and the International Monetary Fund in late 2010 was the transfusion of cash so badly needed. Today, Ireland, which exited its bail-out around two years ago, is resurgent. It is the fastest growing economy in Europe, with growth of 6.3 percent forecast for this year.[54]

For all countries of the region the crisis acted as a wakeup call. Along with bail outs the European Union imposed strict rules and regulations as a form of bitter medicine to be swallowed mandatorily. Several economists wildly criticized austerity policy as counterproductive and inhumane, serving German interests only. They maintained that compulsory cuts weakened the repayment capacities of affected countries and that their relative debt burden would actually increase on account of related GDP declines. Although this criticism was not without merit, stringent restrictions, painful as they were, still were badly needed. The austerity measures, forced by the German-led European Union, at last led to a cutting-back of reckless spending. Pension systems were reformed and cut and retirement ages increased. Very painfully the populations of this region learned not to spend beyond their means. In some cases – again extremely painfully – living standards fell backwards into closer alignment with the economic fundamentals of particular countries, and away from the patterns and imagined richness of life in more the prosperous Northwest. All these developments gradually restored growth capacities in Ireland, Spain, and Portugal.

Spain, having suffered disastrous blows in 2008 and in June 2012, and then having requested European funding of €100 billion "to recapitalize Spanish banks that need it," met the EU requirements, and thus the country provides one example of the potentially beneficial effects of austerity. The government increased the value added tax by 2 percent and also raised taxes on the wealthiest layer of the population, reformed the labor market, increased the retirement age from 65 to 67 years. Following EU requirements, it enacted a constitutional amendment that made a balanced budget compulsory. After three decades of permanent deficit creation, the trade surplus just since 2013, has doubled. Being a member of the eurozone, Spain could not devalue its currency, and therefore the only means for reestablishing the balance lay in so-called internal devaluation; that is, in decreasing expenditure levels and wages. By such means the country halved its wage bill. In the aftermath of these various austerity measures, exports increased from 25 percent of GDP in 2008 to 33 percent by 2016. After the years of economic decline, growth returned by 2015 at an impressive 3.2 percent annual rate. In 2016, Spanish growth was twice as much as the eurozone average. By 2014–2015, the country had recovered 85 percent of the income lost during the recession years, and the IMF was projecting full recovery of those losses over the next few years. Early in 2017 Spain was being called "the show case of structural reforms."[55]

The Economist offered the Spanish company Gestamp as a "symbol of the transformation of Spain's economy," and Spain's policies as "lessons for Europe's anxious south."[56] Gestamp, now one of the world's leading auto-body-parts producers, owns 100 plants in 21 countries, runs a research laboratory with scientists and engineers, holds more than 900 patents and had sales of €7.5 billion in 2016. The company's success contributed to making the Spanish car industry the second biggest car producer and exporter of continental Europe after Germany.

The Mediterranean-Irish region has exhibited a mixed development trend since the 2008 financial-economic crisis. The poor Balkan country Greece, which, as the only anticommunist country in the communist Balkans and Eastern Europe during the Cold War decades, "accidentally" became a "Western country," is seemingly dropping out from the regional group and slowly shifting to the lower-income region of Central Europe. In 2016, Greece' $17,806 per capita income level was hardly more than half the Mediterranean region's average and less than one-third the Irish level. Actually, three countries from the Central Europe–Baltic region (Slovenia, the Czech Republic, and Estonia) had higher income levels that year than Greece.

Ireland's fast recovery after the devastating crisis demonstrates its strong potential to continue as a super-rich country leaving behind the remnants of a peripheral, middle-income past. The promising reforms and recovery of Spain and its $26,643 income level locate the country in the high-income zone; in the future it may exhibit tendencies somewhat similar to Ireland. Italy requires drastic reform steps if it would remain grouped with the high-income countries that are gradually becoming a stable part of the Northwest. The country has the best possibility of all its Mediterranean neighbors to achieve that goal. Portugal's future is less certain and will require major efforts to follow in the footsteps of Spain and Italy, rather than Greece.

Notes

1 Quoted by Giorgio Mori, "The Genesis of Italian Industrialization," *Journal of European Economic History* 4, no. 7 (1975): 91–92.
2 *Economic Survey of Europe 1991*, Geneva: United Nations.
3 Stephen Broadberry and Kevin H. O'Rourke, *The Cambridge Economic History of Modern Europe, Vol. 2: 1870 to the Present*, Cambridge: Cambridge University Press, 2010, p. 408.
4 From the rich literature on the "Irish Miracle," see Frank Barry (ed.), *Understanding Ireland's Economic Growth*, London: Macmillan, 1999; Alan Gray (ed.), *International Perspectives on the Irish Economy*, Dublin: Indecon, 1997; John McCarthy, "Foreign Direct Investment: An Overview," *Dublin: Central Bank of Ireland, Quarterly Bulletin, Autom 2*, 1999, 55-65, Antoin E. Murphy, *The Celtic Tiger – The Great Misnomer: Economic Growth and the Multi-Nationals in Ireland in the 1990s*, Dublin: MMI, 1998.
5 "The Luck of the Irish," *The Economist*, October 14, 2004.
6 "How Ireland Became the Celtic Tiger," The Heritage Foundation, June 23, 2006, www.heritage.org/ europe/report/how-ireland-became-the-celtic-tiger, accessed December 18, 2016; hereafter, Heritage Foundation, "Celtic Tiger."
7 Ibid.
8 Antoin E. Murphy, "The 'Celtic Tiger': An Analysis of Ireland's Economic Growth Performance," Robert Schuman Centre for Advanced Studies, RSC No. 2000/16, p. 5.
9 *OECD Education at Glance 2013*, www.oecd.org/edu/Ireland_EAG2013%20 Country%20Note.pdf, accessed December 22, 2016.
10 Murphy, "The 'Celtic Tiger'," pp. 6, 11.
11 A.T. Kearney, "Weekly Indicators: Globalization," *The Economist*, 2000, p. 6.
12 Ibid.
13 *The Economist, Pocket World in Figures 2008*, September 1, 2007, London: The Economist.
14 www.world.tax/countries/ireland/ireland-tax-system.php, accessed March 2, 2017.
15 onlinepdfcatalog.com/c/cadmus.iue.it1.html, accessed January 4, 2017; *The Economist*, May 17, 1997, p. 15.
16 Commission of the European Communities, *European Economy*, 71/2000, The EU Economy 2000 Review, No. 35, Luxembourg: Office for Official Publications, 2000, p. 195.
17 See Nicole Lindstrom and Dora Piroska, "The Politics of Privatization and Europeanization in Europe's Periphery," *Competition and Change* 11, no. 2 (2007): 89–114.
18 Heritage Foundation, "Celtic Tiger"; Murphy, "The 'Celtic Tiger'."
19 Ibid.
20 *OECD Economic Surveys*, Ireland 1995, p. 6, www.oecd-ilibrary.org › economics › oecd-economic-surveys-ireland, accessed February 17, 2017.
21 Quoted in Kenneth Maxwell, *The Making of Portuguese Democracy*, Cambridge: Cambridge University Press, 1995, p. 96.
22 Argyris G. Andrianopoulos, *Western Europe in Kissinger's Global Strategy*, New York: St. Martin Press, 1988, p. 17; Daniel J. Sargent, *A Superpower Transformed. The*

Rethinking of American Foreign Relations in the 1970s, New York: Oxford University Press, 2015, pp. 69, 209.

23 Kristin Archick, "European Union Enlargement," Congressional Research Service Report, February 19 (2014), pp. 1, 10, www.fas.org/sgp/crs/row/RS21344.pdf, accessed March 17, 2017.

24 In the two decades between 1960 and 1980, EU connections helped Greece to nearly treble its per capita income level from $3,204 to $9,071.

25 *El País*, May 7, 2015.

26 *El País*, January 13, 2017.

27 Jorge Nadal, Albert Carreras, and Carles Sudrià, *Les economía Espanola en el siglo XX: una perspectíva histórica*, Barcelona: Ariel, 1987, pp. 271, 274, 292–293, 308.

28 The sweatshops appeared also in Italy and Portugal.

29 "Portugal's Economic Weaknesses: Country Report Portugal," Rabobank, April 24, 2014, https://economics.rabobank.com/publications/2014/april/country-report-portugal/, accessed February 18, 2017.

30 "Is Convergence a Spontaneous Process? The Experience of Spain, Portugal and Greece," *OECD Economic Studies*, 16 (Spring 1991): 177–178, www.oecd.org/eco/growth/34278656.pdf), accessed January 24, 2017.

31 Ibid.

32 Ibid., pp. 179, 192.

33 In Spain, for example, "during the period of 1975–94 the Spanish economy became more fully integrated into the world economy and especially into the European Union." For this, see Richard Gillespie, Fernando Rodrigo, and Jonathan Story, *Democratic Spain Reshaping External Relations in a Changing World*, London: Routledge, 1995, p. 82.

34 "Greek Shipping Is Modernized to Remain a Global Leader and Expand Its Contribution to the Greek Economy," National Bank of Greece, Press Release May 11, 2006, www.nbg.gr/publications/ eco_fin_bulletin/home.html, accessed January 11, 2016.

35 Piero Esposito and Paolo Guerrieri, "Intra-European Imbalances, Competitiveness and External Trade: A Comparison between Italy and Germany," in Stefan Collignon and Piero Esposito (eds.), *Competitiveness in the European Economy*, London: Routledge, 2014, p. 86.

36 "The Real Sick Man of Europe," *The Economist*, May 19, 2005.

37 Roberto Di Quirico, "Italy and the Global Economic Crisis," *Bulletin of Italian Politics* 2, no. 2 (2010): 3–19.

38 Mark Muro, "Making Regions Work – Lessons from Italy," November 11, 2010, https://newrepublic.com/article/79134/making-regions-work-lessons-italy, accessed December 7, 2016.

39 Di Quirico, "Italy and the Global Economic Crisis," p. 16.

40 Ibid.; also ec.europa.eu/economy_finance/eu/countries/italy_en.htm, accessed January 7, 2017; europa.eu/abc/european_countries/eu_members/italy, accessed January 9, 2017; www.oecd.org/italy, accessed January 9, 2017.

41 "Why Does Italy Not Grow?," October 10, 2014, bruegel.org/2014/10/why-does-italy-not-grow/, accessed January 19, 2017.

42 ec.europa.eu/economy_finance/eu/countries/italy_en.htm; *European Bank of Reconstruction and Development Transition Report 2005*, London: EBRD, 2005, p.19; www.oecd.org/italy, accessed January 20, 2017
43 Maria Tadeo and Sharon R. Smyth, "Housing Crash Turns Spain's Young into Generation Rent," *Bloomberg*, November 29, 2016.
44 Ivan T. Berend, *Europe in Crisis: Bolt from the Blue?*, London: Routledge, 2013, p. 24.
45 www.nationmaster.com/country-info/stats/Transport/Road/Motor-vehicles-per-1000-people, accessed March 17, 2017.
46 Esposito and Guerrieri, "Intra-European Imbalances," p. 88.
47 Franz-Josef Meiers, *Germany's Role in the Euro Crisis: Berlin's Quest for a More Perfect Monetary Union*, Cham, Switzerland: Springer International, 2015, p. 17.
48 "Dublin as a Financial Center," *The Economist*, January 28, 2017.
49 Meiers, *Germany's Role in the Euro Crisis*, p. 25.
50 "Bank in Spain Passed Its Tests: Then It Failed," *New York Times*, June 25, 2017; "EU Approves Billions in Aid for Troubled Italian Banks," *New York Times*, June 26, 2017; "The Euro Crisis: A Second Wave," *The Telegraph*, June 16, 2011.
51 "A New Sick Man of Europe," *The Economist*, April 14, 2007.
52 "Bank in Spain Passed Its Tests," *New York Times*.
53 "Irish Lender, Revived from Crisis, Is Valued at $13.3 Billion in IPO," *New York Times*, June 24, 2017.
54 "Is the Celtic Tiger Really Ready to Roar Again?," *The Telegraph*, June 15, 2017.
55 "Spain's Economic Crisis: A Timeline," *The Telegraph*, February 27, 2017; www.telegraph.co.uk/finance/economics/11574536/How-Spain-became-the-Wests-superstar-economy.htm, accessed December 8, 2016; David Ampudia, "Spain: Economic Growth Remains Firm in Q2 Despite Political Impasse," *FocusEconomics*, August 25, 2016.
56 "Spain's Economic Recovery: Stamp of Approval," *The Economist*, June 17, 2017.

6 Central Europe and the Baltics

Trapped in middle-income periphery?

What is Central Europe?[1] The answer to this question is seemingly easy. One has only to calculate the middle longitude – the center area – between the longitudes that border Europe. Experts began trying to do so in the 18th century and continue the project even today. Surprisingly enough, there is no agreement on an answer. Monuments in several places claim to represent the real center point of Europe: in Suchowola (Poland), Purnuškės (Lithuania), Polotsk (Belarus), Tállya (Hungary), and several other places in Slovakia, Ukraine, and Estonia. Ultimately, the answer depends on the definition of the borders of Europe, whether only the mainland is included in calculations, or also remote islands.

The geographic center of the continent itself, however, is basically evident. But which countries belong to that area? The answer again varies. The *Collins English Dictionary*, for example, defines Central Europe as "an area between Eastern and Western Europe, generally accepted as comprising Austria, the Czech Republic, Germany, Hungary, Liechtenstein, Poland, Slovakia, Slovenia, and Switzerland."[2] This belies the fact that for nearly a century, the very definition of Central Europe, even the question whether it is a valid category at all, has been an unsettled question. The debate turns not only on geographically defined borderlines, but also on historical-political considerations. While some categorizations locate Switzerland, Germany, and Austria in Central Europe, others (including my categorizations in this book) assign those countries to the West European region. The outstanding British historian Eric Hobsbawm once stated that the Habsburg empire was Central Europe, par excellence, and that after its dissolution Central Europe no longer existed. He was pointing out the fact that historically and politically some part of that area shifted to the West, others to the East. Péter Hanák, a Hungarian historian, remarked that Central Europe is the area where Johann Strauss's *Die Fledermaus* is performed on New Year's Eve, in homage to the cultural traditions of the Habsburg empire.

Although the term "Central and Eastern Europe," broadly used since World War II, is valid for the geographic Eastern half of the continent, it was tailored with the Soviet bloc in mind and never was wholly accepted in the categorized countries. The Czech writer Milan Kundera wanted to separate his own country, at least intellectually, from the Soviet-dominated area. He maintained that Central Europe had been "kidnapped," cut off and "stolen" from the place where it belongs, in the West.[3] A similar idea prompted the Hungarian historian Jenő Szűcs to separate his country and some of its neighbors from the Soviet Bloc. Resting his argument on an interpretation of history reaching back to the middle ages, he defined Central Europe as a region between the West and the "par excellence" East, which is Russia.[4] Actually interwar German journalism already had used a similar term, *Zwischen Europa,* and interwar Hungarian writers had named the same countries between West and East, either "Karpathian Europe" or "Danubian Europe." I am not going to enter this debate here.

It is interesting to note that the people of these countries also have mixed feelings on the subject. A recent (2017) Bratislava-based Global Security Forum (Globsec) poll of citizens found that 42 and 45 percent of Poles and Hungarians, respectively, believe that their country belongs to the West, while only 38 and 21 percent in the Czech Republic and Slovakia, respectively, define their countries similarly. Furthermore, although the percentage of Hungarians considering their country Western was higher (45 percent) than elsewhere, a slightly larger percentage (47 percent) maintained that their country belongs somewhere in between the West and the East. Among younger people (18–24 years of age), however, a different position emerges: two-thirds of such Hungarians and more than half (54 percent) of such Czechs believe that they belong to the West. In Slovakia, by contrast, only one-third of youth share this feeling, while half place their country between East and West.[5]

In this book the term "Central Europe" (including the Baltic area) applies to a specific region consisting of the present-day Czech Republic, Slovakia, Hungary, Poland, Slovenia, and Croatia, along with the three Baltic countries, Estonia, Latvia, and Lithuania. All are members of the European Union (eight since 2004, Croatia since 2013). Poland is the largest among them, with a population of 38.6 million, while the Czech Republic and Hungary have, respectively, 10.2 and 10.1 million inhabitants. The other countries are much smaller. Slovakia has 5.4 million, Croatia, 4.3 million, Slovenia, 2.0 million, and the three Baltic countries combined have 6.8 million. Altogether the region has about 75 million inhabitants today. With its overwhelmingly majority Catholic, Western Slavic population and culture, this area definitely does not belong to Western Europe, naturally has nothing to do with Mediterranean Europe, and also differs from the Russian-Balkans Orthodox Eastern Slav area, whether from the standpoint of historical development, economic level, or social-cultural and political features.[6]

These countries historically have been bound closely together. Hungary, Slovakia, and Croatia belonged to the same Hungarian Kingdom for nearly a millennium. Together with the present-day Czech Republic and Slovenia, they were part of the Habsburg Empire for about four centuries. Poland and Lithuania belonged to the Polish-Lithuanian Union and later Commonwealth from the middle ages until the 18th century. From the 14th century, Poland and Hungary shared rulers and developed a close, traditional connection and friendship. All of these countries, including the Baltic States, had an extreme rightwing, even fascist past in the first half of the 20th century (especially during World War II), followed by a period of communist rule in the second half of that century. All lost independence at certain points and belonged to huge empires for quite a while. All also became independent countries after World War I and then again in the early 1990s. This area definitely exhibits certain homogeneities.

Belated and partial modernization: the historical background

As northwestern Europe moved through its revolutionary historical transformation from the Renaissance, via the Reformation and scientific revolution, to the Enlightenment, the Central European region was hardly touched. It remained largely frozen in the past even as northwestern countries, undergoing agricultural and industrial revolutions in the late 18th to early 20th centuries, became strongly urbanized and educated. Enlightened members of the Central European noble elite who traveled in the West saw the transformations there with their own eyes and complained about their countries' backwardness.

Hungarians Count István Széchenyi and his traveling companion Baron Miklós Wesselényi visited England, France, and the Netherlands in the early 19th century. Count Széchenyi, the leading early-19th-century reformer aristocrat in Hungary, wrote in his diary in 1822: "I feel profound pain and downheartedness at the situation … of our country. … Our country is sleeping." Eight years later, in his book *Credit*, he added: "Hungary has no commerce … Did we do enough to increase our output … and promote marketing? Many look down on commerce." His friend Baron Wesselényi, also an enlightened nobleman, described with admiration the modern crop rotation system he had seen in France and compared it to the medieval two- or three-field rotation regime – always leaving half to one-third of land fallow to promote soil recovery – still being practiced in Hungary. On his experience in Britain he enthusiastically reported: "One glass factory, coal mine, and iron works next to the other. … The steam engines are used everywhere and they are exquisite."[7]

Polish visitors to the northwestern countries also returned home positively impressed by their observations and critical of conditions and attitudes in their country. Having visited Britain in 1811 and 1819, aristocrat Dezydery Chłapowski established a model farm on his estate, basing his reforms on his experience in England. Stanisław Konarski, an enlightened and educated Piarist priest and writer, similarly advocated for the British example: "Let us govern ourselves like sensible people. … The God of nature did not search for different clay when he made Poles from what he used for Englishmen." After the failure of heroic but fruitless Polish noble uprisings against occupying Russia, the mid-19th-century poet-philosopher Cyprian Norwid accused the "unjustified national religion [with its] mystical heroic deeds" of undermining secular ideals.

In the 1870s, an enlightened intellectual circle, the Warsaw Positivists, advocated replacing heroic national struggles with *praca organiczna,* organic work: "In order to take their place among the modern nations in Europe the Poles must first improve trade and industry ... build towns and railways, and raise the rate of literacy."[8]

These diagnoses and recommendations were well justified, as the Central European region was indeed asleep. The only form of Western revolutionary thinking to take effective root in the region was anti-Enlightenment Romanticism, which arrived via Germany and subsequently generated passionate nationalism and heroic national struggles for independence. The most important fruits of this revolutionary cultural-political import were the Polish uprisings of the 1790s, 1830, and 1861, launched by three consecutive generations of the Polish nobility, and also the 1848–1849 fight for independence and revolution in Hungary.

"Noble values" (discussed in Chapter 2) and the social conditions associated with hierarchical, premodern societies continued to dominate the region throughout the 19th century. Serfdom, for example, persisted until 1848 in Hungary and until 1863 in Poland, effectively freezing agriculture in the past. Until the early 20th century, half to one-third of the land belonged to the exploitative large estates of a handful of aristocratic families. In the Czech lands, for example, 0.2 percent of landowners owned 32 percent of the land. The overwhelmingly dominant peasantry was mostly landless, or owners of dwarf-parcels, and largely illiterate until the last third of the century. In 1910, for example, 36 percent of Hungarian peasants, along with more than one-quarter of wage earners, could not read or write. Of the remaining population, the large majority had attained no more than an elementary school education; only 5 percent had gone on to secondary school.[9]

A modern middle class, including professionals, hardly existed. Until the 1870s, this category represented only about 8–10 percent of the working-age population, and not more than about 15 percent in the early 1910s. Moreover, two-thirds of the gentry, middle class or noble by birth, had become déclassé, having lost their relatively small landed estates. Yet they had not moved into the modern occupations of the Western middle classes but rather had chosen the traditional occupations of the nobility in the military and state-local bureaucracies. In this way they had preserved their elite noble status, even while losing class position.

None of the countries of the region were independent. Politically, all were incorporated into autocratic huge empires, either the Habsburg empire (and after the Austro-Hungarian Compromise in 1867, Austria-Hungary), or the Russian empire, or, in the case of tri-partitioned Poland, mostly the Russian empire, but partly also the Habsburg empire and Prussia. Moreover, excepting in the Czech lands (Bohemia and Moravia), which together with Austria proper belonged to the advanced part of the Habsburg empire bordering the West, the entire region remained economically dependent on traditional agriculture. This situation is clearly expressed by the 80 percent of the Hungarian labor force employed in that sector in 1870, a share that declined only to roughly two-thirds by 1910. In these overwhelmingly agricultural countries, the 18th- and 19th-century Western agricultural revolution, with its modern crop-rotation system, canalization and irrigation, early forms of mechanization, and use of fertilizer, did not arrive until late in the 19th century.

Industrialization and urbanization did not start until the last third of the 19th century. Consequently, when world war broke out in 1914, just 17–20 percent of working-class people in Central Europe labored in industry, while in the West the figure was 40–50 percent. Urbanization was in an embryonic stage, with just 20–25 percent of the population dwelling in cities. (In the 1910s, in Britain already 75 percent of the population lived in cities, and in Germany, the Netherlands, and Belgium, 50–53 percent.) Prague, Warsaw and Budapest, the largest cities of the region, had 677,000, 856,000, and 1.1 million inhabitants, respectively.

Nevertheless, the demonstration effect of the transforming West, together with the impact of belonging to large empires, slowly, mostly from the last third of the 19th century, produced a nascent modernization. The process began with the importation of basic scientific and medical advancements, which ended the devastating effect of the so-called medieval diseases in this region. Improvements in health and nutrition significantly decreased death rates while leaving traditionally high birth rates unaffected. Consequently, the millennium-long stagnation or extremely slow population growth gave way to an explosion. This new demographic trend had emerged first in the Netherlands and Britain in the s17th--18th centuries and had spread quickly to other Western countries. By the turn of the 19th century, the "Malthusian Check" had disappeared. Western European population increased by 360 percent between 1800 and 1910. Central Europe experienced a similar phenomenon, with Poland's population increasing from 9 to 29 million and Hungary's from 9.3 to 21 million during the long 19th century: 322 and 225 percent, respectively. The land could not offer enough jobs or sustenance to its inhabitants. A significant part, about one-fifth, of the younger generations, consequently emigrated to America. Even so, employing and feeding the new millions required more opportunities for work, along with housing and food.

The model to follow was close at hand. Offered by the West it consisted of forms of economic organization and technology. Having accumulated huge amounts of capital quite rapidly, Western countries were seeking opportunities to invest in neighboring, less-developed areas, not only to gain market for their products but also to satisfy their hunger for food and needs for raw materials. Foreign investments and loans flooded Central Europe.

Although British, French, and other West European countries started investing capital in the region in the early 19th century (in 1825, $0.9 billion and by 1870, $6 billion), the high time for foreign investments of European origin began only in the last third of the century. From $6 billion in 1870, this investment increased by 1913 to $46 billion. The significance of this latter figure is evident from the fact that it was equal to 20 percent of the world's aggregate

GDP. More than a quarter of this exported capital went to peripheral European countries, partly to Central Europe.[10] In the early 20th century, 12 percent of French and 23 percent of German capital-export targeted Austria-Hungary. Between 1867 and 1873, when modern transformation began in Hungary, 60 percent of invested capital in the country came from abroad, mostly from Austria and Germany. The amounts of invested capital multiplied in Hungary, yet, when compared to rapidly increasing domestic accumulation, the share actually was 25 percent before World War I.

This capital inflow provided the spark that ignited modern transformation in Central Europe. First came the introduction of a modern banking system after 1867, with central participation by Austrian and German banks. They owned 55 percent of Hungarian banking capital, for example, and financed the country's large landed estates by means of mortgage credits equaling more than half their assets. The newly funded big banks also owned 36 percent of industrial shares. Most importantly, foreign investments were the prime mover of railroad construction. In Hungary, again, the first rail line was opened in 1847, but the real boom started only after 1867 with 60 percent of investment financed by Austria. By 1913, a dense rail network 22,000 kilometers in length (including present-day Slovakia and Croatia) had been created. Each kilometer of line served a 15.7 square-kilometer area and 110 kilometers of line served every 100,000 inhabitants. This rail density was the sixth greatest in Europe, ahead even of some Western countries. In Poland and the Baltic region, French capital played the decisive role in building the 70,000-kilometer-long Russian railroad system. Half the length of the West European network, it connected Poland and the Baltic areas to the heartland of Russia. Rail transportation became the most advanced sector of the Central European economy, with a density more than half its counterpart in Western Europe.[11]

Railroads allowed the delivery of food and raw materials to the industrialized parts of Europe. By enabling access to distant markets, they motivated increased agricultural output. They also inspired the development of certain branches of mining and industry, particularly the mining of coal and iron ore, and the production of engineering parts to supply the railroad networks. Opportunities to work in railroad construction motivated a huge part of the landless peasant population to leave agriculture and the countryside. This was, in fact, their main road to urban industrial employment.

Although revolts against imperial masters occurred, belonging to large empires actually spurred economic modernization and elevation in Central Europe. This held regardless of the overall prosperity of the empire in question: Hungary benefited from association with more developed Austria and Bohemia in the Habsburg empire, but so did Poland and the Baltic states (including Finland), from their incorporation into the backward Russian empire. In the first case, the Western areas of the Habsburg empire not only financed the Hungarian economy but also offered the best market for that country's agricultural products, most of all grain. Access to these markets, in turn, stimulated a belated agricultural revolution in Hungary and rapid growth of the sector.

Hungarian, mostly Jewish, merchants, accumulated significant profit from grain trade to Austria. So that they could sell processed, thus more expensive, grain on the Austrian markets, they became the biggest investors in domestic flour mills. Consequently, Hungary became one of the world's biggest wheat-flour exporters. These food processors were the pioneers of Hungarian industrialization. Total industrial production increased by fourteen times between 1860 and 1913, with 40 percent of that coming from food processing.[12]

Despite the overall backwardness of the Russian imperial economy, demand from Russian markets sparked industrialization in Poland and the Baltic region. During the last third of the 19th century, Poland emerged as the third industrial center of the enormous empire. Between 1864 and 1910, but especially from 1890, the country's industrial output increased by 20-fold. Polish coal, a valuable commodity in the wider European market, accounted for 40 percent of the Russian empire's coal production. The textile industry employed 44 percent of industrial labor and produced nearly half of total industrial products, 80 percent of which went to the Russian markets. Polish textiles represented 20 percent of the empire's textile output, the steel and iron production, 23 and 15 percent, respectively. Export to Russia from Poland increased by 27 times and Polish per capita industrial production rose to twice the comparable Russian figure.

After incorporation into the Russian empire, the Baltic region, and particularly the small provinces of Latvia, Livonia, and Kurland, together developed as an important industrial center producing to Russian markets. This sector employed 35 percent of the region's labor force and produced 53 percent of its GDP. The Baltic metal, engineering and rubber industries sold 90 percent of their product in Russia; just three rubber factories delivered 28 percent of total imperial rubber output. The textile, leather, timber, and chemical industries sold 70 percent of their output to the Russian market, and the glass, china, and paper industries, 60 percent. This small region also produced one-third of the imperial cable and nail output.

Despite its incipient industrialization in the later 19th century, Central Europe could not keep pace with the stormy development of northwestern Europe, and instead remained basically agricultural. Before World War I, about two-thirds of the active population still worked on farms and in fields. An agricultural-industrial structure had emerged, with some deleterious effects. In comparison to the West, for example, Central Europe was more backward in 1913 than in 1870, when modernization began: its per capita GDP amounted to about 54 percent of the average income level of the eight advanced North and Western European countries (Austria, Belgium, the Netherlands, France, Germany, Sweden, Switzerland, and Britain). Although the scattered data available for these calculations makes these figures somewhat uncertain, more estimates than exact figures, the relation they reflect between Central Europe and Western Europe is well-based.[13] This region, compared to the high-income level North-West Europe, stood unquestionably at middle-income peripheral level.

The interwar fiasco

The interwar decades of the 20th century were an extremely troubled period all over the world, in Central Europe much more than elsewhere. After World War I, countries across this region acquired independence. Polish territories were reunited after 150 years of tripartition, the Baltic area liberated itself from Russia after the Bolshevik Revolution. After 400 years in the Habsburg empire (later Austria-Hungary), Hungary regained independence, but it also lost 60 percent of the original territory of the multiethnic Hungarian Kingdom. Czechoslovakia was newly created by combining lands from the historic Kingdom of Bohemia, Moravia, and Silesia with Slovakia, the former Slovak-inhabited Upper Hungary and Carpathian Ruthenia, all formerly part of the Hungarian Kingdom. Now, in the early twenty-first century the Czech Republic and Slovakia are independent countries (separated in 1993), while Carpathian Ruthenia, part of the Soviet Union after 1945, since 1991 has belonged to Ukraine.[14] Slovenia and Croatia, both removed from Austria-Hungary, became part of newly created Yugoslavia.[15]

This matter-of-fact description in itself captures the troubled historical past of the region and the extremely difficult challenges introduced after World War I. All of these countries, whether restored historical units or brand-new constructions, had to adjust to a totally new historical situation, to new borders and a new Europe. Poland, as an example, directed its efforts principally toward unifying its economy. It was not an easy task because each of the three former parts had been integrated previously into different empires. This problem is symbolized by the fact that at the beginning there were four different currencies in circulation.

All of these countries were trying to consolidate their economies in times of tremendous economic difficulty, caused partly by the war and the severe postwar inflation, partly by the new borders, and partly by the international economic situation. As is well known, a few years after postwar financial stabilization, when a quasi-normal economic condition had made possible further economic development, world history's most devastating economic crisis, the Great Depression of 1929–1933, hit the continent and the region very hard. Central Europe had not fully recovered the losses brought by this crisis when World War II broke out. By 1938 Hungary's GDP per capita had almost recovered the 1929 value, but the Czechoslovak and Polish GDPs remained 5 and 10 percent less than the 1929 levels.

World War II not only brought foreign occupation but also devastation, as armies fought heavy battles and, in cities, sometimes house-to-house. Peace rearranged the map again. Poland, literally speaking, was shifted to the West, within new borders, while the Baltic countries were incorporated again into Russia (now the Soviet Union). The entire region was introduced to Soviet-type, centrally planned, one-party governance.[16] Most of the countries came under Soviet occupation or control as parts of the so-called Soviet Bloc. Slovenia and Croatia – although outside the Soviet Bloc after 1948 – were parts of communist Yugoslavia.

The effects of interwar political and economic upheavals were wide-ranging and accompanied by sharp hostilities between neighboring, now independent countries. Ties that formerly had connected economies were cut. All of them introduced aggressive protectionist tariff policies against each other. Economic nationalism became the rule of the game and that generated tariff and trade wars.

Each country had to develop its economy to replace imports it had received from within its former empire, and each also had to look for new export markets to absorb the products previously sold on imperial markets. That was an extremely difficult challenge at the time, nearly insurmountable for Poland and the Baltic countries: 80 percent of Poland's prewar exports had been sold on the Russian markets before the war but after the war, with the collapse of tsarist Russia and subsequent closure of Russian markets in the context of revolution, the figure dropped to a mere 1.5 percent. Estonia's former important trade connection with Russia dropped from 22 to 3 percent; Lithuania and Latvia's export declined to 10 and 1 percent of prewar levels, respectively.[17]

In the near term, the new imperative of self-sufficiency somewhat stimulated the region's economies. Between 1913 and 1938, Czechoslovakia and Hungary, for example, increased their GDP by 14 and 12 percent, respectively. Poland, in contrast, never achieved its pre–World War I GDP level. Slovenia and Croatia, being already much more developed and industrialized than the Serbian-Bosnian-Macedonian parts of Yugoslavia, became the industrial centers of the new country. Despite these improvements, and because northwestern Europe was advancing somewhat faster, Central Europe faced conditions resembling the "Wonderland" where Alice was told that "one has to run twice as fast to stay in the same place." Viewed from this perspective, the very "modest progress" measured by per capita GDP becomes a significant success.[18]

The quantitative aspect of growth is not sufficient in itself, however, to fully evaluate economic development in any particular situation. The record of technological and structural development is more important. Could the Central European countries have followed in the footsteps of the advanced countries, with their technological development and modern economic restructuring? Certainly, they did not; rather, their interwar economic trends moved *against* the international tendency. The Czech lands, for example, had been industrial exporters and agricultural importers before the war. But newly created interwar Czechoslovakia, cut off from the traditional Hungarian agricultural deliveries that had sustained it as part of the Habsburg empire, now developed its domestic grain economy in order to ensure self-sufficiency: against the trend of the advanced world. The country was so successful as a grain producer that it became a grain exporter by the 1930s. Before the war, the especially strong Austro-Bohemian textile industry exhibited a special division of labor: spinning was concentrated in the Czech lands and weaving in Austria. Now these two parts were separated, and each country built up the missing sector, the Czechs the weaving and the Austrians the spinning capacities. Hungary, by contrast, had not developed a textile industry because its role in the imperial division of labor had consisted of delivering grain and food to the Czech Lands and Austria and of buying the Austrian and Czech textiles and other industrial products. In the new situation, to create self-sufficiency, Hungary concentrated on building up its own textile and other consumer goods industries. The fourfold increase in textile output during the interwar decades contributed the most of any sector to the country's industrial growth. The textile sector became the fastest developing branch of the economy, at a time when it was already declining in the advanced world.

Developing the grain economy and textile industry stimulated growth but in sectors that, in advanced countries, belonged to the past. In Denmark and Norway, for example, agriculture's contribution to national income dropped from 30 to 21 percent and from 24 to 14 percent respectively. Between 1913 and 1950, agricultural employment in northwestern Europe decreased from 23 to 13 percent and in Europe as a whole from 47 to 36 percent. Yet in Poland and Hungary more than half of the active population worked in agriculture. Britain's leading textile industry sharply declined between 1912 and 1938: cotton yarn output by 50 per cent, the number of cotton spindles and looms by 70 and 60 percent. (Britain actually sold the old textile machines at scrap-iron prices and Hungary built up its textile industry by purchasing them.) Meanwhile, the manufacture of artificial fibers, electrical goods and cars doubled in the West. In the Netherlands, textile employment dropped to 19 percent, while employment in engineering and chemical industries jumped from 17 to 30 percent. Establishing modern sectors and using new technology led to increases in labor productivity (the value of produced GDP per work-hour): in France, it nearly doubled, in Norway, Sweden, and Switzerland it increased by two-and-half times between 1913 and 1950. Even so, Europe as a whole could not keep pace with the United States: Western Europe's productivity level, 70 percent of the American in 1870, and 59 percent in 1913, dropped to 46 percent by 1950. And, at only half the Western European level, Central Europe fell ever farther behind.[19]

Relative backwardness was also expressed by the consumption of modern electric appliances and cars, which spread in the North-West but remained a rarity in Central Europe. The per capita number of telephone sets in the region was only about one-tenth of the Western level. The so-called motorization index, the number of cars in comparison to territory and population of a country, as an average was 5.7 in Europe, but only 1.8 in Czechoslovakia, 0.5 in Hungary, and 0.3 in Poland.

In the late 1930s, preparations for war in the framework of the Győr Program in Hungary and the Industrial Triangle Program in Poland, which brought investments in iron, steel and engineering, also furthered modernization, but they did not decisively contribute to Central European economic development. In 1934, some parts of the region integrated into the Nazi-initiated *Grossraumwirtschaft*, a trade agreement zone geared toward war. Thus, they subordinated themselves to Nazi interests and moved their economies into a subservient position with only transitory benefits. In other words, their economies primarily developed, not the most modern economic branches but instead those that already had declined in advanced countries or that would have but a temporary relevance as suppliers to the Nazi war effort.

As it did in economic policy, nationalism flooded into the political arena. This led to harsh confrontation between Czechs and Slovaks in Czechoslovakia and to even more deadly conflict between Croats and Serbs in Yugoslavia already in the 1920s. Hungary introduced Europe's first anti-Jewish legislation in 1920, and anti-Semitism permeated politics in the authoritarian Horthy regime. During the 1930s a Hungarian Nazi party was established, and in the first secret ballot election in the country in 1939, it emerged as the strongest party, with 40 percent of the vote. After a few years of democratic opening, newly united Poland also turned to authoritarian, one-party rule. Following the outbreak of World War II fascist parties took over in Slovakia (1939), Croatia (1941), and Hungary (1944). The goal of exterminating the Jewish population, initiated by the occupying or allied Nazi Germany, but assisted and realized by local authorities, produced the darkest chapter of the war, the Holocaust. The Jewish population in Poland was reduced from 3 million to 600,000, in Lithuania from about 210,000 to 10,000–15,000. In Hungary, it was halved. About half of the 1.5 million Holocaust survivors in the Central European and Baltic region emigrated after the war.

During World War II, the region became a battlefield. All of the countries were occupied and became scenes of most devastating warfare, Poland twice. Yugoslavia, under German occupation, experienced partisan warfare and 11 German military offensives. Most of the Czech lands became a German protectorate, but the Sudetenland with its German population was incorporated fully into the German Reich. So also was Slovenia. Throughout the region, the population was decimated. About 6 million Polish citizens perished during World War II, nearly one-fifth of the prewar population. Estonia lost one-quarter of its inhabitants, and Hungary, 8–10 percent. About three million ethnic Germans escaped from the region at the end of the war, along with the withdrawing German troops, or were expelled after the war. Together with the Holocaust, a significant part of the German-Jewish modernized middle class was eliminated.

The stagnation of the interwar period and the severe destruction caused by the total war together prevented Central Europe from escaping its condition of relative backwardness. Still not fully industrialized, the region remained agricultural-industrial structurally. Even with the stimulus provided by successful and surprisingly fast postwar reconstruction, the average income level of the region, calculated in constant prices, increased only by 33 percent during the 37 years between 1913 and 1950. Moreover, by 1950, average per capita GDP relative to the European northwest had fallen by two percentage points from 1913 levels, to just 48 percent. Thus, regional relative backwardness actually had increased.[20]

"Detour from the periphery to the periphery"

After World War II, in the radically changed political environment under Soviet control, the Central European periphery was cut off from Europe for nearly half a century, removed from its former economic ties and relations with the West, as well as from the particulars of their ambiguous effects. In their place the Soviets imposed a non-market, totally state-owned, centrally planned economic system, along with collectivized agriculture and a program of forced capital accumulation and industrialization. This Soviet model, first formulated in the 1920s by Bolshevik economist Yevgeni Preobrazhensky, had been taken over by Stalin and developed in the 1930s in the context of war preparations and of the terrible battles following the Nazi invasion of Russia.[21] When imposed in Central Europe, after the war came to an end, the model undeniably led to the fastest industrialization in the region's history, but the price for this success was high.

To illustrate, let me briefly sum up the main characteristics of the forced industrialization program. The first of the two central pillars of the model, and its merit, lay in stressing low levels of capital accumulation and investment, the principal causes of peripheral backwardness. It is a commonplace, and also a very personal experience of poor people, that a low living standard is naturally accompanied by low savings rates in the affected population. In sharp contrast to the rich, the poor have to spend most of their low income for food, accommodation, and other basics. The situation is exactly the same with poor and rich countries. Capital accumulation is low in the former and high in the latter. Low-income level, in other words, is sufficient in itself to reproduce relative backwardness, because it prevents accumulation and investment. The Soviet economic model, developed in a poor country with a traditionally low level of income and capital accumulation, solved this problem. In 1928, in line with this model, the regime introduced forced capital accumulation, by keeping wages and the living standard brutally low, and most of all by exploiting peasant agriculture with a "price scissor" of high industrial and low, at cost, agricultural prices.[22] In a nonmarket system, with its centrally fixed prices backed by a dictatorial political system, resistance was virtually impossible. The result was an increase of capital accumulation in the 1930s to an unheard of 35–40 percent of the GDP, enabling the tremendous investments of the first Five Year Plan.

In Central Europe, where the accumulation level in the interwar decades was about 6–8 percent of the GDP, hardly more than half of the Western level, the application of this model dramatically increased accumulation to 20–35 percent in the 1950s, and kept it at about 20 percent during subsequent decades. Investments varied between 13 percent in the extremely Stalinist 1950s and about 9–10 percent later on. As a consequence, the ratio of fixed capital investments to GDP was higher in the region than in the West. As in the Soviet Union, a large part of this investment – until the 1980s, 35–40 percent – went to industry.[23]

An emphasis on redirecting huge numbers of workers from agriculture to industry provided the other central pillar of the model. Forced collectivization served this purpose. Begun between 1948 and 1953, and accomplished by 1960, collectivization uprooted 40–50 percent of the Central European peasantry and pushed them into construction and industrial work. Agricultural populations declined to 24–38 percent in Poland, Hungary, and Czechoslovakia. Employment became mandatory; not to take a job became a crime. A permanent high labor input, a steady 7 percent increase in the number of new laborers every year, likewise contributed to rapid growth. This extensive growth model, in turn, generated rapid industrialization.

During the high Stalinism of the 1950s, as an American congressional study revealed, industrial output increased by 8–9 percent per annum and rapid growth continued until the 1970s–1980s, although at a somewhat slower rate. Between 1970 and 1988, according to the United Nations Statistical Yearbook, Czechoslovakia, Hungary, and Poland doubled their industrial production. At the end of the 1980s, the entire Central European region was highly industrialized, with the sector producing 61, 41, and 48 percent of the GDP, respectively, in the aforementioned three larger countries.[24]

After the death of Stalin, subsequent regimes modified the collectivization model to address the stubborn problem of chronic food shortages. For 20 years, agricultural output had been unable to surpass prewar levels and severe food shortages plagued the region. In the modified system, agricultural investments increased by three to five times from the late 1950s until the 1980s, and the use of artificial fertilizer jumped from about 5–12 kilograms per hectare before the war to 200–300 kilograms per hectare in the later 1980s. Rapid mechanization complimented these changes. According to the United Nations Food and Agricultural Organization, agricultural production doubled in postwar Czechoslovakia and Hungary and increased by roughly half in Poland. Average wheat yields in Czechoslovakia and Hungary surpassed the European average by 50 percent, corn and sugar beet yields by 20–25 percent. Agricultural output per capita developed the most in Hungary, reaching 98 percent of the US level in the 1980s.

When compared to its prewar state, Central Europe's economic growth was definitely impressive. The region's per capita income level more than doubled, increasing by 237 percent between 1950 and 1990.[25] Industrialization and rapid economic growth, however, were achieved by huge sacrifices. Low income levels and living standards, shortages of everything for quite long periods, and existence in oppressive regimes were the price to pay for development and growth. Moreover, despite their impressive achievements, these tremendous efforts failed in the end. Backwardness was reproduced in a different way.

Crisis and collapse

From the mid-1970s Central Europe (together with the entire Soviet bloc) declined into a deep crisis. The adopted extensive growth model was exhausted, and the huge labor input of the 1950s and 1960s could continue no longer. Forced capital accumulation also had to moderate significantly in face of riots and revolutions in 1956 in Hungary and Poland, and in 1968 in Czechoslovakia. To pacify the population, governments had to increase living standards and consumption levels. Capital formation transitorily dropped to 13 and 15 percent in Czechoslovakia and Hungary after the mid-1950s. The two oil crises in 1973 and 1979–1980 complicated matters by undermining the trade balance within the Soviet bloc. The "terms of trade," the relations of export and import prices, severely declined: in some of the countries by 20 percent, but in heavily energy importer Hungary by 50 percent between the war and 1989.

Governments began relying on foreign credits from oil-producing countries to fill the gaps and finance trade deficits. A severe indebtedness followed: Hungary accumulated a debt burden of $20 billion, Poland of $42 billion, two times and five times greater than hard currency export incomes, respectively. For political reasons, these credits were directed mostly toward consumption, in order to keep the living standard relatively stable. From its $20 billion credit, Hungary invested only $4–5 billion. Poland, in contrast, sought to exit the crisis by shoring itself up with additional investment in what were the increasingly obsolete branches of industry, which had been central to Soviet industrialization policy. Meanwhile, cheap credits disappeared and interest rates on outstanding loans became almost unbearable. Poland and Yugoslavia became insolvent and asked for a rescheduling of their debt payments.

The crisis that hit Central Europe was actually an international "structural crisis," the type of economic crisis excellently analyzed by one of the leading economists of the first half of the 20th century, Joseph Schumpeter. In his interpretation, structural crises are caused by technological-industrial revolutions, which make the leading sectors in old technology regimes obsolete and declining, while new sectors, based on new technology, emerge. "Industrial revolution[s] ... periodically reshape the existing structure of industry. ... [During] the elimination of antiquated elements of the industrial structure, 'depression' is predominant." New, modern sectors develop during such periods, but until they ignite a new prosperity, stagnation continues, sometimes for 10 to 15 years: "Thus there are prolonged periods of rising and falling prices, interest rates, employment and so on, which phenomena constitute parts of the mechanism of this process of recurrent rejuvenation of the productive apparatus."[26]

With the worldwide structural crisis of the 1970s–1980s, old sectors unavoidably declined everywhere. In the West, however, emerging modern sectors soon counterbalanced the decline of the old and led to new prosperity. Quoting Schumpeter:

> The fundamental impulse that sets and keeps the capitalist engine in motion ... revolutionizes the economic structure from within, incessantly destroying the old one, incessantly creating the new one. This process of Creative Destruction is the essential fact about capitalism.[27]

Exactly that happened in the Western European countries. They gave up the postwar extensive development model and turned to an intensive model, based on their own research and innovation, in order to enter into the new technological age. In Central Europe, however, Schumpeterian "Creative Destruction," the elimination of the old to clear the ground for the new, could not work. Structural crisis there was highly destructive but not creative. Sectors based on new technology could not take root here. The region needed to introduce major market reforms and to end its isolationist practice of import-substitution.

The three leading countries of the region recognized the need to end the Soviet-type extensive, import-substituting industrialization model. Quoting from my own lecture in Budapest, where I lived that time, delivered at the General Assembly meeting of the Hungarian Academy of Sciences in May 1977: "The resources of the extensive industrialization and economic development are exhausted … The only way for further development is the mobilization of the intensive sources of economic growth, the technological-organizational and productivity factors."[28]

Efforts to address recognized needs for change varied from country to country. Croatia and Slovenia, the most advanced parts of Yugoslavia, opened toward the West and developed an independent model of communist economy based on private agriculture and a system of worker self-management. They did not, however, eliminate the basic features of state-owned economy. Hungary and Poland made some efforts toward opening and joined both the international trade and tariff agreement (GATT) and the International Monetary Fund (IMF). Economic reforms started in all of the three countries, but they met with strong Soviet resistance. In the case of Czechoslovakia reform, attempts were brutally cut short by Soviet Bloc military invasion in the summer of 1968. Hungary, in contrast, gained some elbow room after the defeat of its 1956 revolution, also by Soviet military invasion: preferring to keep the delicate political balance in the country, the Soviet government allowed the country to proceed with some reforms. Partial changes to the Soviet model began in the later 1960s. Poland started down the same path after the military suppression of the peaceful Solidarity uprising in 1981, but it was too late for real results, especially because the martial law imposed after the uprising had brought about the total isolation of the country. In the Baltic area that belonged to the Soviet Union, real reforms were impossible, but the region fought for independence and obtained it in 1991. Reforms became possible only after that success.

All in all, Central Europe was unable either to follow the requirements of, or give an adequate answer to, the challenge of the structural crisis. Their economies were based on an obsolete, 50- to 80-year-old structural-technological patterns, with concentration in anachronistic heavy industrial branches such as coal, iron, steel, metallurgy, and certain forms of engineering. The countries could not follow the new pattern of structural change, which, in the West were acquiring pre-eminence from the 1970s on. In particular, Central Europe could not follow along the path of the dramatic new technological-communications revolution, which opened a new age in the 1970s with the breakthrough of the computer revolution.

The Central European region, as the peripheries in general, never at the forefront of innovation, always had to rely on technology supplied by foreign countries. During the second half of the 20th century this imported technology was Soviet-, Czechoslovak-, or East German-made, far beneath standards in the West. It belongs to the truth that American political decisions in the early years of the Cold War played a principal part in creating this situation. The United States Congress, as early as 1947, banned technology exports to the Soviet bloc. This position became institutionalized in 1949, with the passage of the United States Export Control Act, establishment of the Organization for European Economic Co-operation and, in the fall of the same year, foundation of the Coordinating Committee for Multilateral Export Controls (CoCom). In 1952, the CoCom List contained 400 major categories and 150,000–200,000 items. Modern telecommunication and biotechnology, computer and software sales were all banned. In the late 1970s, revisions to the ban added infrastructural areas to the list of prohibited exports and also targeted blocking "cultural preparedness," the learning of modern technology and industrial procedures by studying them in the West. By means of frightening sanctions, the United States forced this policy on all Western countries including neutral Sweden.[29] When Hungary, for example, signed a trade agreement to buy a digital telephone exchange system from the German Standard Electric Lorenz company in the 1980s, the deal was canceled by American veto, and NATO countries had to accept the American decision. Consequently, neither the communications revolution nor high-tech industry, nor even the transportation innovations that were transforming the West, arrived in the region until after the collapse of the Soviet bloc.

The combination of technological backwardness and low income kept the crucially decisive productivity level inferior in comparison to the West. In 1950, the Central European countries average productivity (produced GDP per work-hour by a worker) was $2.90, only half the West European level. Productivity increased to $7.22, 2.5 times, by 1992, but in the same period, West European productivity – because of the new technological revolution – increased by four times to $25.30. Instead of holding steady at 50 percent of the Western level, the region's productivity had declined to one-quarter of it.[30] The "Marxist-Leninist" orthodoxy practiced in the Soviet Union and imposed also on the countries of Central Europe had failed to implement policies based even on Lenin's 1918 observation that "the fundamental task of creating a social system superior to capitalism … [is] raising the productivity of labor."[31]

The state-socialist countries of Central Europe were sucked into a whirlpool which pulled them deeper and deeper below. The regimes lost control of inflation. Between 1986 and 1989 Poland suffered a 251 percent and Yugoslavia a more than 1,200 percent annual hyperinflation. Hungary's inflation rate was 17 and 18 percent in the last two Soviet bloc years.[32] Growth slowed down and lost more ground compared to Western Europe: between 1973 and 1989 the

Czechoslovak per capita GDP declined from 57 percent to 51 percent of the West European average, the Hungarian from 45 percent to 40 percent, and the Polish from 43 percent to 33 percent.[33] Political elites and governments lost self-confidence along with the hope of being able to cope with the unsolvable problems, and opposition movements emerged, especially in Poland. The Soviet regime peacefully collapsed in 1989, first in Poland, then in Hungary, and at last in Czechoslovakia. In Yugoslavia, the communist regime collapsed together with the Yugoslav state, and subsequently both Slovenia and Croatia (as well as Serbia, Macedonia, and Bosnia) – accompanied by a bloody civil war – became independent. The three Baltic countries exploited the crisis of the Soviet Union and in close cooperation with each other declared their independence. Soviet tanks tried to reverse their secession but failed, and the reform-oriented Gorbachev leadership acquiesced to the loss. So began transformation in a region of newly independent states.

Transformation to democratic market capitalism in new state formations

The Central European saga did not come to an end in 1989; rather, the nationalist revolutions of the 19th century and interwar period opened a new chapter, which concluded in a rush of new state creations. Most of the multiethnic, multinational states of the region dissolved after the demise of communism. Czechoslovakia and Yugoslavia, created as independent states only in 1918, broke up in 1993 and 1991–1995, respectively. The Soviet Union itself collapsed in 1991. New and newer state formations dominated the 1990s: 29 independent states now occupied the same area as the eight former states of communist Central and Eastern Europe, with nine of the new entities in the Central European and Baltic region. This meant a permanent adjustment process to new borders and territories from the late 19th century to the 1990s causing a pretty chaotic historical time.

A stormy economic transformation began in parallel with the emergence of new state formations. When the Berlin Wall collapsed, the crisis-ridden countries turned to the International Monetary Fund for assistance. As a prerequisite for loans, the countries had to accept the "recommendations" of the so-called Washington Consensus, a typical neoliberal plan requiring countries accustomed to high protectionism and isolation to privatize their state-owned economies immediately and to liberalize trade by opening their borders and introducing free trade. With some negligible differences, all countries of the region except Slovenia and Croatia adopted the required policy. The two holdouts, having the earlier Yugoslavia as a model, considered an independent and gradualist transformation, with much slower privatization, more appropriate for their economies. Slovenia even restricted foreign investment.

What followed was like opening the windows of a hothouse in the middle of a cold winter, in the expectation that the plants will adjust healthily to "normal" weather conditions: tremendous devastation and decline followed. Millions lost their jobs and poverty rates rose as high as 15–25 percent. Production declined drastically. Between 1989 and 1992, Hungarian agricultural output dropped by 35 percent. Latvia, now independent from the Soviet Union, suffered annual declines of 29, 18, and 15 percent between 1992 and 1994; Lithuania, 23, 6, and 20 percent in the same years. In the three bigger Central European countries crude steel and cotton yarn production declined by 44 and 61 percent by 1993, and total industrial output by 37 percent. Per capita GDP, between 1989 and the nadir in 1992–1993, declined by 21, 19, and 17 percent in Czechoslovakia, Hungary, and Poland, respectively.[34] The successor states of former Yugoslavia suffered the most: the combination of the 1991–1995 civil war and the economic transformation crisis led to a decline of nearly 40 percent. Industrial output halved in Croatia between 1990 and 1996. Losses caused by the transition would not be recovered until 2000, after which nearly a decade of boom would ensue. That boom, however, would be, brought to a sudden halt in the worldwide Great Recession of 2008.[35]

The 1990s "shock therapy," as it was nicknamed, not only was forced on the transforming countries by the IMF and the Washington Consensus, and not only was recommended warmly by the Western experts who flooded Central Europe as advisors of new governments, but also was enthusiastically welcomed by the rising new elites of the region's newly independent countries. They all wanted to go "back to Europe," to quote their favorite slogan, and they thought to be able to do it in a few years, thus rejected gradualism. The World Bank agreed: "This chaotic environment, combining a disintegrating economy with a rapidly weakening government, allowed no scope for gradual reform. For these countries the all-out approach was the only one available."[36] One of the best Hungarian economists, who presented the deepest critical analyses of state socialist economies from the late 1950s, János Kornai, argued along the same lines in December 1992:

> The severe decrease of production is a painful side effect of the healthy process of changing the system. ... Its cause is the transition from socialism to capitalism. .... To end the decline one should ... accomplish even faster the task still remaining.[37]

Some experts, however, disagreed. Nobel laureate economist Joseph Stiglitz, for example, opined that the sudden withdrawal of the state was mistaken because the state should have been allowed to play an important role by creating appropriate regulations and social protections: "We should not see the state and market as substitutes. ... The government should see itself as a compliment to markets, undertaking those actions that make markets fulfill their function better."[38]

Neither scenario came to pass as envisioned. Instead, today, states are resuming their former dominant roles in the economies of some of these countries. The long legacy of history, the path-dependence operative in human societies, has penetrated the transformation process, and in certain respects it has deformed newly introduced Western-style structures and institutions. In several Central European countries, an alternative to the Western democratic free market system, the Asian-Russian "authoritarian state-led economic model," has acquired popularity and power since the turn of the 21st century. A close connection between the state, banks and industry is allowing a kind of neocorporatism, the so-called "state catch," to emerge. Here the state, the new political elite and the newly created oligarchs (the robber-beneficiaries of years of extremely corrupt privatization of the state sector), all closely connected, assist each other in maintaining dominance. Huge amounts of money and wealth are being concentrated in the hands of state-connected individuals.[39] This system has developed across the entire former communist bloc, probably most extremely in Russia and some other successor states of the Soviet Union, but also strongly in Poland, Hungary, and other Central European countries.

In Slovenia and Croatia, despite their gradualist post-Soviet road, the slogan of creating a "national middle class" has offered crony capitalism as a national agenda. Advocating "national capitalism" and "national interest," domestic owners, actually political cronies, often family members and party friends, have taken over banks, telecom, insurance, and energy companies. The deformation of newly emerging capitalism into "crony capitalism" is a phenomenon typical in peripheral countries.[40] Slovenian analysts report that the political elite has used "parallel networks of informal rules. They [have] captured the state and distribute[d] the spoils."[41] A Hungarian author, offering a detailed presentation of facts about the same phenomenon, writes of the creation of a "post-communist mafia state."[42] Institutionalized corruption, as an *Economist* article mentioned earlier in this book has stated, has "replaced communism."

The merger of political and economic elites also has opened the door to authoritarian tendencies. The troubled years of the early 1990s caused a social shock to the population, only partly connected with issues of economic decline and frighteningly rising poverty. As with any major historical transformation, regardless of positive or negative historical role, this one of the 1990s required inhabitants to make fundamental changes to their life strategies and behavior patterns, in a wholly changed social-political environment.[43] For many people, the necessary changes were highly confusing and difficult to learn. With the demise of the former system of poor but egalitarian life, some people grew rich, seemingly overnight, while most people struggled. In these circumstances old social-cultural "values" began to represent lost stability and security. The large numbers of people who had not believed communist anti-capitalist rhetoric now turned against Western-type capitalism and offered a mass base for nationalist rightwing populism. ("What we learned about socialism was a big lie," the saying goes, "but everything was true that they said about capitalism.") Political reaction was often, and inevitably, extreme. The combination of the disappearance of the "socialist value system" and the imperatives of still unlearned new ideas created an ideological vacuum that was filled by religion for some, by racist-rightwing ideas for others and by politics, all having been suppressed for decades. These came to the surface almost immediately after the regime change. Anti-Roma atrocities shocked Prague and Hungary. Rightwing nationalism took over Slovakia and Croatia under the Mečiar and Tuđman regimes. Anti-Semitism openly resurfaced in Poland and Hungary, countries of only a few thousand Jews.[44] Submerged soon, however, because the countries were attempting to join the European Union, these trends and sentiments bubbled back up to the surface in the 2010s, as economic difficulties returned.

Recovery and development based on capital inflow: under the tutelage of the European Union

The entire process of decline and recovery was closely connected with the European Union, which was eager to accept the region's countries as new members. Speaking in Bruges in November 1989, after regime change already had started in Poland and Hungary, but a few days before the collapse of the Berlin Wall, Jacques Delors, the president of the European Commission, stated that Europe would not "close the door to other European countries willing to accept the terms of the contract ... It is the East that is being drawn toward the West. Will the Community prove equal to the challenge of the future?" A few weeks later, in December 1989, Chancellor Helmut Kohl told Secretary of State James Baker that in the future "the Czechs as well as the Hungarians and Poles will join the European Community."[45]

The European Union wanted to create a united, cooperating, peaceful Europe and also to enlarge the integrated Single Market with another 100 million people, hungry to buy its products and willing to work for lower wages than their Western counterparts. Consequently, it did not wait passively as Central European and Baltic countries stepped into their newfound independent status. Rather, it sought to influence the direction of developments in these countries by offering lavish aid packages and EU membership, dependent, however, on implementing specific Western laws and rules. The *acquis communautaire*, an official EU document of more than 80,000 pages, outlined the required changes. From the mid-1990s, almost all of the Central European and Baltic countries introduced enough changes to become candidates, and, in 2004, full members of the European Union. Croatia was the last to join, in 2013.Capital from the West began flowing into the region immediately after the collapse of communism. In November 1989, the month the Berlin Wall fell, the Commission of the European Community hosted a meeting of the representatives of 24 advanced countries and pledged $6.5 billion in aid for Poland and Hungary, the first countries to destroy the communist regime. Four days later, President George H. W. Bush signed a bill authorizing $1 billion in aid for those two countries. Very soon, the 24 advanced countries decided to give another $27 billion to Poland, Hungary, and Czechoslovakia. The creditor countries also forgave the more than half of the Polish debt.

Even more importantly, private investors, major European banks and huge multinational corporations, as well as hundreds and thousands of relatively smaller Western companies, sought to take advantage of the opening of the region by buying state-owned firms and making "greenfield investments"; that is, investments to cut into the market of the region and exploit the tremendous wage difference compared to the West. By 1993, between $13 and $15 billion already was channeled to the area. In the mid-1990s, the transition countries started issuing "Eurobonds," and selling them in the West. In this form loans also arrived in Central Europe and the Baltic countries: in 1998–1999 the amount was $5–6 billion. In 1989, at French initiative, a new European Bank of Reconstruction and Development (EBRD) was also established. Modeled after the World Bank, the EBRD was financed initially with $12 billion capital (doubled in 1997) from 60 countries, to be directed toward transformation. The EBRD became the largest single investor to the region. Between 1991 and 2004, the bank distributed roughly $80 billion among the former Soviet Bloc countries. After these countries (Romania and Bulgaria included) became members of the European Union the EBRD regularly invested an annual $1 billion in the region.[46]

Begun even before the countries became EU members, significant amounts of EU aid continued afterwards. Standard EU policy designated every EU region with a GDP level less than 75 percent of the EU average eligible for aid. In two full budgetary periods, between 2007 and 2014 and from 2014 to 2020, the EU provided billions to the Central European region. The three main beneficiaries were Poland (€67.2 and €76.9 billion), the Czech Republic (€26.3 and €21.6 billion) and Hungary (€24.9 and €21.5 billion). The region's countries altogether received €150 billion in the first budgetary period, and €152 billion in the second. These were enormous amounts, in certain years equaling about 15–20 percent, but usually 4–5 percent of the countries' GDP.[47]

This aid, mostly from the EU's Cohesion Policy Fund, did not account, however, for the entire EU budgetary inflow to the region. The EU's agricultural assistance program (CAP) also contributed. In the case of Poland, the earlier noted €67.2 billion aid from the 2007–2014 budget was accompanied by a significant amount from CAP; the country altogether received more than €101 billion. In the 2014–2020 period, to the €76.9 billion aid another €28.5 billion was added from the agricultural fund, altogether more than $105 billion. Although in the other countries of the region agriculture was less dominant than in Poland, billions of euros directed from CAP to this sector contributed also to their development.

Between 1993 and 2002, loans from sources other than the EU budget accounted for 26 percent of capital inflow, while another 19 percent came from portfolio investment: purchase of stocks, bonds, and other assets. The biggest share came from foreign direct investment (FDI) by companies and individuals, either to establish business operations or acquire business assets. Between 1989 and 2004, Poland received more than $56 billion FDI (nearly $1,500 per inhabitant), the Czech Republic almost $42 billion, Hungary more than $37 billion. Slovakia's share was more than $11 billion, and Croatia's $9.3 billion. (On a per capita basis this amounted in the first two cases to about $4,000, and to more than $2,000 for the other countries.) Slovenia and the three Baltic countries each received $3–4 billion ($1,500–$2,800 per capita). Altogether, more than $161 billion in FDI flew into the region.[48]

European Union aid and FDI inflow became the most important factors in Central European and Baltic transformation, recovery, and economic growth, as clearly reflected in the percentages of GDP as a result of foreign investment. In the Czech Republic, for example, until 1997, the amount received annually equaled 2–3 percent of the GDP, then rose to 9–10 percent between 1998 and 2002. Although somewhat slowed down subsequently, in 2003–2005 it was still 5–6 percent. In Hungary, FDI equaled 8–9 percent of the GDP until 1997, and after 1998, 5–6 percent. In Poland, the comparable figures were 2 percent per annum until 1998, and thereafter, 3–4 percent. In Slovakia until 1998 the annual share was 2 percent, and subsequently, 3–4 percent. In the Baltic region, Estonia integrated its economy quite closely with Sweden and Finland, while in the former Yugoslavia, the gradualist and anti-foreign investment policies in Slovenia privileged the independent "national economy." Slovenia only slowly opened its economy to FDI after 1995, and even then, FDI's annual share of the GDP stayed at a low 1–2 percent.[49]

If, as these figures substantiate, foreign investors during the first post-Soviet years favored Hungary and the Czech Republic, by the early 21st century, they shifted their attention to Poland: in 2005 the country stood as the fifth most-preferred investment location, having risen from a previous 12th place. One in ten global investors indicated in 2005 that they would make first-time investments in the country.[50] Among the smaller countries of the region, Estonia and Slovakia were the favorites.

Foreign direct investment currently continues to underwrite large percentages of GDP in the region. In Poland, original EU countries hold the highest share of foreign-owned productive capacity. Of foreign firms investing in Poland in 2006, for example, the largest number originated from Germany (5,718) while France came in second (1,075), followed by Britain (927) and the United States (733).[51] In 2004, to offer another example, the share of foreign stock as a percentage of GDP in Hungary, the Czech Republic, Slovenia, and Slovakia constituted respectively 43, 34, 24, and 22 percent of GDP, while in Poland the share was 19 percent. These high percentages indicate that foreign capital was playing a vital role in Central Europe and the Baltics in the years before financial meltdown plunged economies worldwide into deep recession. Almost all of this type of investment (88 percent) came from European Union countries.[52] In the banking sector, foreign companies and investors controlled about 87 percent of the total banking assets; in the Czech Republic and Estonia, 96–97 percent of total.

In the uncertain competitive environment associated with the globalized economy, powerful European multinational corporations pushed the European Union to further integrate the economies of the European continent. A regionalized Europe, it was maintained, would be able to compete against American, Japanese and other rivals. The Single Market project established between 1985 and 1992 indeed eliminated most of the roadblocks to the free flow of goods, capital, and people within the EU. Banks acquired "European Passports" and corporations acquired "European Company" status, allowing their free operation throughout the European Union. As Central European countries became candidates to the EU, and then members, this new regionalized Europe moved ahead full steam. Leading Western companies built up value chains and subsidiary networks in Central Europe and the Baltics. Western banks, such as the French BNP Paribas and Société Générale, along with the German Deutsche Bank and the Austrian Erste Group and Raiffeisen Bank International, entered the region. The German Daimler-Benz and Volkswagen, as well as some other Western automakers, built up a large car industry in the Czech Republic, Slovakia, Hungary, and Poland. Slovakia, nicknamed "Volkswagen Land," actually became number one in the world in per capita car production.

In the first years of transition, Western companies signed outward processing agreements with several Central European countries. Under the terms of these agreements, the Western companies provided the materials and design, while the local Central European firms, mostly in low-tech textile, clothing, leather, and furniture industries, manufactured the products. Until 1996, 75 percent of Central European outward processing exports to the EU originated from these sectors. In other words, Western companies took advantage of the low wage level in the region, which in several countries, at exchange rate parity, was only 7 percent of the Western level.

In the later 1990s, however, such businesses began losing importance, as foreign companies turned to mostly semi-high-tech or high-tech production. From then on, Western multinationals needed a well-trained labor force and high-level engineers. Several major Western companies established research and development centers in the region, and engineering, communication technology, and electric and chemical industries developed. These new high-tech and semi-high-tech industries facilitated better outcomes and established new export sectors. In Hungary, for example, their value-added contribution was 24 percent in the early 21st century, the same level as in Japan and higher than the average of the G-7 countries. In the same years the share in total industrial output of high-tech combined with semi-high-tech industries in that country, and also in the Czech Republic, reached the G-7 level of 67 percent. But the benefits of these developments were not spread evenly, either geographically or socially. Poland, for example, had only a 33 percent share.[53] Moreover, the companies in the region producing for semi-high-tech and high-tech were (and still) in fact only parts of the value chains of Western companies, and their products required mostly unskilled, low-paid labor. In Hungary the share of unskilled labor in these sectors was almost 40 percent in 2006, in Estonia nearly 60 percent. In the Netherlands, by contrast, unskilled labor accounted for only 17 percent.[54]

In general, Western corporations built up a modern export sector in Central Europe and the Baltics. In Hungary multinationals provided 82 percent of total industrial investments, employed 47 percent of the industrial labor force, delivered 73 percent of sold products and 89 percent of industrial exports at the turn of the century. Four Western multinationals, Philips, Audi, Opel, and IBM, produced 30 percent of Hungarian exports. In the Czech Republic, foreign, mostly European multinational companies provided 53 percent of investments, 27 percent of industrial employment, and 61 percent of exports. This share was lower in Poland.

None of these important developments could have happened without the positive role and contribution of the European Union in the transformation process and later, in the 2010s, in management of crisis in the region. That role is well-documented by the fact that between 2013 and 2016, EU members contributed 25–75 percent of total investments. In Hungary, about 2.5–4.0 percent of economic growth was generated by EU transfers.[55] Similarly, more than half of the crucially important infrastructural investment in Poland and Hungary was financed by EU money.

However, during the postcommunist transformation, the characteristics of a so-called *dual economy* emerged in the region. In addition to the modern technology-based competitive export sectors, mostly established and financed by Western corporations, a significant part of the economy was represented by domestically owned and technologically not advanced or competitive small and middle-sized companies producing for the domestic market.

Throughout the transformation decades the nine countries of Central Europe and the Baltic area have shared certain characteristics, yet the Baltic countries (Estonia, Latvia, and Lithuania) also have stood somewhat apart, not least because of their close connections with the Nordic countries (Scandinavia and Finland). Estonia, home to speakers of a Finno-Ugric language very near to Finnish, even explicitly identifies itself as Nordic, not Baltic. It is not an entirely new idea. As early as 1917 when the reestablishment of independence from Russia began, the charismatic Estonian politician Jaan Tönisson advocated creating a Scandinavian-Baltic Bloc of 30 million people.

After acquiring independence from the Soviet Union in 1991, these three countries experienced particularly rapid development by comparison with their Central European counterparts. The strong support of Nordic neighbors most certainly played a role, not least by establishing banking systems and supplying capital and technology. To the effects of new economic ties must be added those of older social-cultural connections with the West: some of those areas belonged to Sweden and also had a history of a long-established enclaves of German population, of habits encouraged by Protestantism, and of historical associations with Sweden and the Hanseatic League. Together, these left the people in these countries more open to pursuing business activities than their counterparts in Central Europe. These factors allowed a region already industrialized under Soviet rule to adjust relatively easily to a West-dominated economic regime after the initial post-1991 shocks.

In just a few years around the turn of the millennium, their growth achieved levels seen only in Asia. In 2006, for example, the economy in Estonia and Latvia grew by 11.2 and 11.9 percent and in Lithuania by 7.5 percent. All three countries saw their rates of unemployment fall below the EU average. The world started to speak of the "Baltic Tigers." Between 1995 and 2014, these three countries had average annual growth rates of 4.5 percent, the highest in Central Europe. In 1995, their income level was only 25–30 percent of the EU-15 countries average, but by 2014 it had elevated to 65 percent, thus from hardly more than one-quarter to nearly two-thirds of the EU-15 average. It is highly interesting to note that, as Karsten Staehr calculated, without the tremendous capital inflow, the average growth rate of these countries would have been only about 2 percent per annum.[56] Despite having suffered Europe's steepest depression after 2008, a 14–18 percent contraction of their GDP, they nevertheless recovered surprisingly soon and resumed their growth. By 2016, their average per capita income level was nearly one-quarter higher than in Hungary and Poland, the two countries considered the "transformation and development stars" of the former Soviet Bloc.

Although the effects varied from country to country, European Union aid, as described, strongly contributed to development in the Baltic and Central European countries. Its role was especially important in agricultural modernization and infrastructure development, urban construction and renewal, highway building, and the modernization the entire communication system. The latter can provide an example. The region's backwardness in the crucial telephone system is well-documented by the fact that the Soviet Bloc altogether reached only one-third of the OECD level and only 14 percent of the population had access to telephones before the collapse of the regime. By 2005, however, the region had become a major participant in the mobile phone revolution, with five of its countries ranked among the world's top 30 in mobile phone saturation. The Information and Communication Technology Index, which combines the telephone and computer density of a country, reflects a real breakthrough: early in the 21st century Estonia surpassed Ireland, Slovenia surpassed Belgium, the Czech Republic was passed by both Italy and Spain, and the countries of the region stood among the top 44 countries of the world.[57]

During the transition years, all these developments led to structural modernization along the line of Western Europe. The obsolete heavy industrial and other branches of state socialist economy were decimated. Deindustrialization decreased the dominance of this sector in the national economy to 23–28 percent in four countries (the same level as the eurozone), although Slovenia, the Czech Republic, Poland and Lithuania had still 33–38 percent. In five countries, the share of industry in the production of the GDP was basically similar to the eurozone, around 30 percent. The Czech Republic, Slovakia, and Slovenia had a higher share, around 38–40 percent. The earlier important weight of agriculture also declined. In the Czech Republic, Hungary, Estonia, Latvia, Slovakia, Poland, and Slovenia agricultural employment declined to 3–4 percent, compared to the eurozone's 2 percent level. This sector produced between 4–6 percent of the GDP in four countries of the region, close to the eurozone's 4.4 percent. However, in Poland and Lithuania, agricultural employment still remained at 18 percent and, in Latvia, 14 percent. The fastest developing sector was the service sector: 67–70 percent of the GDP was produced by services in the early 21st century, with 55–60 per cent of the labor force so employed. This level approached the 66 percent of the GDP and 70 percent of the labor force in the most advanced EU-15 countries.[58] All in all, structural modernization basically followed the Western pattern.

The years between 1995 and 2008, and especially between 2000 and 2008, saw fast economic growth, much faster than in the West. The region's per capita GDP recovered the postcollapse decline and by 2000 once again registered at levels prior to 1989. It would surpass those levels by about 50 percent during the boom years of the early 21st century.

Crisis: major weaknesses surface after 2008

As in the other peripheries of Europe, credit fueled most of the turn-of-the-millennium boom in the Central European and Baltic countries. By relying on foreign loans, in some countries taken in Swiss francs, large numbers of people spent two times more than they earned. Debt levels elevated into the danger zone. External debt in Croatia, for example, jumped from 60 to 90 percent of the GDP between 2000 and 2004. Current account deficits reached 13 percent in Estonia, 9 percent in Hungary and Latvia, and 7 percent in Croatia and Lithuania. This consumption bubble burst after 2008 and repayment of the loans became impossible in some countries. In Hungary, the government had to intervene to save the indebted people because the country devalued its currency and thus repayment of debts in Swiss francs cost nearly twice as much as before. In 2011, the government partly burdened the mostly foreign-owned banks by a repayment scheme to relieve Hungarian families.

Some of the countries of the region were hit very hard. Foreign investment and capital inflow stopped. Lending by the European Union to its newest member countries, declined by $35 to $80 billion.[59] Export possibilities for these countries quickly diminished, dropping 5–15 percent in comparison to the fourth quarter of 2007, by the fourth quarter of 2008, and 10–25 percent by the first quarter of 2009. The European Bank for Reconstruction and Development stated in its 2009 report on the transition countries: "Export and financial shocks magnified the reversal of credit booms that had already been under way in many countries before the September shock."[60] In the same year, the GDP in Latvia, Lithuania, Estonia and Slovenia suffered the sharpest contraction of the crisis, 18.0, 17.4, 14.3, and 8.1 percent, respectively. Hungary also suffered a severe decline, with its industrial output dropping by 17.4 percent and its GDP, by 6.7 percent in 2009, and another 2.5 per cent in 2010. The debt burden soared above 100 per cent of the GDP in Hungary, Latvia and Estonia. Unable to meet their loan obligations, the former two became bankrupt. Hungary sought help from the IMF and the European Union in the first months of the credit crisis. *IMF Survey Magazine* reported on October 28, 2008, "The IMF, the European Union, and the World Bank announced a joint financing package for Hungary, totaling $26.1 billion."[61] The IMF and the EU also bailed out Latvia.

Growth rates turned negative in six countries of the region during the years between 2007 and 2012: Latvia's annual decline was −2.8 percent, Slovenia's −1.1, Hungary's −1.0, and Estonia's −0.8 percent. The Czech Republic had 0.3 percent annual growth. Croatia suffered a decline every year between 2009 and 2014: for example, −7.4 in 2009, −1.7 in 2010, and as high as −2.2 percent in 2012. In short, everywhere in the region, stagnation set in, pushing aside the previous exceptional boom conditions.[62]

It is interesting to note that even the richest country of the region, Slovenia, lost its way after 2008, as it tried to cope with the crisis. The Swiss Institute for Management Development found in its 2015 analysis of 61 countries, that Slovenia's competitiveness ranking had declined from 28th place in 2002 to 49th in 2015, ahead only of Greece, Bulgaria, and Croatia in the EU. Just since 2010, the country had slipped 20 places. Political destabilization followed after 2011, with anticapitalist and anti-EU sentiments emerging, including "the rise of leftist radicalism."[63]

Developments in Slovenia apart, the crisis eventually stopped and some of the countries of the region returned to economic growth already in 2010–2011. Once again integration into the European Union played an important role in producing favorable conditions. First of all, the fact that the Western member countries had established the banking sector of the region and owned 87 percent of its assets turned out to be a great advantage. Neither the Central European nor the Baltic countries had to recapitalize their banking systems, as had been the case for overburdened, bankrupt Ireland and Spain. The Western-owned banks recapitalized their Central European branches, while Nordic banks consolidated their affiliates in the Baltic countries. Crediting continued and growth returned.

The European Union itself took important steps to shore up its new members. In March 2009, it initiated a meeting in Vienna with the IMF, World Bank, the European Bank of Reconstruction and Development, and about 40 banks involved in cross-border crediting. Participants hammered out an agreement, the Vienna Initiative, committing their institutions to refraining from withdrawing capital and to continuing to finance the transition countries. In January 2012, this effort was repeated, and a Second Vienna Initiative was signed. Meanwhile, the EU also reached an agreement in Brussels with the European financial regulators to not force Western banks to withdraw from risky business ventures in the region. A top official of the Austrian Raiffeisen Bank International, one of the strongly involved banks in Central Europe stated: "We welcome the agreement reached in Brussels as a further important step to supporting the stability of Central and Eastern Europe's financial sector."[64] Thus supported, the crisis-ridden countries of the region returned to growth.

Most surprisingly, some of them actually did not decline at all into deep financial crisis. The main reason behind this was their willingness, as new members of the European Union eager to join the common currency system as soon as possible, to keep strict order in their financial households. Unlike several longtime member countries, including those in the Mediterranean region, these new members observed the EU's rules on budgetary deficits (3 percent or less) and debt (60 percent of GDP or less). Slovenia, Slovakia, the Czech Republic, and Poland fulfilled the EU requirements between 2002 and 2007, and thus successfully prevented the collapse of their state finances. Five of the region's nine countries joined the common currency just before or during the crisis: Slovenia in 2007, Slovakia in 2009, Estonia in 2011, Latvia in 2014, and Lithuania in 2015. Poland and Hungary, however, preferring to remain financially "sovereign," chose not to join the eurozone. László Csaba, a Hungarian economist, argues that in rejecting eurozone membership in the 2010s, these countries marginalized themselves and that this marginalization contributed to their slowing down and failure to continue catching up with the West in the later years of that decade.[65]

Similarly interesting are the records of Slovakia and Poland during the crisis. Slovakia, barely impacted, achieved an impressive 1.9 percent annual economic growth between 2007 and 2012. Poland, an absolute exception in all of Europe, not only did not decline for even a short while, but between 2007 and 2012, actually continued its rapid, 3.5 percent average annual growth. Two factors played central roles in preserving that momentum. First of all, Poland was the biggest beneficiary of European Union's financial aid program. Having received one-quarter of the total EU aid to Central and Eastern Europe between 2000 and 2006, it continued to receive one-third of that total during the crisis years, 2007–2014: "It is reported," one writer observed, "that the transfer from the Union made it possible for the Polish government to minimalize effects of the crisis of 2008–2010."[66] For another thing the Polish economy was not export-oriented and thus its markets did not shrink to the extent they did in the export-dependent Czech Republic and Hungary; the large Polish domestic market absorbed the majority, roughly 60 percent, of output. Clearly, during the crisis years, this domestic orientation offered an advantage, however transitory it might be in the longer run.

To manage the crisis and meet combined EU, IMF, and World Bank demands, most of the Central European and Baltic countries had to introduce austerity measures and cut social expenditures, including health care financing, quite severely. The cuts undermined welfare systems and increased income inequality (see Chapter 2). After some hopeful years a great part of the regional population lost faith in the promise of a better future at home. Mass migration followed, encouraged in part by the extension to these countries of the EU right to work anywhere in the Union. There were not enough jobs at home. The number of job seekers in Hungary and Latvia, for example, increased by 58 and 39 percent, respectively. Skilled workers and the university-educated young, in particular, left the region for Western Europe, attracted by better living conditions, opportunities and wages. A Polish worker, for example, might earn 48 Deutschmark per hour in Germany, as compared to the equivalent of 5.5 DM at home. Perhaps unsurprisingly, then, about 3–3.5 million people, or 20 percent of the

Polish labor force left the country to work abroad. During the 2010s, about 500,000 people left Hungary, 5 percent of the population, to work in the West. For Central Europe and Eastern Europe as a whole, the IMF has reported that about 20 million people left their home countries between 1995 and 2012; that number equals the entire population of the Czech Republic and Hungary. Some of the migration, it should be noted, occurred between countries of the region, for example, from Slovakia to the Czech Republic or from Lithuania to Poland.

By 2016, the standard of living in Central Europe had improved, but it still lagged well behind standards in the advanced northwest. Wages, despite increases, remained far below northwestern levels and cash remittances to the home country from migrant workers, as the Hungarian Statistical Office reported, had become the second largest amount of financial support from outside the country.[67] "Eastern Europe's economies," [meaning the Central European region] a 2016 Peterson Institute analysis concluded,

> are not catching up with their Western neighbors as quickly as many had hoped. The latest Eurostat figures on economic growth in Europe, released earlier this month, show a troubling trend. While growth is returning to Europe after several difficult years, Eastern Europe is not converging with "old Europe," the pre-2004 EU members.[68]

Estonia, Croatia, Latvia, Lithuania, Hungary, and Slovenia, the report found, all were growing more slowly than the euro area average. Even Poland, the perennial star performer during the first crisis years, had not surpassed the EU growth average of 1.8 percent of GDP in 2016. This lack of economic vigor is surprising, opined the analysis, as Eastern Europe has enjoyed significant energy price declines, a devalued euro (for the six countries already in the euro area or with a currency board pegged to the euro), and falling interest rates.

The main reason for this lethargy, the analysis concluded, is the declining labor force. Between 1990 and 2015, the working-age population decreased because of low birth rates and increased emigration. The birth rate in Eastern Europe fell from 2.1 children per woman in 1988 to 1.2 children by 1998. Economic uncertainty was the single most important reason for this trend. Since then, birth rates have slowly increased, to 1.44 children per woman in Hungary, 1.53 in the Czech Republic, and 1.58 in Slovenia, the highest rate in Eastern Europe. But this rate is still insufficient for population growth. In addition, the Peterson Institute's analysis observed, labor participation by women is also very low. In 2014, it reported, just 47 percent of all East European employees were women. As principal causes it named traditional ways of thinking about the role of women in family and society, and a lack of both sufficient childcare and flexible part-time work. Only 6 percent of Slovakian and Latvian women were working in part-time jobs in 2016, for example, whereas between one-quarter and one-half of their northwestern European counterparts were so employed.[69]

The Peterson Institute's analysis, however, overlooks the complexity behind the Central European slow down. The 2013 report, "Stuck in Transition," issued by European Bank of Reconstruction and Development, better captured the full picture. This report pointed to the political change in several countries of the region: the challenge to democracy and the rejection by large numbers of disappointed people of transformation modeled after the Western road. The report assigned most of the cause to the austerity restrictions instituted after 2008, which fueled populist trends in several countries, especially in Hungary, Poland, Slovakia, and Slovenia. "Progress in transition is closely correlated with political systems," the Executive Summary of the report stated. "Public opinion turned against market reform after the 2008–09 financial crisis. ... Economic growth remains well below pre-crisis levels and many countries have turned their backs on the reforms that could put economic expansion back on track." Another major cause of slowdown in the region, according to the report, is that the

> pre-crisis growth in many countries in the transition region was boosted by large and ultimately unsustainable inflows of debt and foreign direct investment. The crisis triggered a sharp reduction in FDI and portfolio flows, which have not recovered and are forecast to remain below of those earlier levels in the medium term.

Further contributing to the complexity, the report noted, was a natural slowing down, as countries adapted to the reality that the boom of the early transition years could not continue indefinitely. "Economies in the region," it concluded "are likely to grow more slowly in future."[70]

Conclusion

Between 2000 and 2014, Central Europe and the Baltics increased their income level by nearly three times, thus faster than Western Europe, where the level doubled. In United States dollars, this meant that the level in the Central European–Baltic region rose from $5,722 average per capita GDP to $15,635, while in slower growing Western Europe it increased from $25,399 to $49,317. Income level in Central Europe now registered at 32 percent of the Western level, up from 23 percent in 2000. Despite this improvement, the region remained stuck at the middle-income level. Moreover, its average per capita income level relative to the West was lower than it had been in 1990. (Hungary reached its earlier level only in 2017.)

Table 6.1 presents the region's per capita income level between 1870 and 2014, as a percentage of the level in advanced West European countries:

These figures cover nearly 1.5 centuries, the entire modern period of Central European development. The region has been unable to climb up from its middle-income level; indeed, has declined over that period from more than one-half to one-third of the West European level.

Table 6.1 Central Europe GDP per capita in percentage of Northwestern Europe

Year	*Central Europe as percentage of the West*[a]
1870	54
1913	50
1950	48
1990	37
2000	23
2016	32

Note:

a The calculations up to 1990 are based on Maddison, *Monitoring the World Economy*; the 2000 and 2014 figures are calculated from *The Economist, Pocket World in Figures 2004* and *The Economist, Pocket World in Figures 2017*; the 2016 figure is based on statisticstimes.com/economy/countries-by-projected-gdp-capita.php, June 7, 2017.

The eleven highly advanced northwestern countries average per capita income, according to a mid-2017 calculation, is $49,317. The entire region belongs to the upper 20 percent of the high-income level group of countries above $20,000 per capita income. The nine Central European and Baltic countries, in contrast, had an average $15,635 income, thus a middle-income level. It is about 50 percent higher than the $10,562 world average and nearly three times higher than the lower 50 percent of the countries of the world, with lower than $5,500 income level. Even so the Central European level only reaches 32 percent of the Western European level. Slovenia has the highest level in the region ($21,062). The country is the only one in the region to have climbed into the high-income ranks, albeit just barely. The Czech Republic ($18,534) comes in next, and then Estonia ($17,891). These three countries are listed as 39th, 41st, and 42nd among the world's 190 countries, clustered around the lowest rung of the high-income level. Within the region, Slovakia, Lithuania and Latvia occupied the middle zone, with $16,412, $15,090, and $14,188 per capita income, respectively. They rank as 49th, 53rd, and 56th on the world list. At the lower level among the region's countries are Hungary ($12,767), Poland ($12,722), and Croatia ($12,046). They rank as 59th, 60th, and 61st among the 190.[71]

Are Central Europe and the Baltic area fatally trapped in middle-income peripheral status? The experience of the last century, especially the persistent relative decline of the region as compared to northwestern Europe, certainly points in this direction. The social-cultural characteristics of the region, developed in the peripheral past and changing very slowly (see Chapter 3), only strengthen the portrait. And should the post-2008 antidemocratic and anti-EU political trends persist much longer, as exemplified in the embrace by Hungary, Poland, and Slovakia of the Asian-Russian model of political-economic organization, with its "state catch" and "business catch" effects, the result may well be a hindrance of further transformation and growth.

However, there are promising signs suggesting the possibility of an opposite outcome, at least in the long run. Slovenia, the Czech Republic, Slovakia, and especially Estonia and the other Baltic countries already are knocking at the door of the high-income group. Catching up may not be happening quickly, but given that these countries embarked on the new road leading to this door only about a quarter of a century ago, probably better to say, just over a decade ago, in tandem with European Union membership, their record is outstanding. Still, recent forecasts for these countries have been gloomy, should they neglect to introduce certain market and financial reforms. The previously cited 2013 report by the European Bank of Reconstruction and Development, for example, has observed:

> Assuming an absence of reform, most countries would continue converging, but far more slowly than over the past decade. ... In 20 years' time the CEB countries would have incomes per working member of the population that were in access of 60 percent of the EU-15 average. It is not very impressive given that all CEB [Central European and Baltic] countries except Latvia already exceed the 60 percent thresholds. Only the Czech and Slovak Republics are projected to have incomes in excess of 80 percent of the EU-15 average in the baseline scenario.

But, in an alternative scenario, the case of continued reforms that create the required institutions and rules that would add an annual 0.2–0.5 percent additional growth, the report does not exclude the possibility that convergence might be restored, so that the entire region, including Hungary, Croatia, and Slovenia, could possibly approach 80 percent of the EU-15 average income level.[72] In an ideal 21st-century environment and in the framework of a well-progressing European Union integration, the Central European–Baltic region just might follow the gradual road of convergence and slowly elevate to the high-income zone.

Notes

1 In this chapter I broadly have used several of my publications on this region: *An Economic History of Nineteenth Century Europe: Diversity and Industrialization*, Cambridge: Cambridge University Press, 2013; *From the Soviet Bloc to the European Union: The Economic and Social Transformation of Central and Eastern Europe since 1973*, Cambridge: Cambridge University Press, 2009; *Central and Eastern Europe 1944–1993: Detour from the Periphery to the Periphery*, Cambridge: Cambridge University Press, 1996; *Europe in Crisis: Bolt from the Blue?*, London: Routledge, 2013; *An Economic History of Twentieth-Century Europe: Economic Regimes from Laissez-Faire to Globalization*, 2nd ed., Cambridge: Cambridge University Press, 2016; *Decades of Crisis: Central and Eastern Europe before World War II*, Berkeley: University of California Press, 1998.

2 *Collins English Dictionary*, www.collinsdictionary.com/us/dictionary/english/central-europe, accessed February 20, 2017.

3 Milan Kundera, "The Tragedy of Central Europe," *New York Review of Books*, April 26, 1984.
4 Jenő Szűcs, *Vázlat Európa három történeti régiójáról*, Budapest: Magvető, 1983.
5 www.globsec.org/wp-content/uploads/2017/09/globsec_trends_2017.pdf, accessed March 2, 2017.
6 In the region only Hungary and the Baltic countries are not Slavic-populated, but the Baltic countries do have considerable Slavic minorities: in Latvia 34.5 percent, in Estonia 28.8 percent, and in Lithuania 13.8 percent.
7 István Széchenyi and Miklós Wesselényi, *Feleselő naplók: Egy barátság kezdetei*, Budapest: Helikon, 1985, p. 212; István Széchenyi, *Hitel*, Pest: Petrózai Trattner, 1830, pp. 155–156.
8 See Peter Brock, *Nationalism and Populism in Partitioned Poland*, London: Orbis, 1972, p. 12; Norman Davis, *Heart of Europe: A Short History of Poland*, Oxford: Oxford University Press, 1986, p. 170.
9 In Poland, the situation was much worse.
10 Simon Kuznets, *Modern Economic Growth*, New Haven: Yale University Press, 1966, p. 324; A. G. Kenwood and A. L. Lougheed, *The Growth of the International Economy 1820–1960*, London: Allen & Unwin, 1971, p. 43; W. Woodruff, "The Emergence of the International Economy 1700–1914," in Carlo Cipolla (ed.), *The Fontana Economic History of Europe*, Vol. 4, Pt. 2, London: Collins/Fontana, 1973, p. 707; W. Woodruff, *The Impact of Western Man: A Study of Europe's Role in the World Economy, 1750–1960*, London: Macmillan, 1966.
11 W. S. Woytinsky, *Die Welt in Zahlen*, Vol. 5, Berlin: Mosse, 1927, pp. 34–35.
12 Ivan T. Berend and György Ránki, *Hungary: A Century of Economic Development*, Newton Abbot: David & Charles, 1974.
13 These calculations are based on Angus Maddison, *Monitoring the World Economy, 1820–1992*, Paris: OECD, 1995. The numbers, however, are scattered and not available for all periods, for all Central European and Baltic countries. The numbers for 1870 are based on two major countries (later, Czechoslovakia and Hungary), the numbers for 1913 on three major countries (later, Czechoslovakia, Hungary, and Poland). For Poland, data exists only from 1929. This figure is definitely higher than the one for 1913. All of these data shortcomings introduce uncertainties in the calculations. The figures used in the text thus are more estimations than exact figures.
14 The small Carpathian Ruthenia's fate is emblematic of the troubled history and frequently changing borders of Central Europe. An old joke expressed it well: if someone had a long enough life there, even if never ever left his village, he would have lived in four different countries.
15 Slovenia too exhibits the troubled history of the region: during a single century, it was part of Austria before World War I, then, after that war part of Yugoslavia, but during World War II, incorporated into the German Reich, only to return to Yugoslavia after the war. With the disintegration of Yugoslavia, it became an independent country for the first time in its history.
16 Poland lost 70,000 square miles of its Eastern territory to Russia and was compensated by 40,000 square miles from Germany.
17 John Hiden and Patrick Salmon, *The Baltic Nations and Europe: Estonia, Latvia and Lithuania in the Twentieth Century*, London: Longman, 1991, p. 85; Irena Kostrowicka,

Zbigniew Landau, and Jerzy Tomaszewski, *Historia gospodarcza Polski, XIX i XX wieku*, Warszawa: Ksiazka i Wiedza, 1966.

18 Maddison, *Monitoring the World Economy*.

19 Ibid., p. 249.

20 Based on ibid.

21 Yevgeni Preobrazhensky was one of Stalin's victims during the Terror of the 1930s.

22 Yevgeni Preobrazhensky, *The New Economics*, Oxford: Clarendon House, 1965.

23 János Kornai, *The Socialist System: The Political Economy of Communism*, Princeton: Princeton University Press, 1992; Paul Marer, *Historically Planned Economies: A Guide to the Data*, Washington, DC: The World Bank, 1991.

24 *National Accounts Statistics: Main Aggregates and Detailed Tables*, New York: United Nations, 1988, 1990.

25 Based on Maddison, *Monitoring the World Economy*.

26 Joseph Schumpeter, *Capitalism, Socialism and Democracy*, 5th ed., London: Allen & Unwin, [1943] 1976, pp. 67–68.

27 Ibid., 82–83.

28 Ivan T. Berend, *Öt előadás gazdaságról és oktatásról*, Budapest: Magvető, 1978, pp. 200–201.

29 Michael Mastanduno, *Economic Containment: CoCom and the Politics of East-West Trade*, Ithaca, NY: Cornell University Press, 1992, pp. 193–194, 215; Douglas E. McDaniel, *United States Technology Export Control: An Assessment*, Westport, CT: Praeger, 1993, pp. 11, 112–113.

30 Based on Maddison, *Monitoring the World Economy*, p. 249

31 Vladimir I. Lenin, "Immediate Task of the Soviet Government," *Selected Works*, one-vol. ed., New York: International Publishers, [1918] 1974, p. 415.

32 *European Bank of Reconstruction and Development Transition Report 2001*, London: EBRD, 2001, p. 61.

33 Maddison, *Monitoring the World Economy*, p. 201.

34 *European Bank of Reconstruction and Development Transition Report 1996*, London: EBRD, 1996; *European Bank of Reconstruction and Development Transition Report 2000*, London: EBRD, 2000; Maddison, *Monitoring the World Economy*; Angus Maddison, *The World Economy: A Millennial Perspective*, Paris: OECD, 2001.

35 The sharp, post-Soviet economic declines stopped in 1992–1993 and recovery started. The region's annual growth rate was between 3.3 and 5 percent per year between 1994 and 2004. In 2005–2007, it even reached 5–6 percent per annum. Slovenia, Croatia, and the Baltic countries belonged to the fastest growing countries of Europe. See *European Bank of Reconstruction and Development Transition Report 2005*, London: EBRD, 2005, p. 48; European Commission, *Employment in Europe 2006 – Archive of European Integration*, 2006, aei.pitt.edu/40717.

36 World Bank, *From Plan to Market: World Development Report*, Washington, DC: World Bank, 1996, pp. 11, 19, 21.

37 János Kornai, *Magyar Hírlap*, December 24, 1992.

38 Joseph Stiglitz is quoted in Ben Fine, Costas Lapavitsas, and Jonathan Pincus (eds.), *Development Policy in the Twenty-First Century: Beyond the Post-Washington Consensus*, London: Routledge, 2001, p. 3.

39 Robert Gilpin, *The Challenge of Global Capitalism: The World Economy in the 21st Century*, Princeton, NJ: Princeton University Press, 2000, p. 51.
40 In Latin America, the phenomenon is called *capitalismo de amigos*.
41 Alenka Kuhelj and Bojan Bugarič, "Slovenia in Crisis: From a Success Story to a Failed State?," in Frane Adam (ed.), *Slovenia: Social, Economic and Environmental Issues*, New York: Nova Science, 2017, p. 61.
42 Bálint Magyar, *Post-Communist Mafia State: The Case of Hungary*, Budapest: CEU Press, 2016.
43 Karl Polanyi called our attention to this phenomenon by presenting historical examples of social shocks, including the British Industrial Revolution. See Karl Polanyi, *The Great Transformation: The Political and Economic Origins of Our Time*, Boston: Beacon Press, [1944] 1957.
44 Joseph Held (ed.), *Democracy and Rightwing Politics in Eastern Europe in the 1990s*, Boulder, CO: East European Monographs, 1993.
45 Address by Mr. Jacques Delors, President of the Commission of the European Communities, Bruges, October 17, 1989, Europa.eu/rapid/press-release_SPEECH-89–73_en.htm?locale=FR, accessed January 9, 2017; Helmut Kohl, Gespräch des Bundeskanzlers Kohl mit Aussenminister Baker, Berlin (West), 12 December 1989, in Dokumente zur Deutschlandpolitik, Munich: Oldenbourg, 1998, p. 640.
46 www.ebrd.com, accessed December 8, 2016.
47 KPMG, "EU Funds in Central and Eastern Europe. Progress Report 2007-2015," 2016, https://assets.kpmg/content/dam/kpmg/pdf/2016/06/EU-Funds-in-Central-and-Eastern-Europe.pdf, accessed May 12, 2018.
48 *European Bank for Reconstruction and Development Transition Report Update*, London: EBRD, May 2005, p. 19.
49 United Nations Economic Commission for Europe, UNECE Statistical Database, Economic Statistics, http://w3.unece.org/pxweb/Dialog/statfile1_new.asp.
50 www.paiz.gov.pl/index/?id=59112692262234e3fad47fa8eabf03a4, accessed January 7, 2017.
51 Lucyna Kornecki, "Foreign Direct Investment (FDI) in the Polish Economy: Comparison with Central and Eastern Europe (CEE) Countries," *Problems & Perspectives in Management*, 4, no. 3 (2006).
52 Lucyna Kornecki, "FDI in Central and Eastern Europe: Business Environment and Current FDI Trends in Poland," *Research in Business and Economics Journal*, www.aabri.com/manuscripts/09348.pdf, accessed December 11, 2016.
53 Krzysztof Piech (ed.), *Economic Policy and Growth of Central Eastern European Countries*, London: School of Slavonic and East European Studies, 2003, pp. 256–257.
54 Anna Kadeřábková, "Skills for Knowledge-Based Economy in Central Europe," in Krzysztof Piech and Savo Radocevic (eds.), *The Knowledge-Based Economy in Central and Eastern Europe: Countries and Industries in a Process of Change*, Houndmills: Palgrave Macmillan, 2006, pp. 157, 159.
55 László Csaba, *Válság, Gazdaság, Világ: Adalék Közép- és Kelet Európa három évtizedes gazdaságtörténetéhez (1988–2018)*, Budapest: Éghajlat Kiadó, 2019, chaps. 8, 10; Miklós Losoncz, "A globális és regionális integrálódás és a fenntartható növekedés néhány kérdése a visegrádi országokban," *Közgazdasági Szemle*, 64, nos.7–8 (2017): 677–697.

56 Karsten Staehr, Economic Growth and Convergence in the Baltic States: Caught in a Middle Income Trap?, https://ec.europa.eu/economy_finance/events/2015/20150616_vilnius/paper_baltic_states_en.pdf, June 16, 2015.

57 *The Economist, Economic Intelligence Unit 2005*, pp. 60, 91, 93.

58 *The Economist, Pocket World in Figures 2006*, September 1, 2005, London: The Economist; *The Economist, Pocket World in Figures 2007*, September 1, 2006, London: The Economist.

59 The 30 million to 80 million range arises from the fact that various methods of calculation have been applied in assessing the impact of crisis on lending.

60 *European Bank of Reconstruction and Development Transition Report 2009*, London: EBRD, 2009, pp. 10–11.

61 *IMF Survey Magazine*, October 28, 2008, www.imf.org/external/pubs/ft/survey/so/2008/car102808b.htm, accessed November 18, 2016.

62 *The Economist, Pocket World in Figures 2015*, September 1, 2014, London: The Economist.

63 Frane Adam (ed.), *Slovenia: Social, Economic and Environmental Issues*, New York: Nova, 2017, pp. 42, 43, 49, 123.

64 European Bank for Reconstruction and Development, "Vienna Initiative – Moving to a New Phase," www.ebrd.com/downloads/research/factsheets/viennainitiative.pdf, accessed June 6, 2017.

65 Csaba, *Válság, Gazdaság, Világ*, esp. chaps. 8 and 10.

66 Steelguru, "Manufacturing Economy in India Rebounds from Rupee Demonetization Downturn," February 2017, https://steelguru.com/steel/manufacturing-economy-in-india-rebounds-from-rupee-demonetisation-downturn/471360, accessed February 2, 2017.

67 Philip Ther, *Europe since 1989: A History*, Princeton, NJ: Princeton University Press, 2016, p. 309; Heti Világgazdaság, July 20, 2016; "Hazautalások Kelet- és Közép Európába, Statisztikai - Központi Statisztikai Hivatal, január 18, www.ksh.hu/statszemle; http://archive.rec.org/e-aarhus/files/legal1998.pdf, 2010, accessed May 7, 2017.

68 Simeon Djankov, Eastern Europe's Lethargic Economies, PIIE, November 21, 2016, www.piie.com/blogs/realtime-economic-issues-watch/eastern-europes-lethargic-economies, accessed April 8, 2017.

69 Ibid.

70 *European Bank for Reconstruction and Development Transition Report 2013*, pp. 4, 11, 13.

71 statisticstimes.com/economy/countries-by-projected-gdp-capita.php, June 7, 2017.

72 *European Bank for Reconstruction and Development Transition Report 2013*, p. 17.

7 The Russia-Turkey-Balkans low-income region

Outside Europe?

What justifies grouping the 11 countries – Russia, Belarus, Ukraine, Moldova, Bulgaria, Romania, Serbia, Bosnia, Albania, Montenegro, and Turkey – together as a distinct region? As usual, some geographic and ethnic factors are important. Most of these countries are located on the east and southeast half-circle of the European continent, but two, Russia and Turkey, are transcontinental, partly European, partly Asian. Turkey has only a small edge in Europe, part of Istanbul. Of the country's territory, 99 percent is Asian and home to 95 percent of its population. Three-quarters of Russia's territory lies in Asia, but only 23 percent of its population lives there. With the exception of three Muslim or majority-Muslim countries (Turkey, Bosnia, Albania), these countries mostly are inhabited by Slavic peoples who belong to the Greek-Russian Orthodox cultural sphere and speak Slavic languages. There are a few, relatively small spots with populations of Catholic background.

More importantly, history has hammered these countries into a region. The entire area and its population had the experience of belonging to two empires, the Russian (or later Soviet) and the Ottoman Turkish, for nearly half a millennium. Before that the Mongol and Ottoman invaders who occupied the region introduced Asian influences. In the second half of the 20th century, except for Turkey, the countries fell under communist rule, as part of the Soviet Bloc, and thus did not have market economies or multiparty democratic governments. With the collapse of the Soviet regime in 1989–1991, these countries began a period of transformation, as they attempted to reform their political and economic systems according to the Western European model.

In spite of the transcontinental character of the two dominant countries of the region, historically the region belongs to Europe. Russia has always been a European power. Turkey, for 400 years also a partly European power, began an explicit Europeanization of its culture in the early 20th century, after the collapse of the Ottoman empire. Under Kemal Atatürk, the new leader, Arabic script was dropped in favor of the Latin alphabet, and the Muslim country was secularized. Turkey even joined the Western military alliance (NATO) in the second half of the 20th century and became the only non-European official candidate of the European Union.

The Russian and Ottoman empires were strong and expansionist military powers. Russia incorporated huge Asian territories and tried to expand its influence into the Balkans. Ottoman Turkey, expanding in several directions, incorporated the Middle East, North Africa, and the Balkans. It even challenged Venice and Vienna but failed militarily. Both powers waged several wars against the West and sometimes against each other. This history permanently impacted the society and culture of the region.

The early 20th century: the most backward periphery of Europe

This part of Europe followed a long historical road to the early 20th century rather different than in the West or other European regions (see Chapter 1). The lack and failure of the transforming effects of the Renaissance, Reformation, French Revolution, and of the two modern-era industrial revolutions to reach this region left it "outside" Europe, frozen in *ancien régime* structures and practices.

Russia remained a nearly exclusively rural, peasant country until World War I, with about 80 percent of its population working in the agriculture sector. Until the last third of the 19th-century agriculture was quasi-medieval in its practices and structure, reliant on serf labor, or, after its abolition (in 1861), on the *otrabotochnaia sistema*. In the latter, which persisted until the end of the 19th century, former serfs cultivated the land of the big estates with their own tools, in exchange for an allotment of sharecropping plots. The big estates, unlike in other parts of Europe, did not transform to capitalist enterprise, and wage labor was marginal. (In Turgenev's excellent, late-19th-century novels, the landowners who used wage labor were very proud of their modern attitudes.)

The medieval village community (*obschina* or *mir*) remained intact until 1906. Peasant land was not privately owned but rather belonged to the community, which preserved the medieval communal life, including common work and egalitarian distribution. The community paid taxes collectively and redistributed parcels among families from time to time. Investing into the land was discouraged by this system, and by 1915, still only 10 percent of peasant households had created independent farms. No longer tied by law to their former lords' estates, peasants nevertheless remained virtually bound to their communities. To leave the community required the approval of the collective. Without that permission, no one could get a passport, a document still required, even for travel within Russia. At the end of the 19th century, these domestic passports were issued for less than a year, mostly for three months. Mobility, therefore, even after the 1861 emancipation, was very limited.

Agriculture remained monocultural, with grain the chief product and traditional production techniques persisting. As late as 1870, 97 percent of the land still was given to grain, while the traditional three-field rotation system dominated. Even in the last third of the century about 28 percent of the arable land would be fallow each growing season. However, in the same era agricultural output began increasing and the state began a program of requisitioning grain for export. Output increased 2.5 times by the end of the 19th century, but exports by 5.5 times. Minister of Finance Vyshnegradsky declared: "We may go hungry, but we will export!" Indeed! The result of the export program was domestic food shortage. Sergei Witte, the reform-oriented minister to Tsar Nicholas II, would inform the tsar in March 1899 that "per capita consumption in Russia stood at only one-fourth to one-fifth of what was considered the minimum of Western Europe."[1]

The seeds of change already had been sown, however, and some elements of modern agriculture appeared in Siberia and in the black-soil area in the Ukrainian part of the Russian empire. Well-to-do peasants bought more than half of the sold noble lands and, in the latter region, modern crop rotation methods replaced the practice of three-field rotation. Grain output doubled between 1860 and the war. Choosing to move to newly colonized Siberia brought settlers relief from compulsory military service for ten years, along with 270 acres of land and 20 years of tax exemption. After 1861, about 3.3 million Russian peasants decided to take advantage of these incentives, along with 4 million German migrant peasants. The population of Siberia increased from 2.7 million to 10.3 million between 1858 and 1913. This enclave of modern agriculture, with its cattle and milk economy, butter and cheese production, signaled the beginning of modernization.

Turkey and the Balkans remained totally agricultural, moreover lacking any significant elements of agricultural revolution. True, the 19th century, a crucial period of tentative modernization in peripheral regions, was disastrous in that area. Virtually unending warfare against the Ottoman army and, upon liberation, against each other, troubled the entire century until World War I. The weakening of central power and the gradual disintegration of the Ottoman empire led to rule by local warlords and bandit Janissary hordes that terrorized and robbed the population and isolated the area from Europe.[2]

In the last third of the 19th century, when the Balkans became independent, egalitarian peasant societies, still organized in village communities (*zadruga*), as in Russia, distributed the Ottoman land equally, creating small family plots, mostly under 20 hectares. These were large enough for basic self-sufficiency but too small to produce also for market. The *zadruga* started disappearing, but collective communalism survived in the forms of collective cultivation of land (in Serb areas called *moba*), mutual harvesting and labor sharing (*pozajmica*), and reciprocal loans of livestock and equipment (*sprega*).

In areas such as Romania, Bosnia, and Macedonia, large estates worked in a special organizational form predominated. In the most characteristic Romanian system, three-quarters of estates larger than 3,000 hectares were rented out by their absentee landlords to merchant-speculators who did not cultivate the lands, but rather sublet them to peasants for sharecropping: half their output constituted their rent obligation. This double-renting system was the most exploitative of all forms of "irresponsible landlordism," as Robert Seaton

Watson called it.[3] It also preserved the traditional, obsolete, virtually medieval cultivation methods.

Nevertheless, the expanse of land under cultivation significantly increased in the last third of the 19th century. Much arable flat land had been abandoned in earlier centuries, in response to the onset of the Little Ice Age and also to dangers posed by marauding Ottoman hordes. Now, as both of those conditions disappeared and as countries gained independence under the terms of the 1878 Congress of Berlin, peasants began resettling and reclaiming these lands. Predatory elites, however, controlled the political-state organization from Russia to the Balkans, and they did not hesitate to rob their people ruthlessly. The extremely autocratic Russian and Ottoman rulers as well as the new Balkan military-bureaucratic elites, conserved an *ancien regime*, which served only a small segment of the population. This political environment did not create the institutional-legal systems that served modern social-economic transformation elsewhere in Europe.

Balkan agricultural development, however, gained some impetus with the resettlement of formerly abandoned areas. In Romania, cultivated land increased from 2.1 million to 5 million hectares by 1900, and then grew another 50 percent before the outbreak of World War I. In Bulgaria and Serbia, the land under cultivation grew from 2.8 million to 3.6 million hectares. The production of grain, the principal crop by far, increased threefold in Romania and doubled in the other countries. Corn production increased from 39 million to 72 million quintals. Grain also accounted for 80 percent of total exports in Romania and two-thirds in Bulgaria. In Serbia, prunes (sun-dried or oven-dried plums) made up one-quarter of exports. Altogether, half to two-thirds of Balkan export consisted of agricultural (and some raw material) products.

Cultivation technology remained mired in the past. In Bulgaria wood plows were most common, as they had been for centuries. Before the war, still 46 percent of arable land was kept fallow and used for transhumant animal husbandry, reflecting the perseverance of the medieval two-field rotation system. In Serbia, peasants harvested with sickles, and animal husbandry relied on grazing (stall-feeding was unknown). In Romania, signs of mechanization in the form of steam-threshing and horse-driven sowing machines appeared, but machine numbers were so few that each machine served three times more hectarage than in neighboring Hungary. In Bulgaria, mechanization just started and each machine served a huge landed area, 20 times bigger than in Romania. This was only the very beginning of the mechanization of agriculture. Systems of modern credit did not exist and the medieval usurious crediting was still prevalent. If peasants had to borrow, they paid 200 percent interest in early-20th-century Bulgarian villages.

The backward agricultural economy was hardly able to feed the dramatically increasing population in the Russia-Turkey-Balkans region. One of the most important imports from the West, namely the inventions that decreased regional death rates from 35–36/1,000 to 22–25/1,000 (still much higher than the Western 15/1,000), generated a belated demographic revolution during the

19th century. Birth rates, unlike in the West where they dropped to 26–27/1,000, remained traditionally high, around 40/1,000 inhabitants. Decreased death rates occurring along with conserved high birth rates caused a quadrupling of population in Russia and a trebling in the Balkans between 1800 and 1910. Only in war-ridden Turkey did population stagnate.[4] Small wonder then that per capita agricultural production declined by 28 and 14 percent in Serbia and Bulgaria, respectively. Or that per capita livestock production stagnated in Bosnia and Bulgaria and halved in Serbia. Or that all farm production per capita decreased by one-third in Serbia and by one-sixth in Bulgaria and stagnated in Bosnia and Montenegro in the second half of the 19th century.

Industrialization did not start in most part of this region, although Russia at least took a few first steps. This development was closely connected with two international factors: globalization and military pressures. The half-century before World War I became the period of the "first globalization."[5] During that time Western Europeans started investing in food- and raw material-producing countries lying to the east and connecting them to the west by rail. Russia, until then outside the world system, started integrating as a major deliverer of agricultural and raw material, and together with the Balkans began providing about one-third of the world's grain exports. Military considerations also contributed in Russia. Backward as it was, this country was a major military power, valuable to the West as an ally. For quite a while France and Russia, for example, worked together against the Ottoman empire and then, when the two confronting European blocs emerged in the 1870s and 1880s, against Germany and Austria-Hungary. Strengthening the mobilization capacity and the armament industry in Russia became a par excellence French interest.

Railroad construction started in the enormous Russian empire in the 1860s. With the support of mostly foreign investments, 70,000 kilometers of line were laid and opened before World War I. An achievement without a doubt, this construction still produced a density of only 42.3 kilometers per 100,000 inhabitants, less than half of the West European 90.2 kilometers per 100,000 inhabitants. The picture is even worse if we compare the territory served by each kilometer of railroad: it was somewhat more than 10 square kilometers in the West, but 324,000 square kilometers in Russia.[6]

Nothing similar happened in the Ottoman empire and the Balkans. Although the very first railroad line, 130 kilometers long, opened in Turkey in 1856, by the collapse of the empire only 8,000 kilometers of line existed, just 3,660 kilometers of which crossed the territory that would lie in postwar Turkey. In the Balkans, the only line was the Balkan part of the Berlin-Baghdad Oriental Railway with some sidelines. Even short lines, however, can bring benefits. To take an example from the 1980s: the Anatolian Railways lines connecting Eşkisehir to Konya and Ankara to Istanbul most certainly encouraged cotton and grain cultivation on the Adana plain. Rail allowed less expensive and much faster delivery to the Black Sea and to the Mediterranean ports than caravans did.[7]

The Russian railroads had a much more important influence on industrialization than in the Balkans. The traditional and obsolete Ural iron industry was replaced by modern, Western-financed iron and steel industries in the Donets Basin. Iron ore extraction increased by eightfold and iron production by a similar amount between the 1890s and the outbreak of World War I. Western companies started oil production in Baku in the last third of the 19th century. Between 1900 and 1913, iron and steel production increased by 50–60 percent, while coal and sugar output, the number of cotton spindles and industrial production in general doubled in less than 1.5 decades. Three industrial enclaves emerged: around the Donets Basin, St. Petersburg, and Moscow.

Nevertheless, by comparison with the rest of Europe, Russia was scarcely industrialized. Horsepower capacity was only one-tenth of the German level and six percent of the British level. The value of industrial production was only a third of the Italian or Austro-Hungarian. Only 18 percent of the labor force worked in industry. Raw cotton consumption by the embryonic textile industry stood at one-third the Western level and iron production at one-fifth. Overall, the per capita level of Russian industrialization was just 36 percent that of the West.

In the Ottoman empire the arrival of Western forms of industrial production had a devastating consequence: a sharp de-industrialization, which lasted into the 1850s. Domestic consumption demand had been satisfied earlier by home- and handicraft-production. In 1820, for example, 97 percent of consumption was covered domestically. Then came trade agreements with the West, which were forced on Ottoman Turkey in the 1830s by the militarily victorious Britain and Western powers. Traditional, home-based Turkish goods could not compete with the cheap products of highly productive Western factories: Turkish spinning output, 11,550 tons in the early 1820s, dropped to 3,000 tons by 1870–1872, and by 1910, 75–80 percent of domestic textile consumption was being satisfied by imported Western products. Traditional home- and handicraft-industries survived only in more remote territories that imports could hardly reach.[8]

Mechanized factories scarcely existed in either Ottoman Turkey or the Balkans. Nor did modern industrial enclaves develop, as they did in Russia. The labor force in modern industry in these countries was tiny, numbering fewer workers in total than might be employed in just one large Western European factory. The average number of workers per establishment was 45 in Bulgaria, 35 in Serbia and 167 in Bosnia (after it was annexed by Austro-Hungary). Per capita industrialization levels in Bulgaria, Serbia and Romania stood at 10–13 percent of those in the West.[9]

Isolated from Europe by developments largely beyond its control, the Ottoman empire, including the Balkan region, fell into economic decline. Between 1870 and 1913, the economy grew a mere 0.5 percent annually. Its per capita income level, 45 percent of the German level in 1870, dropped comparatively to 33 percent by 1913.[10] In the freshly independent Balkans, there

Table 7.1 The region's per capita GDP in 1913, as a percentage of Western Europe

Countries	*Per capita GDP in 1913 in 1990 $*	*Per capita GDP in % of West*
Russia	1,488	36
Turkey	979	23
Romania	1,000	24
Bulgaria	1,498	36
Serbia, Bosnia, Macedonia, Montenegro	1,029	25

Source: Based on Angus Maddison, *Monitoring the World Economy 1820–1992*, Paris: OECD, 1995.

was total economic failure. Russia, it must be noted, fared only a little better, despite its small pockets of mostly foreign-established modern industry.

As can be extrapolated from Table 7.1, the average per capita income level of the entire region equaled just 29 percent of the West European level. This sign of peripheral backwardness represented a position in the low-income category, or in the best case at the bottom of the middle-income level. By comparison, in 1913, the neighboring middle-income Central European periphery had an average income level about 60 percent higher than the Russia-Turkey-Balkan level, equivalent to about 50 percent of the West European per capita GDP.

In life expectancy and education, as in income level, the Russia-Turkey-Balkan region remained far behind the other parts of Europe. Turkey's 1913 life expectancy of 30 years, for example, hovered near the medieval level, and only 10 percent of the adult population was literate. This country registered at the lowest level (0.190) in the region on the Human Development Index, 33 percent of the West European level (0.580). Romania (0.345), the relatively best performing country of the region, stood at 59 percent of the Western level.[11]

Given this economic condition World War I caused a cathartic and humiliating shock to the backward countries of the region. They had to face the tests of a demanding modern war, the first mechanized war in history, when tanks and airplanes appeared and trucks transported soldiers. They had to face the more advanced world. They failed miserably.

A new opening to the European world, new states, and regimes after World War I

The war drew in all the countries of the region, on one or the other side. Serbia and Russia joined the Entente with United Kingdom, France, and Italy. Russia had an army with the world's most limitless number of soldiers; 12 million men were mobilized and attacked the enemy in endless lines. An unheard-of 76 percent of these men were lost, with 7 million killed or wounded, the others simply unaccounted for. Famine and disease killed another1.5 million civilians. Serbia, occupied by the Central Powers in 1915, lost nearly half its mobilized men. Romania, after long hesitation, joined the Entente in August 1916. In December that year most of the country (except Moldavia) was occupied by the Germans. German military administration lasted until November 1918. Turkey, on the German side, mobilized 2.8 million men and lost 975,000, while Bulgaria, aligned with the German side, mobilized 1.2 million men and lost one-quarter of them.

Turkey suffered a most humiliating defeat combined with an unheard-of devastation. In the two Balkan wars of 1912–1913, then World War I, followed by the War of Independence in 1920–1922, a total of about 2 million people died. The Armenian genocide led to the loss of 1.5 Armenian Turkish citizens, while another 1.2 million people, Greeks who lived in Anatolia, moved back to Greece. Overall, the population of what became the Republic of Turkey in 1922, declined from 17 million in 1914 to 13 million at the end of 1924.

Across the Russian-Turkey-Balkan region, terrible civilian population losses, hunger and humiliating occupations led to an elemental upheaval, as outdated political and economic systems proved incapable of adapting to the transformed world of their European neighbors to the West. The war provided a wakeup call, which mobilized small groups of people to take action. In Russia, despite alliance with the victorious Entente, the tremendous military and civilian casualties and resulting desperation led to the collapse of the tsarist empire in the two revolutions of 1917. The first of these, a democratic revolution, was followed after a few months by the Bolshevik Revolution. Led by Vladimir Lenin, the Bolsheviks answered the postwar challenges by destroying capitalism, cutting off relations with Europe, isolating their country from Europe and building up the world's first communist regime. Several years of bitter civil war and foreign attacks followed until 1921. In the process Russia lost huge parts of its Western territory, partly to Poland, which launched and won a war against the new Bolshevik state, partly to Finland, and finally to the three Baltic states, which successfully asserted their independence in the postrevolutionary chaos.

Most of the other countries of the Russia-Turkey-Balkan region started down the road, not of communism, but of national revolution. In Turkey, Mustafa Kemal Atatürk and a small group of enlightened soldiers and intellectuals who saw in the humiliations and defeats of the war signs of the need to change, launched a national revolution in 1922. The Ottoman empire collapsed as a result. All of its Middle Eastern and North African territories were lost and from the ruins a modern Turkey emerged, intent on secularizing and Europeanizing.

In the Balkans, nationalist desires for modern, territorially enlarged, more powerful and efficient states merged with the goals of the victorious Entente powers in ways that made the Great War a turning point in the region's history. France, the leading continental military power, played a lead role. The aim of the Entente was to rearrange the political configuration of Central and Eastern Europe by creating an allied ring of countries behind Germany and its "natural ally," Austria-Hungary, in order to isolate Bolshevik Russia. The maneuver actually eliminated Austria-Hungary as a great power by slicing it apart. The resulting alliance system, the "Little Entente," connected a significantly enlarged Romania and the postwar creations Czechoslovakia and Yugoslavia in a *cordon sanitaire.*

Across the Balkans, nationalist drives met with mixed success. Bulgaria, allied with the losing side in World War I, failed to realize its enlargement dream, the Great Bulgaria that would have required annexation of Macedonia. Romania, in contrast, acquired large new territories and thus succeeded in creating Romania Mare, Great Romania. The Entente, in a secret treaty in 1916, had promised this outcome to Romanian leaders if they chose to enter the war on the Entente side, which they did. Honoring the secret treaty, the Entente awarded to Romania the regions of Transylvania, a part of the Great Hungarian Plain, Bukovina, and Bessarabia. As a result, the Romania of 137,000 square kilometers and 7.5 million inhabitants before the war became after the war a country of 304,000 square kilometers and 18 million inhabitants. Paradoxically, however, this national revolution produced a new multiethnic state with large minorities: 2 million Hungarians and another 1.6 million Russians, Germans and Bulgarians. Another 5 percent of the population was Jewish, therefore, according to an 1879 constitutional amendment in force until 1923, prohibited from obtaining Romanian citizenship.

Farther south, the Serbs tried a new road of "nation building" based on the idea that south Slavic peoples of similar, if not identical ethnicity could be homogenized as a nation. The result was Yugoslavia, a new, small, multinational, south Slavic state, joining Bosnia, Croatia, Slovenia, Macedonia, and Montenegro to Serbia. Separately, the mostly tribal and Muslim Albania also started existence as an independent state. The last in the Balkans to break free of Ottoman control, it acquired legal independence just before the outbreak of war in 1913.

Successes and failures in the interwar decades

This new opening to Europe naturally required tremendous adjustments, adjustments certainly unattainable in the mere 21 years of peace that followed upon the end of the world's first total war. International economic and political situations were partly responsible for the problems. Financially stabilizing the war- and inflation-ridden countries required almost half of the first postwar decade. In the second half of that decade the Great Depression hit Europe and this region very hard. Before that crisis ended, a new war-coalition formation and war preparation started, followed by the most devastating World War II. Domestic conflicts fueled other troubles.

The new communist Russian state, for example, required a decade to transform into the Soviet Union. The structural changes began only in 1928, under the terms of the first Five Year Plan, and continued during the 1930s as Josip V. Stalin cemented his ruthless dictatorial rule, eliminated rival factions in bloody purges, established an institutional framework for the regime and launched his collectivization and industrialization drives, accompanied by famine, mass deportations and the death of about ten million people.

Turkey, also searching for a road, took most of the interwar decades to find one. The 1924 constitution provided a foundation with the declaration of the "Turkish nation," but major reforms continued to be enacted until 1935. The model was the West and its representative, parliamentary, secular democracy, based on the separation of the branches of power. The Atatürk regime emancipated women, declared equality before the law and banned all Islamic institutions, including the traditional Muslim fez, turban and clothing. The Hat Law in 1925, mocked as "the hat revolution," prohibited the wearing of traditional hats and required public servants to wear Western hats. Similar traditional clothing bans followed in 1934. The Atatürk regime also introduced compulsory education in 1928, the national railway system in 1927, and the National Bank in 1934.

To realize these radical reforms, Atatürk turned to absolute power and introduced a strict one-party regime. The only political party was his social-democratic type party, the Republican People's Party (*Cumhuriyet Halk Partisi*). Atatürk did not allow any power-sharing, nor, after his death in 1938, did his successor, Mustafa İsmet İnönü, until 1945. Highly impressed by the successes of Stalin's modernization program in the Soviet Union, Atatürk embraced harsh statist measures. The new strategy, officially announced in 1930, promoted the state as a leading economic agent, producer and investor, and introduced the Soviet planned economy model. The state planning organization subordinated each economic sector to a directorate. Sectoral holding companies set prices centrally. Indeed, Soviet advisers assisted the Turkish regime with the first Five Year Plan to jump-start industrialization. State enterprises started their operations in 1933 and by the end of the decade dominated the key sectors of the economy: textiles, sugar, iron and steel, glass works, cement, utilities and mining.[12] Central planning remained in place and Five Year Plans followed one after another even after World War II and the deaths of both Atatürk and İnönü. The fourth Five Year Plan was realized in the early 1980s.

Left- and rightwing extremism flooded the highly exhausted, frustrated and unstable Balkan countries after World War I. Bulgaria offers a typical example. In September 1918, a leftwing peasant revolution started in Vladaya, and peasant troops marched against the capital, seeking to oust Tsar Ferdinand. However, they were defeated and their leaders, Raykov Daskalov and Aleksandŭr Stamboliyski, imprisoned. The regime played the nationalism card, attempting to realize the "Great Bulgaria" dream by incorporating Macedonia. That effort failed and the defeated country had to adjust to postwar European rules. Tsar Ferdinand resigned in favor of his son Boris, and free elections subsequently were held in September 1919. The desperate peasant country turned toward the revolutionary Agrarian Union, headed by Stamboliyski, who had been released from prison. He received 31 percent of the votes. More than 18 percent was given to the Communist Party and nearly 13 percent to the Social Democratic Party. A peasant-worker's coalition government was formed and soon established a leftwing populist peasant dictatorship. Stamboliyski's paramilitary "Orange Guard" terrorized the opposition, including the rival communists. In 1920, after a second election, and a third one in April 1923, Stamboliyski introduced his one-party dictatorship. He enacted a radical land reform that limited the maximum size of estates to 30 hectares (75 acres) and introduced compulsory labor service, progressive taxation, and state monopoly of grain trade to eliminate "parasitic" merchant activity. Imprisonment of wartime cabinet ministers and leading businessmen accompanied these reforms. Stamboliyski also rejected nationalism and territorial expansion and suggested a Balkan Confederation with Yugoslavia.

This peaceful revolution revitalized the Bulgarian extreme right. The Internal Macedonian Revolutionary Organization (IMRO), a rightwing terrorist organization dating back to the end of the 19th century, resurfaced and launched attacks to regain Macedonia by force. The IMRO also attacked the left. Another rightwing organization bearing the name Naroden Sgovor (National Concord) also attracted support, and its leader, Colonel Damian Velchev, launched a coup d'état in June 1923. These rightwing groups defeated the peasant troops and captured Stamboliyski, who was tortured, beheaded, and mutilated by IMRO terrorists. The Communist Party organized a new revolution, and uprisings erupted in various places. These also were defeated, and 10,000–30,000 communists were killed. Bulgaria turned to rightwing dictatorial rule and aggressive nationalism. When the 1931 elections, held during the misery of the Great Depression, produced an absolute majority for the Agrarian Union in coalition with some other opposition parties, the hard right did not hesitate to take action. Colonel Velchev launched a second coup d'état in May 1934. The chaotic situation, conflicts, and frequent terrorist attacks offered the possibility to Tsar Boris in January 1935, of imposing a nonparliamentary royal dictatorship. Tsar Boris also established a close alliance with Hitler and Mussolini.

Bulgaria's troubled interwar history was not at all unique. Just the opposite, it well represents the general instability in the Balkans countries. Newly created Yugoslavia was also unable to consolidate or turn to peaceful reconstruction and development. Ten years after its foundation this new country nearly exploded because of heated national conflict between its Serbs and Croats. The trigger was the assassination of the leader of the leftist Croat Peasant Party, Stjepan Radič, in 1928, during the session of the Parliament. King Alexander banned all parties, shut down democratic institutions and introduced his personal royal dictatorship in January 1929, a model followed by all the Balkan countries between 1929 and 1938. Five years later, in October 1934, King Alexander met the same fate as Radič, assassination. This time the venue was France, where the king was making an official state visit, and the perpetrators, Croatian fascists of the Ustašha movement, who were working in collaboration with the Bulgarian IMRO. Croatian fascism gained ground under Ante Pavelić, and after the Nazi attack against Yugoslavia in 1941, Hitler created an independent, fascist, Croatian, Ustašha state.

Despite having introduced a democratic system after the war, Romania, too, shifted toward rightwing extremism. One of Europe's biggest fascist parties was established there in the 1920s, under the leadership of Corneliu Zelea Codreanu. This party challenged the regime and organized terror actions, which led to the introduction of royal dictatorship in 1938. As in Croatia, during the war, the Romanian fascists entered the government as part of a coalition. In the interwar Balkans, no place could be found for democracy, peaceful construction, and modern transformation.

Economic performance of the region during the interwar decades

As in Central Europe, economic nationalism emerged during the interwar decades as the dominant economic model in this region. To guarantee both their independence and their stability, the newly sovereign countries of the Russia-Turkey-Balkans region, with their newly formed regimes, chose economic self-sufficiency over interdependence. All the countries started replacing imports with their own production and building up their missing and weak economic sectors. The exemplar for this kind of policy was the communist Soviet Union.

The isolated Soviet regime, surrounded by enemies, survived civil war and foreign intervention after the revolution, but never could exclude the possibility of new attacks. This fear was given extra fuel by the rise of violent fascism and Nazism, especially in the 1930s. Preparation for possible war was thus one of the central motives of Soviet economic policy. In a speech, delivered in February 1931, Stalin explained his industrialization plans in the following way:

> One feature of the history of old Russia was the continual beatings she suffered because of her backwardness. She was beaten by Mongol khans … by Turkish beys … by Swedish feudal lords … by the Polish and Lithuanian gentry … by the British and French capitalists. … All beat her because of her backwardness. … We are 50 or 100 years behind the advanced countries. We must make good this distance in 10 years. Either we do it, or we should go under.

At the 1933 Party Congress, he added: "We could not know just when the imperialists might attack us. … The Party could not afford to wait. … It had to pursue the policy of accelerating development to the utmost."[13]

The other main source of Stalin's economic policy was Marxist communist ideology; in particular the emphasis on eliminating private ownership of the means of production. From that came the idea of planning the economy, with egalitarian distribution as a chief goal. Stalin also took over Friedrich Engels's idea of collectivizing peasant agriculture. Most of the genuinely Marxist ideas were applied in a distorted form. Engels presented his collectivization idea as a strictly voluntary, if needed, long process, but it was implemented under Stalin as a mandatory measure, over just a few years, with brutal force and inhumane actions. In Marx's conceptualization, socialism would win in the most advanced, high-income countries, with the international proletariat acting together. Egalitarian distribution, subsequently, would assure high standards of living. In backward Russia the application of this concept produced instead a distribution of poverty, as when two to four families, for example, were assigned to share one, relatively small apartment. Furthermore, the investment capital required for successful, rapid industrialization could be accumulated only by subjecting peasants to a "price scissor" (keeping agricultural prices very low and fixing high prices for consumer goods) and by significantly depressing workers' wages. The strategy of directing capital to industry caused permanent shortages of consumer goods, sometimes even food and clothing rationing (individual clothing purchases might be limited to one winter coat and one pair of shoes per year, for example). The Marxian egalitarian principle thus was deformed into a regime approaching the frightening utopian society of communal *phalanstères* envisioned by Charles Fourier.

The Soviet communist regime launched its development strategy in the late 1920s and early 1930s. The first Five Year Plan, a 1,700-page document put forth in 1929, targeted increasing industrial output by 2.5 times and heavy industrial goods investment by nearly four times, all by 1932. Several new industrial centers were created, the industrial labor force was doubled, and the country was on its way to "guaranteeing us economic independence."[14]

Forced capital accumulation and industrialization policy worked. During the 1930s when the world average economic growth was 2 percent and the West increased its per capita GDP by 8 percent, the Soviet Union achieved a robust growth of 61 percent. In 1929, per capita GDP was only 28 percent of the advanced West, but by 1938 it stood at 43 percent of it. Already in 1934 Stalin triumphantly announced that the country has eliminated "backwardness and medievalism. From an agrarian country it has become an industrial country."[15] The Soviet Union trebled its industrial output by the end of World War II. Furthermore, between 1913 and 1950, it almost doubled its income level, to 49 percent of the Western level, far surpassing the moderate all-European increase of 37 percent.[16]

None of the other countries of the region were able to repeat this breakthrough in industrialization. Turkey, for example, started its new chapter in economic development after the creation of the Turkish Republic in 1922 with a dramatic 20 percent decline of population and 40 percent decline in per capita incomes compared to 1913. As a result, the GDP per capita for Turkey was sharply lower than before. The greatest achievement of the country in the interwar decades thus lay mostly in its recovery from this devastating downturn and its attainment of a modest increase of income per capita. Population growth was extremely fast, and the population of the country consequently increased by 60 percent during the interwar period. Agricultural output increased by 50–70 per cent during the 1930s.

Most of the institutional changes did not influence the still majority-rural population or alter the dominance of agriculture in the economy. Consequently, the efforts of the 1930s contributed only modestly to economic growth and structural change. Economic nationalism and protectionist policy definitely favored the creation of a more inward-oriented economy and it reduced imports from more than 15 percent of GDP in 1928–1929 to less than 7 percent by 1938–1939. Import repression created attractive conditions for the emerging domestic industry, but mostly for small and medium-sized workshops. Modern industrialization did not break through. In 1938, employees at large modern enterprises accounted for only one percent of the total in the country. Approximately 75 percent of industrial employees were working in small-scale private enterprises. In the 37 years between 1913 and 1950, the per capita income consequently increased by a mere 32 percent.[17]

Modest economic growth was the norm in that troubled period. Except for the Soviet Union, with its robust growth in isolation, not hit by the Great Depression, the countries of the region could not improve their relative position in Europe. Bulgaria and Romania exhibited 10–20 percent growth in the 37-year period 1913–1950, and the four countries of the region together (without the Soviet Union) had an unweighted average of 26 percent per capita growth. That growth was much slower than in the eight top northwestern countries, which progressed from the 1913 per capita income average of $3,933 to the 1950 average of $6,241 (in constant prices). Per capita income of this region, expressed as a percentage of the same in the West consequently declined from 30 to 27 percent between 1913 and 1950.[18]

New political environment and troubled history after World War II

In two countries of the region, the Soviet Union and Yugoslavia, World War II was especially devastating. The Soviet Union lost nearly 27 million people, 17–20 percent of its population and Yugoslavia, counting demographic losses and emigration, nearly 2 million of its 15 million inhabitants, thus 13 percent of its population. These belong among the heaviest losses anywhere during the entire war. German attacks and Soviet counterattacks crossed the European part of the Soviet Union twice, causing tremendous physical destruction: the loss of 1,700 towns, 70,000 villages, 32,000 factories, and 65,000 kilometers of railroad line.[19] In Yugoslavia three years of partisan warfare and 11 German counteroffensives also caused severe damages. Most of the other parts of the region, however, were spared. Turkey did not enter the war until February 1945, when it joined the Allies; Romania exited the German-led Axis when the Soviet troops arrived at its border and thus saved itself from becoming a battlefield.

Postwar reconstruction was fast and successful. In the Soviet Union the losses in the badly devastated European part of the country were partly compensated by the evacuation of industry from those parts and by massive wartime economic development in the Asian parts of the country. All in all, in 1948–1950, the whole region recovered and started on a new development road. But the region also experienced a decisive regime change. Excepting Turkey, all the other countries became part of the Soviet Bloc: Yugoslavia and Albania voluntarily, Bulgaria and Romania involuntarily, after occupation by the Soviets. Most of the region, consequently, introduced the Soviet-type political and economic regime, one-party dictatorial rule and a nonmarket, state-owned, and centrally planned economic system. The 1950s brought numerous shocks: all round nationalization, basic institutional changes, radical elite shifts and, after Stalin's death in 1953, the de-Stalinization of the later years of that decade. The Soviet-Yugoslav conflict that erupted in 1948, followed by the exclusion of Yugoslavia and Albania from the Soviet Bloc and the establishment of national communism in those two countries, as in Romania, also undermined consistency and stability. After 1973, the region's communist regimes – as in the neighboring regimes in Central Europe – declined into a deepening crisis that ended with their collapse in 1989 (1991 in the Soviet Union and Albania). With these collapses the multinational Soviet Union and Yugoslavia disappeared from the map. Instead of five states, the region now had 11. The imperative to adjust and reorient continually, repeatedly, disrupted peaceful development.

Turkey's postwar history has been rather different but not at all undisturbed. The country changed political orientation, turned to multiparty democracy, and hesitantly taken steps to embrace the free market economy. It joined the West in 1952, by becoming a member of NATO, thus part of the Western military alliance. But the turn to the free market really did not begin seriously until 1980, and politically the country never has become fully Westernized. From time to time, military coups have occurred, and dictatorial regimes have been put in place. This happened in 1960, 1971 and 1980. Domestic terrorist organizations, the leftwing Turkish People's Liberation Army and the rightwing Islamist Grey Wolves organization, have threatened the population. An Islamist political resurgence, begun in the 1980s with the rise of the antisecular Welfare Party, has intensified since 2002, under the so far unbroken rule of the initially moderate Islamist Justice and Development Party (*Adale ve Kalkinma Partisi*, or AKP) of Recep Tayyip Erdoğan. Since the 2010s, Erdoğan has turned increasingly against the West, and has moved the country back toward dictatorship and its Islamist past. Turkey during the second half of the 20th century and at the beginning of the 21st century, in other words, has not been a stable democracy at all. There, as elsewhere in the region, the years after World War II have not been the best of times for undisturbed economic development and catching up to the European core.

Rapid growth and industrialization

In the new, postwar, political framework, most of the Russia-Turkey-Balkans region (Turkey being the exception) introduced the Soviet-type regime of collectivized agriculture, state-owned, centrally planned economy, and forced capital accumulation and industrialization. The introduction of the new policy and institutions, as in the Soviet Union in the 1930s, shocked economies. First of all, in the dominantly agricultural countries, collectivization, with its accompanying elimination of well-to-do peasantry (dekulakization à la Stalin), caused tremendous destruction and decline, the slaughtering of a huge part of the animal stock, the disappearance of meat and other food products from shops. Nearly two decades and major shifts away from the Soviet model (a reinstitution of private agriculture in Yugoslavia, for example) would be required for agriculture to recover from these losses and return to precollectivization output levels. Secondly, forced capital accumulation dramatically changed the situation. Instead of registering at the average of 6 percent, capital accumulation elevated to 20–25 percent of the GDP, and investment became and remained high until the 1980s. Fixed capital formation increased to twice that in the West.[20] In line with the Soviet model, nearly 50 percent of investment across the region in the 1950s was concentrated into industry. More specifically, in Bulgaria and Romania during the 1960s, industrial investment reached 42–45 percent and 48–49 percent, respectively, and hovered quite consistently in these ranges until the second oil crisis in the 1980s.[21] By contrast, such investment in the 1960s in Western Europe commanded just 24–25 percent of total investment.

Forced accumulation and high investment, together one element of the extensive development model followed by all the communist countries, were supplemented by high labor input, a second, equally important element. In the dominantly agricultural countries collectivization combined with the mechanization of large-scale production well-served the goal of generating an exodus from the countryside. In two decades about 40–50 percent of the agricultural labor force was uprooted. In Bulgaria the rural population decreased to 32 percent, in Romania and Yugoslavia, to 53 and 57 percent, respectively. Labor input to industry increased annually by 9 percent in Yugoslavia, 8 percent in Bulgaria, and nearly 5 percent in Romania in the 1950s. During the 1960s, it slowed down somewhat but remained very high, more than 5 percent, in Romania and Bulgaria, and continued during the 1970s at a slower pace. This high labor input, the prime mover of industrialization, did not come to a halt until the 1980s.

After the slow economic growth in the interwar decades, the postwar region shifted gears to high speed. According to various modern Western calculations, annual growth in the Balkans even in the second half of the 1960s, was 8–9 percent.[22] Other estimates suggest about 4–5 percent annual growth over the entire period between 1950 and 1980.[23] Fast growth rates and strong concentration in industry, the centerpiece always in Soviet economic strategy, caused a page turn in the history of the communist countries of the region: they now became industrialized. According to an American Congressional Paper, annual industrial output in the 1950s increased by nearly 13 percent in Bulgaria and 9 percent in Romania and Yugoslavia. Between 75 and 90 percent of investments targeted the so-called heavy industries during the first Five Year Plan period, and these sectors remained preferred later as well, although somewhat less one-sidedly

Table 7.2 Stagnation between 1973 and 1990 in Bulgaria, Romania, Yugoslavia, and the Soviet Union

Year	*Soviet Union*	*Bulgaria*	*Romania*	*Yugoslavia*
1973	6,058	5,284	3,477	4,237
1989–1990	6,871	6,217	3,830	5,917

Source: Angus Maddison, *Monitoring the World Economy 1820–1992*, Paris: OECD, 1995.

so. During the 1950s coal, iron and steel production basically doubled. From the 1960s to the 1980s, several engineering branches and basic chemical materials production also emerged. According to the United Nations statistical yearbooks, Yugoslavia increased its industrial production by 2.5 times, Bulgaria by three times and Romania by five times by the 1980s. In 1988, between 45 and 62 percent of the GDP in these countries was produced by industry.[24]

The Soviet Union basically continued its industrialization policy, especially by modernizing and developing its armament industry and by further decreasing the labor force in agriculture from 54 percent in 1940 to 20 percent by 1984. Production expanded until the early 1970s, and the GDP increased by more than two times between 1950 and 1973. Cold War confrontation and tension, however, paralyzed Soviet economic development. With less than half of the income of the United States, the country kept military expenditure at a competitive level, an unbearable burden on the economy. About 70 percent of industry served military purposes. Research and development focused on defense, producing the exceptional successes of developing an arsenal of atomic weapons and missiles, and, in the first period, of surpassing the United States in space programs. The country, however, had to pay a tremendous price for these achievements: economic stagnation overall, from the early 1970s to 1990. Per capita GDP in 1973 reached a peak at $6,058 and then remained at the same level for 17 years. In 1990 it amounted $6,871.

With the exception of Yugoslavia, the other communist countries of the region shared the Soviet destiny of stagnation or near stagnation from the mid-1970s until the regime collapse in 1989.

The four communist countries of the region, on average, achieved only a 20 percent increase of unweighted per capita GDP over 17 years, representing a fraction of their growth between 1950 and 1973.

Ambivalent modernization in Turkey

Through the postwar period, Turkey remained an entire stage behind the other countries of the region, with its most striking development being its strongly belated demographic revolution; that is, its conspicuous population explosion, similar to the one that happened a century before in Europe. In the second half of the 20th century, even as European demographic growth slowed down significantly, the annual rate of population growth in Turkey, as in the so-called developing countries, reached around 2.4–2.5 percent. In 1960, as an average, a Turkish woman had 6.2 children and about two decades later still 4.3 children. The birth rate declined around the turn of the millennium, but even in 2008, it still hovered somewhat above the reproduction level of 2.1 percent, much higher than the European 1.3–1.6 percent average.

This belated demographic revolution actually copied the Central and Eastern European pattern of the 19th century. Thus, the mortality rate, and especially the infant mortality rate, declined with the arrival of Western medical achievements. In 1960, 166 of every 1,000 newborns died, but at the turn of the millennium already only 20. The birth rate, however, remained premodern, typical of peasant societies. Consequently, as in 19th-century Europe, the Turkish population increased by more than three times in the second half of the 20th century. After the high population losses in the era of World War I, the population grew to surpass 13 million in the mid-1920s and then to reach almost 21 million by 1950. By the early 21st century, the country's population was nearly 73 million (although 3.5 million people emigrated, 3 million of them to Europe).[25]

Such a tremendous increase of the population required more food to feed the people, more housing to accommodate them and more jobs to offer income for a living. These needs could not be met easily. Agriculture was rather backward in the country. The legacy of the interwar decades made matters worse: output per capita had dropped by a shocking 50 percent during the decade of wars between 1912 and 1922 and did not recover until the 1930s. After World War II, Turkey was still a rural agricultural country with 16 million of its 21 million people, more than three-quarters of the population, living in the countryside in 1950, for example. Agriculture employed 79 percent of the population (nearly the same level as in 1880) and produced 53 percent of the GDP. The sector stood at the center of development for decades after the war, the 50 percent increase of land under cultivation being one of the most important elements of development. Intensive cultivation gained ground, irrigation was introduced in the Euphrates Valley and agricultural labor productivity increased fourfold between 1950 and 2000. Shifting from agriculture to industry and services required almost the entire second half of the 20th century. By 2000, the rural population had dropped to 35 percent (24 million of a total population of 68 million). Still agricultural employment, although sharply decreased, accounted for 35 percent of the total, very high by European standards.

As these figures suggest, the second half of the 20th century saw the role of agriculture in the economy shrink dramatically. This is clearly expressed by the fact that in 1960, 80 percent of Turkish export consisted of agricultural products, during the 1970s still 60 percent, but by the late 1980s, only 20 percent; also by the fac that by the turn of the millennium, agriculture contributed only 14 percent to the Turkish GDP and 3 percent to its exports.[26]

Turkey's economic policy in its industrial and service sectors, at first glance surprisingly, did not differ much from the policies of its communist neighbors in the region. Until roughly 1980, the country typically followed the same import-substituting industrialization strategy aimed at developing a strongly state-owned economy. The state was the chief entrepreneur, and a local bourgeoisie hardly existed. The state overwhelmingly dominated the postwar banking, mining, energy, transport and communication sectors. Foreign investment was insignificant, representing only one percent of private investments in the first period after the war. In 1970, scarcely more than 2 percent of the fixed capital formation was covered by foreign investments. The savings rate was low, even in 1980 only 12 percent of the GDP. With the exceptions of food, textiles, iron and steel, the country depended on imports. Its principal export items were agricultural products and textiles. The country did not have a modern banking sector, and finances were always in trouble. A huge current accounts deficit, along with 32 years of inflation (in the second half of the 1990s, climbing to 80–85 percent) and heavy indebtedness characterized the last decades of the 20th century. To stabilize the economy, the IMF contributed about $50 billion in loans between 1961 and the 1990s. Historians and economists speak of the "lost years" of the 1970s and 1990s.[27]

Economic development in Turkey had to support a sharply increased population, and therefore any growth of the GDP had to be spread over a greater number of people. As a result Turkish per capita income level barely more than doubled (210 percent) between 1950 and 1973, a period of exceptionally rapid development all over Europe; the period when the eight highly developed northwestern countries, starting from a much higher base, increased their income level by 214 percent and Turkey's communist next-door neighbors recorded even faster growth, 264 percent. Turkey's relative position in the Russia-Turkey-Balkans region thus declined markedly, from 72 percent of the per capita income of its four communist neighbors in 1950, to just 57 percent in 1973.

During the last third of the 20th century the trend reversed course dramatically. The region's communist countries declined into a deep and gradually deepening crisis while Turkey took a positive turn: it stopped import-substituting and started down the road of integration into Europe, modernizing by adjusting to the West, changing its economic model to one of export-oriented development.

Reproduced backwardness in Russia and the Balkans

The most devastating problem facing the regions' communist countries after 1973 was not stagnation per se but rather the lack of the market and entrepreneurial flexibility so necessary if economies are to adapt to new challenges and market requirements. Rigid, bureaucratic central planning was a heavy burden on these economies in a time of radical worldwide changes. Unlike in some of the Central European communist countries, in this region reform was not on the agenda. Romania and Bulgaria did not change policies at all. Yugoslavia distanced itself from Soviet-type institutional system after 1948, by reprivatizing agriculture and introducing workers' self-management as a kind of collective ownership system, but the country still did not follow a flexible market economic model. When the leadership paralysis in the Soviet Union was solved by the appointment of Mikhail Gorbachev in 1985, it was already too late. Moreover, Gorbachev started reforming from the "wrong end," loosening the authoritarian grip and democratizing the system by *Glasnost,* replacing Cold War confrontation with *détente* and giving up the close and rigorous control of the Soviet Bloc countries, but hardly progressing with *Perestroika*, changes to the economic system. His reforms were powerless to change and modernize the country. Collapse became unavoidable.

In most of the countries in the region, a deep leadership crisis long-paralyzed action. The Brezhnev regime in the Soviet Union blocked the road to significant change for nearly two decades. After Brezhnev's death, two old, sick persons were elected to the leadership, one after the other. Both died after a very short time in office. Then came Gorbachev, too late, as I have noted already. In Romania, Nicolae Ceauşescu, an egomaniac dictator, decided to eliminate his country's debt by means of the harshest austerity. He ruined and impoverished the country. After the debt was repaid, a revolution erupted, the only violent one in the region, and the army, which joined the revolution, tried and executed both Ceauşescu and his wife. In Yugoslavia, during the critical 1980s, after the death of Josip Broz Tito, a collective, rotating leadership proved unable to direct the country. Beset by nationalist sentiments and revolution in the various, increasingly independent republics, the country soon was torn apart in a brutal civil war. In general, a lack of leadership caused political chaos and paralysis in the region's communist countries.

Meanwhile a deadly structural degradation, which actually had been unfolding all through the postwar period, came to a culmination in the communist world. Modernization based on tremendous efforts and forced sacrifices, aimed at transforming agricultural or agricultural-industrial economic structures into fully industrialized ones, proved to be the wrong road, reliant on a pattern made obsolete by the postwar, new revolution of technology. Hints of what was to come had been signaled by the invention of the first main frame computer and radar in Britain, the use of nuclear energy in the United States, the development of rocket technology and jet flight in Germany. In the 1950s two key inventions in the United States, the transistor and the chip, quickly led to a radical breakthrough, the invention of the personal computer in 1974. The age of the communication revolution had begun, a revolution comparable in historical importance to the first industrial revolution.

As usual, none of the European peripheral nations numbered among the pioneers of revolution. The Soviet Union, with its tremendous scientific capacity, concentrated its efforts to military technology by creating special scientific-research enclaves, closed from the world, with different financial system, wages and supply; small isolated "Western islands," in effect, able to command anything needed to support innovation. This military research and innovation had no connection to the civilian economy, which was neglected and deprived of necessary resources. Across the entire Soviet Bloc, countries that prior to the 20th century had imported modern technology from the advanced West were prevented from buying and adopting the new, modern technology by an American ban on its export. This ban was in place from 1947 and internationalized through The Coordinating Committee for Multilateral Export Controls (CoCom), discussed in Chapter 6. Excluded from the possibility of acquiring and thus benefitting from the new technology, the communist countries of Russia and the Balkans remained distant by "light years" from the economic revolution in the West.

The economies of the communist countries of the region were becoming obsolete, therefore, even as they were trying to modernize. The regional energy system, for example, was frozen in the coal-economy, although Soviet oil extraction did increase and begin to play a more important role. The old-fashioned, raw-material-wasting dominant "heavy industries" were less and less competitive. High-tech sectors did not emerge, and the regional infrastructure, barred from access to revolutionary technologies, deteriorated. Concomitantly the countries experienced a strong, in some cases 20–30 percent decline of the terms of trade, brought on by the pairing of increasing import prices with stagnating or decreasing export prices. On top of that, trade within the region, particularly with the Soviet Union, was collapsing. Since such trade accounted for large percentages of total trade in the individual countries – 50 percent in Romania and 80 percent in Bulgaria, for example – the countries had to turn to Western markets.

Trade deficits created huge holes in national budgets and set in motion the conditions for subsequent crisis. Budgetary deficits were "filled" by foreign credits. Romania's debt burden equaled its total export income in 1985; Bulgaria's, at nearly $10 billion, 75 percent. Meanwhile the cheap "oil dollars" of the mid-1970s disappeared and interest rates on new credit sharply increased. Repaying old debts by taking on new ones became impossible. At the end of the 1980s, Yugoslavia and Bulgaria became insolvent and asked for rescheduling. Romania was totally broken by the burden of debt repayment. In the brewing atmosphere of crisis in the 1980s, with the Solidarity movement gaining strength in Poland, the Romanian dictator, Ceauşescu, turned to the Soviet Union, suggesting military action against Poland to save the regime. Gorbachev rejected this possibility. What followed was the collapse of state socialism across the whole region, following similar collapses in Poland and Hungary. It happened at the end of 1989 in Yugoslavia, Bulgaria, and Romania; in Albania and the Soviet Union, in 1991. The two multinational states of the region, the Soviet Union and Yugoslavia, dissolved. In their place national revolution created 22 new independent states.

The Russia-Turkey-Balkan region and the European Union

The collapse of communism and close of the Cold War ended the separation of the two halves of Europe. In this new international situation, the road toward the integration of all of the four regions of the European continent into a gradually homogenizing union opened up. The European Economic Community, which had become the European Union of 12 countries by the end of the 1980s, was more than ready to accept and incorporate other European countries.

The history of the EU actually is the history of permanent enlargement. In 1973 the number of member countries increased from the founding six to nine, then by 1986, to 12, and in 1995, to 15. By means of the postwar Marshall Plan, the United States, the leader of the Western world during the Cold War decades, played a role in the integration process from the very beginning. Ever since it has urged and pushed EU enlargement. It has aimed to hammer out a closely integrated, allied, anticommunist world in Europe and has pushed the EU to accept all European NATO countries as new members. Efforts to attain this goal were quite successful in the 1960s when even dictatorial regimes (in Greece, Portugal, and Spain) were accepted as associates and part of a customs union, the first steps on the road toward membership.

As part of this policy, the United States also "suggested" accepting Turkey, indeed pressed for this result. A US congressional analysis of 2013 noted that successive administrations:

> have long backed EU enlargement. … Over the years, the only significant US criticism of the EU's enlargement process has been that the Union was moving too slow, especially with respect to Turkey. … The United States believes that Turkey's membership in NATO has demonstrated that Turkey can interact constructively with … countries that belong to the EU. … The US has been disappointed that it has not been able to use its influence to help shape a more constructive EU-Turkey relationship.[28]

Encouraged by the United States, Turkey first applied for membership in1959, but politically and economically it was far from being prepared for such a step. Nevertheless, the European Economic Community (EEC, the precursor of the EU) cautiously yielded to American pressure and in 1963 signed an association agreement (the Ankara Agreement) with Turkey. In 1971, the EEC removed almost all of its tariffs on Turkish products and established a customs union with Turkey. The relationship remained always troubled, however, especially because consecutive military coups introduced dictatorships in Turkey in 1960 and 1980. Nevertheless, in the 1990s, Turkey officially became an associate member. But since then the process has stalled, as the Erdoğan government has begun reinstituting dictatorial policies. His hostile anti-European policy of the 2010s has not only set back progress toward full Turkish membership but also pushed it from the realm of the acceptable.

When communism collapsed, the European Union was ready to admit the formerly communist Central and Eastern European countries. The Copenhagen Community meeting declared in 1993 that the "countries in Central and Eastern Europe that so desire shall become members of the European Union … as soon as … [they have fulfilled] the obligations of membership by satisfying the economic and political conditions required."[29] Eight Central European and Baltic countries, along with Romania and Bulgaria, applied for EU membership. The eight were accepted in 2004; Bulgaria and Romania, in 2007. Both sets of admissions were hazardous, the latter more so than the former. The average per capita income level of the "eight," just over $9,000, already placed them in a category separate from the other EU members, with their $29,000 average. The two Balkan countries differed even more. Their mere $4,000 income level, less than half that of the Central European countries, encapsulated their non-Western economic, social and political backwardness. As a prerequisite to membership, the EU demanded from Bulgaria and Romania, successful interventions against their devastating, non-European levels of corruption (ranked by the World Bank as 101st and 104th among the world's most corrupt countries). The EU accepted their preparations as convincing and satisfactory. After acceptance, Bulgaria, however, immediately stopped its formal anticorruption fight.

The admission of several of the Central European countries, and especially of the Balkan countries, was definitely premature. Despite this, the EU started negotiations with nearly all the other Balkan countries: Macedonia, Albania, Montenegro and Serbia filed their membership applications between 2005 and 2009. Negotiations then began on ways to meet the requirements, which were laid out in the 35 chapters of the so-called *acquis communautaire*. Albania became an official candidate in 2014 but as of this writing, negotiations with the other applicants have yet to come to fruition. A kind of anteroom for candidacy, the Stabilization and Association Agreement, has been signed with several of these countries, including Kosovo, which the United Nations has recognized as an independent country. In other words, the West Balkan countries are all on the waiting list and standing before the EU door.[30] Meanwhile the people of several Western member countries clearly have expressed their dissatisfaction with further enlargement. In 2014, the newly elected president of the European Commission, Jean-Claude Juncker, announced that acceptance of new members would not be on the agenda for at least five years and then extended further.

This halting of further enlargement has occurred in close connection with the spectacular failure of the European Union's overly ambitious eastern enlargement initiative. In 2003–2004, in the framework of a new Neighborhood Policy, the EU started building connections with, even offering aid to six former Soviet republics, the now independent countries Armenia, Azerbaijan, Belarus, Georgia, Moldova and Ukraine. Then in 2007, the European Commission presented the so-called Black Sea Initiative to the European Council and Parliament. It stated that this region is "rich in natural resources and strategically located at the junction of Europe, Central Asia and the Middle East … [thus] opens a window of fresh perspectives and opportunities."[31]

Actually, already in 1996, the Commission announced its desire to add Ukraine to "the European architecture." The Council of Ministers immediately added that the EU "wishes to see the Partnership and Cooperation Agreement" with Ukraine. The ministers stated that such an agreement would be not only economically advantageous but also would prevent "any possible return to the former ways [and] loosen the grip of dependence upon their powerful neighbor [Russia]."[32] Parallel with the EU initiative, the Bush administration in the United States attempted to rush inclusion of Ukraine into NATO; this failed because of French and German opposition. Still, in November 2013 a thousand-page "further Europeanization" EU Association Agreement was ratified with Ukraine, Moldova, Armenia, and Georgia.

This proved to involve a catastrophic miscalculation, putting the interests of Russia and the EU into direct confrontation. Ukraine, a fatally divided country with a Western-oriented Catholic Western Ukraine and a Russian-oriented, Russian Orthodox Eastern Ukraine, the latter with a large Russian minority population, exploded in a civil war. The fighting was initiated primarily by Vladimir Putin's Russia, which also annexed the Crimea, after a military intervention. Trying to incorporate into the EU orbit (and NATO), a country lying without a doubt in the Russian sphere of interest, naturally invited Russian counter actions. A special subcommittee of the British House of Lords stated:

> Britain and the European Union made a catastrophic misreading of Russia ... and sleepwalked into the Ukrainian crisis." The European Union self-critically added in 2014: "we set in motion a chain of events ... Thus we learned about the geopolitical implication of technical cooperation, export of norms and trade relations the hard way.[33]

Yet the European Union had a natural interest in influencing and even in incorporating the Russian-Turkish-Balkans region, or at least part of it, into its own circuit. The enlargement policy was an attempt to secure peace and friendly relations across the entire continent by pacifying the Balkans, a traditional "powder keg" of Europe (especially after the bloody Yugoslav civil war in the early 1990s) and the highly troubled, neighboring, European former Soviet Bloc successor states. The policy also spoke to the elemental economic interest of the EU and its corporate businesses, which would be well-served by adding another 100–150 million new consumers and an extremely cheap, unlimited labor force to the European common market.

In addition to igniting conflict in Ukraine, the overly ambitious EU expansion plans set off other Russian responses detrimental to peaceful economic development and relations between the various European regions. After the collapse of the Soviet Union and the humiliating decline of the country during the 1990s, Putin began taking Russia back to its traditional policy of compensating for internal weaknesses by supporting a backward economy, while isolating the country from the West and relying on military buildup and provocations at EU borders to protect the country. Over its entire modern history, Russia has been an economic dwarf and a military giant. During Putin's presidency the country has built political and military connections (joint military exercises) with China, as well as friendly relations with Turkey, Serbia, Hungary and Bulgaria, all as a counterweight against the West.

To counterbalance the European Union, Russia not only intervened militarily in the Ukrainian crisis but also, in 2000, established the "rival" Eurasian Economic Community with five successor states of the Soviet Union. In 2010, Russia, Belarus, and Kazakhstan established a customs union, then, in 2015, Kyrgyzstan and Armenia joined with those three countries to create the Eurasian Economic Union. This organization copied the structure of the European Union by setting up supranational and intergovernmental institutions, a Commission and a Court of Justice on the one hand and a Council of member countries on the other. It also took over the EU's Single Market model (in this case creating a market of 183 million people) and the "four freedoms" idea and practices (free flow of goods, services, capital and people). Russia is trying to attract as many former Soviet republics as possible, using a "stick and carrot" policy, pressure couple with proffered advantages. A hostile Russia is challenging the European Union and wants to be a global power again.

While the relatively smaller Balkan countries of the region are looking to the West and to the European Union now that they are members or candidates of the latter, the two largest and strongest powers, Russia and Turkey, are hostile to the EU and trying to counterbalancing its influence and power. This political situation in the early 21st century will determine the future of the entire region.

Transformation: rising or declining relative income level? The 21st century

Transforming from nonmarket state socialism and one-party authoritarian systems in the interest of realizing the dream of a "Return to Europe," as a popular slogan expressed it, required the establishment of pluralistic democracy and free market capitalism. In reality, such a return was not possible, as was repeatedly demonstrated in the late 1980s and early 1990s. Several of the newly independent, former communist countries, had no history of real pluralistic democracy or of functioning, efficient free market capitalism. The task of establishing these forms, therefore, was gigantic: a Sisyphean task. Even if the task of returning to Europe by transforming economies and polities in Russia and the Balkans should one day be accomplished, or in other words, should prove not to be Sisyphean, its daunting challenges are such that its extremely ambiguous results to date should scarcely be surprising.

The following subchapter covers the period around the turn of the millennium and explores its results in the Russia-Turkey-Balkans region. The term "transformation" requires some explanation. It is evident that most of the region has begun shifting away from authoritarian, nonmarket state socialism to democratic market capitalism; moreover, that the large political entities of the region, the Soviet Union and Yugoslavia, have been replaced by many smaller, independent states, some of them belonging to the region under consideration. For

Russia, Ukraine, Belarus, Moldova, Serbia, Bosnia-Herzegovina, Macedonia, and Montenegro, both forms of transformation have occurred.[34]

Can we also speak of transformation in the case of Turkey? Certainly, in this case state formation and borders did not change, nor was this country part of the communist group. Nevertheless, successful participation in the emerging postwar world economy, as well as entry into the EU, required major transformations in the country. Haluk Haksal characterizes the Turkish economy until the 1980s as "highly regulated and state dominated. Its major feature was import substitution industrialization policy, which protected the economy from competition in international markets." In that decade Turgut Ozal began a program of deregulation. The so-called January 24th Measures not only "broadly aimed at introducing the 'Washington Consensus' principles in Turkey," Haksal writes, but also aligned with the terms of IMF stand-by agreements. The later Stabilization Program, negotiated in 1999 with the IMF, "was in line with 'Washington Consensus' principles as well as EU requirements."[35] These requirements determined Turkish economic policy and institution-building around the turn of the millennium. All strongly paralleled the transformation policies of the former communist countries of the EU. Thus Turkey, although not a former communist country, followed a road from the 1980s into the early 21st century rather similar to the one taken by its former communist regional neighbors. Around the turn of the millennium a major historical change and transformation toward privately owned, export-oriented market capitalism began here too.

Şinasi Aksoy describes the new Turkish policies of the 1980s with celebratory language:

> 24 January 1980 represents a turning point in the Turkish economic history. The import substitution strategy which has been practiced since the early years of the Republic (1930s) has been replaced by export-based, outwardly-oriented economic development and growth policy. A shift of emphasis towards a free market economy accompanied by economic liberalization measures were determined to be the future path to follow. Along with flexible exchange rates, export drive … privatization has been an important policy ingredient in this new era.[36]

Indeed, the government, as announced, targeted the "transfer of the decision making process in half of the economy from the public sector to the private sector to make the economy more responsive to market forces."[37]

Nevertheless, there was not much cause for celebration. The new policy could not break through easily. Turkey did not have an efficient financial market or an entrepreneurial class. In fact, the Morgan Guaranty Bank did not include domestic participants in its preparation of a Master Plan for privatization. Privatization actually started in 1986 but until 1993 had very limited success, not least because when the first company was sold to foreign investors at the end of the 1980s, a major political resistance exploded. In the end, the

Council of State (Danistay) rejected deals with Société des Ciments Français and Scandinavian Airlines, and it also ordered the government to offer the shares to employees with a ruling that privatized companies should be offered to Turkish citizens first. "Government credibility was inexcusable undermined."[38] In the end, between 1986 and 1998 eight successive governments managed to privatize only $4.5 billion worth of assets, representing less than 10 percent of state-owned assets.[39]

Those years were unstable economically, with an average 40 percent inflation rate that doubled to 80 percent in the decade after the turn of the millennium. A push from outside the domestic system was needed and at last was given during the 1990s, but external and internal shocks still followed one after the other: in 1994, a foreign exchange crisis, in 1997 and 1998, the Asian and Russian financial crises, respectively, in 1999, an earthquake. In December 1999, Turkey had to turn to the IMF for a $4.0 billion stand-by credit. The agreement required government efforts to continue reforms and privatization. In late 1999, the government finally set in motion a comprehensive economic reform program, the aforementioned Stabilization Program.

An OECD report from that time summarized the major points of progress, which I note here. First, a series or laws and regulations had been enacted, including the Competition Law, complying with the European Union (EU) standards, and the Electricity Market Law of 2001, which regulated the competition and privatization policies in electricity production and distribution. In addition, the Central Bank of Turkey had gained independence from the government and a Banking Regulation and Supervision Agency (BRSA) had been established, while a new Public Procurement Law made EU and United Nations standards compulsory and ensured competition, equal opportunity, accountability, and effective supervision. A strategy to improve governance and combat corruption had been adopted by the Council of Ministers in 2002. Significant reforms had been introduced to ensure a merit-based recruitment of the civil servants without political influence. And at the end of 2001, Turkey had even put into effect some constitutional amendments regulating the government and addressing civil rights issues. Around the same time, further privatization had begun.[40]

This momentum was nurtured by the Justice and Development Party (AKP) of Recep Tayyip Erdoğan, which started its rule in 2002 with a program of liberalization and faster adjustment to the requirements of EU membership. In 2007, voters rewarded the AKP with almost 47 percent of the votes (instead of 34 percent in 2002), a landslide victory. Turkish transformation, at last, started. European Union candidacy and implementation of certain market reforms attracted foreign investments and capital inflow. Between 2002 and 2006 – the high prosperity years in Europe – $87 billion speculative "hot money" and $30 billion FDI flooded the country, with nearly two-thirds (63 percent) of that coming from EU countries. The stock value of FDIs reached $174 billion. The record level in one year, 2007, was $20 billion capital inflow. Nearly two-thirds (63 percent) of foreign capital arrived from European Union countries. Western capital inflow was crucial because domestic accumulation was rather low, only 10 percent in 2011.[41] In the first decade of the 21st century capital inflow was closely connected with the increasing number of foreign multinational companies that established business in Turkey. Their number increased from 5,000 to 42,000.

Foreign capital targeted several sectors. The financial sector, where foreign investment decisively contributed to building up modern banking, was the principal target; also manufacturing, which received almost one-third of FDI, and construction. Modern industries, including car and electronics, were established. The country was integrated organically into the global network of motor vehicle production. In 2008, more than 1.2 million motor vehicles were produced. A 2016 World Bank report placed Turkey 5th in Europe and 12th in the world in this sector. In shipbuilding the country placed as 12th, in steel production as 8th in the world.[42] All of this progress was partly connected with foreign investment and capital inflow. With this help, the previously permanent inflation (in 2000 it was 55 percent) was curbed to just 5 percent by 2014–2016.

Seeking to liberalize and modernize, the ambitious Erdoğan government initiated a policy of mega-programs, best symbolized by the three "pride of the government" projects: a third bridge across the Bosporus, a third airport on a 7,500 hectares land, and the 43-kilometer-long, 400-meter-wide, 25-meter-deep Canal Istanbul, parallel to the Bosporus, crossed over by six bridges and surrounded by a new city.[43] These projects, financed with IMF loans and other forms of foreign investment, helped to stimulate an economic boom. Structural modernization finally could break through. The OECD recategorized Turkey as a high- and sustained-growth country. The annual growth of real GDP, 2.5 percent between 1991 and 2001, 4.1 percent between 1995 and 2005, 5.4 percent between 2009 and 2014, was impressive indeed.

With structural modernization taking hold, agriculture gradually lost its role as the leading sector of the Turkish economy. Between 1913 and 1950, agriculture employed about 80 percent of the active population. That share dropped to 34 percent by 2005 while the share of industry increased from 9 to 23 percent and services from 11 to 43 percent. Although agriculture still produced 60 percent of the country's exports in 1980, by the end of the century its share was only 20 percent. In 2001, its contribution to the GDP was still 13 percent, half a decade later only 8 percent. At the turn of the century, industry produced already more than 30 percent of the GDP and services nearly 60 percent. By 2014, the contribution of services increased to 65 percent and that of industry decreased somewhat to 27 percent (within manufacturing 18 percent), percentages near those in advanced countries.[44]

The international economic crisis that began in 2008, hit Turkey hard, with deleterious effects for the project of EU membership. In response, the already overly self-confident Erdoğan government, intoxicated by its successes, changed its policy and embraced "an authoritarian and undemocratic form of Keynesianism," with increasing state interventionism. Between 2009 and 2014, state ownership of immovable property increased by 20 percent.[45]

Concomitantly the government started a gradual re-Islamization of the country and claimed dictatorial powers. A large country with a strong army, Turkey now is investing in military equipment and demonstrating its military power by intervening in neighboring Syria. Just as Russia seeks to be a global power, Turkey aims to emerge as a local power in the Middle East. As a step toward this goal, the country is building close connections with the Central Asian, Turkic former Soviet republics and friendly relations with Russia, while launching a war of words against the European Union.

Meanwhile, major weaknesses associated with traditional backwardness and able to undermine progress persisted. A still low educational level underscores the point. Less than half of people 25–34 years old possessed even a high school diploma in the 2010s. The country came in at nearly last place (32nd out of 34 among OECD countries, which have as an average 80 percent high school graduates in that age group). Similarly, labor participation in 2016 was only 56 percent while the OECD average was 74 percent.[46]

Dependence on imports (72 percent in 2014) to meet energy needs ranks as one of the most troubling economic weaknesses of the country. The share of energy imports in trade balance was 22 percent in the late 1990s but increased to 45 percent by 2007. An organic permanent weakness of the export-oriented country is that virtually all its exports (except food) are created from imported materials; thus, Turkey depended on imports for raw materials. In 2005, for example, to realize $78 billion export value the country had $112 billion worth imports. In 2013, the $152 billion exports income required spending $251 billion for imports. In 2001, the ratio of exports to imports was 76 percent but in 2013 it declined to 60 percent. Balance of trade thus perpetually exhibits huge deficits; in 2014, 64 percent, for example. For 12 years in the early 21st century the country has run a 6–10 percent current accounts deficit. Debt service began absorbing one-quarter of the GDP in the mid-2010s.[47]

Inequality is also extremely high. The upper 20 percent of the population on the income-scale commands almost half of the income, while the lowest 25 percent has only a 6.2 percent share. The GINI coefficient of Turkey (0.404) places the country 48th among 113 countries. Internet and computer users are only half of the population, far behind the European standard. In efficiency of the government and competitiveness of the country, Turkey is only 59th, in ease of starting a business, 71st, and in corruption, 122nd.[48] None of these rankings meet European standards.

One of the main contributors to economic weaknesses is political instability, the uncertainty associated with the historical record of repeated swings from liberalization back to dictatorship. As he has returned Turkey to dictatorship (a process strengthened by his 2018 electoral victory) and stabilized an almost unlimited presidential power after the failed military coup attempt in May 2016, Erdoğan has had 50,000 arrested and 150,000 suspended from their jobs. He has purged the country of his opposition and eliminated freedom of press. The purges have extended to the business elite. In 2016, the government seized nearly 900 businesses and appointed party loyalists to run them. Economic activity has nearly stopped. The number of tourists has dropped from more than 32 million in 2014 to 22 million in 2016. Morgan Stanley has ranked Turkey among the "Fragile Five."[49] Foreign investments and loans may well dry up. (As a precautionary take, one must not forget that between 1998 and 2000, before Erdoğan's early liberalization programs took hold, economic difficulties caused $70 billion investments to be withdrawn from the country in just a few months.) Sharp conflict with Germany, including the arrest of German citizens in Turkey, may lead to severe economic destruction, not least because Germany is the number one trading partner of Turkey, buying 30 percent of its exports and delivering 20 percent of its imports. The annual 3–5 million German tourists visiting the country and the 7,000 German companies that operate there have made Turkey strongly dependent on preserving good relations with this powerful EU country.[50]

Despite recent setbacks, Turkey overall has had the most successful transformation of all the countries in the Russian-Turkish-Balkans region. Its per capita income level, which showed a significant increase (a one-third increase between 1980 and the mid-1990s), testifies to its first-place position. So, too, the fact that between 2005 and 2016 the level doubled again, nearly reaching the world's average and coming in second in its region in that latter year, very near to leading Russia. Heightening the significance of these figures is the fact that in the mid-1970s Turkey's per capita income level was the lowest in the region, reaching only 57 percent of the average for the region, yet had surpassed the region's average by nearly 50 percent in 2016. The country – according to the categorization in this book – elevated to the top level of the European low-income category, at the border of the middle-income zone: impressive and important, yet still little more than 20 percent of the northwest European and 62 percent of the Central European-Baltic average.

As already implied, the transition of the region's former communist countries was much less successful. The collapse of regimes, destruction of former polities, in some cases civil wars, such as in Russia (two Chechen wars in 1994–1996 and 1999), Moldova (Transnistria war in 1990–1992), Yugoslavia (civil war in 1991–1995), and Ukraine (2014–), led to a catastrophic economic collapse in the first period of transformation. Opening borders to free trade from one day to the next in previously closed economies ruined a great part of the non-competitive domestic companies. Previous Russian and eastern (Comecon) markets, undemanding, highly interdependent and operating within a closed system, ceased to exist. The countries that sold their products on those markets were unable to shift their exports to the highly competitive Western markets.

An often chaotic and slow privatization also contributed to the difficulties. By the mid-1990s, 77 percent of the big and medium-sized firms in Russia, and 82 percent of the small ones were privatized. After that time private industry employed 60 percent of the workforce and produced two-thirds of the output. But in Russia and Ukraine, privatization also involved criminal-type action, open robbery of the state by newly "appointed" clients of the government, who became billionaire oligarchs over just days or weeks.[51] In an instant, as a 2013

Credit Suisse report phrased it, "the highest level of inequality in the world [was created]." In postcommunist Russia, by the mid-1990s, just 110 people owned 35 percent of total household wealth.[52]

Devastating financial chaos and decline hit some of the countries. Romania, for example, experienced inflation of 200 and 250 percent in 1992 and 1993, while Serbia-Montenegro, between 1992 and 1994, suffered history's second biggest hyperinflation: at the peak in January 1994, prices were rising 313 million percent per month.[53] In Russia, the Asian financial crisis of 1997 began undermining the economy and in 1998 caused the collapse of the financial system. This in turn quickly generated high inflation (84 percent per annum, equivalent to a decline of real wages of 40 percent) and a capital flight of $1.5 billion per month. Russia had to turn to the IMF and received a $22.6 billion loan to stabilize.

The case of Russia exemplifies the stubborn and broad effects of financial crisis. Capital outflow continued for a long time after the IMF released the stabilization loans. According to a 2002 estimation by the European Bank for Reconstruction and Development, it amounted to $20–25 billion per year.[54] Some calculations suggest that without this capital flight, Russian domestic investments could have been much higher for years, reaching as much as 2 to 6 percent more of the GDP. Instead the Russian market in 2016 was $191 billion, thus smaller than the Czech ($42 billion) and Slovak ($75 billion) markets combined.[55] The financial crisis had a strong negative impact on neighboring Belarus, Ukraine and Moldova, countries that had strong trade connection with Russia (in the case of Moldova 50 percent, in Ukraine and Belarus 33 percent of foreign trade with Russia), and Russians, themselves, suffered to a great degree. Workers did not receive their salaries for months, while starvation and sickening alcoholism killed even young people. The generation born in the 1990s in Russia and in some similar former Soviet republics is even one centimeter shorter than generations before and after.[56]

In sum, upon the collapse of the communist economic system and sudden immersion in the Western system of free trade, the successor states of the Western Soviet Union (Russia, Belarus, Ukraine, and Moldova) and of eastern Yugoslavia (Serbia, Montenegro, Bosnia-Herzegovina, and Macedonia), together with Romania, Bulgaria and Albania, all suffered a free fall. A few statistics will illustrate. Between 1990 and 1993, Albanian industrial output declined by an enormous 77 percent, Romanian industry by 22 percent in 1992 alone, and then by another 6, 17 and 9 percent in 1997, 1998, and 1999, respectively. Balkan industrial output declined by 50 percent and Bulgarian agriculture in 1992 and 1993 halved.[57] Per capita income almost halved, dropping from $5,139 percent in 1990 to $2,872 as each country reached the nadir of its trajectory of decline.[58] Recovery was very slow, with economies requiring 20 years to reach precollapse levels. During the entire decade 1991–2001, growth rates were mostly negative: −1.2 percent in Bulgaria and Romania, −3.3 percent in Russia and −6.6 percent in Ukraine. One of the most striking shocks of transition was the drop in life expectancy, especially in Russia, where between 1991 and 1994, it fell from 74 to 71 for women and from 64 to 57 for men. Even in the spring of 2017, men's life expectancy was just 64 years, 15 years less than in Western Europe.

After the turn of the millennium, with recovery accomplished, the region enjoyed a few years of prosperity and fast growth. Between 1995 and 2005, Russia's average annual growth rate was already 3.9 percent, Ukraine's 2.7 percent, Romania's and Bulgaria's 2.1 and 2.0 percent, respectively. In the early 21st century, Romania and Bulgaria achieved an annual 4–6 percent growth rate. In the five countries just named, per capita income level increased by more than five times between 2000 and 2014. Romania recovered its precollapse level by 2004 and until 2008, together with Bulgaria, it somewhat surpassed the 1989 level. Serbia and Bosnia-Herzegovina, to the contrary, remained still about 40 percent behind their earlier levels.

The West Balkan countries had experienced one tragedy after another after the collapse of the regime and the Yugoslav state. The bloody Yugoslav civil war had killed a quarter-million people and displaced two million. About 100,000 houses had been destroyed. The devastation until the mid-1990s had had severe consequences. The short period of recovery before the 2008 international finance crisis was not long enough for complete recuperation. Huge trade deficits of 35 percent and unemployment rates of 28–30 percent in Bosnia, Montenegro, and Kosovo made the West Balkan's situation even in 2006, just before the crisis, "mostly miserable."[59]

Still, before the 2008 crisis, clear signs of recuperation had appeared. FDI, for example, had started flowing in: in 2007, its amount was almost 22 percent of GDP in Montenegro, 6 percent in Albania, 14 percent in Bosnia and Herzegovina, 13 percent in Kosovo, 9 percent in Macedonia and more than 4 percent in Serbia. Remittance sent from workers abroad to families at home provided significant sums that contributed to growth of consumption and investment. The World Bank noted that:

> the SEE6 countries (Albania, FYR Macedonia, Kosovo, Montenegro, Serbia, and Bosnia and Herzegovina) are among the top migrant-sending regions in the world. Today the equivalent of one-quarter of the current population of SEE6 lives outside their home countries. ... Since the early 1990s, there has been a steady flow of migrants from the SEE6 to the EU with roughly 4.9 million people having left their countries ... [and] people continue to emigrate in search of better economic opportunities.[60]

At the time of this writing, economic growth at last has regained some of the impetus it lost after 2008. Countries in the Western Balkans grew around 3 percent per year in both 2016 and 2017. Serbia and Albania, which made up half of the GDP of West Balkan countries in this Russia-Turkey-Balkans region, have experienced steady acceleration as a result of sustained fiscal consolidation. Private consumption and investment also has increased and Serbian export has accelerated. Nevertheless, these Balkans countries are still some of the poorest places in Europe. Neither Albania nor Kosovo has reached minimum European or Central European standards. Kosovo has the highest rates of illiteracy and infant mortality. The region's average ranking is 86th in the World Economic Forum's Global Competitiveness Report. On average, firms in the Western Balkans lose more than 13 percent of their annual sales due to a combination of crime, electricity issues, poor transport infrastructure and corruption.[61]

In the Romanian and Bulgarian cases, returning prosperity began in the 1990s, in close connection with EU candidacy. Foreign capital started flowing in. The Bulgarian minimum wage, €1.56 per hour in 2013, was still extremely low, less than one-tenth of the wage in France, Belgium or the Netherlands.[62] In Romania today, the minimum hourly wage, after a 16 percent increase in 2017, is just $2.18. The EU's calculations show that the median disposable Romanian and Bulgarian income is less than 10 percent of the Swedish or Austrian. Low wages are combined with a well-trained labor force and the relative political stability offered by EU membership after 2007. This has made both Bulgaria and Romania very attractive to Western investors. Between 1998 and 2004 Bulgaria received $8,241 million and Romania $16,185 million in foreign investments (Serbia and Bosnia-Herzegovina received only $4,088 and $1,493 million, respectively). Their foreign trade increased by leaps and bounds: the value of trade in Bulgaria, for example, jumped by 1,500 times over those years.[63]

In the first half of 2017, Romania, with a 5.8 percent growth rate, became one of the fastest growing economies in Europe. However, this record did not have a solid base. It was caused by an irresponsible populist policy of raising wages: 16 percent for workers, 25 percent for medical workers and 25 percent for the entire public sector. As one of the parliamentarians said: "The government gives money for the chosen people" and generates an artificial consumption-heated prosperity. Indebtedness, meanwhile, has been increasing even in boom times and the extremely backward infrastructure continues to be neglected.[64]

Russia's recovery, with its nearly sevenfold increase in income level, has had a rather different cause. There, the exceptional boom has been based on the country's oil and natural gas richness. Russia is one of the largest oil producers and exporters in the world, with the world's eighth largest oil reserves. Additionally, the country is the world's number one natural gas producer (in 2015–2016, 630–640 billion m^3). The country is also the largest exporter of natural gas and possesses the largest known reserves of that resource. (At current estimations oil reserves could be depleted in 30 years, gas reserves in 160 years.) In the summer of 2006, crude oil and condensate production reached the post-Soviet maximum of 9.7 million barrels (1,540,000 m^3) per day, more than three times the 2000 production level. Russia produced an average of more than 10.8 million barrels (1,722,000 m^3) of oil per day in December 2015, 12 percent of the world's oil production and exports. By 2017, the output increased to 11.7 million barrels.[65] Although Russia is not an "oil country," the oil and natural gas sector plays the central role in its economy, generating approximately one-fifth of the Russian GDP in the 2000s and nearly 30 percent of the state's budget revenue. Although this sector employs only 1.5 percent of the labor force, it provides over half of export revenues.[66]

Russia's recovery, however, has been the consequence not only of the resurrection of the oil and gas industry (in the latter case output had declined to half its 1990 level in the decade after the collapse) but also, most of all, of the international price movement of oil products. Inflation-adjusted crude oil prices (in $/barrel at July 2017 price) reached an all-time low of $18 level in 1998 (lower than between 1946–1973 when it moved to around $23–27). But ten years later in June 2008, crude oil prices were at a nearly all-time high of $103. (In 1980, the price per barrel was $111.) Oil prices started rising at the turn of the millennium, elevating from $39 per barrel in 2000 to $70 in 2006, and, after further rises to the peak in 2008, settling at $60–90 until 2014. This bonanza for the oil producers ended in 2015 when per barrel price declined to $43. It fell even further in 2016 to $37.[67] In other words, Russia's oil and gas income skyrocketed in the first 1.5 decades of the 21st century, and then dropped sharply from 2015.

The reconstruction and increase of oil and gas production and exports, combined with the sixfold increase of oil prices in the early 21st century together have been responsible for the new prosperity of Russia. Nevertheless, their effects have turned out to be a mixed blessing. True, the wages and living standard of the population have increased sharply. According to the International Labor Organization (ILO), real wages in Russia have risen almost 3.5 times between 2000 and 2013, and even though they started declining in 2014, in November 2015 they were still three times higher than in 2000.[68] With more income, people could begin using credit cards and before long they owned 150 million of them. Millions have become car-owners: in 1999, 900,000 cars were sold, in 2012, nearly 3.2 million. In that later year, 48 million Russians traveled abroad for vacation and every 100 people had 145 cellphones. In 1999, only 1 per 100 people used the Internet, in 2012, already 64. For the first time in history and after hundreds of years of shortages and deprivations, Russians are living in a consumer society. Since all of this has happened since 2000, during Vladimir V. Putin's presidency, his popularity seems to be cemented. In 2000, he was elected by 53 percent of the votes, in 2004 by 72 percent, and polls since then indicate an 80 percent approval rate. In 1999, only 31 percent of the people viewed their country as a great power; in the fall of 2015, 65 percent did. The Russian regime has become stable.[69]

Nevertheless, the country never has embraced a real Western economic and political system. In Chapter 3, I asked whether the various political regimes of its history formed Russia or whether Russia shaped the various regimes. In the early 21st century, it must be noted, President Putin adopted a political ideology of adjusting and aligning everything to Russian characteristics and traditions. He announced clearly that Russia wanted neither to follow Western liberal-democratic patterns nor to become a "second edition of the United States or Britain … For us, the state, its institutions … have always played an exceptionally important role. … [It is] the initiator and main driving force of change."

Putin argued for adjustment of market system and democracy to "Russian realities."[70] Under his presidency the state has remained omnipotent. The political system, however, contains certain democratic features, operating on an increasingly autocratic base. Some call it a "militocracy," a polity dominated by the military, secret police and law enforcement people who form a closed circle around Putin, the former KGB officer.[71] The state is dominant in the economy. About 4,100 enterprises have some state ownership and they employ almost 40 percent of the labor force. The banking sector is 64 percent state-owned, as is almost half of the oil and gas industry. Under Putin the state does not hesitate to renationalize private companies. It is easy to arrest and imprison the oligarchs who emerged after the collapse of communism, and to confiscate their possessions. Their tax evasion, money laundering, and other compromising behaviors (*kompromat*) provide easy justification. From the "Kremlin banker," Sergei Pugachev, for example, the state expropriated $15 billion business assets, from Mikhail Khodorovsky and Vladimir Yevtusenkov, the state took over two major oil companies the Yukon and Bashneft, respectively.[72]

Steven Rosefielde has characterized the Russian road since the fall of communism with the following acerbic words:

> Neither structural demilitarization nor a democratic free enterprise transition, was ever in the cards. … They were down instead to the traditional Russian patrimonial pattern of "rent granting"; shifting administrative usage rights … from one group of servitors to another at the autocrat's discretion. Aspiring oligarchs and other favorites were granted indulgencies to seize "prolonged warfighting material reserves" … and profit from foreign weaponry sales. … Defense material reserves worth tens of billions of dollars were illegally sold abroad, a large portion to Asia. … Rosvooruzhenie (the Russian arms sales agency) became a lucrative sinecure and control of the crown jewels (i.e. Russia's mineral wealth) was transferred … [to the] oligarchs.[73]

That road has enabled Putin's return to the traditional Russian strategy of strengthening the country's world-standing by means of military power. In 1998, Russia already had twice as many tanks (16,210 in contrast to 8,369) and more than twice as many artillery pieces (16,453 against 7,225) as the United States. It had more submarines and especially many more strategic ballistic missiles (1,575 against 755).[74] Militarily, therefore, Russia remained competitive. President Putin has further strengthened this position. Relying on the huge Russian state oil income, he has increased to 30 percent the portion of state expenditure dedicated to modernizing and strengthening the army and the nuclear arsenal of the country. His Reform and Development of the Defense Industrial Complex Program of 2002–2006 has started reorganizing the military complex. As of 2005, the wholly state-owned Russian armament industry had 1,700 enterprises in 72 regions. Putin's military reform has led to the building of fifth-generation armed forces. The huge expenditures are partly financed by global arms sales, one of the biggest businesses of the country.[75] Among the customers are China and India, along with some Latin American and Near Eastern countries. The scale of this business is clearly shown by the fact that in 2009, the worst year of the recent financial crisis, Russia still exported $7.4 billion of weapons.[76]

By 2017, in the aftermath of the Ukraine crisis, the combination of drops in the price of oil after 2015 and Western sanctions against Russian producers had caused serious deterioration of the Russian position. The *Washington Post* opined in March 2017 that "Russia lacks the resources to fund the great power pretension." As proof the reporter noted that already in 2016, for the first time since 1990, military spending had declined; furthermore, that NATO was spending $41 billion a year, while Russia could not afford more than $1.8 billion; thus the gap between Russia and the Western alliance was increasing.[77] An economy overly reliant on oil production and sales proved to be vulnerable.

The most important negative outcome for Russia associated with its so-called oil jackpot has been the neglect of overall economic modernization. This is a well-known disease of resource-rich countries, often called the "resource curse" or the "paradox of plenty" or even the "Dutch disease."[78] This concept explains that countries rich in natural resources often overlook the advantages to be accrued by developing new modern economic sectors. They fail to develop other sectors and therefore become extremely dependent on one source of wealth. Thus, they also become less modern and less resilient than other countries. This is not an absolute "law," but among the 51 countries of the world categorized as "resource-rich" by the IMF – countries which have at least 20 percent of exports or 20 percent of fiscal revenue from natural resources – 29 are low- and low-middle-income countries.[79] In Russia this paradox of plenty definitely has been operating. During the early 21st century years of prosperity, industrial production stayed at 85 percent of its 1990 level. Of all industrial sectors, only that of oil-gas surpassed 1990 production levels, while every other major industrial sector experienced decreased outputs. In 2015 the size of the machine-building sector, for example, was barely more than 16 percent, the chemical industry just 50 percent of 1990 levels.[80] The structure of the country's economy stayed bound to an obsolete economic model.

Russia's postcommunist prosperity thus has been built on an extremely weak base. With the exception of a few years, foreign investments have always been very limited. Moreover, political instability and the almighty power of a state that could confiscate a company and arrest any billionaire at will have made the oligarchs, the holders of so much Russian wealth, extremely cautious. One author flatly stated that "the arrest of Mikhail Khodorkovsky, [one of the richest of the oligarchs] head of the Yukos oil company, in October 2003, was a key turning point in modern Russian history."[81] Indeed, the weakness of the rule of law (Russia belongs to the lowest quarter of the countries of the world from this respect) has produced a permanent and significant capital flight. For example, in the 2010s, companies borrowed $170 billion from the West over just two years but invested only a small fraction of it. Most of it, the Chief Economist of the Sberbank CIB, Yevgeny Gavrilenkov, estimated, found its way into off-shore bank accounts. In 2011, $80.5 billion fled the country, in 2013 $60 billion and in 2014, when the Ukrainian crisis exploded, $160 billion.[82] Meanwhile, a great part of the population, about 40 percent, has faced serious difficulties just to buy food and clothing. Nearly 15 percent of Russian fell below the state's official poverty line in 2016.[83] In sum, Russia has missed a huge opportunity to modernize and restructure its economy or elevate its people nearer to European levels.

Other countries of the Russia-Turkey-Balkans region have not been able to follow even the positive parts of the Russian road. They have been caught in a vicious and seemingly unbreakable circle and show no signs of real recovery or development. Their history in the last quarter of a century has been one of underachievement and failure, almost unparalleled in Europe. Ukraine, for example, could have become a rich country. Nearly three-quarters of its territory is agricultural land, half belonging to the world's most fertile, famous, humus-rich, black-soil region. The country has vast natural resources, including coal and iron ore, Europe's largest graphite deposits and 40 percent of the world's manganese ore deposits, as well the world's biggest deposits of ozocerite (a naturally occurring form of paraffin wax) and sulfur. The known natural gas resources (estimated at several trillion cubic meters) could almost create energy independence in two decades. With its location on the border of the European Union, the country has access to a huge export market, and it has a well-educated population.

Yet Ukraine has been unable to exploit these possibilities. Several factors have blocked its way. Among the most important is this: Ukraine, as I have noted previously, is not one but two countries culturally speaking: the one in the north and west being West-oriented, Catholic, Ukrainian-speaking, the other in the south and east being Russia-oriented, Russian Orthodox, Russian-speaking, and partly Russian-populated. This separation has fueled instability, conflicts, revolutions, and civil wars. During the quarter-century period of transition, as a clear sign of instability, the country has had 24 prime ministers. The potential for reform promised by two revolutions, the Orange Revolution in 2004 and the Euromaidan Revolution in 2014, so far remains unexploited. Ukraine is in the hands of a corrupt oligarchic elite, in the closest of connections with political power – such connection being the path to individual enrichment – and this elite has robbed the country: "Sometimes the dividing line between legitimate capitalists and plain criminals is blurred," Pekka Sutela has stated, "and elected politicians may be little more than covers for their interests."[84]

True, in Ukraine the process of transforming from communism and adjusting to independent statehood after 1991 began in an atmosphere of unique disaster. The country started the process from a very weak position. First of all, it had suffered more than others during World War II, with armies twice crisscrossing its territory, decimating its population, especially its male population, and largely obliterating its business-oriented, significant Jewish minority. And second, in the 1991 collapse, it had inherited one of the lowest income levels of all the

Soviet successor states: according to very uncertain estimations, about $1,300 per capita GDP. Over the next few years, as transformation was supposed to be taking place, this low income further declined by more than 40 percent. Then in 1993, came a hyperinflation, reaching reached the 10,256 percent rate. In the entire first decade of transformation real market institutions could scarcely be created.

The early 21st century seemed to be more promising. After a decade of decline in the 1990s, the GDP grew by more than 33 percent in 2000–2003, and it continued growing rapidly for five more years, sometimes reaching 10–12 percent per annum. This boom was closely connected with the European Union attempts to move Ukraine into the EU orbit. In July 2008, those attempts led to the preparation of a Stabilization and Association Agreement. Various political obstacles postponed this progress, but in 2014, the agreement was signed. These moves toward Europe provided automatic guarantees of European investment in Ukraine, and between 2005 and 2010, $5 to $10 billion foreign direct investment indeed arrived annually. The World Bank provided a $5 billion modernization loan. Credits also flooded the country, increasing in just a few years from 7 percent to nearly 80 percent of the country's GDP. This foreign capital hardly reached the industrial sectors, however, where it might have aided modernization. As OECD recognized,

> most knowledge-intensive and high value-added industrial sectors remain outside the line of vision of foreign investors. As yet, Ukraine remains a source of raw materials, an assembler of industrial components and as a large and promising market for foreign-based goods and services.[85]

Instead, FDI mostly targeted the banking and retail sectors. About 40 percent of banking assets consequently ended up in foreign hands.

Even the inherited, traditional, Soviet industrial sectors began prospering again. In conditions of international boom, Ukraine was able to increase and export metal, metallurgy, engineering and chemical products. In 2000, metals, mineral, and chemical products together with food accounted for 70 percent of exports. In 2008, the shares remained quite similar, with the share of food exports increasing from 11 to 16 percent. Export prices were very favorable for most of these goods. Steel prices grew more than four times between 2000 and 2008. Meanwhile, imported oil and gas prices dropped and the country's terms of trade, the relation between export and import prices, improved by 50 percent. Consequently, economic growth from the turn of the millennium until the 2008 economic crisis averaged an impressive 7.4 percent per year.

Unfortunately, Ukrainians did not know how to use their steeply increased income. The greatest part was stolen by oligarchs and politicians, but mostly not invested. The country had some high value-added export products, such as aircraft components, helicopters, electrical machinery, and some pharmaceuticals, inherited from the its time as part of the Soviet Union, but export volumes from these products did not increase, and very few new export products emerged. Imports contributed to rising consumption (15 percent annual increases) and living standards, but not to economic modernization and growth. Trade balances, meanwhile, stayed mostly negative, together with the current accounts. The pension burden was one of the worst worldwide, with 14 million of 46 million citizens retired, and pension payments as a percentage of GDP increasing steeply: payments consumed 9.2 percent of the GDP in 2003, nearly double that (18 percent) in 2009. A balanced, modernized, and well-developing economy simply did not emerge, despite the boom years.

The boom came to an end in 2008, and in the third quarter of that year, the developing international crisis hit the country hard. The banking sector was undermined. The national currency lost 60 percent of its value. A 29-month, $15.2 billion stand-by arrangement from the IMF provided the first aid. However, public and private foreign debt, which had risen during the boom years from more than $10 billion in 1997–2002 to over $100 billion in 2008–2009, now jumped from 56.4 percent of GDP in 2008 to 92 percent by 2009 and then to a unsustainable 192 percent in 2011.

Ukraine was still in economic crisis when political and military crisis exploded in 2014, after President Yanukovich declined to sign the agreement with the European Union. The ensuing Euromaidan Revolution removed him. The resulting pro-EU orientation, together with NATO and EU ambitions to incorporate the country, provoked a Russian response. Putin would not allow Ukraine to move into the Western camp and with assistance from East Ukrainian followers started the civil war that ultimately led to direct Russian intervention and the annexation of the Crimea. As one of the consequences, Ukraine lost its eastern industrial base in the Donetsk and Luhansk areas. These two centers concentrated 20 percent of the country's industrial production.

In the aftermath Ukraine's economy once again has declined. Most of the industrial enterprises in its eastern territories have shut down. Of coal mines in the separatist-controlled region, 93 have shut down permanently, and another 69 have suspended operations. Food production has decreased by 25–30 percent, and 40,000 small business have become bankrupt. Thousands of kilometers of roads, 30 bridges, and nearly 5,000 apartment buildings have been destroyed, and 58 thermoelectric power stations have been damaged. In 2014 Ukraine's economy contracted by −6.8 percent, then by another −15 percent in 2015. Retail trade shrank by nearly −9 percent and then more than −20 percent in those years. Exports declined by more than 30 percent in 2015. Even three years after the tragic events, the country is in a crisis, albeit a stable one. The summer of 2017 signaled the first signs that the country "has turned a corner," with forecasts for 2017 of 2.8 percent growth, coming on top of 2 percent growth the year before.[86]

It has turned out that Ukraine's geographical location, a natural advantage, also can be a liability, the cause of an unbreachable obstacle to the project of joining Europe. The cradle of Kiev Rus, the birthplace of Russia, a natural as well as history-based Russian sphere of interest, remains closely controlled by

Putin's Russia. This situation paralyzes the country's movement toward Europe. Ukraine hopelessly exists at the low-income level.

Only neighboring Moldova is similarly trapped in such a non-European income standard and tragic situation. It is one of the poorest in Europe, on the same income level as Nicaragua and Ghana, registering at half the level of Albania, another very poor country. In this small territory with a small population, transformation from the Soviet-type system to free market democracy exhibits all the deformations of the larger region but in a magnified way. Moldova looks like an anatomy chart in a doctor's office, signaling all the possible illnesses in human body. Privatization of the state-owned economy is still, after a quarter of a century, far from being accomplished. Between 2001 and 2004, the government planned to continue the process and privatize 480 enterprises. In reality, only 60 were sold and today the public sector still plays a dominant role in the economy. The foundations of economic freedom are not yet firmly institutionalized, and the judiciary remains vulnerable to political interference and corruption.

Moldova, in other words, is far from becoming a free market country.[87] Its business elite is tiny and its politicians corrupt. If in Russia, Ukraine, and several other transforming countries, the political and business elite numbers in the several hundreds or even thousands, in Moldova it consists of just three or four families who virtually own and rule the country: Pavel Filip, Veceslav Platon, Vlad Filat, and especially Vlad Plahotniuk, the richest and most powerful figures, also heads of parties and governments, presidents of the country. When one party gains power from another in elections, the incoming government often has its political rivals arrested and sentenced. Filat, for example, was sentenced to nine years in prison, Platon to 18 years.

The list of maladies continues: Under the best of circumstances, embarking on independent statehood after the collapse of the Soviet-controlled regime was very difficult, but in tiny Moldova, the situation was complicated by a civil war between the Romanian majority and the Russian and Ukrainian minority of the province of Transnistria in the East. As in Ukraine, this led to Russian military intervention. If free fall in the 1990s characterized quite a few countries in the region and led to dramatic increase of poverty and shortened life expectancy, in Moldova it was so tragic that the moderate poverty rate (measured by $5/day income level) increased to 41 percent in 2015. Life expectancy for males under 65 years of age decreased by 12 years and for females by 6.4 years.[88] If lack of jobs and life possibilities generated mass migration in the transition countries and significant layers of their working age population looked for work abroad, in Moldova this phenomenon became so extreme that 40 percent of the labor force now works outside the country. Moldavian guest workers abroad send home remittances equaling 25–30 percent of the country's GDP, a world record. Finally, if corruption is a paralyzing mass disease of peripheral countries, in Moldova it has produced the most gigantic and spectacular example, a $1 billion asset-stripping of three Moldovan banks (Banca de Economii, Unibank, and Banca Socială) in late 2014, with that money finding its way into various private bank accounts abroad. The amount was equal to 12 percent of the country's GDP and caused a major shock to the entire economy. Moldova's transformation to free market democracy thus is a caricature of the transformation process. Still, the European Union's ambitious Eastern Neighborhood policy has tried to influence and assist the country. Negotiations for an Association Agreement and a Deep and Comprehensive Free Trade Agreement began in 2010 and the resulting documents were signed in June 2014.[89] These EU gestures, no doubt hopelessly, seek to stimulate the highly required major reforms and cleaning.

In spite of such dismal experiences and conditions, it is unquestionable that the relative prosperity of the early 21st century stabilized most of the countries of the Russia-Turkey-Balkans region. The four most significant former communist countries, Russia, Ukraine, Romania, and Bulgaria, increased their per capita income level by five times between 2000 and 2014, even with the negative impact of the 2008 crisis. Yet that upward increase has not yet been sufficient to improve the region's overall situation; just the opposite, compared to the other regions of Europe, a further relative decline has been the result. In 2016, Ukraine and Moldova had the lowest, and non-European, per capita income levels, $2,262 and $2,089, respectively. Although much better than Ukraine and Moldova, Belarus, Serbia, Bosnia, and Albania also had per capita GDP (ranging from $4,300–$5,800) in the lowest category in Europe. At the top in the region are Russia, Turkey, and Romania, with around $9,000–$10,000 per capita income, at the borderline of the middle-income level in Europe.

The tragic decline in the 1990s, then the few years of prosperity in the early 21st century followed by the new decline after the 2008 crisis together have made the transformation decades quite miserable in this region. The average $6,241 per capita GDP in 2016 represented a further relative decline compared to all other regions of Europe: the countries reached only 13 percent of the northwest level of $49,317, about 20 percent of the Mediterranean-Irish level of $31,198, and 40 percent of the Central European-Baltic level. Seeking to make distinctions among the peripheries of Europe, some authors, such as economic geographer Martin Sokol, call these non-EU countries of the East and Southeast the "Super Periphery."[90] I am inclined to agree.

Notes

1 William L. Blackwell, *The Industrialization of Russia: An Historical Perspective*, 2nd ed., Arlington Heights, IL: Harlan Davidson, 1982, p. 26; Theodor H. Laue, *Sergei Witte and the Industrialization of Russia*, New York: Atheneum, 1969, p. 231.

2 Michael Palairet, *The Balkan Economies c. 180–1914, Evolution without Development*, Cambridge: Cambridge University Press, 1997, pp. 37–38, 147.

3 Robert W. Seton-Watson, *A History of the Roumanians*, London: Archon, 1963, p. 369.

4 D.V. Glass and E. Grebenik, "World Population 1800–1950," in H. J. Habakkuk and M. M. Postan (eds.), *The Cambridge Economic History of Europe*, Vol. 6, Cambridge: Cambridge University Press, 1965, pp. 68–69; Palairet, *Balkan Economies*, p. 20.

5 See Kevin H. O'Rourke and Jeffery G. Williamson, *Globalization and History: The Evolution of a Nineteenth-Century Atlantic Economy*, Cambridge, MA: MIT Press, 1999.

6 Ivan T. Berend and György Ránki, *The European Periphery and Industrialization, 1780–1914*, Cambridge: Cambridge University Press, 1982, p. 100.

7 Şevket Pamuk, *The Ottoman Empire and European Capitalism: Trade, Investment and Production*, Cambridge: Cambridge University Press, 1987, p. 104.

8 Şevket Pamuk, Jeffrey G. Williamson, "Ottoman De-Industrialization 1800-1913: Assessing the Shock, Its Impact and the Response," NBER Working Paper No. 14763, Issued in March 2009, The National Bureau of Economic Research. https://www.nber.org/papers/w14763, accessed January 16, 2020; A. Kander, P. Warde, "Energy Availability from Livestock and Agricultural Productivity in Europe, 1815-1913: A New Comparison," *Economic History Review*, 64, no. S1 (February, 2011): 1–43..

9 Palairet, *Balkan Economies*, p. 222; Paul Bairoch, "How and Why? Economic Inequalities between 1800 and 1913, Some Background Figures," in Jean Batou (ed.), *Between Development and Underdevelopment: The Precocious Attempt of Industrialization of the Periphery (1800–1870)*, Gèneve: Librairie Droz, 1991, p. 3.

10 Bryan Christiansen and Mustafa Erdoğdu, *Comparative Economics and Regional Development in Turkey*, Hershey, PA: IGI Global, 2016, p. 128.

11 Based on Angus Maddison, *Monitoring the World Economy*, 1820-1992, Paris: OECD, 1995

12 Ibid., p. 277; Jacob M. Landau (ed.), *Atatürk and the Modernization of Turkey*, Boulder, CO: Westview Press, 1984.

13 Joseph Stalin, *Problems of Leninism*, Peking: Foreign Language Press, 1976, pp. 528–529, 599–560.

14 This goal was declared in the Party journal *Pravda* in September 1927. See Edward H. Carr and Robert W. Davis, *Foundation of a Planned Economy, 1926–1929*, Vol. 1, Harmondsworth: Pelican Books, 1974, p. 867.

15 Stalin, *Problems of Leninism*, p. 672.

16 Maddison, *Monitoring the World Economy*.

17 Pamuk, "Economic Change in Twentieth-Century Turkey," pp. 278–279; Maddison, *Monitoring the World Economy*.

18 Based on Maddison, *Monitoring the World Economy*.

19 Mark Harrison, "The Soviet Union after 1945: Economic Recovery and Political Repression," April 14, 2010, https://pdfs.semanticscholar.org/a9f8/18a73a11680033aef1442e05ecbb4346d72b.pdf, accessed February 3, 2017.

20 Frederick Pryor, *A Guidebook to the Comparative Study of Economic Systems*, Englewood Cliffs, NJ: Prentice Hall, 1985.

21 János Kornai, *The Socialist System: The Political Economy of Communism*, Princeton, NJ: Princeton University Press, 1992, p. 175.

22 Michael C. Kaser (ed.), *An Economic History of Eastern Europe 1919–1975*, Vol. 3, New York: Oxford University Press, 1987.

23 Pryor, *Guidebook to the Comparative Study*.

24 *American Congress Joint Economic Committee Papers*, Washington, DC, 1970; *National Account Statistics: Main Aggregates and Detailed Tables, 1988, 1990*, New York: United Nations, 1990.

25 See United Nations Statistical yearbooks and Maddison, *Monitoring the World Economy*.

26 Based on Maddison, *Monitoring the World Economy*.

27 Christiansen and Erdoğdu, *Comparative Economics and Regional Development*, pp. 154, 155, 209, 213, 221, 340–342.

28 The Congressional Research Service Report, quoted by Ivan T. Berend, *The Contemporary Crisis of the European Union: Prospects for the Future*, London: Routledge, 2017, p. 67.

29 The European Councils 1993, Conclusions of the Presidency, 1992–1994, Report of the European Council in Copenhagen, 21–23 June 1993, quoted by Berend, *Contemporary Crisis of the European Union*, p. 69.

30 ec.europa.eu/environment/enlarg/candidates.htm, accessed February 4, 2017.

31 Archive of European Integration, "Black Sea Synergy – A New Regional Cooperation Initiative," Communication from the Commission to the Council and the European Parliament, COM (2007) 150 Final, April 11, 2007.

32 Archive of European Integration, "Action Plan for Ukraine," Communication from the Commission to the Council, COM (96) 93 Final, November 20, 1996.

33 "Britain and Europe 'Sleepwalked' into the Ukrainian Crisis, Report says," *New York Times*, February 20, 2015; Sven Biscop, "Game of Zones: The Quest for Influence in Europe's Neighborhood," Archive of European Integration, Egmont Paper 67, June 2014.

34 A reminder: This chapter does not cover all of the successor states of the Soviet Union and Yugoslavia. See Chapter 6 for the three Baltic countries, and former Yugoslav Slovenia and Croatia. The Asian and Caucasian successor states of the Soviet Union, such as Tajikistan, Kazakhstan, Georgia, and Armenia, as well as Kosovo, lie beyond the scope of this work.

35 Haluk Haksal, *Financial Reforms, Stabilization and Development in 21st Century Turkey*, Wilmington, DE: Vernon Press, 2017, pp. 55, 56, 61, 158.

36 Ibid., 55.

37 Ibid., p. 43.

38 Ibid., p. 11.

39 Aysun Ficic, "Political Economy of Turkish Privatization: A Critical Assessment," cevdetkizil.com/cevdetkizil/tr/admin/editor/ccv/genel/poleconomy.pdf, accessed February 19, 2017.

40 OECD, "The Importance of Regulatory Reforms for Turkey," www.oecd.org/turkey/1840711.pdf, accessed December 11, 2016.

41 Christiansen and Erdoğdu, *Comparative Economics and Regional Development*, pp. 275–343. See also the various OECD reports and analyses at www.oecd.org/turkey/, accessed January 9, 2017; https//data.oecd.org/turkey.htm; www.oecd.org>Tur key>puublications&Documents, accessed November 29, 2016; Binici Erşen, Elif, "Turkey Upgrades to High and Sustained Growth Country," OECD Reports. *Daily Sabah*, December 26, 2016, www.dailysabah.com/economy/2016/12/26/turkey-upgrades-to-high-and-sustained-growth-country-oecd-reports, accessed February 9, 2018; OECD, "Country Statistical Profile: Turkey 2009," Key Tables from OECD, www.oecd-ilibrary.org/economics/country-statistical-profile-turkey-2009_20752288-2009-table-tur, accessed October, 7, 2017.

42 The World Bank in Turkey Overview, 2016, www.worldbank.org/en/country/turkey/overview, accessed January 3, 2017.

43 Fikret Adaman, Bengi Akbulut, and Murat Arsel (eds.), *Neoliberal Turkey and Its Discontents: Economic Policy and the Environment under Erdoğan*, London: I.B. Tauris, 2017, pp. 105–107.
44 *The Economist, Pocket World in Figures 2004*; *The Economist, Pocket World in Figures 2017*.
45 Adaman, Akbulut, and Arsel, *Neoliberal Turkey*, pp. 18, 37.
46 The World Bank in Turkey Overview, 2016.
47 *The Economist, Pocket World in Figures 2004*, September 1, 2003, London: The Economist; *The Economist, Pocket World in Figures 2017*, September 1, 2017, London: The Economist.
48 Christiansen and Erdoğdu, *Comparative Economics and Regional Development*, pp. 347–349.
49 "Turkey's Economy: The Next Casualty of Erdoğan's State of Emergency," *Politico*, August 13, 2017; "Turkish Economy Heading toward Crisis under Erdogan," *Spiegel Online*, www.spiegel.de, March 31, 2017.
50 "For Turkey and Germany, Chill in Relations Puts Much at Stake," *New York Times*, August 26, 2017.
51 Ibid. Bernard Black, Reinier Kraakman, and Anna Tarassova, "Russian Privatization and Corporate Governance: What Went Wrong?," September 15, 1999, https://papers.ssrn.com/sol3/delivery.cfm?abstractid=181348, accessed February 18, 2017.
52 Ariel Cohen, "Russia's Avoidable Economic Decline," September 17, 2014, www.heritage.org/europe/report/russias-avoidable-economic-decline, accessed January 28, 2017.
53 Pavle Petrovic and Zeljko Bogetic, "The Yugoslav Hyperinflation of 1992–1994: Causes, Dynamics, and Money Supply Process," *Journal of Comparative Economics*, 27 (1999): 335–353.
54 Willem H. Buiter and Ivan Szegvari, "Capital Outflows from Russia: Symptom, Cause and Cure," May 30, 2002, www.ebrd.com/downloads/research/economics/workingpapers/wp0073.pdf, accessed December 18, 2016.
55 László Csaba, *Válság, Gazdaság, Világ: Adalék Közép- és Kelet Európa három évtizedes gazdaságtörténetéhez* (1988–2018), Budapest: Éghajlat Kiadó, 2019, chaps. 6, 10.
56 *European Bank of Reconstruction and Development Transition Report 2016–17*, London: EBRD, 2017, p. 4.
57 Ivan T. Berend, *From the Soviet Bloc to the European Union: The Economic and Social Transformation of Central and Eastern Europe since 1973*, Cambridge: Cambridge University Press, 2009, pp. 75, 76.
58 Based on Angus Maddison, *The World Economy: A Millennial Perspective*, Paris: OECD, 2001.
59 Mirna Flögel and Gordan Lauc, "War Stress – Effects of the War in the Area of Former Yugoslavia," www.nato.int/du/docu/d010306c.pdf, accessed February 5, 2017; "The Balkans Economy: Mostly Miserable," *The Economist*, www.economist.com/blogs/easternapproaches/2012/06/balkan-economies, accessed January 27, 2017.
60 Balkan Economic Forum, www.balkaneconomicforum.org/wp/balkan-economic-developmentoutlook/, accessed February 7, 2017; World Bank, *Western Balkans*, Regular Economic Report No.11, Spring 2017, www.worldbank.org/en/region/eca/publication/western-balkans-regular-economic-report, accessed June 2017.

61 European Bank of Reconstruction and Development, www.ebrd.com/news/2016/how-the-western-balkans-can-catch-up.html, February 19, 2016; EBRD, "What Is Holding Back the Western Balkans Economies?," www.ebrd.com/news/2017/what-is-holding-back-the-western-balkans-economies.html, March 7, 2017.

62 Tuissaint, Eric, "The Euro Crisis, Contradictions between Countries in the Periphery and Centre of the European Union," GlobalResearch, November 26, 2013, www.globalresearch.ca/the-euro-crisis-contradictions-between-countries-in-the-periphery-and-centre-of-the-european-union/5359408, accessed December 1, 2013.

63 *The Economist, The World in Figures 2006*, September 1, 2005, London: The Economist, p. 67.

64 "Romania, Europe's Hottest Economy, Could Be Headed for Trouble," *New York Times*, October 19, 2017.

65 Euan Mearns, "Oil Price Scenarios For 2016," December 16, 2015, http://euanmearns.com/oil-price-scenarios-for-2016/, accessed June 20, 2017; www.businessinsider.com/when-will-russia-run-out-of-oil-2017-4, April 5, 2017.

66 Heli Simola and Laura Solanko, "Overview of Russia's Oil and Gas Sector," BOFIT Policy Brief 2017 No. 5, https://helda.helsinki.fi/bof/bitstream/handle/123456789/14701/bpb0517.pdf?sequence=1, accessed June 7, 2018.

67 Ibid.

68 "Russia's Economy Drops to a Lower Category," *Central European Financial Observer*, www.financialobserver.eu/cse-and-cis/russias-economy-drops-to-a-lower-category/, May 13, 2016; Paul T. Christensen, "Labor under Putin: The State of the Russian Working Class," New Labor Forum, CUNY, December 2016, https://newlaborforum.cuny.edu/2016/12/08/labor-under-putin-the-state-of-the-russian-working-class/, accessed May 9, 2017.

69 Timothy J. Colton, "Paradoxes of Putinism," *Daedalus, Journal of the American Academy of Arts and Sciences* (Spring 2017): 8–18, pp. 10, 16, 17.

70 Ibid., p. 9.

71 Brian D. Taylor, "The Russian *siloviki* & Political Change," *Daedalus, Journal of the American Academy of Arts and Sciences* (Spring 2017): 53–63, p. 53.

72 Ibid., p. 56; Stanislav Markus, "The Atlas That Has Not Shrugged: Why Russia's Oligarchs Are an Unlikely Force for Change," *Daedalus, Journal of the American Academy of Arts and Sciences* (Spring 2017): 103–104.

73 Steven Rosefielde, *Russia in the 21st Century: The Prodigal Superpower*, Cambridge: Cambridge University Press, 2005, pp. 63–64.

74 International Institute for Strategic Studies, *The Military Balance 1998–99*, London: Oxford University Press, 1999, pp. 20–27, 108–112.

75 Rosefielde, *Russia in the 21st Century*, p. 86.

76 Andrei P. Tsygankov, "Russia's Power and Alliances in the 21st Century," *Politics* 30, no. S1 (2010): 43–51, esp. 47.

77 "Why Russia Is Far Less Threatening than It Seems," *Washington Post*, March 8, 2017.

78 This term was introduced after the Netherlands discovered a huge natural gas field in Groningen in 1959, a discovery that in the end harmed the country's ability to use other elements of the economy to perform well.

79 On this topic see Michael L. Ross, "The Political Economy of the Resource Curse," *World Politics* 51, no. 2 (January 1999): 297–322; Anthony J. Venables, "Using Natural Resources for Development: Why Has It Proven So Difficult?," *Journal of Economic Perspectives* 30, no. 1 (February 2016):161–184; Jeffrey Sachs and Andrew Warner, "Natural Resource Abundance and Economic Growth," NBER Working Paper (5398), 1995.

80 Christensen, "Labor Under Putin.".

81 Richard Sakwa, *Putin and the Oligarchs: The Khodorkovsky-Yukos Affair*, London: I.B. Tauris, 2014.

82 "The End of the Line," *The Economist*, November 20, 2014; Cohen, "Russia's Avoidable Economic Decline."

83 "Why Russia Is Far Less Threatening," *Washington Post.*

84 Pekka Sutela, "The Underachiever: Ukraine's Economy since 1991," Carnegie Endowment for International Peace, https://carnegieendowment.org/2012/03/09/underachiever-ukraine-s-economy-since-1991-pub-47451, March 9, 2012. I used this study in the following paragraphs on Ukraine, as well as www.ukraine-arabia.ae/economy/history/, accessed February 23, 2017.

85 *Development in Eastern Europe and the South Caucasus: Armenia, Azerbaijan, Georgia, Republic of Moldova and Ukraine*, Paris: OECD, 2011, p. 239.

86 "Ukraine's Economy Has Turned a Corner," *Financial Times*, July 4, 2017; "The Stable Crisis: Ukraine's Economy Three Years after the Euromaiden," April 5, 2017, www.osw.waw.pl/en/publikacje/osw-commentary/2017-04-05/stable-crisis-ukraines-economy-three-years-after-euromaidan.

87 *CIA World Factbook*, www.cia.gov/library/publications/the-world-factbook/geos/md.html.

88 World Bank Update, Moldova, www.worldbank.org/en/country/moldova/brief/moldova-economic-update, October 5, 2016; http://data.euro.who.int/hfadb/, accessed November 28, 2016.

89 *The World Bank Overview*, www.worldbank.org/en/country/moldova/overview, accessed January 9, 2017.

90 Martin Sokol, *Economic Geographies of Globalisation: A Short Introduction*, Cheltenham: Edward Elgar, 2011.

Conclusion

Of the several results to emerge from the *longue durée* historical approach to Europe's regional division, two in particular command attention. Most dominant and striking is the stubborn and surprisingly constant survival of a stratification arising from economic developments in centuries past: several countries quasi-cemented into middle- or low-income zones. Equally noticeable, however, is the evidence of inconsistent rates of development within and between ranks, producing a deterioration of some positions within the overall structure: some countries in the southern and eastern border regions actually slipping downward, while quite a few others, partly in the south and more consistently in the north, steadily increase their income levels at faster than average paces, and therefore move upward into higher income zones.

The differentiation has become more pronounced during the 1.5 centuries since 1870. On the one hand, most countries of North and Mediterranean Europe have found their way from middle-income to high-income or even super-rich levels of the West. This upward motion has held despite the persistence of pockets of weakness inherited from peripheral pasts in some of the more *nouveau riche* members of this group. A few countries from the Central European and Baltic region, most of all the Czech Republic, Estonia, and probably the other Baltic countries, have begun traveling along the road toward the higher income zone. On the other hand, most countries of Central Europe, Eastern Europe, and the Balkans, along with Russia and Turkey, remain behind, lodged in their traditional rankings as places of relatively lower income. In most cases, instead of narrowing, the gap between these countries and the advanced core of Europe has grown significantly and sometimes even unevenly from one country to the next.

Lying behind the persistence of economic regionalization, that is, behind the conservation of wealth and increasing richness in some countries and the preserved, even exacerbated backwardness in others, is an economic logic driven by historical economic factors. High income levels allow critical economic strengths to accrue to a country, and these strengths, in turn, underwrite conditions favorable to further development. Put another way, high income levels create the conditions for economic growth: the possibility of higher saving, therefore of higher capital accumulation and investment in new enterprises. In such conditions, education levels, research and development, and the ability to attract and retain foreign talent likewise become more probable. All these possibilities and the higher productivity levels associated with them enhance the position of high-income countries relative to other countries and regions.

The experiences of lower-income countries likewise reflect the operation and effects of this logic. These countries have lower capacities to accumulate and invest capital, thus more limited possibilities for research, invention, and innovation. In comparison with their high-income counterparts, these countries also often exhibit greater degrees of social and economic inequality. Such inequality curbs consumption levels and thus slows down economic growth. Lower living standards and reduced research and advancement opportunities encourage harmful brain drain, which in turn tends to exaggerate disadvantages and to increase backwardness. Thus, the logic produces an overall structure and dynamic across Europe in and through which countries that attained high income levels earlier in history continue to pull ever farther away from their lower income counterparts. The regional differentiation that appeared at the outset of economic modernization persists, even during periods of marked improvement in lower income areas.

Social-cultural factors have worked and still work hand-in-hand with economic factors to conserve the division of Europe into regions of rich and relatively poor countries. Here the acceptance or rejection of new social-cultural habits and values in the early modern period plays a determinative role. In the rich north and west, the 17th and 18th centuries saw the stabilization of new habits and values that had appeared in preceding centuries. These favored business activities, entrepreneurship, the accumulation of money, solid lifestyle, respect for governance by law and for new institutions, desires for education, and for individual and familial progress from one generation to the next. Since the 18th century, these deeply rooted ways of thinking and behaving have well served further economic development in the north and west. By contrast, in Central and East Europe and some Mediterranean countries traditional noble-aristocratic values, mentalities, and cultural habits continue to dominate, preserved in part by the historical accidents that caused these regions to spend centuries subjugated to rule by foreign, imperial powers.

The combination of persistent aristocracy with foreign rule favored the emergence of predatory states in Central and East Europe, with societies notable for their extreme degrees of income inequality and for the exploitation of their majority populations by their aristocratic or oligarchic minorities. In these states, a very small segment of the society almost always has owned the largest part of national income. Indeed, having been forcibly suppressed under communist rule, this pattern of wealth distribution quickly reemerged after the late-20th-century collapse of the communist Soviet Union and its European bloc. The era around the turn of the millennium became a time of a new "primitive accumulation" in these countries, with new billionaires, members of a tiny elite personally connected to postcommunist leaders, being minted "overnight." Remarking on the rise of extreme inequality in post-communist Russia, Serbia, and Bosnia-Herzegovina, the European Bank of Reconstruction and Development's Transition Report 2016–2017 concluded that "economic growth mostly benefitted the rich minority, in some cases just the top 10 or 20 percent of the households." The report also noted that nearly one-quarter of the population was worse off at the moment of writing than in 1989.[1]

In contrast with their counterparts in the rich north and west, the inhabitants of these predatory states have tended to distrust the justness of law, to use whatever strategies they can to work around its restrictions, and to avoid state institutions as much as possible. Cheating the state, the law, and social rules, using kinship connections, looking for patrons, bribing unavoidable officials, all have been and still are the way of everyday life. Through the nineteenth century and even into the early 20th century, illiteracy and semi-illiteracy, considered God-given, reigned *en masse*. Education was undervalued, often officially, while children were directed into jobs as early as possible.

Operating somewhat like natural reflexes, these behavioral patterns pass easily from generation to generation. In this sense, they function to perpetually indoctrinate families and small community circles. Therefore, in modern times, even if the economic and income level elevated in the countries with predatory state structures, these patterns exhibited surprising stability and continuity. Traditional social structures and behavioral habits, "institutions" based on personalized connections, change very slowly, in contrast to economic levels, legal environments or state institutions, which may change more rapidly, sometimes overnight. In the end, just as the social-cultural characteristics of a rich environment assist further economic development, those gradually evolved and solidly cemented in poor societies block such an outcome. Regionally different social-cultural features, therefore, contribute to stabilizing or even broadening economics-based regional divisions.

Given this historical situation, how could a country or group of countries break out from peripheral backwardness? How did it happen that some countries were able to defeat and destroy economic and social-cultural obstacles? What are the factors that may assist with the elevation from backwardness, from lower to higher income level and better life for the population? Historical experience, the performance of several countries, offers a well-based answer to these questions.

First of all, certain objective factors, built into a country's history, must be taken into account. Shared basic social, political, and cultural characteristics could provide great advantages. The Scandinavian countries, for example, while economically peripheral until the 1870s, enjoyed just such a relation with the northwestern region. Similarities in the social, political, and cultural spheres allowed them to exploit the rising European market of that period, the era of "first globalization," and thus to catch up with the West. A little farther to the east, Finland and some Baltic countries once had belonged to Sweden and had shared its social-legal systems. Here too social-cultural familiarity enabled the lagging countries to cope successfully with peripheral backwardness. Another objective factor, geographical location, particularly proximity to centers of vibrant economic activity, markets and financial resources, provided major advantages. Sweden, Norway, and Denmark in the 19th century, Finland in the 20th century, and the Czech lands, Hungary, Poland, and Estonia in the early 21st century all benefited in this respect. Such objective conditions offered the possibility to profit from trade or foreign direct investment, or to copy the more beneficial economic models of rich neighbors, all factors that work against the reproduction of backwardness within the logic and structure of the international economic system.

One of the most important factors underlying successful elevation, however, is the history of domestic policy and government action in relatively backward countries. The economic nationalism adopted by many countries during the interwar decades had a very negative impact, cutting them off from the connection-building, trade promotion and foreign investment, which could have contributed to their economic progress. Historical examples clearly underline the key importance of educational policy, by showing that one of the main weapons against backwardness has been, and still is a strong, efficient educational system and well-educated population.

Governments also have the responsibility to promote fair income distribution. Here the history of peripheral countries, with their stark inequality, differs substantially from their wealthier counterparts. There are well-known policy measures, including taxation and welfare, wage and labor market policy, which may positively influence income distribution. Several peripheral countries, however, have a power structure where political and economic elites are virtually amalgamated with the political elite, with an autocratic state of extreme inequality the result. While this is a social-political problem par excellence, it is also a situation negatively impacting economic growth. It is a commonplace in economics that sharp inequality, widespread poverty and low living standard drastically curb the growth potential of a country: "Most research shows that, in the long term, inequality is negatively related to economic growth and that countries with less disparity and a larger middle class boast stronger and more stable growth." Or, as the European Bank of Reconstruction and Development, investigating the transforming Central and Eastern European countries, recently stated: "There is growing evidence that excessive inequality hurts long-term growth prospects. Specifically, the concentration of earning in the top quintal (20 percent) of the income distribution may hamper subsequent growth."[2]

Finally, governments may alter domestic environments. By establishing and defending the rule of law, or creating efficient state institutions, they can make a country more competitive, clear the way for opening new businesses and establish motivating taxation systems. No less important, governments can and must struggle against the negative cultural inheritance, and work consistently to fight against corruption, against black market activity, and for cleansing government institutions of unlawful practices.

The importance of domestic policy and government action is clearly expressed in the 2013 Transition Report issued by the European Bank of

Reconstruction and Development. The reporters presented the experience of the quarter-century of transformation, made forecasts for future development and calculated that rapid and efficient further reforms might create the possibility for the Central European and Baltic countries to reach 80 percent of the income level of workers of the EU-15 countries in 20 years. It predicted that if further reforms were not to progress well, as actually has been the case, these countries would elevate only to 60 percent of the EU-15 level. Such an outcome would represent an underachievement since these very countries were approaching that level already a decade ago, before the 2008 crisis.[3]

All the factors discussed here may help in challenging backwardness and promoting faster than average growth to catch up with more advanced countries. Backwardness, as history proves, is not an eternal destiny but a historically developed situation and therefore open to the possibility of change.

Historians are not futurologists and most of them do not like making forecasts. However, the *longue durée* approach allows for making some predictions on the basis of long-term trend analysis. A century from now, in the 2110s, on a higher income level than nowadays, Europe certainly will be more homogenized than it is today. A more or less equalized income level is definitely not foreseeable, but some countries and regions will possibly elevate to the high-income zone and thus become equal in this sense to the European core. It should be added, however, that although the relative high, middle, and low income levels all will be higher than today, the relative differences and gaps will be present on that higher level as well.

This developmental pattern is already becoming evident. Ireland and some Mediterranean countries as well as some Baltic and Central European countries seem likely to achieve a stable high-income level and eliminate their still-extant internal social-economic weaknesses. But the future of Portugal and especially of Greece and some Central European countries is much less certain. They easily may remain trapped in the middle-income zone, albeit probably in its higher strata. The mostly backward Russian-Turkish-Balkans region, in the best case scenario, may elevate to the middle-income zone, some countries even to the zone's top level, but an economic miracle will be needed to achieve more than that. Miracles may indeed happen but only if the countries in question create the conditions to allow such results. Above all, they must not repeat the history of missed opportunities that characterized their late-20th-century and early-21st-century road.

Future development is far from guaranteed or logically necessary and dependent at the very least on Europe's meeting certain prerequisites. Of these, the most important is the further development and integration of the European Union and preservation of its homogenization policy, all of which have been challenged in the crisis of the 2010s. Only since 2017 have strong economic signs of returning normalcy appeared. And this recovery is fragile, easily endangered, especially if negative political trends strengthened by populist breakthrough in some of the countries undermine the integration process. An even more decisive prerequisite is the domestic policy in peripheral countries. Success at meeting the required reforms that were briefly mentioned above will play a central role in shaping the future. Without the further development of European integration and especially without the appropriate domestic policy of peripheral countries, regional divides will sharpen further and remain the harsh reality.

Europe also must avoid certain traps standing in its path. The first of these is the trap of ongoing demographic crisis; that is of declining population. Reproduction rates started decreasing in the last third of the 20th century, reaching 1.4–1.8 children per couple in the early 21st century. According to estimates by the Population Division of the United Nations Department of Economic and Social Affairs, at present rates, the population of Europe will be 632 million in 2050, down from 728 million in 2000. By 2100, when the world population will have jumped to 11.2 billion from the present day 7.5 billion, a further decline in Europe will leave just 538 million inhabitants. Europe's share in world population is dramatically shrinking: it was 28 percent in the 19th century but only 12 percent in 2000 and, according to the forecasts, it will be only 7 percent in 2050 and less than 6 percent by 2100. (Meanwhile Africa's population share will almost double from 13 to nearly 25 percent over this same time frame.[4])

These figures already reflect the possibility, or better to say, the reality of the other major trap on the road to the future for Europe: the immigration crisis. Until the mid-20th century, Europe was a continent of emigration. About 60 million people left the continent. That pattern was replaced by immigration during the second half of the 20th century but, until the early 21st century, immigration numbers were moderate. Then they began swelling, reaching a peak in 2015–2016 of more than 2 million, as Africans, Middle Easterners, and some Asians began fleeing civil and religious wars, as well as the consequences of the unfolding climatic tragedy, the global warming that is destroying the possibility of life in some areas on some continents. According to well-based estimations, about 60 million people are endangered, partly already uprooted and wanting to move, most of them to the advanced world, including Europe. The United States, Australia, and some other parts of the advanced world have barriers that slow down entry, but Europe had, for some time, an overly liberal policy and did not defend its borders until the mid-2010s. Europe, of course, needs immigrants, but the numbers of newcomers in 2015–2016 have generated strong political resistance and political crisis, ongoing today. A continued migration crisis may undermine the European Union and destroy its growth potential as well. Very recently, important signs of change, however, signal a new European policy with more secure defense of the borders and close control of immigration.

Any projections regarding the future of regional divide within Europe must therefore be made with caution. The forces able to bring about a harmonization of income levels and elimination of sharp divides are present but dependent on several unpredictable circumstances. In the best case, forecasts involve intelligent guessing, the grounds for which can be undermined easily in a rapidly changing, chaotic world.

Notes

1 *European Bank for Reconstruction and Development Transition Report 2016–2017*, London: EBRD, 2017, p. 9.
2 Ibid., p. 12.
3 *European Bank for Reconstruction and Development Transition Report 2013*, London: EBRD, 2013, p. 17.
4 *World Population to 2300*, New York: United Nations, 2004, p. 22, www.un.org/esa/population/publications/longrange2/WorldPop2300final.pdf, accessed March 23, 2017.

Index